Napoleon and Berlin

CAMPAIGNS AND COMMANDERS

Napoleon and Berlin

The Napoleonic Wars in Prussia, 1813

Michael V. Leggiere

UK edition first published 2002

PUBLISHED IN THE UNITED KINGDOM BY:

Tempus Publishing Ltd
The Mill, Brimscombe Port
Stroud, Gloucestershire
GL5 2QG
www.tempus-publishing.com

PUBLISHED IN THE UNITED STATES BY:

University of Oklahoma Press
1005 Asp Avenue
Norman
Oklahoma 73019-6051

British Library Cataloguing in Publication Data.
A catalogue record for this book is available from the British Library.

ISBN 0 7524 2333 9

Napoleon and Berlin: The Napoleonic Wars in Prussia, 1813 is Volume 1 in the Campaigns and Commanders series.

Cover Image: *Napoleon at Fontainebleau*. Paul Delaroche.
Courtesy of Sotheby's Picture Library

CONTENTS

Illustrations

Photographs

All photographs are courtesy of the Anne S. K. Brown Military Collection, Brown University Library.

Maps

Preface

A study of French military operations in North Germany not only highlights the breakdown of Napoleonic strategy in 1813 but constitutes a fascinating study in coalition warfare, international relations, and civil-military relations.[1] In early 1813 Prussia faced a choice between dependency on France or on Russia. At the moment of Napoleon's greatest calamity, the Prussian army pushed the state into a war of liberation. Not only did the Prussian army pressure the monarch, but a patriotic uprising swept the kingdom as well. To meet the demands of modern war, save his capital, and liberate his country, the conservative Prussian king Frederick William III reluctantly and momentarily embraced a popular uprising that transformed the struggle from a dynastic conflict to a national war: a Franco-Prussian war.[2] The growing patriotic movement, made evident by anti-French demonstrations, influenced public opinion, especially the attitude of the educated classes. Despite Frederick William's "diplomatic anxiety and his dislike of the patriots' enthusiasm, the king was pressured into supporting a patriotic liberation struggle."[3]

Nineteenth-century German historians referred to the war against Napoleon in 1813 as a struggle for freedom, a *Befreiungskrieg*, or war of liberation. A popular uprising occurred in Prussia, which, according to historian Paul Schroeder, "was broad and deep enough to be called 'national,' and closely connected with the ultimate peace settlement in 1814–15, as well as with the rise of German nationalism later in the nineteenth-century—so closely connected, in fact, that one cannot see how these developments could have come without it."[4] Although the poor still filled the ranks of the regular army, the moderately wealthy served in the newly established militia, the *Landwehr*, which was Prussia's authoritarian answer to the egalitarian French *levée en masse*.[5] Moreover, older men between forty and sixty years of age enlisted in the irregular insurrectionary force—the *Landsturm*—to wage a guerrilla war against the hated French. In Berlin civil authorities launched an ambitious plan to fortify and flood the region to prevent the national capital from falling into French hands. Thus the war was conceived as a struggle between peoples and nations, a crusade against tyranny and a quest for emancipation and freedom.[6] Despite the national rising in Prussia, the war was fought by states and powers whose monarchs were concerned about "dynastic rights and claims, power interests and a balance of power, about the restoration of stability."[7] Ultimately, Prussia, Russia, and Austria molded a coalition whose "central goal and purpose would not be a military victory, but durable cooperation among its members; a peace settlement which would not rest on defeating France . . . but on balancing and pacifying Central Europe under the aegis of their own alliance."[8] Although Prussian impetuosity did not always suit this multinational coalition, the Prussian army carried its hatred of the French into the Grand Alliance of 1813.

In early 1813 the Prussians found themselves not only engaged in an epic struggle for survival but also searching for the true meaning, definition, and purpose that could explain their state's existence. Would centuries of political conservatism be sacrificed in the name of a people's war that would lead to constitutional government? Or would the Crown, army, and people work together within absolutist bounds to liberate Prussia from French control? Napoleon's obsession with Berlin provided the Prussians a unique opportunity to test the resolve of their new patriotism. Based on archival research, published official documents, and eyewitness testimony, this book describes how Prussians—from peasants to urban laborers to aristocratic officers—coped with the issues unleashed by a people's war. It combines a social-historical perspective with traditional operational history to show that the Prussians achieved success in North Germany because they viewed the conflict as a Franco-Prussian war, despite the multinational aspect of the struggle. By no means is this book a discourse on diplomatic history, yet it illustrates the impact of Prussian patriotism, as well as the desire for revenge, on coalition warfare.

The hundred years between 1813 and 1913 witnessed the publication of numerous German, French, English, and Swedish works that mostly claimed credit for the defense of Berlin along nationalist lines. Since the loss of the Prusso-German General Staff archives during World War II, few historians have been able to piece together an operational history of the Prussian army of 1813. No work has provided a comprehensive study of both the military operations around Berlin and the Prussian efforts to defend their national capital. Based on German, French, and private archival documents, this book is the first history of the war in North Germany that combines all aspects of Prussia's War of Liberation: the mobilization, the strategy, the militia, the plans for home defense, and the trials and tribulations of the civilian population. The book also builds on historian Gordon Craig's noteworthy treatise on coalition warfare by offering fresh insight into how the defense of Berlin affected relations between the Prussians and their allies. By reconstructing the principal campaigns and operations in North Germany, this study charts how the epic Battle of Nations at Leipzig was made possible by Prussian victories. By thwarting Napoleon's plans to capture Berlin and by carrying the war to the French, Prussian impetuosity changed the course of the war in 1813.

The unceasing and generous assistance of several people and institutions made the completion of this work possible. I must first thank Joachim-Albrecht Count Bülow von Dennewitz and his son, Hasso. Count Bülow kindly gave me two privately printed volumes of his ancestor's correspondence. For several years both he and Hasso produced a constant stream of documents and information that greatly broadened my knowledge of Frederician and Napoleonic Prussia. I would like to thank the helpful staff of Germany's Geheimes Staatsarchiv Preußischer Kulturbesitz zu Berlin for locating pertinent archival material relating to the defense of Berlin in 1813 and for providing the surviving Repositoria of the Prusso-German General Staff archives. The helpful staffs of the Service historique at the Archives de la Guerre in Vincennes and Archives Nationales in Paris patiently handled my requests for photocopies and microfilm. I also wish to thank Stephen Bowman for five days of companionship and expert assistance while I conducted topographical research on the battlefields around Berlin.

Research trips to Germany and France would not have been possible without generous grants provided by Florida State University and Louisiana State University in Shreveport. I offer a special note of thanks to my advisor and mentor, Donald D. Horward, director of the Institute on Napoleon and the French Revolution at Florida State University. My attempt to sort through the diplomatic history of the period was greatly facilitated by Frederick Schneid. Llewellyn Cook brought clarity to my first drafts and provided much moral support. Two superb readers, Peter Paret and Charles White, offered valuable insight and constructive criticism; I owe much of my knowledge of the Prussian army to their scholarship. I would also like to thank John Gill, John Gallaher, John Weinzierl, Geoffrey Wawro, and Owen Connelly for their support and advice over the years. Dennis Showalter has provided years of great encouragement. I am indebted to series editor Gregory J. W. Urwin, and Charles Rankin and Alice Stanton at the University of Oklahoma Press, for their unwavering encouragement and patience. I would also like to thank Ron Chrisman, formerly of the University of Oklahoma Press, and copyeditor Kathy Lewis. I wish to thank Peter Harrington of the Anne S. K. Brown Military Collection at Brown University for locating the artwork that accompanies the text and to thank Frank Bauer of Potsdam for assisting with the maps.

I owe a debt of gratitude to several friends and colleagues at Louisiana State University in Shreveport. My friend, colleague, and chair, Milton Finley, read the manuscript twice and provided much useful advice. Jason Mackowiak of the Fine Arts Department spent much of his Christmas vacation meticulously preparing the maps. I would also like to thank Helen Taylor of the English Department and Michael Williams of the Foreign Language Department for proofing parts of the manuscript. Fermand Garlington, Brian Sherman, and Rich Collins of Noel Library diligently obtained books for me on the shortest notice. John Vassar, Ann McLaurin, and Cheryl White provided great moral support. Last but not least, I would like to acknowledge the support of LaMoyne Batten, chair of the Department of Fine Arts, Foreign Languages, and Humanities, as well as Merrell Knighten, dean of the College of Liberal Arts. Many others have contributed in many ways. To them I offer thanks and an apology for any omission. The merits of this work are due in part to their contributions; its faults are my own.

Finally, I wish to thank the three people closest to me: my wife, Michele, and my parents, Rosalie and Thomas. For seven years, my wife talked to the back of my head as I labored over a keyboard, and she waited patiently for me to finish my work. She endured being left behind during four research trips to Europe but has always remained a source of solid support. My parents have also been by my side for years, and to them I dedicate this book. Their love, patience, understanding, and support are beyond words; their steadfast strength and encouragement have provided an unending source of inspiration. This accomplishment belongs as much to my wife and parents as it does to me.

A note on name and rank: to avoid the confusion caused by the differences between German and English rank structures, generals of all grades are referred to here simply as "general." Native spellings of names are used as much as possible except for monarchs, whose names are anglicized.

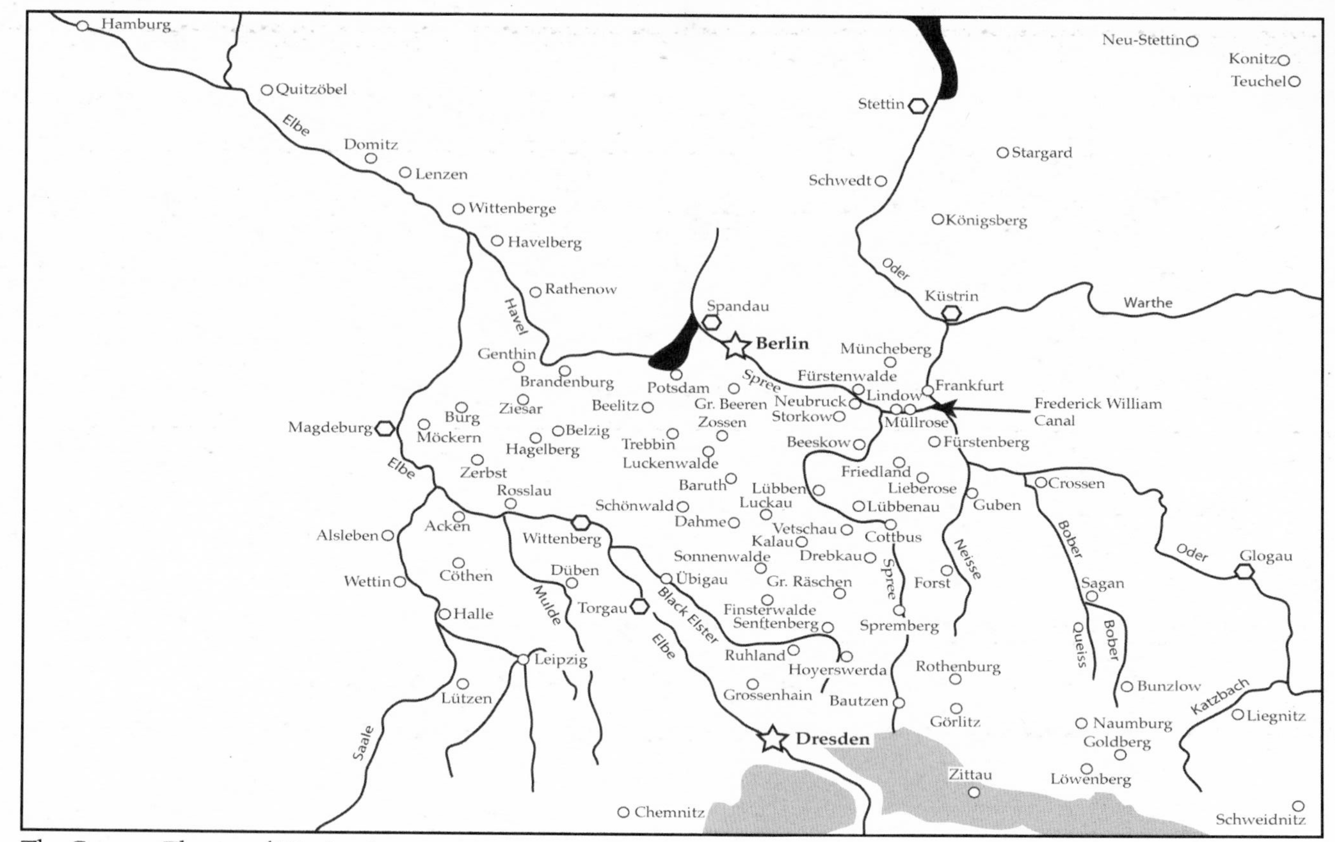

The German Theater of War in 1813

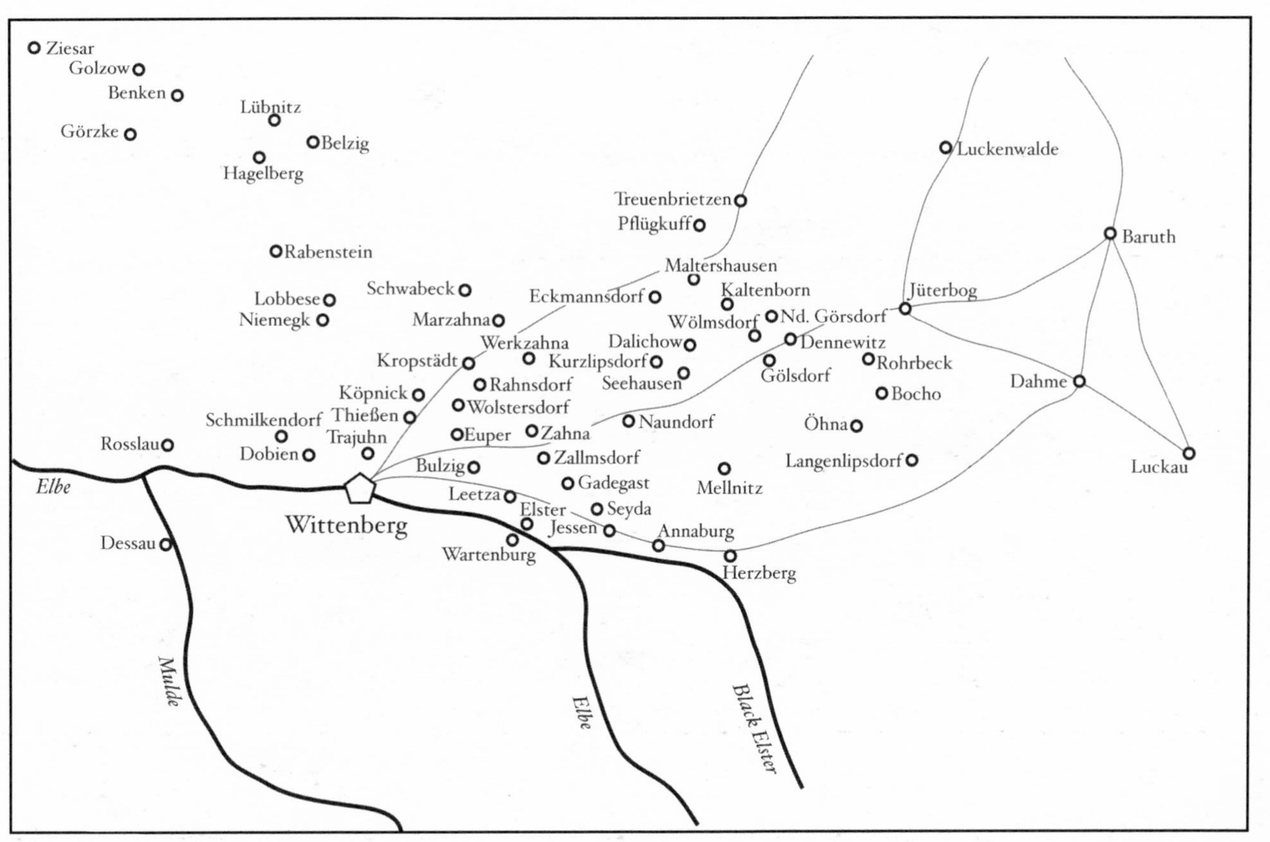

Wittenberg and the Surrounding Area

Napoleon and Berlin

1

France and Prussia

After Frederick the Great's death in 1786, Prussia embarked on a considerable change in foreign policy. Frederick's nephew and successor, Frederick William II, soon became entangled in altercations with Holland, Poland, Russia, Austria, and the other German states. Such aggression excited the Prussian military establishment and catered to the army's lust for glory. The beginning of the French Revolution in 1789, however, trivialized Prussia's police actions. The upheavals in France soon embroiled all of Europe. Frederick William denounced the French and sided with the Austrians in an effort to crush the Revolution. In 1792 a Prussian army rendezvoused with the Austrians on the Rhine River to launch the War of the First Coalition.

The alliance itself proved uncomfortable for many Prussians, especially those who still regarded Austria as the enemy. France's role in the Seven Years' War had faded from memory, and some Prussians sympathized with the French.[1] Despite some disagreement over the war, the Prussians believed that their army would be victorious. Many were happy to display Prussian military prowess not to the French but to the Austrians. Although the Prussians invaded France, defeat at the battle of Valmy on 20 September 1792 brought the first campaign to a shocking end. Berlin continued the war in 1793 but lost interest after two more years, partly due to the lure of Polish territory.[2] The Peace of Basel officially ended the war between Prussia and France on 16 May 1795 and marked the beginning of Prussia's ten-year period of neutrality.[3] During this time France rocked the status quo. Although the War of the First Coalition ended in 1797, continued French expansion in Italy, Switzerland, Egypt and in the Rhineland prompted Great Britain, Austria, Russia, the Ottoman Empire, Naples, and Portugal to form the Second Coalition by 1799. Despite offers from both sides, the new king of Prussia, Frederick William III, remained neutral.[4] Resounding French victories over the Austrians in Germany and Italy in 1800 caused little concern in Prussia. Berlin interpreted French success in Germany as advantageous, since it came at the expense of Austria and the long-defunct Holy Roman Empire. Due to traditional animosity, the Prussians continued to view Vienna as their true rival and enemy. To Berlin, it appeared that France would open the door for Prussian expansion in North Germany.

Changes in the revolutionary governments of France did not stir the Prussians, even after Gen. Napoleon Bonaparte engineered a coup in 1799. Instead they quietly watched Bonaparte's star rise. Although concerned over French expansion in the Rhineland, Berlin remained confident that territorial gains could still be won through diplomacy. British encroachments on the high seas, rather than the establishment of French control over the left bank of the Rhine, finally moved the Prussians. After the disastrous War of the Second Coalition, Russia, Denmark, and Sweden revived the "Armed Neutrality of 1780" in response to British harassment of neutral shipping on the Baltic Sea. Prussia joined the "Second Armed Neutrality" in December 1800, but the league collapsed the following year after the British destruction of the Danish fleet at Copenhagen and the assassination of Tsar Paul of Russia.[5]

Attention then shifted back to Central Europe, where Citizen Bonaparte met with representatives from every German state between 1801 and 1802 to discuss territorial realignment in the Holy Roman Empire. While Napoleon solved the issues of compensation and reorganization in Germany, Austria's leadership over German affairs crumbled. Although Holy Roman Emperor Francis II finally convened the Imperial Recess in 1803 to reassert his leadership, his prestige had suffered irrevocable damage. Bonaparte had already engineered agreements with the medium-sized German states that provided for generous expansion at the expense of the smaller and ecclesiastical states of the Reich. He also rewarded Berlin's patience. Prussia, which had lost

1,674 square miles and 125,000 people to French expansion along the left bank of the Rhine, received compensation in Westphalia and Thuringia amounting to 7,440 square miles and 900,000 inhabitants.[6] It appeared that a good agreement had been struck with Bonaparte, and Berlin continued to benefit from friendship with France. French expansion undermined Vienna's influence over South Germany, while Prussia strove to establish hegemony in the North. In reality Berlin's good relations with Paris existed at Bonaparte's convenience, despite his desire for Prussian neutrality. As long as France benefited from a neutral Prussia, Bonaparte maintained cordial relations with Frederick William. Conversely, Prussia's neutrality puzzled the statesmen of Austria, Russia, and Great Britain, who believed that Prussian diplomacy masked a deeper, sinister motive. At the right time Prussia would resume its traditional role as the jackal of Europe and devour territory after the other powers had exhausted themselves. The resulting atmosphere of international mistrust placed Berlin in a precarious position. An isolated Prussia was considered contemptible and unreliable.

Despite benefiting from Napoleon's reorganization of Germany, Berlin gradually lost international influence. Bonaparte's encroachments in Germany soon challenged Prussia's ability to protect its interests. Although Austria had been displaced as the dominant power in Germany, France rather than Prussia assumed leadership over German affairs. The occupation of Hanover by French forces in 1803 meant that French troops now stood between Brandenburg and Prussia's Rhenish provinces. After Bonaparte's coronation as emperor of the French in 1804, the folly of neutrality became increasingly evident to the Prussians. French aggression violated Prussian interests, but Frederick William clung to his neutrality.[7] In 1804 Austria's special envoy to Berlin, Clemens von Metternich, the future architect of the alliance that would bring Napoleon to his knees in 1814, noted that in Prussia existed "a conspiracy of mediocrities . . . united by the common terror of any decisive action. . . . There is nobody to remind the king that his army might perhaps be utilized to greater advantage on the field of battle than on the plains of Berlin and Potsdam."[8]

The first crisis that shook Berlin came not from France but from Russia. In April 1805 Russia, Great Britain, and Austria formed the Third Coalition to end French expansion. The Russians urged, and then demanded, that the Prussians join the anti-French league. In July Napoleon countered by offering the Electorate of Hanover in exchange for a Prussian alliance. Despite Russia's dictatorial tone and Napoleon's offers, Frederick William still hoped to mediate European affairs. In the end both sides tested Prussian neutrality.[9] In September Tsar Alexander I insisted that 100,000 Russians be permitted to cross Prussian territory while en route to the Rhine. After Frederick William refused, the tsar threatened to force the passage. Prussian troops rushed to the Vistula, and war with Russia appeared imminent. In the midst of the mobilization, attention shifted back to France after Frederick William learned that the French marshal Jean-Baptiste Bernadotte had marched his corps through the Prussian territory of Ansbach in October. Meetings between Frederick William and Alexander soon eliminated the chance of war between the two powers. Bernadotte's transgression, however, so outraged Frederick William that he signed the 3 November 1805 Treaty of Potsdam with Alexander. The agreement required Prussia to act as an armed mediator between Napoleon and the emperors of Russia and Austria. The terms also demanded a complete French withdrawal from Italy and Switzerland; the separation of the French and Italian crowns; and the evacuation of French forces in Germany, Holland, and Naples. Napoleon would be given four weeks to retreat behind his natural frontiers. Should he refuse, 180,000 Prussians would join the ranks of the Third Coalition.[10]

Napoleon's brilliant victory at Austerlitz on 2 December 1805 destroyed the Third Coalition. Broken by French military might for a third time in less than ten years, Austria withdrew from the war. This forced the Russians out of Central Europe and placed the Prussians in an untenable position since the decisive French victory ruined any plans for an armed mediation. Knowing the stipulations of the Potsdam Treaty, Napoleon met with the Prussian foreign minister, Count Christian von Haugwitz, in Vienna shortly after Austerlitz. The French emperor exacted a fitting punishment for Prussia's apparent forfeiture of neutrality. He forced Haugwitz to sign the Treaty of Schönbrunn, which reduced Prussia to a French satellite and gave Napoleon tight control over the Prussians. Bonaparte also ordered the Prussians to annex Hanover, the homeland of the British royal family.[11] Knowing that Berlin could not annex the electorate without earning the enmity of King George III, Napoleon planned to maneuver Prussia into a confrontation with Great Britain.

Berlin had traditionally considered Hanover vital to national security; its annexation would solidify Hohenzollern territory in North

Germany. Although eager to acquire the electorate as a reward for his neutrality, Frederick William first wanted Great Britain's approval before accepting Napoleon's gift. The Prussians actually hoped to mediate a treaty between Great Britain and France; Hanover would be their fee. Armed with these new plans, Haugwitz journeyed to Paris in February 1806, as more Prussian troops marched into Hanover; Berlin continued its dangerous game. During their interview Napoleon berated Haugwitz for Prussia's ingratitude. As punishment he presented new and more stringent conditions. Signed on 15 February, the Treaty of Paris required Prussia to close the North German coast to all British shipping and commerce. As with the Schönbrunn Treaty, Hanover remained a Prussian possession, but it now served as Frederick William's reward for assisting Napoleon in his struggle against Great Britain.

Frederick William could either comply with the new treaty and face a war with Great Britain or rebuff Napoleon and wage war against France. A concentration of French forces in Germany and a partially demobilized army ruled out any thoughts of challenging Napoleon. With no other choice, the Prussian king ratified the Treaty of Paris on 3 March 1806—fitting punishment for an overambitious game of power politics with the new master of Europe. Great Britain responded to the expulsion of its trade from North Germany by blockading the mouths of the Elbe and the Weser Rivers on 5 April. British naval and customs authorities seized over 300 Prussian merchant ships. On 20 April 1806 Great Britain declared war on Prussia.

Although Napoleon brilliantly isolated Prussia, Frederick William finally declared war on France five months later. Several factors ultimately moved him to war.[12] The year 1806 witnessed a continuation of Napoleon's nepotism. The Kingdom of Italy had been formed in 1805, with Napoleon as its king and his stepson, Eugène de Beauharnais, as its viceroy. Less than one year later Napoleon made his older brother Joseph the new king of Naples, while his younger brother Louis became the new king of Holland. Although these events also disturbed the other powers, Napoleon's reorganization of Germany particularly alarmed Berlin. In January 1806 he signed agreements with Austria to dissolve the Holy Roman Empire. Seven months later, on 17 July, he proposed to create the *Rheinbund*, or Confederation of the Rhine, which would consist of sixteen autonomous German states joined in a military and political union under the protection of the French emperor.

Emperor Napoleon I (1769–1821). In the Campaign of 1814 in France, Napoleon brilliantly outmaneuvered the Prussians, inflicting bloody defeats on Blücher's army in four successive battles between 10 and 14 February.

Member states would receive full sovereignty over domestic affairs and meet in a Diet to discuss foreign policy. In return the Confederation of the Rhine would supply Napoleon with an army of 63,000 men.

Napoleon also directed a second territorial redistribution that proved far more effective in bringing order to Germany's fragmentation than the Imperial Recess of 1803. Over sixty princes whose lands and subjects were encompassed by larger principalities lost their sovereignty and their dominions to the larger German states. In appreciation Bavaria, Württemberg, and Baden—the states that benefited the most from Napoleon's proposals—eagerly ratified the treaties to create the Rheinbund. This settlement affected 12,000 square miles and 1.2 million people.[13] At the last meeting of the Imperial Diet of the Holy Roman Empire on 1 August 1806, sixteen German princes withdrew from the empire in a strong show of support to end the Austrian-dominated Reich. Five days later Holy Roman Emperor Francis II renounced his title, which effectively dissolved the thousand-year empire. He retained an imperial title as Francis I, emperor of Austria. Despite Bonaparte's vague suggestion of forming a North German Confederation under Berlin's leadership, Prussia remained outside of this new French-dominated satellite.

After the formation of the Rheinbund, the French emperor momentarily turned his attention to the Mediterranean. In the Kingdom of Naples a British victory over the French at Maida on 4 July 1806 prompted Napoleon to bolster Joseph's regime. To entice the British away from Naples and Sicily, Napoleon opened secret negotiations with London. In early August 1806 the Prussian ambassador in Paris informed Frederick William that Napoleon had offered to return Hanover to George III if the British withdrew from Sicily. A hawkish anti-French party led by Prussian queen Luise now made court—not to mention his personal life—almost unbearable for the cautious Frederick William. This pressure, combined with his own refusal to become a French satellite, finally prompted the king to go to war.

Prussia opted to confront France before gaining any concrete assurances of Russian support. With France and Russia technically still at war, Frederick William was confident that the tsar would come to his aid. Years of mistrust, however, meant that Berlin would have to take the lead in order to convince the Russians that the Prussian army would finally march against France.[14] The British also dropped their grievances and agreed to subsidize an anti-French alliance: the Fourth Coalition. In a fit of confidence the Prussians drafted an ultimatum that demanded the end of French influence in Germany. It arrived in Paris on 25 September, but the emperor had already departed for the Prussian frontier. When the document reached him on 7 October, he responded by ordering his troops to begin the offensive. Without hope

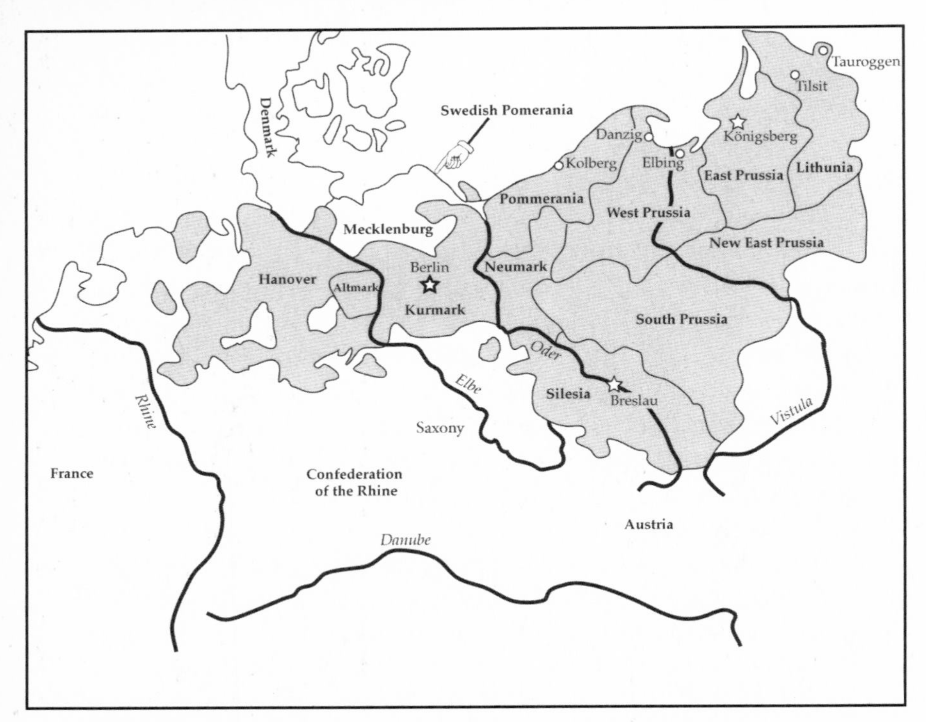

Prussia in 1806

of Austrian support and with the Russian army far away, Prussia prepared to challenge Napoleon's Grande Armée.

Under the emperor's personal supervision, the Grande Armée was a powerful weapon. Bonaparte exploited the form of warfare waged by modern nation-states, where commanders harness the power of universally conscripted mass armies to break "the enemy's will to resist through short, rapid, and destructive strokes against his main force."[15] In developing his art of war, Napoleon, a voracious reader, modified and applied the ideas he found in the writings of eighteenth-century military theorists and commanders. Superior strategy and the development of grand tactics mark his true contributions to the art of warfare. To achieve his political objectives Napoleon sought to outmaneuver and annihilate his opponent's main army.[16] He had inherited an army that already practiced modern tactics based on regulations issued to the royal army in 1791 and then developed during the Revolutionary Wars.[17] Napoleon perfected French tactics by developing a sequence based on four principles: offensive action, relentless pressure, mobility, and a flexible combined attack that included bombardment, skirmishing, cavalry attack, infantry attack, and light cavalry exploitations.[18]

Central to the Grande Armée, the corps system has been described as "the preeminent executive instrument of French conquest and military success during the Napoleonic wars."[19] Although it was not a new concept, Napoleon did refine the *corps d'armée* so that it contained all three arms: infantry, cavalry, and artillery. The typical French corps featured two or three infantry divisions, a cavalry division complete with horse artillery, field artillery, one battery of heavy twelve-pounder artillery, and support personnel. By adding or detaching divisions, an individual corps could become as small as 9,000 men or exceed 40,000 men. Napoleon knew the strengths and weaknesses of each marshal or senior general who commanded a corps; he devised all strategy and they decided the tactics to implement his plans.

Napoleon exploited several intrinsic benefits of the French Revolution, which had produced a highly motivated and ultrapatriotic citizenry. The levée en masse of 1793 had created armies of unprecedented size to protect France during the War of the First Coalition. France had become the first true "nation in arms." Moreover, the mass exodus of nobility during the Revolution had purged the army's leadership and opened the officer corps to "natural-born" commanders. The effects of Liberty, Equality, and Fraternity carried over to the battlefield and produced success. Unlike the reluctant peasants and capricious mercenaries who served in the armies of their absolutist foes, French armies consisted of men who enjoyed the benefits of a constitution that protected their civil rights and guaranteed them a society and career based on merit.[20] Napoleon's comment that a marshal's baton could be found inside the knapsack of every soldier adequately describes the real possibility of promotion based on talent rather than a noble pedigree. To motivate his men he awarded generous incentives such as medals, decorations, monetary grants, and titles. With a vested interest in their country, more could be demanded and expected of the French soldiers than of their Austrian, Prussian, or Russian counterparts.

French tactics reflected the advantages of an open society. On the battlefield the French utilized unprecedented numbers of skirmishers and light infantry. Deployed in open order and instructed to make use of the topography, French skirmishers poured round after round into the ranks of the enemy as they formed their battle line. The French adopted a simple logistical system that dispensed with depots and the traditional eighteenth-century supply system. Napoleon's soldiers lived off the land by foraging while on the march. This added flexibility, mobility, and speed to the French armies. Napoleon also created a reserve system, which invariably consisted of artillery, heavy cavalry, and the infantry of his elite Imperial Guard. With the reserves under his personal command, he waited for the right moment in battle—after the enemy had committed all available forces—to unleash these fresh troops to deliver the *coup de grâce*. Napoleon also employed his artillery in mass batteries that allowed him to direct overwhelming firepower against any point on the battlefield. Enemy infantry, forced to form squares to ward off French cavalry, often experienced the full weight of a barrage from Napoleon's massed artillery batteries.

One shortcoming in Napoleon's system manifested itself particularly after 1808, when he could not be present in the theater of war. With the exception of Marshals André Massena and Louis-Nicholas Davout, few of the men Napoleon chose for independent command in the latter years of the empire could match his ability to improvise, adapt to conditions, scramble, and exploit the enemy's mistakes. With a General Staff system that functioned as a mere secretariat, many French field commanders lacked the skills to formulate strategy on a par with their emperor. Napoleon's system of command excelled at training his marshals to be tacticians but failed to prepare his officers for independent command.[21] Like Frederick the Great, Napoleon was sovereign, commander-in-chief, and chief of staff; his subordinates viewed strategy as the emperor's domain. Pride and jealousy among the corps commanders also hindered the coordination of French forces, particularly in Iberia and Russia.[22] Although hundreds or even thousands of miles from the area of operations, the emperor had to issue detailed orders and instructions to his subordinates. Napoleon's inability to grasp the concept of a competent General Staff system contributed to the eventual breakdown of the French command structure. This deficiency became acute when the number of forces and theaters of war multiplied between 1808 and 1813.

The antithesis of the Grande Armée and epitome of a classic eighteenth-century fighting force was the Prussian army of 1806.[23] The Prussian army dutifully respected the cult of Frederick the Great.[24] Frederick had perfected eighteenth-century linear tactics and the oblique order of battle.[25] After his death, Prussian military leaders studied his battles in search of a universal formula for success. Prussian military theory thus experienced minimal change. In fact, twenty years after the passing of Old Fritz many of the same generals remained in command or held advisory positions. Prussian generals, numbering 142 in 1806, included 4 over the age of eighty, 13 over the age of seventy, and 62 over the age of sixty.[26] Although reform had become a hot topic in Prussia military circles after the turn of the century, the command, doctrine, logistics, and structure of the Prussian military system badly needed to be overhauled before the army challenged France. Some had recognized the need for reform, but change came slowly and with much opposition.

Frederician warfare—with its emphasis on position, maneuver, and attrition—differed fundamentally from Napoleon's emphasis on a war of annihilation. Frederick the Great had waged war to attain specific objectives that could be won just as easily at the peace table as on the battlefield. "The optimal way to achieve these," notes historian Dennis Showalter, "was neither to exhaust one's adversaries nor to destroy them, but rather to establish, by an initial victory or series of victories, the wisdom of negotiation as an alternative to further struggle."[27] After the horrors of the Seven Years' War, Frederick viewed his army as a strategic deterrent. Military readiness and the *capacity* to wage war, rather than waging war itself, became the bedrock of Prussian national security from 1763 to 1806.[28] A well-disciplined army was the key ingredient of Prussian deterrence. Since the state lacked the material and human resources to wage prolonged wars, the mere threat of Prussia's rapid first-strike capability had to suffice to deter larger neighbors from helping themselves to Prussia's disjointed territories. For this reason, the army had to be a well-oiled machine, controlled from top to bottom and built on "strict discipline, unconditional obedience, [and] prompt execution of orders."[29]

Tactically the Prussian army employed the Frederician linear system. Linear tactics required the planning of the entire operation from the approach march to the actual engagement itself.[30] Frederick's emphasis on a closely supervised, cohesive infantry attack that featured massed volleys shaped Prussian tactics. Frederick stretched his battalions into long thin lines to maximize firepower.[31] Prussian regulations required the infantry to advance shoulder to shoulder in rigid, close-order lines that resembled parade ground drill and limited maneuverability.[32] According to historian Peter Paret, "the extent, complexity, and brittleness of the tactical patterns, as well as the difficulty of maintaining an orderly and rapid fire, demanded intensive training of the soldiers, and their most stringent supervision, particularly in combat. For the man in the ranks . . . this meant renouncing his will to reason and his total submersion into the unit, the strength and safety of which resided largely in the degree to which its members could act as one."[33] Frederick insisted on strict discipline and drill as combat facilitators that would maintain cohesion and eliminate friction.[34] He did not, however, view discipline and drill as ends in themselves. "Frequent negative references to the Prussian soldier as a machine or automaton," argues Showalter, "have obscured the fact that he was seen as part of an integrated weapons system."[35] Unit cohesion remained the hallmark of the Prussian company; soldiers performed twenty-two separate actions to load and fire a single round. Regulations stressed high rates of *unaimed* fire to demoralize the enemy through rapid and continuous volleys.[36] The Prussians also preferred muskets that were easy to load rather than accurate.[37] By 1806 the Prussian "moving batteries" still used the 1782 model, which Carl von Clausewitz described as the worst in Europe.[38]

Close supervision and discipline proved essential not only for tactics but also to hold together the Frederician army. Historian Martin Kitchen describes the bulk of the Prussian army as "demoralized men, often the dregs of society, press-ganged foreigners and prisoners of war, unwilling peasants and unreliable mercenaries, the whole motley crew held together by violent brutal discipline and ferocious punishments."[39] Frederick sought to shield his population from the effects of war as much as possible and thus recruited foreigners and the least productive elements of his population. Ideally he sought professional soldiers, whether foreign or native, without roots in their society.[40] "Useful hardworking people should be guarded as the apple of one's eye," notes Frederick in his *Testament of 1768*, "and in wartime recruits should be levied in one's own country only when the bitterest necessity compels." Iron rule had to be imposed to mold social outcasts and foreigners into a cohesive army; Frederick feared that slack discipline would lead to "barbarization."[41] Linear formations provided both tactical and disciplinary control, while fear, compulsion, habit, and in some cases even *esprit de corps* motivated the individual soldier.[42] "If during an action a soldier appears ready to flee," wrote Frederick, "or so much as steps off the line, the non-commissioned officer standing behind him will run him through with his bayonet and kill him on the spot."[43] Deserters were executed, while those found guilty of less serious offenses "ran the gauntlet" of two hundred men armed with salted whips. The goal of this discipline was to transform the army "into an instrument of a single mind and will." Prussian commanders broadly interpreted Frederick's remark that the men should fear their officers more than the enemy. Frederick's opinion that stern discipline was needed to guarantee the army's success remained long after the great king's death.[44]

Supervision of the men and the requirements of linear cohesion limited the options and flexibility of Frederician generals. Although the number of foreigners that served in the Prussian army fluctuated between twenty-five and seventy-five percent during Frederick's reign, army doctrine at the turn of the century still reflected Frederick's goal of preventing desertion.[45] This influenced the Prussians to continue their reliance on closed-order linear tactics, since fighting in open formations could increase desertions. A night march had to be avoided except when absolutely necessary.[46] Moreover, woods and hills undermined the effectiveness of the volleys, broke linear cohesion, and limited the tactical control of the commanding general.[47] Bound to Frederick's system of sophisticated maneuvers and tight formations, Prussian generals preferred to move their units slowly and methodically over open terrain. Unlike Napoleon, the Prussians had to hold precision above speed and flexibility.

As for provisions, the Prussians supplied their army through a system of food and fodder magazines. Since Frederick fought many campaigns in his own territory, he established a logistical system to spare the Prussian countryside. Although the system shielded the fragile Prussian economy, it forced the army to advance with large quantities of food in huge supply trains. "Soldiers would desert if left to forage in small parties," explains historian R. R. Palmer, "or if not furnished with a tolerable standard of living, since to make a living, not to fight or die for a cause, was the chief aim of the professional soldier."[48] Dependence on magazines and depots further added to the army's inflexibility. Since aristocratic officers traveled in style, and the morale of soldiers who lacked political passion would suffer without a steady supply of food, enormous baggage trains followed the army.[49] In contrast to the light, highly mobile units of Napoleon's army, the numerous baggage trains further compounded the problems of an already slow-moving, inflexible army.[50]

Unlike the revolutionary governments of France, the Hohenzollern monarchs failed to enlist the support of the masses. Prussia, like many other absolutist states, lacked a true focal point for national aspirations. Despite the great social upheaval in France, Prussia still maintained a feudal structure based on the principles of caste. Prussian peasants owed their lord fidelity, respect, and obedience, while a constitution guaranteed the rights of French citizens.[51] Like the serf on the manor, the Prussian soldier was "trained to direct all his psychic and physical energies towards the prompt and precise execution of the command."[52] The winds of change did stir some Prussian military theorists to demand reform, yet the emphasis remained on strict obedience and harsh discipline rather than initiative.[53]

Perhaps more detrimental to the Prussian army of 1806 was the fact that Frederick's high degree of precision had sought to achieve the "full scope to the art of generalship."[54] Frederick's successors, both dynastically and militarily, could have reaped the benefits of such a disciplined fighting force had they possessed some of his abilities. Instead the army of 1806 would suffer from command by committee and the vacillation of a man-child king. Conversely, it would be inaccurate to label the Prussian army obsolete. Reforms that reflected the revolutionary changes in the art of war were slowly being introduced. Aside from the French, no other power could match the tactical and administrative levels of the Prussian army just prior to 1806.[55] As Showalter convincingly agues, the Prussian army fulfilled its role as a deterrent for almost fifty years by allowing three successive monarchs to live the gambler's dream: winning without betting. In the 1778 War of the Bavarian Succession, or "potato war," the Habsburgs abandoned their designs for the Bavarian throne rather than risk a general war with Prussia.[56] Moreover, fear of the Prussian army facilitated Frederick William II's aggression in Eastern Europe. Prussian demands for Polish territory resulted in the Second and Third Partitions of Poland, in part a result of the fact that no European power wanted to challenge Prussia, the least of the great powers.[57]

Finally, it was international respect for the Prussian army that allowed Frederick William III to remain neutral for over ten years. From 1795 to 1806 both revolutionary and imperial France opted to placate rather than fight Prussia. Conversely, anti-French coalitions believed that Prussian participation would guarantee victory.[58] When Frederick William finally declared war on France in 1806, he did not intend to use his army to fight a prolonged war.[59] Instead he looked for a decisive strike that would slow Napoleon and provide time for both the Russians and the winter to arrive and alter the circumstances.[60] Had the Prussians faced a foe other than Napoleonic France, the outcome probably would have been much different. Yet a new age of warfare had dawned, and the Prussian military establishment had to confront the harbinger of that new age: Napoleon and his Grande Armée.

After mobilizing in August, the Prussian army marched to meet the Grande Armée in a showdown between Frederician "limited" war and Napoleon's "unlimited" war, between the Frederician strategy of attrition and the Napoleonic strategy of annihilation.[61] The Prussian commander, Duke Charles of Brunswick, initially planned to take the offensive before French forces entered Prussian territory. Reconnaissance reports, however, revealed that Napoleon had already concentrated 180,000 men on the Prussian frontier along a front of 38 miles; Brunswick had dispersed his army across a front of 190 miles.[62] After losing the opportunity for an offensive, the Prussians divided the army into two groups under Brunswick and Prince Friedrich Ludwig von Hohenlohe.[63]

Napoleon anticipated Brunswick's decision to protect his line of communications by concentrating a force between Erfurt and Weimar. To intercept the Prussians, he ordered Marshal Davout to advance along the Weimar-Naumberg Road. On the morning of 13 October the main Prussian army under Brunswick evacuated Weimar. Reports that French forward troops had reached Weimar caused the king to order a retreat to the Elbe River by way of Auerstädt. That evening Brunswick failed to send a sufficient cavalry force either to clear the road or to make an initial advance in strength on Davout's position. Forewarned of the Prussian advance, Davout had sufficient time to prepare his forces.

Davout's forward troops made contact with the Prussians at 8:00 A.M. on the morning of 14 October. Although outnumbered more than two to one, Davout's corps of 26,000 men and 44 guns held against a Prussian army of 39,000 infantry, 9,200 cavalry, and 230 guns. While leading an attack, Brunswick fell, shot through both eyes. The Prussian command lapsed into confusion and disarray after Frederick William failed to name Brunswick's successor or take personal command. At 12:30 P.M. the Prussians began an orderly retreat. According to Davout, the Prussians lost 15,000 casualties, 3,000 prisoners, and

Marshal Louis-Nicholas Davout (1770–1823). In 1814 Davout "the terrible," arguably Napoleon's ablest general, successfully held Hamburg against 60,000 Allied besiegers until the restored Bourbon king Louis XVIII ordered him to surrender the city.

115 guns. French losses amounted to 7,000 men, almost one-fourth of Davout's corps.

Meanwhile Napoleon had discovered what he thought to be the main Prussian army and began concentrating his corps for a battle of annihilation at Jena. Hohenlohe had foolishly scattered his army in isolated units along the road to Weimar. He eventually realized the danger and ordered his regiments to converge and meet the French advance. An attempt to turn the French right flank failed and resulted in Hohenlohe's left being separated from his center for the entire battle. Hohenlohe's 50,000 Prussians bravely resisted the 90,000 men that Napoleon brought to bear against them, but they began to yield after sustaining tremendous losses. Hohenlohe's center finally broke at 2:00 P.M., and French cavalry relentlessly pursued the retreating Prussians. Hohenlohe's army became nothing more than a mass of helpless fugitives; all resistance ended by 4:00 P.M. In just one day the French crushed the Prussian army; Frederick William lost 25,000 prisoners, 200 guns, and 60 regimental standards.

In a rapid succession of calamities that followed the army's defeat, it became exceedingly clear that the Prussian military establishment had been swept away by modernity. On 27 October Napoleon entered Berlin. The French celebrated their great victory by helping themselves to the city's wealth. Official plundering and unofficial looting disillusioned the urban population.[64] After a respite in Berlin, during which he appeased the monied classes with empty promises of political reform and a modern constitution, Napoleon rejoined his marshals to continue the pursuit of the exhausted and disorganized remnants of the Prussian army. With a handful of stragglers, Frederick William and the royal family fled to Königsberg, the provincial capital of East Prussia, to unite with the approaching Russians; yet Prussia collapsed after a series of feeble and unparalleled surrenders. The Jena campaign ended with the fall of Magdeburg and its garrison of 22,000 men on 6 November. In a little over one month the Prussian army lost 165,000 men, including 25,000 killed and wounded.

Although some Prussian auxiliaries helped the Russians check Napoleon in East Prussia at the battle of Eylau on 7–8 February 1807, the French army quartered for the winter and recovered. Once the campaign resumed, the French defeated the Russians at Friedland on 14 June. With his army unable to continue the war, Alexander abandoned Frederick William and opened negotiations with Napoleon. On 25 June *bilateral* peace talks began on a raft moored in the middle of the Niemen River not far from Tilsit. Frederick William did not receive an invitation to this epic meeting between the two emperors. Days passed while he nervously awaited his fate. The waiting finally ended on 7 July 1807, the day Napoleon and Alexander signed the Treaty of Tilsit. The tsar agreed to Napoleon's plan to create the Grand Duchy of Warsaw by stripping Prussia of the Polish territory gained in the Partitions of 1793 and 1795. A French protectorate and member of the Rheinbund, the Grand Duchy of Warsaw later became a point of contention in Franco-Russian relations. In the meantime the tsar remained content with Napoleon's promise to support Russia's war against the

Ottoman Empire. Alexander also agreed to participate in Napoleon's Continental System by closing his ports to British shipping. At Tilsit Napoleon believed that he had maneuvered Russia into the position of a client state under the pretense that he and Alexander would divide Europe as equals.

Two days later, on 9 July 1807, a dejected Frederick William concluded his own peace with Napoleon. Although the tsar intervened to save Silesia, the Treaty of Tilsit reduced Prussia to a third-rate power. Prussia's prewar population of 9,752,731 inhabitants shrank to 4,938,000, and the state's 5,570 square miles to 2,877.[65] In addition to being stripped of new Prussian Poland, Frederick William lost all territory west of the Elbe.[66] Danzig on the Baltic Sea became a free city under French authority. Other conditions stipulated that French troops would occupy the three great fortresses on the Oder River—Glogau, Küstrin, and Stettin—until the Prussians paid a considerable indemnity. Berlin would also have to pay the cost of provisioning the imperial garrisons that would be spread throughout Prussia and of maintaining the imperial highways that would be built to connect the Grand Duchy of Warsaw with the Rheinbund: an estimated total cost of over 200 million francs.[67] Finally, Tilsit impressed Prussia into Napoleon's Continental System, which led to a sharp drop in trade.[68]

In Prussia the lower classes accepted the army's defeat with quiet apathy.[69] Only the monied classes' outright collaboration with the French invader eclipsed popular indifference. This not only sealed Prussia's humiliation but offered decisive proof that a Prussian nation did not exist to match the energies unleashed by the French. If Prussia ever hoped to oppose the French and regain its independence, a nation that generated patriotic energy had to be created. Shortly after the war a group of Prussian civil servants and army officers sought to resurrect the Prussian state as a nation rather than effect a mere restoration of the Hohenzollern kingdom. Collectively called "reformers," they sought to foster patriotism and exploit national energies that had been repressed by Prussia's social structure.[70] Their success was mixed, and their motives, prerogatives, and goals have been the subject of scholarly debate. As historian Hans Rosenberg notes, "the worst cracks on the surface of the social and political order were patched up and a few narrow but solid bridges were built over the old caste barriers."[71]

Universal conscription formed the key component of military reform. The reformers understood that universal conscription could be achieved only after the implementation of sweeping social reforms since Prussia's social order and military establishment were so intertwined that a change in one would have a profound effect on the other.[72] To create citizen-soldiers to match the French, Prussian subjects had to possess a vested interest in the state. Developing the conditions that would produce *national* honor and patriotism became the philosophical goals of reform.[73] The reformers hoped a new Prussian state would generate what historian Thomas Nipperdey terms a "neuer Mensch": a reborn, educated, autonomous, and patriotic human being.[74] To reinforce these emerging concepts, Johann Gottlieb Fichte and Ernst Moritz Arndt led an intellectual and moral revival to provide a sense of purpose and personal dedication.[75]

The appointment of Baron Heinrich Friedrich Karl vom Stein as principal minister of domestic and foreign affairs in October 1807 launched Prussia's era of civil reform.[76] Emancipation of the peasantry, a key ingredient in Stein's program, served as the counterpart of military reform. The reformers hoped that Prussian peasants would be much more valuable to the state as free citizens.[77] Clausewitz insisted that, like the French, Prussians too could fight for their beliefs and ideals.[78] Stein's domestic reforms climaxed with the great Edict of Emancipation of 9 October 1807 that abolished serfdom as of 11 November 1810.[79] One Prussian official expressed hope that the edict would "give birth to a new generation that will form a people armed with strength and will, a people that will wipe out the country's shame and reestablish the glory of its honored name."[80] Such revolutionary changes, however, could only be tested in "total" war, when the "shift from the dynastic to the national form of state" would be tested by a clash between peoples rather than crowns.[81]

As for military reform, the king took steps to resurrect his army by appointing the Military Reorganization Committee in 1807.[82] Chaired by the leader of the military reform party, Gerhard Johann von Scharnhorst, the committee directed the rebirth of the army.[83] Although conservatives who were opposed to certain aspects of Scharnhorst's program received representation on the committee, he and his followers labored to transform the army by adopting and improving the revolutionary principles employed by the French.[84] To achieve a level of nationalism parallel to the French, changes had to occur within the army itself.[85] The most important concerned the recruitment and composition of the officer corps, military education, discipline, and military administration. A cabinet order of July 1808 officially created a centralized war ministry. Scharnhorst also molded the Prussian General Staff—in existence since 1801—into the army's intellectual nerve center. The reformers ended the nobility's monopoly of the officer corps and based commissions on education, talent, ability, and merit rather than birth right.[86] Scharnhorst and his staff also implemented tactical changes that corresponded to the new civil liberties. Field exercises, target practice, and skirmishing replaced mindless drill. New regulations stressed open-order tactics that employed aimed fire as opposed to the unaimed, massed volleys of the tight linear formations.[87] To create a "nation in arms" and elevate soldiers to "citizens in uniform," reforms abolished the harsher punishments. The reformers hoped to base discipline on reason rather than brute force, and obedience on patriotism rather than terror.[88]

Scharnhorst tried but failed to convince Frederick William to issue a universal conscription decree. Conservative opposition, the state's impoverishment, and treaty limitations prevented the expansion of the army through conscription or a militia.[89] Nevertheless, on 15 March 1808 the reform commission unanimously recommended the introduction of universal military service. "In the future," responded the king, "every subject of the state, without regard to birth, will be obliged to perform military service under conditions of time and circumstances yet to be determined."[90] Despite the ambiguity of this answer, Scharnhorst remained hopeful that a universal conscription decree would replace the traditional canton system of recruitment, which transferred the feudal rights that the lord of the manor exercised over his serfs to the officer commanding his soldiers.[91] Although the universal service law and abolition of the canton system did not come until prompted by the necessities of war in 1813, Scharnhorst did revive the eighteenth-century Krumper reserve system in which each company and squadron discharged a portion of its men at fixed intervals; recruits took their place and received military training. In turn they too rotated to reserve duty.[92] Such foresight provided 36,500 additional soldiers for the mobilization in early 1813.

As the reformers labored, Prussia's deplorable political situation worsened.[93] French vigilance increased in every part of the empire after the Spanish revolted on 2 May 1808.[94] Four months later Napoleon forced another Treaty of Paris on Frederick William that reduced his army to 42,000 men and prohibited conscription, a militia, and a national guard.[95] This repression came as a result of Napoleon's growing commitment in Spain and his mounting concern over manpower. As increasing numbers of French troops crossed the Pyrenees, units that served in Central Europe also moved westward. A significant percentage of the occupation force left Prussia, but numerous garrisons remained behind to insure the payment of reparations. Tension in Prussia somewhat relaxed later in 1808 after the Erfurt Conference between Napoleon and Alexander. Meeting from 27 September to 14 October, the conference was prompted by Napoleon's anxiety over Iberia, where events in Spain warranted his presence. At Erfurt Napoleon hoped to bolster the agreements made at Tilsit and gain Alexander's assurance to maintain the status quo in Central Europe. Alexander tacitly agreed and persuaded Napoleon to reduce the Prussian indemnity by twenty million francs.[96]

French reverses in Spain and Portugal brought hope to the conquered peoples of Central Europe. Napoleon's setbacks in Iberia eroded the belief of French invulnerability and inspired the Habsburgs to make another attempt to restore their shattered power. Hostilities opened between France and Austria on 9 April 1809 in the War of the Fifth Coalition. Austrian propagandists called for the support of all Germans and made the first attempt to transform the war against Napoleon into a German *national* struggle. The Austrians urged all Germans in the Confederation of the Rhine, the Tyrol, and North Germany to arm against the French. Prussian patriots who yearned for revenge heard their pleas. Many Prussian army officers wanted to avenge the humiliations of 1806. Ferdinand von Schill, a Prussian cavalry major and fervent nationalist, attempted to foment rebellion throughout North Germany. In late April 1809 he led a renegade Prussian cavalry force of 500 men into the Kingdom of Westphalia. His attempt to force the king of Prussia into the war against France failed by the end of May, and Schill lost his life in the process. After being warned by the tsar to stay out of a Franco-Austrian conflict, Frederick William refused to declare war on France and so condemned Schill's insubordination.[97]

While the Prussian army anxiously awaited orders that never came, French forces occupied Vienna on 13 May. One week later the Austrian commander, Archduke Charles, shocked all of Europe by defeating Napoleon at the battle of Aspern-Essling. Although Napoleon suffered his first defeat, he recovered and won retribution at Wagram in early July. The Austrians requested an armistice, and Habsburg resistance came to an end. After four destructive wars Vienna attempted to foster a durable peace with Napoleon and perhaps enjoy the benefits of his friendship. These ambitions culminated in March 1810, when a recently divorced Napoleon took Marie-Louise, the nineteen-year-old daughter of the Austrian emperor, as his second wife. Attempts to secure a Romanov bride had failed due to Russian balking. Now it appeared that Austria would replace Russia as Napoleon's partner; relations between Russia and France had steadily deteriorated. Caught between France and Russia since 1805, Prussia now had reason to fear the traditional enemy: Austria.

Frederick William's impotence in 1809 sparked widespread discontent in his army, where Schill was portrayed as a martyr. Just before Schill's death, Gen. Karl von Borstell, who had the reputation of an arch-conservative in military circles and was one of Scharnhorst's bitterest opponents, had warned the king that any disciplinary action against the insubordinate major might spark a revolution in Berlin. Moreover, two key reformers, August Wilhelm von Gneisenau and Karl Wilhelm von Grolman, resigned in disgust.[98] The reformers, especially the military men eager to get another crack at Napoleon, were sickened by Frederick William's apparent fear of the French emperor. The king instructed the reformers "not to prepare a rising against France, but to secure Prussia a more tolerable existence under French hegemony," a point not unnoticed or appreciated by many Prussian officers.[99]

A fresh series of dilemmas beset the Prussian government in the spring and summer of 1811 due to the growing rift in Franco-Russian relations. By 1811 both Napoleon and Alexander were preparing for war. Many Prussians believed an alliance with Russia might save the state. Yet the tsar's own encouragement offered the Prussian king no solace. After listening to Russian proposals, Frederick William noted that "all of this reminds me of 1805 and 1806, when the Tsar's court was seized with the same excitement. I am afraid that the final result will again be an ill-conceived war that brings misfortune to Russia's friends instead of delivering them from the yoke that oppresses them."[100] The king recalled how Tilsit had reduced the kingdom by half; another unsuccessful war against Napoleon could result in total dissolution.

By January 1812 rumors of an impending war between France and Russia had turned into a nightmare for Frederick William. On 24 February 1812 Napoleon forced another Treaty of Paris on the Prussians. The terms opened Prussia's borders to imperial troops en route to the Russian frontier. Frederick William also had to furnish the Grande Armée with an auxiliary corps of 20,842 men, considerable quantities of provisions, and thousands of pack-horses and wagons. With French forces amassed along Prussia's frontier, the king ratified the agreements on 5 March. This new affront triggered dissent among Prussian patriots who yearned to launch their own struggle for liberation. They based their hopes on the Spanish example and British subsidies. After five years of humiliating occupation, most Prussian officers detested the French. Consequently, the new treaty caused a wave of resignations. Gen. Gebhard Leberecht von Blücher had already resigned his command in January. Once the treaty was publicized, the architect of military reform, Scharnhorst, resigned his post as chief of the General Staff. Two of his assistants, Clausewitz and Hermann von Boyen, went to Russia. Over 300 officers, almost one-fourth of the officer corps, left the army in protest.[101] Many went to Russia, some to Spain, and a few to Great Britain.[102] "We shall receive the fate we deserve," lamented Gneisenau. "We shall go down in shame, for we dare not conceal from ourselves the truth that a nation is as bad as its government. The king stands ever by the throne on which he has never sat."[103] Seldom before was the censure of a Hohenzollern monarch so clearly expressed.

Regardless of his hapless ally's troubles, Napoleon assembled his invasion force in East Prussia. On 24 June 1812 the Grande Armée crossed into Russian territory and embarked on one of history's greatest military disasters. The Prussian contingent, commanded by Gen. Hans David von Yorck, did not follow Napoleon's main army toward Moscow but advanced on St. Petersburg as part of Marshal Jacques Macdonald's Tenth Corps. As for Napoleon, he marched deep into Russia. After the burning of Moscow on 15 September, reports of French victories grew less brash. News from the East then ceased altogether as rumors spread of a French disaster. Despite French propaganda, nothing could conceal the Grande Armée's destruction. The proud host of nearly 500,000 men had been reduced by two-thirds. Napoleon's main army staggered out of Russia on 14 December with barely 7,000 men under arms.[104]

Behind the lines in Königsberg and other East Prussian towns, the population bore full witness to the devastation of Napoleon's forces when the remnants of the Grande Armée returned. Innumerable wagons

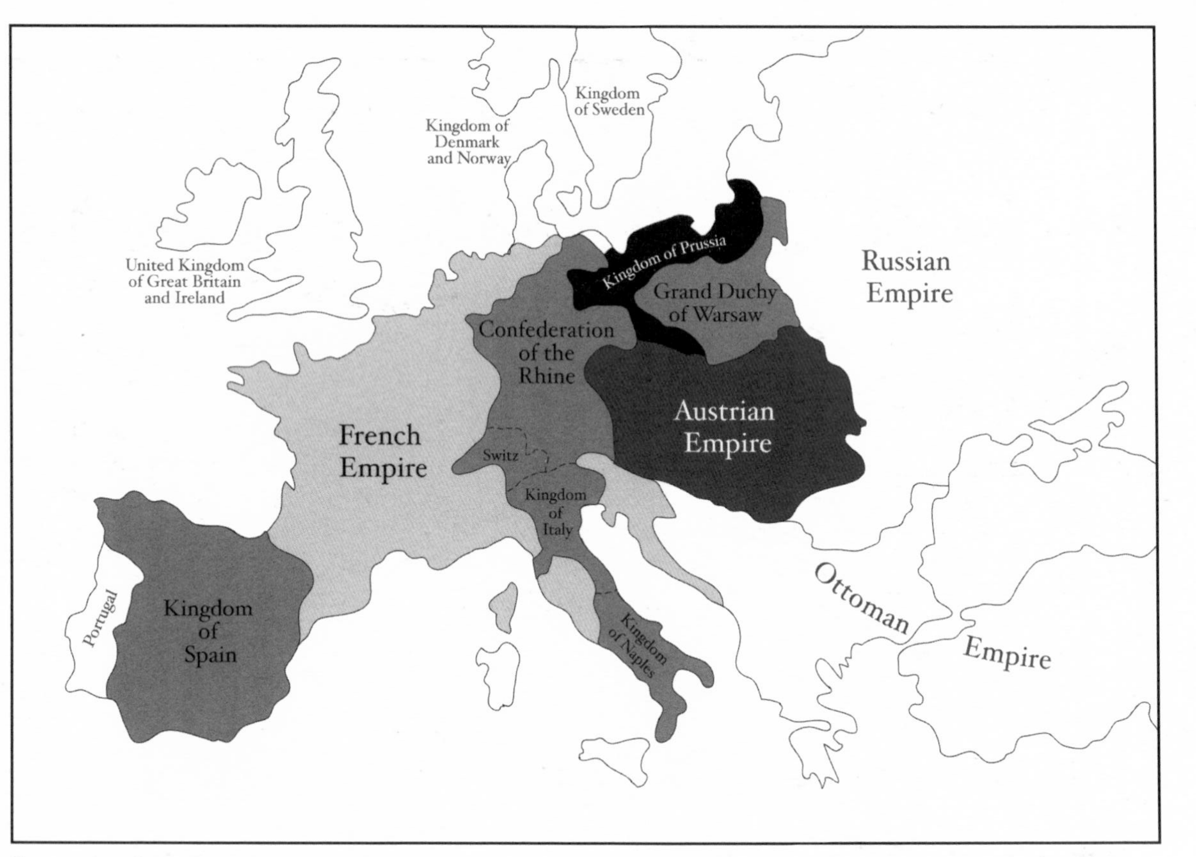

Europe in 1812

appeared daily with cargoes of wounded and sick escorted by exhausted foot soldiers. Deathly pale faces, glazed eyes, and frostbitten limbs provided horrifying testimony of the Russian winter's potency. All semblance of military order had dissolved long before the straggling units reached the safety of East Prussia. It became obvious that tens of thousands had perished.[105] The acting Prussian governor of East and West Prussia and Lithuania, Gen. Friedrich Wilhelm von Bülow, observed this endless train of misery.[106] He later confessed that nothing in his lifetime had been more shocking than the scenes in Königsberg. Bülow described the retreating units of the French army as a "disorderly herd" that one had to see to believe.[107] In Berlin, however, some Prussian statesmen refused to believe these reports.[108] Remembering that Wagram had followed Aspern-Essling, Frederick William understood that Napoleon still controlled immense resources and only needed time to reestablish his dominance. The king prohibited any ministerial action aimed at exploiting Napoleon's setback.[109] As was typical of Prussia's feeble position, Frederick William did not decide his state's next move. Instead a Prussian general took the first step in Prussia's war of liberation.

2

THE SIXTH COALITION

While the statesmen in Berlin contemplated Prussia's next step, Napoleon's energetic will stirred Western and Central Europe during the waning months of 1812. General mobilizations occurred in France, the Rheinbund, and Italy to replace the men lost in Russia. As early as September Napoleon had ordered the conscription of 140,000 men in France and 30,000 in Italy.[1] On 15 December Frederick William received a letter from Napoleon. Giving few details concerning the Grande Armée, Napoleon simply stated that he had left his army and would reach Paris in four days. He expressed his wish that Prussia increase the number of its active soldiers in order to form another corps.[2] Despite growing bitterness, Prussia, like the rest of Napoleon's vassal states, obeyed. The emperor still had powerful weapons to employ against his satellites: outright terror, control of propaganda and information, the threat of force, their persistent belief in his military superiority, and the fact that many princes owed their political existence to him.[3] In France most of the recruits had already reached their depots by the time Napoleon returned to Paris in December; they completed their training as they marched to the front. As they waited for the arrival of these reinforcements, French commanders in the East made herculean efforts to reorganize the remnants of the Grande Armée that trickled out of Russia.

As Prussia's fate once again seemed uncertain, the army refused to allow a repeat of the mistakes made in 1809 and 1812. Despite Berlin's timidity, Bülow proceeded to secure East Prussia's military stores. In the middle of December he halted all convoys and march units en route to Yorck's corps.[4] Bülow also ordered all replacements, recruits, horses, and supplies to move closer to Königsberg. In addition he mobilized all reservists and furloughed soldiers in both East and West Prussia. Bülow instructed the men to report to the fortress of Graudenz on the Vistula, where Col. Heinrich Ludwig von Thümen would form them into reserve battalions. He also summoned several depots to Königsberg and recalled the cavalry patrols from the Baltic coast. Men and horses went to Königsberg, military supplies and equipment to Graudenz.[5] He explained to the French that he was forced to take these measures to save the men and material from the Russians.[6] With both French and Russian troops moving into East Prussia, Bülow had to be prudent. On 19 December the king of Naples and new commander of the Grande Armée, Joachim Murat, established his headquarters in Königsberg. Believing that Bülow commanded 10,000–12,000 men, he demanded that these troops be placed at his disposal. From the outset Bülow evaded French orders and insisted that his small corps consisted only of unarmed recruits.[7]

On 24 December Bülow finally received instructions from Berlin. The king approved Bülow's actions and directed him to form a reserve corps on the Vistula. As soon as Yorck returned from Russia, he would resume his position as governor of East and West Prussia. Bülow, however, would remain in command of the reserve corps. With this royal sanction he doubled his efforts to extract East Prussia's military resources.[8] Frederick William's instructions offered no indication that Berlin would break its alliance with France, yet Bülow did not want to help the French defend East Prussia. On Christmas day Bülow notified Murat that he would move all soldiers capable of bearing arms from Königsberg to the Vistula, away from both the French and Russians.[9] Although Murat knew of his orders to form a reserve corps on the Vistula, Bülow wanted to keep his activities secret. Concealing the movement of men and material throughout the province proved difficult. Notwithstanding Murat's careless compliance, Bülow's work did not escaped the vigilance of the French *intendant-général*, Count Pierre Daru. Charged with supplying the Grande Armée, he noted that Bülow's measures exclusively benefited the Prussians. Daru complained that

Bülow was depriving the French army of supplies, but the Prussians continued to strip the countryside.[10]

Caught between the two warring empires, Prussia had to make a stand. Secret contacts had been maintained throughout the war between the Russians and the Prussians, and Alexander accepted Frederick William's explanation that Napoleon had forced him into the war.[11] Now Alexander needed Prussian assistance to drive the French from his own western frontier. Due to the losses of the previous year, the Russian advance into Central Europe simply could not continue without Prussian support. Frederick William, however, received numerous reminders from the French authorities to remain faithful to their cause.[12] As a result, hope and fear divided Prussia's leadership in the wake of Napoleon's greatest catastrophe. "The Prussian Cabinet," explains Henry Kissinger, "contemplating events from the perspective of past impotence, was paralyzed by the risks inherent in all contingencies: a renewed French advance, great Russian victories, popular passions, or Austrian neutrality."[13]

Frederick William remained terrified of Napoleon's ability to destroy Prussia.[14] Many of his advisors concluded that Prussia's security lay in a firm union with France. They claimed that a pact with St. Petersburg meant far greater dependency on Russia than the French alliance had demanded. The immediate need was to mobilize enough men to help stop the Russians at the Vistula. This would enable Napoleon to rebuild his army, resume the campaign, and secure a victory or at least an advantageous peace. They hoped Prussia would be the recipient of his gratitude. Neither the king nor his chief advisor, Johann Friedrich Ancillon, favored exchanging dependency on France for becoming a Russian satellite. Instead they wanted to exploit Prussia's increased importance and possibly mediate a Franco-Russian peace.[15] As late as 4 February Ancillon proposed that in return for mediating between the two empires, Prussia be restored to a middle-sized state between the Elbe and the Vistula. To entice the belligerents, the Prussians offered East Prussia to Russia and assured the French control of the Rheinbund. Napoleon rejected this offer; but Frederick William's approval of it, which meant that he was ready to sacrifice East Prussia in return for peace and a partial restoration, is telling evidence of the king's fear of war.[16]

Prussia's chancellor, Karl von Hardenberg, believed that Berlin should exploit Napoleon's weakness by demanding a revision of the

Franco-Prussian alliance of 1812.[17] Hardenberg saw an opportunity not only for Prussia's liberation but also for territorial expansion in Germany and possible political hegemony over all of North Germany.[18] Nevertheless, he went along with the pro-French party to gain time. On 26 December Hardenberg wrote that it "is of the utmost importance to show for the present devotion to Napoleon's system and alliances, and to give all our measures the appearance that they are being taken to support France."[19] He recognized that the moment to renounce the hated French alliance and join the Russians had arrived, but Prussia was hardly prepared—either militarily or diplomatically—for such a bold step. Hardenberg also had to harness the prowar patriotism that was sweeping the kingdom. Ultimately his main goal became intertwined with that of the army: getting Frederick William to take a stand.[20]

Napoleon's request for additional Prussian troops encouraged Frederick William, but the king remained wary. The numerous imperial garrisons between the Elbe and the Oder were ominous symbols of French power. With imperial troops quartered in Berlin itself, Frederick William could not risk the same brash conduct that had characterized Prussian foreign policy in 1805–6. Officially at war with Russia, he looked for friends and turned to Vienna, also Napoleon's ally in the war against Russia. By this time most Prussian statesmen had shed their traditional hatred of Austria and hoped to forge a new partnership with Vienna to either wage war against France or jointly mediate a peace.[21] As early as October 1812 Metternich, Austria's foreign minister, had actually taken the initiative and conveyed peace plans to Berlin that included a French withdrawal behind the Rhine and Pyrenees. Of more significance was his suggestion that the Rheinbund states be liberated from Napoleon's control and that Prussia and Austria would jointly protect their independence. According to Metternich, Russia would resume a position similar to its status after Tilsit.[22]

Although the ideas behind these proposals survived, the plans came to naught in the wake of Napoleon's debacle in Russia. As a result the Prussian envoy Col. Karl Friedrich von dem Knesebeck arrived in Vienna on 12 January to revive Metternich's ideas for an Austro-Prussian partnership. Hardenberg still sought an alternative to total dependence on Russia and instructed Knesebeck to request that Vienna join Berlin in an armed neutrality designed to force France and Russia into peace negotiations.[23] Should the Austrians refuse, Knesebeck would then seek Austrian approval of a bilateral Russo-Prussian alliance.[24] Knesebeck's mission entailed a degree of risk, since Austria was still linked to Napoleon through treaty obligations and dynastic ties. Should he succeed, however, an alliance with Austria might offend the Russians and provoke France.[25] Metternich, who insisted on the symmetry of Austro-Prussian interests, assured Knesebeck that an explicit treaty would be superfluous.[26] He realized that an Austro-Prussian alliance would encourage the Prussian peace party and frustrate his own plans to mediate a peace. Moreover, he knew that time would soon run out for Frederick William and that the king would be forced to stand with either the French or the Russians. For this reason Metternich also withheld Austria's official approval of a Russo-Prussian alliance.[27] Instead Knesebeck received only encouragement for the Russo-Prussian alliance and "noncommittal expressions of Austria's goodwill."[28] With the failure of Knesebeck's mission, no other alternative remained for the Prussians but to turn to Russia and hope for fair alliance terms.

News from the East, however, proved just how unpredictable and unstable the situation had become. Since October Yorck had been inundated with Russian offers to defect. He informed Frederick William of the Russian proposals but received no instructions. Yorck had no other choice than to meet with the Russians after they surrounded his troops. On 30 December, just twenty-five miles east of the Russo-Prussian border, he signed the Convention of Tauroggen. This agreement neutralized his corps, thus opening the Prussian frontier to the advancing Russian army.[29] No convincing evidence has ever been produced to prove that Yorck acted on royal authority. Contemporaries claim that permission for such an agreement had been verbally granted by the king, but Frederick William renounced Yorck after news of the convention reached him. This treasonous act, regarded by many Germans as the patriotic gesture that launched the War of Liberation, enabled Russian troops to enter East Prussia unopposed and forced the French to abandon the Niemen.[30]

Despite the weighty decisions that confronted Frederick William, he made a bold stab at power politics. As the price for Prussia's continued loyalty, he demanded territorial restitution and the payment of 90 million francs that France owed for military supplies.[31] Napoleon scornfully dismissed the Prussian envoy who delivered the terms. Now Frederick William either had to obey Napoleon or resolutely follow

Gen. Hans David Ludwig von Yorck (1759–1830). Clausewitz described Yorck as one of the most distinguished men in the Prussian army but claimed that he was gloomy, choleric, reserved, and a bad subordinate who "talked loud when his hopes were lowest and assumed despondency when he entertained no apprehension."

Yorck's lead and ratify a treaty with the Russians. Breaking with France still seemed perilous. A French force of 22,000 men had already assembled on the Vistula.[32] Another 25,000 men occupied Prussia's main fortresses.[33] In Berlin Marshal Pierre Augereau commanded 19,300 men. Despite the Russian disaster, French troop strength in and around Prussia neared 150,000 men.[34] Under these conditions Frederick William could not openly defy Napoleon. Most of his available units were scattered in depots throughout East and West Prussia, Pomerania, and Silesia. His impoverished state could barely afford the equipment and supplies to place the regiments on a war footing. Finally, and most troubling, Russia's intentions remained a mystery. Frederick William could only wonder what the tsar intended for Central Europe. "Russia," as historian Enno Kraehe contends, "was too strong to be resisted and too weak to be trustworthy."[35]

Not knowing of Yorck's negotiations, Bülow continued his own operations during the final days of 1813. On the evening of 29 December the king's adjutant, Maj. Count Wilhelm Ludwig Henckel von Donnersmarck, arrived at Bülow's headquarters; he was returning to Potsdam with Yorck's report of the proceedings at Tauroggen. He informed Bülow that Yorck had separated his troops from the French and that the Russians should be considered allies. The major also claimed that the Russian and Prussian commanders would soon negotiate an agreement to end hostilities between the two countries. A declaration of war against France would be forthcoming. Through Donnersmarck, Yorck urged Bülow to treat the French as the enemy.[36] Donnersmarck only stayed long enough to change horses and then hurried on to Berlin.[37] The news both pleased and disturbed Bülow. He saw his own danger increased by Yorck's unauthorized act. Thus far the French had viewed Bülow's activities as friendly, but Tauroggen could jeopardize all of his work.

On 1 January Bülow received the details of Yorck's convention. Murat, of all people, officially informed him of his countryman's treason.[38] A letter sent by Yorck and carried in secret then reached Bülow's headquarters in Königsberg. He finally learned the full details of the convention. Yorck also requested his cooperation to attack the French with all available forces in East Prussia.[39] Bülow's concern mounted as he considered the dilemmas that Yorck's actions posed for him. Yorck's situation was very different from his. Yorck commanded a battle-ready and experienced force. Furthermore, the Russians were not far away and were obviously willing to cooperate with him. Bülow looked at his recruits—only a small number had received any military training in Scharnhorst's reserve system. His regular troops formed the East Prussian garrisons and were surrounded by superior French forces. Like the king, Bülow had to exercise caution. At any moment his soldiers could be interned, disarmed, or disbanded. One option was to flee eastward with the troops he had in Königsberg to join Yorck. Bülow soon realized that this road was blocked. Macdonald, who was scheduled to arrive in Königsberg on 3 January, stood between him and Yorck. As Bülow contemplated his next step, Murat's fears settled the matter. Distraught over Yorck's defection, the king of Naples transferred his headquarters westward to Elbing. He ordered Bülow to remain in Königsberg and unite with Macdonald. With Murat's departure on 1 January and Macdonald's arrival expected on 3 January, Bülow had two days to escape Macdonald and the pursuing Russians. On the first he sent all military supplies in and around Königsberg to Graudenz. He assembled his 5,000 regulars, reservists, and march detachments in the area of Kreuzberg.[40] Bülow left Königsberg early on the second and arrived in Kreuzberg around noon. He took everything that could be useful, including all of the money and foodstuffs found in the provincial capital.[41] On the following day Macdonald's advance guard reached Königsberg, and Bülow continued his retreat to the Vistula. His columns eventually crossed the frozen river on 9 January.

Bülow planned to complete the mobilization of his corps west of the Vistula, between Neuenburg and Schwetz. French troop movements and demands for his cooperation made this too risky, however. On 8 and 9 January he received two letters from the king of Naples. According to Murat, Frederick William had disavowed and relieved Yorck. Murat insisted that Bülow's troops now formed the auxiliary corps that Prussia had to provide according to the treaty obligations. He ordered Bülow to participate in operations against the Russians.[42] Around the same time Bülow received a communiqué from the Prussian war ministry, dated 6 January. This letter likewise informed Bülow of Yorck's dismissal, ordered him to end all communication with the renegade, and strictly forbade a union with Yorck's troops.[43] On 10 January Bülow informed Murat that his raw recruits could not fight in the field. He also claimed to have orders from his government to move as far westward as necessary to organize the reserve corps. As a result, he decided to move further away and chose the direction of Neu-Stettin in Pomerania, halfway between the Vistula and the Oder Rivers.[44]

There, in Pomerania, another brigade of 6,000 men was being formed by Borstell, who purportedly harbored pro-Russian and anti-French sentiments.[45] Before departing for Neu-Stettin on 11 January, several of Thümen's newly formed reserve battalions from Graudenz united with Bülow's corps. He garrisoned the Vistula fortresses with manpower he had withdrawn from smaller depots in East Prussia.[46] These forces served as the nucleus for eight additional reserve battalions that Thümen soon formed.[47]

Meanwhile Russian Cossacks converged on Bülow's corps as it withdrew to Pomerania. The French initially formed a barrier between the Prussians and Russians, but this screen soon thinned and disappeared altogether. On 12 January Bülow's main body reached Osche, but the Cossacks surrounded his rearguard near Neuenburg.[48] Commanded by Gen. Alexander Ivanovich Chernyshov, the Cossacks arrested three Prussian officers before allowing the rest of the contingent to continue.[49] Bülow, who had reached Tuchel, did not learn of the affair until the fourteenth.[50] When he requested the release of his men, Chernyshov claimed that he would only deliver the captives to Yorck.[51] At Osche Cossacks again surrounded the Prussian rearguard. The Russians demanded their surrender and repeated the promise to deliver them to Yorck. Osche was soon full of Cossacks. They bivouacked in the streets, while the Prussians remained in the barns and stables.[52] Bülow continued to demand the release of his men but could get nowhere with Chernyshov, who responded that the captives would be sent to Yorck. Chernyshov finally yielded after Bülow threatened to attack.[53] Although Bülow secured the release of his cavalry, he eyed the Russians with caution. Until Berlin officially changed its position, he had to protect his corps from both the French and Russians.[54] On 17 January he finally arrived in Neu-Stettin, where he continued to organize his corps for the next several weeks.[55]

As for Yorck, between 26 December and 5 January he dispatched three officers to Berlin with an account of his negotiations at Tauroggen. No reply came. On 8 January he arrived in Königsberg, where his seven battalions and eight squadrons rested for several days. Now behind the Russian army, he met with its commander, Gen. Ludwig Adolf von Wittgenstein. Although Yorck reaffirmed his earlier commitments, he refused to fight the French without royal authorization. To make matters worse, couriers delivered the king's repudiation of the convention as well as instructions for Yorck's dismissal.[56] Yorck refused to surrender his command and declared that he would lead his men against Napoleon, contrary to the king's will.[57] "What are the views held in Berlin?" wrote a distraught Yorck to Bülow on 13 January. "Has one already sunk so deep that he fears to break the chains of slavery, the chains that we have meekly carried for five years? Now or never is the time to regain our freedom and honor." According to Yorck, he had broken his bonds of servitude and would now wage war on his own if necessary. He reasoned that both the army and the people wanted war against France. Even the king himself wanted war but lacked the freedom to act. Yorck explained that it was the army's responsibility to liberate the king and insisted that further hesitation only benefited the French. Although he had broken his oath of obedience, Yorck claimed to have acted "as a faithful servant, as a true Prussian, and without personal regard." He urged "all loyal servants of the king" to take matters into their own hands. "Act, general," he pleaded, "or all will be lost!"[58]

Bülow's agreement with Yorck's views, which is evident from his own letters to Frederick William, cannot be attributed to any personal friendship between the two generals. Their paths had crossed for the first time in September 1797, when both received command of new fusilier battalions. Often forced to cooperate in joint exercises, the two officers developed a mutual disgust. They shared similar views regarding the role of light infantry, but their polar personalities clashed.[59] Later, during the Reform Era, Bülow served with Yorck on a subcommittee chartered to develop new infantry regulations based on open-order tactics, but their mutual hatred did not abate. During the Franco-Austrian War of 1809 their relationship further deteriorated after Yorck attempted to convince Bülow to support the army's prowar party. Conversely, Yorck had developed an intimate relationship with Scharnhorst and many of the reformers. Although Yorck had been a sharp critic of reform, Scharnhorst had won his support on the key issues of universal conscription and light-infantry tactics.

Despite Yorck's rapprochement with the reformers, his relations with Bülow remained icy. In 1811 the two men found the East Prussian town of Marienwerder too small to share as quarters. Yorck revealed his feelings to Scharnhorst in a letter on 22 August 1811: "I will repair my old pistols immediately because I am as sure as I am alive that Bülow and I cannot be together for one week without fighting. . . . As for Bülow and I, you must understand that we cannot stand each other . . . an ugly scene will occur."[60] Scharnhorst encouraged prudence. "Concerning Bülow, I wish that he would retire or take leave," wrote Scharnhorst. "He does not suit our current needs. . . . For the honor of the nation, our military, and especially for the King, I beg you to change your mind and plans about what might happen between you and Bülow; proceed according to the law as soon as he gets out of line."[61]

Fortunately for the Prussians, Yorck was not prophetic: the two parted before an incident occurred. In the current crisis Yorck turned to his old nemesis for support; they put aside their differences for the sake of Prussia. Bülow embraced Yorck's cause and assured the king that recent events would serve to liberate Prussia but cautioned that the state would be dismembered if Frederick William remained faithful to Napoleon. He insisted that an alliance with Russia would result in Germany's liberation and that all of North Germany would unite under the king's protection. He warned that the Russians could not be stopped and that when they reached the Oder the king would have to make a stand. Bülow also expressed his fear that Napoleon would sacrifice Prussian territory in order to make peace with Russia. According to his view, the entire nation had only one wish: a war against France in which the people would "make the greatest sacrifices and make available resources once believed to have been long exhausted."[62]

Bülow's letter, one of many that influenced Frederick William during these pivotal days, arrived at a time when events in the East continued to defy the royal prerogative. In late January Stein, serving as the tsar's commissar of East Prussia and chief advisor on German affairs, returned to Prussia after Napoleon had forced his dismissal five years earlier. At Königsberg Stein summoned a meeting of the East Prussian Diet to discuss armaments and provincial defense.[63] East Prussia faced an uncertain future. Yorck's small force could not prevent the French from stripping the land, as they did prior to the 1812 Campaign. Now the Russians would also be burdening the population with endless requisitions. This concern, along with a call to arms by nationalists such as Arndt, made provincial defense a top priority of all classes. Yet most of the province's eligible manpower had been swept westward by Bülow. This meant that a militia needed to be created from classes that had been traditionally exempt from military service. With Yorck presiding as provincial governor, the East Prussian Landtag decreed the creation of a Landwehr infantry force of 20,000 men and a Landsturm home defense force.[64] Stein, Yorck, and the chairman of the East Prussian Committee of the Estates, Count Alexander Dohna, thus instituted the very process that Scharnhorst had pleaded the king to endorse since 1807: universal conscription. Based on the revolutionary principle of universal military obligation, the East Prussian Landwehr implied universal rights.[65] The East Prussian model helped Scharnhorst overcome Frederick William's resistance to a universally conscripted militia and influenced the mobilization of Prussia's national Landwehr.[66] For now, however, the events in Königsberg served to limit Frederick William's options.[67] The Russians increased their pressure by treating the occupied zones of East Prussia as conquered territory and speaking openly of annexation. National disintegration or war with France appeared to be Frederick William's only alternatives.[68]

Several considerations still prevented the king from breaking his alliance with Napoleon and joining the Russians. The French garrison in Berlin provided Frederick William with a clear reminder of Napoleon's long reach. French officials maintained tight surveillance over their hosts, and the threat that they might seize the king remained constant. Hardenberg finally convinced Frederick William to flee to Breslau, the provincial capital of Silesia. The king left Potsdam on 21 January and reached Breslau four days later. There events similar to those in Königsberg had already taken place, and recruits were streaming in from all over the kingdom.[69] Although Frederick William had escaped the French forces that controlled his capital, the much-anticipated Russian alliance was not the immediate result. At this time demands for war did not correspond with Prussia's diplomatic needs.

As for the Russians, they were prepared to carry the war westward in a great effort to drive the French from Central Europe.[70] The destruction of the Grande Armée offered an opportunity to build a Russian-dominated coalition to liberate Europe. Russia's diplomatic offensive, however, had not fared well from the start. Continued activity in the Balkans and the Transcaucasus kept Vienna and Constantinople suspicious of Russia's intentions.[71] To the north Alexander had stepped forward as the patron of the new crown prince of Sweden, the former French marshal Bernadotte, after Napoleon occupied Swedish Pomerania in January 1812. Four months later the tsar agreed to Sweden's conquest of Norway to compensate Stockholm for Russia's annexation of Finland.[72] In August 1812 Alexander and Bernadotte signed the Convention of Abo, which called for a Swedish military operation in North

Germany with approximately 30,000 men. According to the preliminary terms, Bernadotte would spark a German uprising behind the lines of the Grande Armée as Napoleon struggled to master Russia. For the Prussians, the convention's controversy stemmed from Russia's claim to the Vistula as its future frontier. This caused concern in Berlin over the fate of East Prussia and Silesia and prompted London and Vienna to view Russian war aims as imperialistic.[73]

Notwithstanding Frederick William's flight to Silesia, Napoleon expected the Prussians to defend their frontiers against the Russians. On 29 January Hardenberg received Napoleon's demand for the prompt formation of a second Prussian corps.[74] He promised the emperor that the new contingent would be organized quickly and be commanded by Bülow.[75] Despite the positive dialogue with the Prussians, Napoleon remained concerned that rebels now controlled the Prussian army.[76] Even more disconcerting was the news that Prussian mobilization had received popular support. Eugène de Beauharnais, viceroy of Italy and new commander of the French army in Prussia after Murat departed for Naples, informed Napoleon that Prussian peasants offered their government cloth and money and sold horses for ridiculously low prices.[77] French officials could no longer ignore Prussia's military preparations, despite assurances that the recruits would fight under the French flag. Recruiting substantially increased after the king relocated to Breslau, and the emperor thought better of leaving these troops under the command of a Prussian general.[78] Hardenberg explained that unless the king mobilized his army to control the insurgency he risked being overthrown.[79] Napoleon remained suspicious; with Yorck's defection as a precedent, he decided to place Bülow's corps under the command of Marshal Claude Victor.[80]

Victor received the difficult task of convincing Bülow to accept his orders. The Prussian continued to disobey on the grounds that his corps consisted of unarmed recruits. He would do nothing until he received orders from his government.[81] Bülow's continued defiance convinced Eugène that this Prussian general had also defected. The inaccurate report that Bülow had honored Chernyshov with a ball on 10 February only intensified French suspicion. On the fifteenth Victor informed Eugène of Bülow's refusal to cooperate.[82] This news, along with the continued Russian advance, appeared daunting. In a letter to Napoleon Eugène complained of Bülow's evasive responses. "Your Majesty can see how little one can depend on these troops and, on the other hand, how much to distrust them," he complained. "In his letter, Bülow claims that he will only proceed according to the orders of his sovereign. . . . He pushes the limits of imprudence by throwing balls for the enemy's generals and he is continually in negotiation with them; Cossacks camp in the same villages as Prussian battalions!"[83]

Uncertainty over Prussia's next move, the continued Russian advance, and manpower shortages prompted Eugène to abandon the Vistula and withdraw to the Oder in mid-February. As the French retreated to the Oder, one of Eugène's attachés, Van Zuylen Van Nyevelt, met with Bülow at Neu-Stettin. During their meeting Bülow rejected a request to furnish mounts for the French army on the grounds that he was not obligated to obey the viceroy's commands. Moreover, after refusing to march to Stettin to hold the fortress against the Russians, Bülow hinted that he might withdraw to the Baltic fortress of Kolberg. To add insult to injury, Van Zuylen informed Eugène that Bülow had made a very dubious agreement to release 400 Russian prisoners to a delegation of Cossacks.[84] Without Prussian support Eugène knew that he could not hold the Oder. He expected to receive a Prussian declaration of war at any moment. Due to this fear, the viceroy continued the retreat to Berlin on 18 February.[85]

While Eugène surrendered land for time, direct negotiations between the Russians and Prussians had commenced on 3 February. Although Hardenberg claimed that the Convention of Tauroggen was the least of his concerns, he strove to prevent Prussia from becoming "compromised with France too early."[86] He understood the likelihood of a rupture with France and the crucial need for an alliance with Russia. Thus, after Knesebeck returned from Vienna, Hardenberg sent him to join Alexander's headquarters as it moved through the Grand Duchy of Warsaw with the main Russian army. On 15 February Knesebeck met with the Russians, who eagerly expected to receive a copy of Frederick William's declaration of war on France. Instead Knesebeck demanded an official alliance and Russia's firm commitment to restore Prussia. Like Metternich, Alexander claimed that the current circumstances rendered a formal treaty between Prussia and Russia unnecessary since he too desired Prussia's liberation.[87] This may well have been sincere, yet the tsar's unpredictability—as well as uncertainty over Russia's ambitions—made the situation too risky for verbal assurances: the Prussians had not forgotten the Abo Convention.[88] Paul Schroeder describes the tsar's zeal to liberate Prussia and Europe as "messianic" but adds that Alexander was only willing to befriend Prussia "as a forgiven sinner to be watched, kept on the right path, and not permitted to question his decisions and leadership on vital questions, especially Poland."[89]

Russia's foreign minister, Count Karl von Nesselrode, hoped that a Prussian general would cause a decisive rupture between France and Prussia. Once this happened, the Russians would be able to impose conditions on a desperate Frederick William. As soon as Knesebeck arrived at the tsar's headquarters, the Russians demanded that he order Bülow to unite with Wittgenstein. "Before the adoption of this measure," countered Knesebeck, "it is necessary to discuss the alliance." Nesselrode replied that while they "attended to discussions, [Gen. Paul] Grenier's corps would move to a safe distance, that it would soon be impossible to reach it, and that it was absolutely indispensable to force Bülow to march so that Wittgenstein had support after crossing the Oder." Knesebeck then claimed that he had no authorization to write such a note; nor did Bülow have the authorization to obey any order from him. The Russians lamented that the opportunity to annihilate Eugène's forces would be lost if the Prussians continued to hesitate. Although Nesselrode made every effort to secure Prussian support for Wittgenstein's advance to the Oder, Knesebeck displayed more savvy than the Russians expected.[90]

Two days later, during a council of war at Kolo on the Warthe River, the Russians again demanded that Knesebeck order Bülow to unite with Wittgenstein. With the main Russian army just a few marches from the Prussian frontier, Nesselrode presented a plan that would position Yorck, Bülow, and Wittgenstein to attack Eugène as soon as Prussia declared war on France. With Bülow's 10,000 men on the right, Yorck's 20,000 in the center, and Wittgenstein's 10,000 on the left, this combined army would concentrate east of Berlin on the lower Oder, between Stettin and Küstrin. From this position the Russians believed they would be able to drive Eugène from the Elbe. Meanwhile, the Russian commander-in-chief, Mikhail Kutuzov, would move the main Russian army from Kolo to Magdeburg. Kutuzov would take a position to engage Eugène if he turned on Leipzig or Dresden. From Silesia Blücher's Prussians would simultaneously advance on Dresden.[91]

Knesebeck agreed with the Russian plan and informed Bülow that it would be "completely appropriate" for him to position his corps near Stettin on the left bank of the Oder. He advised Bülow to march westward from Neu-Stettin to observe the various French and Russian troops marching to the Oder. Knesebeck suggested that Bülow could move closer to Wittgenstein by marching to the Oder in accordance with Eugène's orders to hold Stettin against the Russians. Knesebeck wrote Bülow on the urging of Nesselrode, but the letter stressed prudence rather than calling for an offensive. He insisted that Bülow could not open hostilities against the French yet presumed that the situation would be clarified by the time Bülow and Yorck reached the Oder. In his report to Hardenberg, Knesebeck explained that Bülow's movement would "save face and not provide cause for the French to complain. The pretext to cover Stettin will justify Bülow's march in the eyes of this power. However, if this General remains in his current position without moving, while the Russians advance by forced marches, the French will view our inactivity as an agreement with the Russian court."[92]

Wittgenstein had crossed the Vistula on 13 January and proceeded westward. After sending two-thirds of his force to mask the French garrison in Danzig, he was left with an advance guard of 10,000 men. To increase his numbers he requested that Yorck and Bülow join him in a rapid advance to the Oder. Yorck agreed but would not commit to offensive operations. The Russians made similar approaches to Bülow, who claimed neutrality. Wittgenstein could not continue offensive operations without Prussian support, but they refused to open hostilities against the French without explicit orders from Frederick William. On 22 February Bülow met Wittgenstein and Yorck in Konitz to discuss Kutuzov's plan.[93] Yorck, who still had not received any pardon or instructions from the king, admitted to Wittgenstein that the situation was nothing short of embarrassing.[94] Bülow informed Yorck and Wittgenstein of Knesebeck's call for prudence. Ultimately the Prussians proved more patient than the Russians expected. Both Prussian generals claimed that they would not participate in an offensive against the French. Despite their refusal, they agreed to preliminary movements to the Oder in anticipation of Prussia's declaration of war on France.[95] Prussian tenacity, however, frustrated the tsar. Since Bülow and Yorck declined an offensive role in the plan, he canceled the entire operation.[96] Wittgenstein received orders to halt—as soon as the Prussians rendered a decision, the movement would continue.

Despite the failure to implicate Bülow or Yorck, diplomatic negotiations continued at a heated pace. Suspicion stood in the way of compromise, and Poland emerged as a point of contention. Alexander dreamed of reestablishing a Polish kingdom under Russian hegemony. He promised German territory in return for Prussian Poland, but Knesebeck refused. Knesebeck either misunderstood or deliberately ignored Hardenberg's instructions regarding Poland and Prussia's restoration. Hardenberg was willing to sacrifice some of Prussian Poland in return for Russian guarantees to support Prussian expansion in Germany and Berlin's political leadership of North Germany.[97] The Russians offered to support Prussia's pre-1806 material restoration, but Knesebeck sought Alexander's commitment to restore Prussia's pre-1806 frontiers. Negotiations incomprehensibly dragged on for another two weeks before culminating on 28 February with the signing of the Treaty of Kalisch—the much-anticipated Russo-Prussian military alliance. The Prussians agreed to field an army of 80,000 men to assist a Russian contingent of 150,000; both states pledged not to make a separate peace with Napoleon. Alexander promised to restore Prussia's pre-Jena material status, and Frederick William acknowledged that he would lose most of his Polish territory. Prussia would be compensated by Allied conquests in Germany, specifically Saxony.

Thus the Polish-Saxon Question, which, according to historian Rory Muir, "bedeviled Allied relations for the next two years," was officially born.[98] Prussia did assume the role of Russia's junior partner—a logical position considering Frederick William's vulnerable position, financial weakness, and foreign policy record.[99] Frederick William understood what the Russo-Prussian pact required of him. In return for Russia's pledge to restore his state, the king accepted a subordinate role. "To be safe in the arms of the strong power," explains Enno Kraehe, "the weak one must be absolutely unswerving and devoted in its loyalty."[100] More importantly, the Prussians received a treaty that did not enslave them as Napoleon had the previous year; nor did it reduce the state to a Russian satellite. Alexander pledged to fight for Prussia's restoration in terms of territory and population. Although the Russians offered no assurances of Prussian hegemony in North Germany, Hardenburg could count on his position being considerably strengthened by Alexander's support. With Russian backing, he would be able to deal with Metternich as an equal.[101]

Like the Prussians, Alexander had also hoped for an Austrian alliance in early 1813, but Metternich feared that Russian success would be accompanied by territorial expansion.[102] With Russian armies approaching Central Europe, the Austrians declared neutrality. According to historian Steven Ross, Metternich intended to bargain with all belligerents in order to "enhance Austrian power, severely reduce but not destroy French influence, and prevent any other state from replacing France as Europe's dominant power."[103] He had hoped to use Prussia to check Russian ambitions, but the Treaty of Kalisch altered the diplomatic landscape. A grateful Frederick William now stood firmly behind his Russian benefactor, and not even Metternich would be able to change this fact. This setback proved minor compared to the broader meaning of Kalisch and subsequent Russian actions. Rather than digest the immediate gains of East Prussia and Poland, Alexander opted to press the war into Central Europe. Russian armies moved west to liberate the peoples of Europe from French rule. Although Kalisch said nothing of the liberation and unification of Germany, Alexander dreamed of directing its reconstruction.[104] The tsar's zeal to liberate Europe on his own terms jeopardized Metternich's plans and strengthened the hand of the pro-French party in the Habsburg court.

Signing the Treaty of Kalisch did entail a large risk for the Prussians. All reports warned that considerable French forces were moving into Germany. Frederick William delayed issuing a formal declaration of war against France to allow the army more time to mobilize, but all signs indicated that war was inevitable. On 10 March he decreed the creation of the Iron Cross—the new military decoration that became the symbol of the Prussian and future German armies. Six days later Frederick William finally declared war on France. On 17 March he issued his *An mein Volk* proclamation that summoned the Prussian people to fight for their freedom and make sacrifices for their king, Fatherland, and honor. Although it appeared that Frederick William had just decreed a patriotic people's war, the cautious king laid the groundwork to control and subvert the efforts of "the people" just two days later.[105] The long road that led to the triumph of conservatism in Prussia began on 19 March, when the Russians and the Prussians signed the Treaty of Breslau—the diplomatic supplement to the military alliance forged at Kalisch. According to its terms, the Russians affirmed their agreements to restore Prussia's pre-Jena material strength and renounced the clauses concerning East Prussia in the Russo-Swedish Convention of Abo. Alexander also relinquished his dream of uniting all of Poland. For now the tsar promised Frederick William enough Polish territory to connect East Prussia and Silesia. Prussia would be compensated for the loss of other Polish territory with German land; Saxony remained the target of future Prussian expansion. For Prussia, the Kalisch and Breslau agreements—conventional state treaties—meant that the struggle ultimately would be a "cabinet war" rather than a people's war.[106]

The British did their part to bolster the new coalition by reestablishing diplomatic relations with the Prussians. They promptly dispatched 54 cannon along with arms and ammunition for 23,000 men to the Baltic to be split between the Russians and Prussians.[107] The Allies needed much more, and for this reason London launched a diplomatic initiative aimed at Sweden. Although Bernadotte had disappointed the British and Russians by failing to participate in the 1812 Campaign, the British again offered subsidies for a Swedish army to fight on the Continent. Like Napoleon, Bernadotte tied his popularity to the success of his foreign policy. In 1810 the Swedes had elected him to be King Charles XIII's heir. Bernadotte, or Charles John (his adopted name), dreamed of attaining Norway as a gift for his adopted country and as means to secure his dynasty. Denmark, a French ally, had no intentions of handing over Norway to the upstart Swedish prince-royal. After Napoleon refused to help, Bernadotte turned to Russia and Great Britain. By healing long-standing diplomatic rifts with Russia, he won support for attaining Norway as long as Sweden participated in the struggle against France. In early 1813 the British hoped that generous concessions would stir Bernadotte. They pledged to support Stockholm's claim to Norway and discussed the possibility of Sweden's acquisition of the Caribbean island of Guadeloupe. Bernadotte, however, could not be bought that easily. In negotiations that lasted for three months, the crown prince insisted that his army first be used against Denmark. The British countered with more funds; on 3 March Bernadotte finally accepted London's condition that his Swedes fight on the Continent first.[108]

As for Alexander, the burden of waging war in Central Europe fell on him in this early stage of the contest. Russia's front-line army consisted of 51,745 men, 12,283 Cossacks, and 439 guns when it crossed the Prussian frontier. Reinforcements, not expected to reach the front until the beginning of April, amounted to 12,674 men, 2,307 Cossacks, and 48 guns. Russian second-line troops—56,776 men, 9,989 Cossacks, and 319 guns—conducted sieges on the Oder and the Vistula.[109] A reserve of 48,100 men had still not left Russia.[110] Directly opposing the

Russian front line, Eugène fielded a force of 44,110 men and 81 guns.[111] French garrisons stranded on the Elbe, Oder, and Vistula and in the Grand Duchy of Warsaw totaled 69,250 men.[112] By February Eugène had 80,000 men in the field.[113] One month later he was able to deploy 113,360 men and 185 guns to confront the smaller and equally exhausted and disorganized Russian army.[114] Additional French reinforcements between the Rhine and the Elbe amounted to 142,905 men and 320 guns.[115]

As the Russians struggled to move their army to the front, several factors hampered Prussian mobilization in January and February. French troops still occupied half of the country and held all of Prussia's significant fortresses. Tedious negotiations with the Russians also hampered the process. Concentration of the field army, scheduled to begin on 12 February, had to be postponed until the signing of an alliance. Mobilization then continued at an accelerated pace for the next two weeks and culminated with the 17 March decrees that created a national Landwehr. At the beginning of the war the Prussian army consisted of 127,394 men and 269 guns. Only 65,675 of these men had received sufficient training to be utilized in the field; only half of Prussia's armed forces were trained regulars or reservists.[116]

After Prussia's declaration of war, Allied strategy moved from theory to practice. Russian advance troops had crossed the Oder and attempted a *coup de main* on Berlin on 20 February. The appearance of enemy forces west of the Oder convinced Eugène to evacuate the city. On 5 March the viceroy withdrew his forces and marched toward Magdeburg on the Elbe River.[117] Berlin was free from French control for the first time in over six years. Since Eugène's retreat suggested that he could not offer much resistance, Kutuzov ordered a general advance to the Elbe in three main groups. Wittgenstein's army of 19,000 Russians supported by 30,000 Prussians under Bülow and Yorck formed the right wing. Blücher's force of 27,000 Prussians and 14,000 Russians advanced on the left wing from Silesia to Dresden. Kutuzov's main body of 30,000 men followed Blücher. At the Elbe the Allies extended their forces southward in order to maintain communication with Austria. They expected that the Austrian war hawks would sway Francis I into declaring war against his son-in-law.

Although the offensive finally began, hesitation marked Allied war planning from the start. Russian councils of war had been divided for some time. While Alexander fashioned himself as the liberator of

Germany, Kutuzov opposed carrying the war into Central Europe to liberate the same countries that had supported Napoleon's bid to conquer Russia. Other Russian commanders expressed concerns over their long line of communications. Kutuzov favored a slow advance that would allow him to reorganize his army after a deadly winter campaign that had devastated invader and defender alike. After being reappointed as chief of staff of the Prussian Army, Scharnhorst attempted to coordinate operations with Kutuzov, who placed little value on his new Prussian allies. Scharnhorst urged a combined offensive to destroy Eugène's forces before Napoleon arrived with a fresh army. After some modification the plan that finally emerged called for Wittgenstein to cover Berlin by striking the Elbe southeast of Magdeburg. As soon as Blücher reached supporting distance, Wittgenstein would cross the Elbe at Rosslau, and both armies would proceed to Leipzig. The Allies hoped that the appearance of Wittgenstein's advance guard on the lower Saale River and that of Blücher's army on the Pleisse would prevent Eugène from attempting to retake Berlin.[118] Allied forces would also be in position to thwart Napoleon's inevitable counteroffensive.

Two letters from Frederick William explained Bülow's role in the upcoming offensive. Dated 24 and 26 March, the king's extensive instructions all pointed to the same objective: Bülow was to defend Berlin with all possible means to avoid a repeat of 1806, when Napoleon triumphantly rode through the Brandenburg Gate at the head of the victorious Grande Armée.[119] In a meeting with Wittgenstein in Berlin on 29 March, Bülow received additional orders to send a portion of his 11,000-man East and West Prussian Brigade to observe the French-occupied fortress of Spandau while he led the majority of his troops to Ziesar. Bülow's assignment was to defend Brandenburg from Eugène's army, which Allied intelligence placed at Magdeburg. For this task he was to unite with and take command of Borstell's Pomeranian Brigade, much to the chagrin of Borstell, who proved to be a difficult subordinate.[120] After concluding their conference by assigning Bülow the weighty responsibility of defending Berlin, Wittgenstein left the Prussian capital to rejoin Yorck; their combined forces were already on the march to Rosslau. Not only had Yorck persevered during the uncertain days that followed Tauroggen, but he had received command of Prussia's Second Corps after a board of inquiry exonerated him on the pretext that military necessity had prompted him to sign the Convention of Tauroggen.[121] The East and West Prussian Brigade along with the

Pomeranian Brigade formed the Second Division of Yorck's corps; Bülow was divisional commander and was subordinated to Yorck. As operations shifted deeper into Saxony and farther away from Berlin, however, Bülow assumed independent command over his division, which was soon termed a corps in Allied correspondence.[122]

As for Eugène, once he learned that Wittgenstein had led his army to Rosslau, he took a position east of Magdeburg with 54,000 men and 186 guns.[123] Wittgenstein attacked him at Möckern on the morning of 6 April. Alarmed over his communications with Magdeburg, Eugène ordered a general retreat across the Elbe. Although both sides suffered minimal losses, the clash proved significant for several reasons.[124] Most importantly, the Prussian troops that participated achieved success in their first combat. The soldiers purportedly assailed Eugène's troops with intensity. Bülow, who arrived in time to participate in the battle, informed his wife that his troops had fought with "an indescribable bitterness."[125] Moreover, Allied propaganda exploited the engagement as another French calamity: another sure sign that Napoleon's empire teetered on the verge of collapse. After Möckern, Wittgenstein, who replaced Kutuzov as Allied commander-in-chief, advanced into Saxony to unite with Blücher. Wittgenstein then concentrated the Allied army at Leipzig with the intention of driving the French out of Saxony and inducing the Austrians to enter the war.[126] Should the Allies be defeated, Bülow had orders to assemble as many units as possible and take a position between Brandenburg, Potsdam, and Wittenberg to guard Berlin against an inevitable French counteroffensive. In the meantime, from his position between the Saale and lower Mulde Rivers, Bülow was to observe the lower Saale, monitor the viceroy's movements, launch cavalry raids across the Saale to disrupt French communications, and cover the Allied siege of Wittenberg.[127] Although he was separated from the decisive events in Saxony, his fate depended on Wittgenstein's success.

Napoleon originally based his strategy on the hope of reaching the Vistula River. He envisioned a drive through the North German plain that would reassert his dominance over Prussia and rescue the Oder and Vistula garrisons. The emperor noted that "after conducting demonstrations to convince the enemy that I will march against Dresden and into Silesia, I will probably march to Havelberg, reach Stettin by forced marches with 300,000 men, and continue the march to Danzig, which I could reach in fifteen days. On the twentieth day of the movement . . .

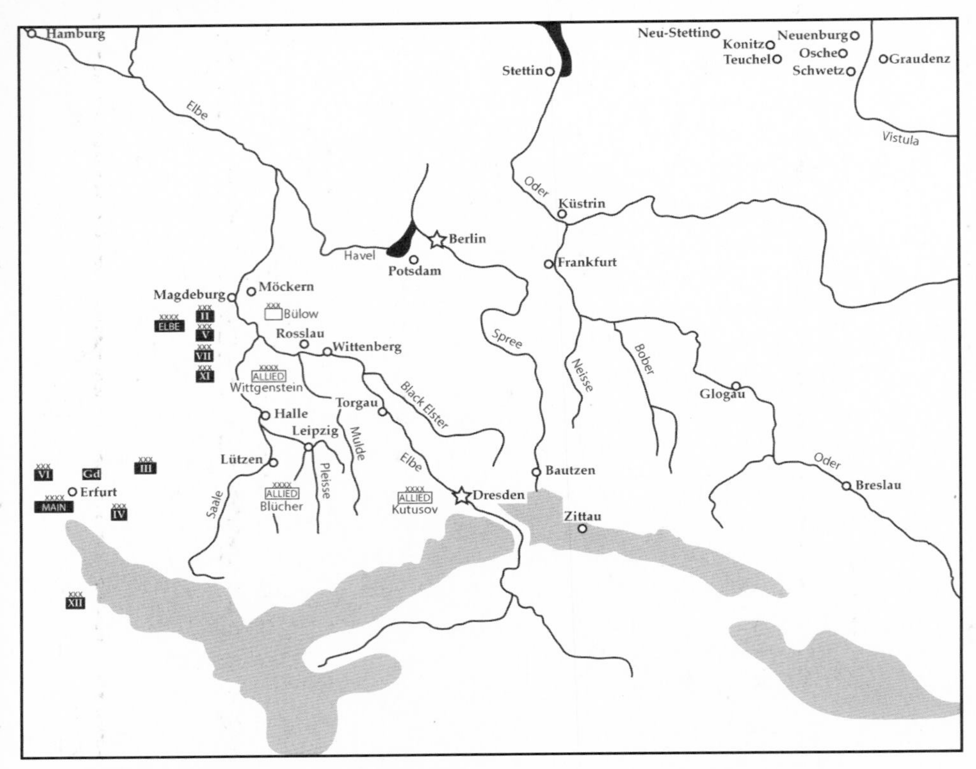

The Situation on 25 April 1813

I should have relieved that place and be master of Marienburg, of the Island of Nogat, and of all the bridges of the lower Vistula."[128] Prussia's declaration of war, the Russian advance, and Eugène's successive retreats forced Napoleon to postpone this operation. Thus he concentrated fresh forces on the left bank of the Saale River throughout April. He correctly assumed that the Allies knew nothing of his movements.[129] On 30 April the emperor began his counteroffensive by leading 120,000 men across the Saale to confront the Allied army near Leipzig. Two days later Wittgenstein found Marshal Michel Ney's French corps isolated near the farming village of Lützen, southwest of Leipzig. Not knowing that the rest of the French army was close enough to support Ney, Wittgenstein attacked with 73,000 men.[130] A few hours later Napoleon reached the battlefield, summoned his reserves, and had 110,000 troops on the field by late afternoon. Although the Russians and Prussians fought well, an attack by the Imperial Guard decided the day. Each side lost 20,000 men. Napoleon's shortage of cavalry prevented him from exploiting the victory and allowed the Allied army to escape. Nevertheless, Allied morale plummeted as the army retreated eastward. Napoleon once again proclaimed himself the master of Europe.

While Wittgenstein contested Napoleon at Lützen, Bülow's mobile corps of 4,500 men drove a French garrison from Halle after a tough day of street fighting.[131] Prussian losses numbered 8 officers and 225 men dead or wounded, while the French lost approximately 700 men.[132] Bülow could not enjoy his success for long; rumors soon reached Halle that Napoleon had defeated Wittgenstein near Leipzig. Bülow dispatched numerous patrols in the hope of discovering the fate of Wittgenstein's army. He even aimed the telescopes in Halle's observatory at the horizon in an attempt to discern distant troop movements. Fugitives and deserters from both sides rendered inconsistent accounts. On the evening of 4 May his scouts finally returned from Wittgenstein's headquarters and reported that the Allies had been defeated at Lützen and were now retreating to Dresden. Knowing that he had to defend Berlin, Bülow also ordered a retreat.[133] The corps left Halle within two hours and reached Dessau on the following afternoon. Bülow sent cavalry detachments to comb the left bank of the Elbe. Rumors indicated that strong French forces had left Lützen and marched in the direction of Wittenberg, but his patrols found no evidence to support these claims.[134]

During the night of 5–6 May Bülow received a message that Wittgenstein intended to hold the upper Mulde and wanted Bülow to retake Halle. Moreover, Bülow was encouraged by a report that Thümen and his detachment, which had been relieved from the siege of Spandau, had reached Rosslau after marching for twenty-four hours.[135] Later that same evening he received an order from the king that instructed him to retreat north through Rosslau and over the Elbe to cover Berlin. Frederick William assured him that a guerrilla war would erupt in the countryside if the French advanced against Berlin.[136] Such conflicting orders from Allied headquarters remained a discomforting norm that all Allied commanders faced. Like most generals, Bülow obeyed the orders of his monarch rather than those of the commander-in-chief. As it was, Wittgenstein abandoned Dresden and continued his retreat eastward to the Spree River.

After Lützen, Napoleon pursued the Allied army in the direction of Dresden but placed an army of 45,000 men under Ney's command. The

Marshal Michel Ney (1769–1815). After Waterloo and the second Bourbon Restoration, Ney was found guilty of treason by the French Chamber of Peers and executed by a firing squad in the Luxembourg gardens on 7 December 1815.

marshal had orders to march down the Elbe, raise the sieges of Wittenberg and Torgau, threaten the right flank of the Allied army, and force Wittgenstein to abandon the Elbe. Once Napoleon learned that Wittgenstein had retreated farther eastward to the Spree River, he ordered Ney to take Berlin.[137] At forty-four years of age Marshal Ney, the duc d'Elchingen and the prince de la Moskowa, one of Napoleon's most decorated senior officers, enjoyed a well-deserved reputation for being "the bravest of the brave."[138] Purportedly the last Frenchman to leave Russian soil in 1812, Ney had commanded Napoleon's rear guard during the final phase of the retreat from Moscow. A capable tactician, Ney typified the marshalate of the First Empire. Although revered by his men—as well as Napoleon—for his fearlessness, Ney was no strategist. When not under his master's watchful eye he often succumbed to his fiery personality, which featured a savage temper governed by pride.[139]

Ney began his march to Torgau on 5 May. He dispatched two divisions of his Third Corps to relieve Wittenberg, while Victor also moved east from Bernburg toward Wittenberg.[140] On the sixth an impatient Napoleon urged Ney to get his forces to Torgau and Wittenberg. The emperor hoped that the appearance of a French army seventy miles south of Berlin would induce Frederick William to direct his Prussians northward to save their capital. Should the Prussians and Russians split, the emperor planned to mask the Russians and destroy the Prussians as they marched to Berlin.[141] If the Prussians remained in Saxony with the Russians, Ney would easily capture Berlin. The fall of Berlin represented the first and most crucial step in implementing Napoleon's "master plan." He believed that the suppression of Prussia had to begin with a morale-breaking conquest of Berlin, which would presumably end Prussia's mobilization. Napoleon also wanted to control the plain between the Elbe and the Oder Rivers. Not only would the two rivers and their fortresses protect his left flank, but as the campaign lengthened and taxed the resources of Saxony he believed that North Germany would better sustain his forces. Napoleon's preoccupation with relieving the besieged garrisons on the Oder and Vistula Rivers and augmenting his armies with the almost mythical numbers of French veterans was another key component of the "master plan." Finally, the emperor believed that a drive through North Germany to the Vistula would force the Russians out of Central Europe by threatening their lines of communication.[142]

A successful French operation against Berlin followed by a drive over the Oder to the Vistula offered strategic advantages. Since Napoleon's conscript army and depleted cavalry did not allow him the mobility to force the Allies to accept battle under adverse conditions, he hoped a secondary operation in North Germany would create opportunities in Saxony. According to this strategy of maneuver, the emperor believed that a *coup de théâtre* would enable him to outflank the enemy army by reaching the Oder or the Vistula before his adversaries did.[143] Numerically superior French forces would allow Napoleon to place an army in North Germany that was considerably larger than anything the Allies could muster, while his Grande Armée still outnumbered Allied forces in Saxony. If the Prussians remained with the Russians, Napoleon planned to drive the retreating Allied army out of Saxony, through Silesia, and into Poland, where Ney would be waiting on the Vistula with 100,000 men. But would Napoleon violate his own principles and divide his forces rather than concentrate them for the annihilation of the main enemy army?

The Defense of Berlin

A short man with a curved nose and deep blue eyes, Bülow benefited from a wealthy and eccentric father who provided his five sons, raised during the Enlightenment, with a private yet thorough education.[1] Bülow's emotional and turbulent personality represented Jean-Jacques Rousseau's romantic ideals, while his aesthetic reverence for culture and education reflected Voltaire's rationalism. Although cheerful, Bülow had a ferocious temper. He considered himself a gourmet and loved a full table graced with good wine. Born in 1755, Bülow served three Prussian kings from the age of thirteen until his death in 1816. As a captain he received his first combat experience against revolutionary France in 1793. In 1806 Colonel von Bülow remained in garrison during the debacle at Jena-Auerstädt. After seeing combat in East Prussia, he emerged from the war of the Fourth Coalition with a sound reputation but faced the agony of losing his wife to complications after the birth of their only child, Marianne, on 29 June 1807. In 1808 Bülow served on the Superior Investigating Commission that examined the reasons behind the army's collapse in the recent war. In June of that year the fifty-three-year-old Bülow married Pauline, the eighteen-year-old sister of his late spouse. Although sorrow brought them together, their relationship became intimate. In 1809 Frederick William appointed him to be Blücher's adjutant. The two men had a turbulent relationship

Gen. Friedrich Wilhelm von Bülow (1755–1816). For his victory over Ney, Bülow received the rank and title of Count Bülow von Dennewitz; in 1814 a snubbed Tauentizien challenged Bülow to a duel, claiming that Bülow had robbed him and his men of their honor.

and parted as enemies. The rift with Blücher did not prevent Bülow from advancing. In 1811 he received command of the West Prussian Brigade and assumed the post of governor of East and West Prussia and Lithuania during the war against Russia. In 1813 the king honored him with the tremendous responsibility of guarding the nation's capital.[2]

Bülow shared this task with the recently formed Military Government in Berlin. On 15 March 1813 Frederick William had partitioned his kingdom into four autonomous Military Governments whose main tasks were to mobilize the Landwehr and arrange local defense measures.[3] Prior to the war a persistent theme among the military reform party had been the creation of a Prussian militia. The reformers believed that a Landwehr could provide the fusion of *Volk* and army that would create a "nation in arms," where citizen-subjects championed the virtues of civic pride and soldierly honor.[4] Aside from hopes and speculation, they failed to agree on the Landwehr's organization or purpose. Conservatives feared that a popular levy would nationalize the army; their persistent opposition had restricted the theoretical development of the Landwehr between 1807 and 1812. The king's refusal to approve plans for the establishment of a militia actually benefited the reformers, who desired to keep the Landwehr separate from the army—only Prussia's chronic shortage of manpower in 1813 allowed the Landwehr to develop as an independent institution. This fulfilled the reformers' intentions of creating a popular national defense force that would counter the "more militaristic, more isolated and more feudalistic" regular army.[5]

The king did establish universal conscription in 1813, but its form corresponded to Prussia's caste society. Rather than a revolutionary levy modeled after the French, the Prussians created a military organization for each social group: the Landwehr for the landed peasants and middle class; the *Jäger* for the upper class; and the regular army for the masses.[6] Men between the ages of eighteen and forty would serve in the Landwehr, while older men between forty and sixty years of age would serve in the Landsturm insurrectionary force. The Landsturm would be summoned when the enemy threatened a specific location. Units would then conduct scorched-earth operations to sabotage and disrupt enemy lines of communication.[7] The Spanish guerrillas provided the philosophical inspiration for the Landsturm, but the cautious king never accepted the principle of a popular insurrectionary force. On 21 April 1813 a hesitant Frederick William signed the Landsturm decrees.[8] In its original form the Landsturm would only last three months before conservative opposition prompted the king to curtail its role sharply.[9]

Despite the ideological efforts of the reformers to win the hearts and minds of their compatriots, each Prussian province experienced obstacles in the recruitment of the militia except for East Prussia, where the hardships of the French occupation had embittered the population.[10] Raising the Landwehr in the Kurmark province—the very heart of the kingdom—proved to be a problem. Bordered by Mecklenburg to the north, the Elbe River to the west, Saxony to the south, and the Oder River to the east, the Kurmark, or Electoral Mark, formed the core of Brandenburg. The Kurmark province fell under the jurisdiction of the Military Government between the Elbe and the Oder—one of the four administrative units created in March.[11] From Berlin civil governor Dr. Johann August Sack and military governor Gen. Anton Wilhelm von L'Estoq jointly administered the Military Government. They worked closely with the president of the Kurmark General-Commission for Landwehr and Landsturm, Magnus Friedrich von Bassewitz, to raise the Kurmark militia's projected twenty-eight infantry battalions and twenty-eight cavalry squadrons from a population of 700,000. In addition to organizing the Landwehr, the Military Government in Berlin also controlled the Kurmark's Landsturm.

When Bülow received the task of guarding Berlin, he hoped to be supported by the Kurmark's irregular forces. According to Bülow's plan, the Landwehr and Landsturm would hold the Havel River from Potsdam to Havelberg, while his army corps assumed the direct defense of Berlin.[12] Delays in the mobilization of the Landwehr, however, meant that the available manpower for the defense of Berlin remained minimal for much of April and May. To compensate for the shortage of troops the Military Government in Berlin devised a comprehensive scheme to flood the countryside surrounding Berlin by damming the region's river network. The dams and other strategic points would be guarded by an extensive system of fortifications.[13] This plan called for the construction of fortifications at the crossings over the Nuthe, Nuthe Canal, Notte, Havel, Spree, and Oder Rivers, as well as around the capital itself.[14]

With Napoleon's victory at Lützen on 2 May and the subsequent Allied retreat, Saxony fell to the French. On 3 May the king of Prussia informed both the Military Government in Berlin and Bülow that a French operation against Berlin appeared likely.[15] Three days later

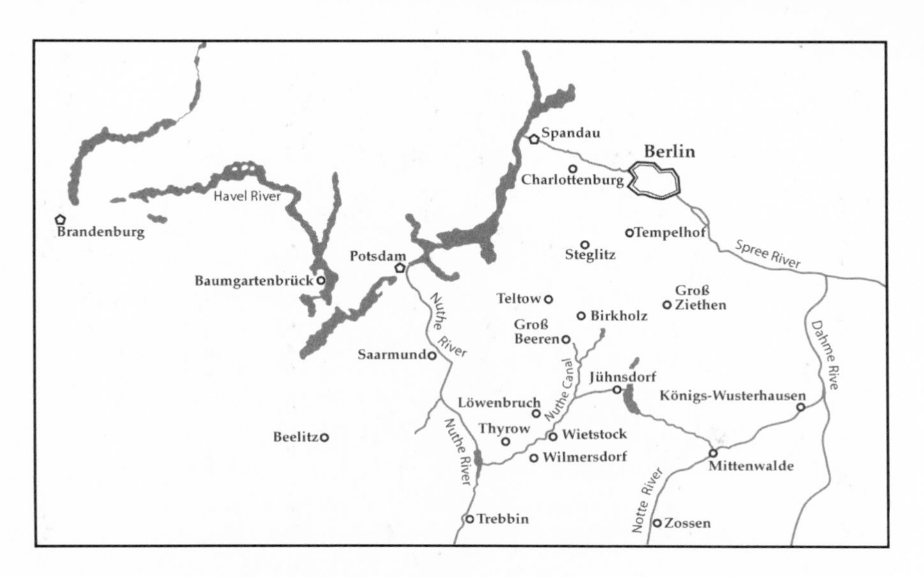

The Nuthe-Notte Defense Zone

Colonel Boyen, reinstated on the Prussian General Staff, left Allied headquarters in Saxony and traveled to Berlin to help prepare a defense.[16] Sack and L'Estoq organized a meeting between Boyen, Oberbaudirektor (building director) Johann Albert Eytelwein, and Bülow's chief engineer, Maj. Johann Ludwig Markhoff. On the ninth they agreed on the construction of a fortified line along the Havel, Spree, and Oder Rivers.[17] Engineers would also dam the Nuthe, the Nuthe Canal, and the Notte in order to flood the southern approaches to Berlin. Fortifications would be constructed at the main passes through the flood zone at Saarmund and Trebbin on the Nuthe; Zossen, Mittenwalde, and Königs-Wusterhausen on the Notte; and Wilmersdorf, Wietstock, and Jühnsorf on the Nuthe Canal. Redoubts would also be built directly south of Berlin on the Tempelhof hills near the Halle Gate.[18] Markhoff received the task of building the fortifications along the Nuthe and Notte; construction began on 11 May. Work on the dams fell under Sack's civil jurisdiction; he assigned the Wasserbaudirektor (waterworks director) August Günther to supervise the dam construction on the Nuthe, while Geheime Oberbaurat (chief of the Building Control Office) Ernst Cochius oversaw the work on the Nuthe Canal and the Notte. Three pioneer companies were assigned to the construction; the Landsturm received the odious task of providing manual labor on the earthworks.[19]

Meanwhile, at Dessau, Bülow awaited the approach of a French army. Allied cavalry patrolled as far as Leipzig and Halle but reported nothing.[20] Bülow concluded that while Napoleon had pursued the Allied army east from Lützen with his main force, Ney occupied Leipzig with a smaller force, and Victor's Second Corps had marched to Bernburg. On 9 May he received a note from Wittgenstein that warned of a French offensive against the Kurmark and placed all Allied units near Berlin and observing Wittenberg and Magdeburg under his command.[21] A subsequent order from the king implored him to prevent the French from taking Berlin. Frederick William expected Bülow to attack any French units that threatened the capital. To facilitate this task he placed the completed units of the Kurmark Landwehr under Bülow's command and authorized the Military Government in Berlin to mobilize the Landsturm at its discretion.[22] Other than his faith in Bülow's untested abilities, he offered his general no direct assistance; the main Prussian army would follow the Russians. Frederick William chose to maintain the unity of Allied operations at the risk of his capital.

At this time Bülow's corps consisted of 11,500 Prussians and 3,800 Russians.[23] Although two months into the mobilization, the Kurmark Landwehr was not ready to support Bülow.[24] The lack of experienced noncommissioned officers to train the recruits and a shortage of experienced officers to command them remained the worst of the numerous problems that hindered the mobilization.[25] This meant that the Landwehr could not assist with the defense of the capital. Since all reports indicated that Wittenberg would serve as the French base for an operation against Berlin, Bülow's position at Dessau southwest of the fortress appeared untenable. He could only hope that the French would not advance from Magdeburg. To cover the capital against an attack from that direction he ordered any available Landwehr battalions to hold the Havel River from Potsdam to Havelberg.[26]

Bülow's situation grew worse with each day. News arrived that the Allies had abandoned Dresden and retreated toward Bautzen.[27] With the return of French troops, the king of Saxony again declared his allegiance to Napoleon, and the fortress of Torgau on the Elbe opened its gates to Gen. Jean Reynier's Seventh Corps. In addition, two other divisions from Ney's army were rumored to be on the march from Düben to Wittenberg. Ney's 45,000 men actually crossed the Elbe at Torgau on the eleventh. Two days later, when the marshal received Napoleon's orders to take Berlin, his army numbered 84,000 men.[28]

With French forces either in or on the march to Wittenberg and Torgau, Bülow could no longer remain at Dessau. Reports that a strong French force had reached Torgau prompted him to cross the Elbe at Rosslau and lead his troops northeast to Coswig on 10 May. He also summoned Borstell's three battalions and one battery from Magdeburg. The Prussian rearguard dismantled the bridgehead at Rosslau and made preparations to burn the wooden bridge if the French approached. With less than 20,000 men to stop Ney, Bülow considered a retreat to the Nuthe-Notte defense line.[29] He also goaded the Military Government in Berlin to complete the Kurmark militia and directed all available Landwehr battalions to Potsdam, Baumgartenbrück, Saarmund, and Trebbin.[30] Much to his dismay, one of the Kurmark Landwehr's two divisional commanders, Gen. Karl Friedrich von Hirschfeld, informed him that the militia was still far from ready.[31] Ney's numerical superiority and the lack of support limited Bülow's options. Although a retreat to the Nuthe-Notte line offered the chance of slowing Ney's advance, Bülow did not want to confine himself to a localized defensive until pressed by the enemy. He decided to maintain his position at Coswig in order to be able to execute offensive operations and would only withdraw to the Nuthe-Notte line if forced by superior numbers. Bülow's belief in an offensive-oriented defense of Berlin became the basis of his strategy throughout the war.

During the night of 11–12 May news arrived at Bülow's headquarters that two French divisions had reached Wittenberg. Other reports placed 8,000 French troops at Dessau and Cöthen.[32] It appeared that French forces were poised to cross the Elbe at Rosslau, Wittenberg, and Torgau, but the task of determining the direction of the main French advance proved arduous. Bülow had a screen of light troops observe the Black Elster River to monitor French activities around Torgau. On the twelfth the Prussians watched three French columns issue from the fortress and march north. Bülow could only hope to hold the French for as long as possible before being forced to make a final stand behind the swamps of the Nuthe.[33]

A glimmer of hope emerged when Bülow learned that a Swedish army of 30,000 men had recently landed in Stralsund. He dispatched Major von Kalkreuth to seek an audience with the crown prince of Sweden, Jean-Baptiste Bernadotte. Kalkreuth carried a letter from Bülow that urged the crown prince to take up the sword and "inflame the hearts of Germany," just as Gustavus Adolphus had in the Thirty Years' War.

Jean-Baptiste Bernadotte, Marshal of France and Crown Prince of Sweden (1733–1844). The former marshal of France became king of Sweden in 1818 and reigned until 1844; his line still rules today.

Bülow offered to subordinate himself to Bernadotte's command in a joint attack on the flank and rear of the Grande Armée.[34] In a letter to Frederick William, Bülow accepted full responsibility for inviting the Swedish army to Berlin and placing himself under Bernadotte's command. He explained to the king that he had "to use every possible means in order to convince the crown prince (who as a Frenchman is probably easy to flatter) that he could be a second Gustavus Adolphus and savior of Germany."[35]

While he awaited an answer from the Swedish prince-royal, on 13 and 14 May Bülow moved his brigades closer to Wittenberg and to the small Russian brigade under General von Harpe that observed the fortress; his Cossack patrols on the left bank of the Elbe had kept Bülow informed of French movements.[36] It appeared certain that Ney's forces at Torgau and Dessau would operate against Berlin. Bülow believed the corps at Dessau would cross the Elbe at Wittenberg in an attempt to hold him, while the force from Torgau advanced to Berlin. Once the French marched from Dessau toward the Elbe, he planned to make a stand in the open terrain north of Wittenberg, where he would be able to utilize his cavalry to threaten the flank of the French army marching north from Torgau. Should the two French forces unite against him, Bülow would have no other choice than to withdraw to the Nuthe-Notte defense line.[37]

As the probability of a French invasion increased, Bülow requested a status report on the Nuthe-Notte defense line. The military governor, L'Estoq, optimistically informed him that the engineers had completed the initial measures with noteworthy speed and efficiency. To build the dams they first closed the existing sluices and dikes, creating a natural accumulation along both rivers. The construction of additional dams to effect a deep flooding of the lowlands had already commenced. "If only the enemy grants me a few more days," expressed a confident L'Estoq, "I will almost be sorry if he does not come."[38] He estimated that 55,000 men could be mustered to defend the capital. These numbers included Bülow's mobile corps of 20,000; 5,000 reserve and march troops located in and around Berlin; 20,000 Landwehr; and 10,000 Landsturm.[39] Of the Prussian commanders who had fought in the previous war against France, L'Estoq was one of the few to acquire a great reputation. His defense of East Prussia in the winter of 1806–7 had provided a bright spot in Prussia's dismal war effort. Through initiative, determination, patience, and skill he had distinguished himself on several occasions in what appeared to be hopeless situations. Now, in 1813, the Prussians hoped that the seventy-five-year-old general would display the same energy in his new administrative role as military governor.

L'Estoq's quixotic remarks may have encouraged Bülow, but other news forced him to alter his plans. According to his scouts, French engineers had quickly repaired the bridges over the Black Elster, and three enemy columns crossed the river at Jessen, Schweinitz, and Herzberg. Borstell also reported that an advance guard of 12,000 men had already reached Luckau. According to the statement of a Saxon deserter, the army from Torgau contained 40,000–50,000 infantry, 5,000–6,000 cavalry, and 12 batteries. Other estimates put the corps that marched from Dessau to Wittenberg—purportedly commanded by Victor—at 20,000–30,000 men.[40] Victor's corps was indeed on the march to unite with Ney. The emperor wanted Ney's army echeloned between Lübben and Schönwald by 16 May. In this position the marshal would be three marches from Berlin and three and a half from Napoleon's Grande Armée. Napoleon informed Ney that the relief of Glogau and the capture of Berlin and Breslau were "the three important goals" that he wanted to accomplish by the end of May.[41]

On 15 May Bülow's rearguard was driven northward to Kröpstadt by a stronger enemy force advancing from Wittenberg. Bülow correctly assumed that as many as four French corps could be moving against Berlin. Since his field units amounted to 15,000 men, a battle against such superior numbers was out of the question. With no other choice, he prepared to retreat toward Berlin.[42] He requested an account of Markhoff's progress and instructed him to locate a suitable position for his corps in the Nuthe-Notte line.[43] Markhoff submitted a detailed report describing the defense zone between Potsdam, Saarmund, Trebbin, Zossen, Mittenwalde, and Königs-Wusterhausen. His remarks concerning the flood measures only increased Bülow's consternation. At the intervals between the main crossings the floodwaters were unusually low due to a drought. Markhoff confirmed what Bülow already feared. A lower than average water table reduced the effectiveness of the flood zone and its six fortified crossings, thus negating the military value of the posts. The positions offered no mutual support and could be evaded and rendered ineffective. Only a high water level would force an invading army to attempt a passage where entrenchments would counterbalance French numerical superiority. In the end

Markhoff suggested that the line should only serve as a means for delaying a French march on Berlin rather than as the capital's primary defense.[44]

Bülow faced a tough decision. Perhaps he recalled the cold day of 5 February 1807 when his Prussian battalion joined four others in an attempt to drive the 17,000 men of Ney's Sixth Corps from the Vistula. In the ensuing fight Bülow received a severe wound to his left arm that put him out of action until April, and his battalion was practically destroyed. Now it seemed pointless to confront Ney's 80,000 men with his 15,000. Despite Markhoff's report, Bülow decided to occupy the defense line. Should he be forced from this position, he planned to hold the French at the Tempelhof hill chain near Berlin's Halle Gate.[45] News that a large French force had reached Luckau ultimately decided the issue. Bülow chose to take a position in the defense line and so marched to Trebbin on 17 May; Borstell's small brigade moved into Mittenwalde.[46]

Bülow arrived in Trebbin on the seventeenth only to be disappointed with what he found. The general could not believe the condition of the Silesian Landwehr battalion that occupied the entrenchments. He complained to L'Estoq that "the men of the 1st Silesian Battalion are without packs, shoes, equipment, and food. I insist that the Military Government refrain from dispatching troops without supplies and sufficient ammunition."[47] Moreover, construction on the entrenchments that he thought his men would occupy had just started. The meager number of civilian workers employed on the fortifications infuriated him. To escape his wrath, civil authorities blamed the local Landsturm commander for refusing to release his men for the construction. For their part, the Landsturm authorities claimed that other construction sites already employed over 400 of their number and no more could be spared. Consequently, construction halted while the Military Government investigated that matter. Regardless of who deserved the blame for the insufficient manpower, precious time had been lost and the construction had fallen behind schedule.

Bülow discovered that a shortage of workers also existed at the five other main points along the defense line. He complained to the Military Government that little had been accomplished between Trebbin and Zossen. "On a line where 2,000 men can and must be employed," Bülow griped, "only seventy-five have reported." He blamed this on the Military Government's "premature" summoning of the Landsturm that allowed the local labor force to "sit in the bivouac."[48] Multiple factors actually caused the shortage of manpower. Few regular army units remained around Berlin to assist with the construction. The declaration of universal conscription and the formation of the Landwehr had enrolled thousands of able-bodied men in military service. By mid-May only a few battalions had completed their training and moved into quarters around Berlin, where they could work on the defense line. With the summoning of the Kurmark Landsturm, even fewer men could provide labor. Since the defense of the dams on the Nuthe-Notte line had been assigned to the Landsturm, local commanders refused to demobilize their units. Lacking funds to pay both skilled and unskilled civilian laborers, the Military Government did little to force the remaining men to work; patriotic pleas for hard labor went unheeded.

The Military Government replied sharply to Bülow's criticism. L'Estoq curtly reminded the general that since construction had commenced only four days earlier "one could not demand more than one has received." He countered that over 1,000 men were employed at the various sites and "all that can be done has been done in view of the great shortage of resources."[49] The military governor then rebuked Bülow for withdrawing to Trebbin, suggesting that had he not retreated the Landsturm would not have been summoned. According to his sources, the approaching French forces were much weaker than Bülow reported. He believed that the French advance was only a diversion. Bülow, who had served under L'Estoq in the previous war, refused to allow the military governor to dictate to him as if the clock had been turned back seven years. Boyen explains that "an unpleasant situation" now emerged between Bülow and L'Estoq. "Bülow considered the intentions of the enemy before Berlin to be real; L'Estoq only viewed them as a demonstration, at the most a feint. Bülow believed that the enemy forces were significant; L'Estoq held them to be mediocre and based this estimate on reports from the spies of the Berlin police that were active in Saxony. A somewhat pointed correspondence emerged; as a result, the honor of being the mediator was bestowed on me; this was not to be envied."[50]

Meanwhile the drought continued to cause problems for the civil engineers. On 14 May the Nuthe had been dammed from Trebbin to Saarmund, making the adjacent lowlands inaccessible. In a matter of days, however, the waters receded and no longer provided a sufficient obstacle. Only six inches of water covered the tract between Trebbin and Jütendorf.[51] Günther also encountered difficulties flooding the terrain between Saarmund and Potsdam.[52] Stabilizing the wooden dams along the marshy banks became a problem. Cochius had more success and flooded the Notte valley from Mittenwalde to Königs-Wusterhausen.[53] He projected similar results for the region between Mittenwalde and Zossen. As for the Nuthe Canal, the stretch between Trebbin and Thyrow was submerged, but the low water level from Thyrow to Löwenbruch raised concerns. Cochius warned that flooding alone would not suffice to defend his sector. Troops would be needed to hold Trebbin, Mittenwalde, and Königs-Wusterhausen as well as the crossings over the Nuthe Canal at Thyrow, Wilmersdorf, Wietstock, and Jühnsdorf.[54]

As Bülow read these reports and contemplated his next move, he received unbelievable news: French forces had turned around and marched southeast. Saxon deserters reported that after Reynier's vanguard reached Baruth his main body marched east from Dahme to Luckau. Bülow believed that the French had shifted their focus from Berlin to the Oder fortresses, but affairs in Saxony actually accounted for this unexpected change. Although Napoleon had recalled a part of Ney's army from its operations in the North, his orders did not specify if all or only a portion should march southeast. Napoleon actually wanted Victor and Reynier to continue their offensive against Berlin. Ney, however, turned his entire army south by the morning of 18 May.[55]

The extent of Ney's withdrawal still remained a question in the Prussian camp. Based on information from stragglers, deserters, and captured French couriers, Bülow concluded that Napoleon had recalled Ney's army for use against the main Allied army at Bautzen. Bülow considered a counteroffensive but refused to advance into an area that had been stripped by the passage of thousands of men. His own troops needed rest and already suffered from inadequate supplies. Bülow's frequent requisitions had produced few results; Prussian resources were nearing exhaustion. Attentive to the needs of his men, he delayed the march and granted them a day of rest on 18 May.[56] Fortune had indeed favored Bülow and spared him a confrontation with a much larger French army. By misinterpreting Napoleon's orders, Ney forfeited an opportunity to destroy Bülow's small corps since the incomplete entrenchments and the low water level of the floodplain would have afforded the Prussians no advantages.

Bülow's cautious operations throughout May reflected his predicament. With the enormous responsibility of protecting the Prussian

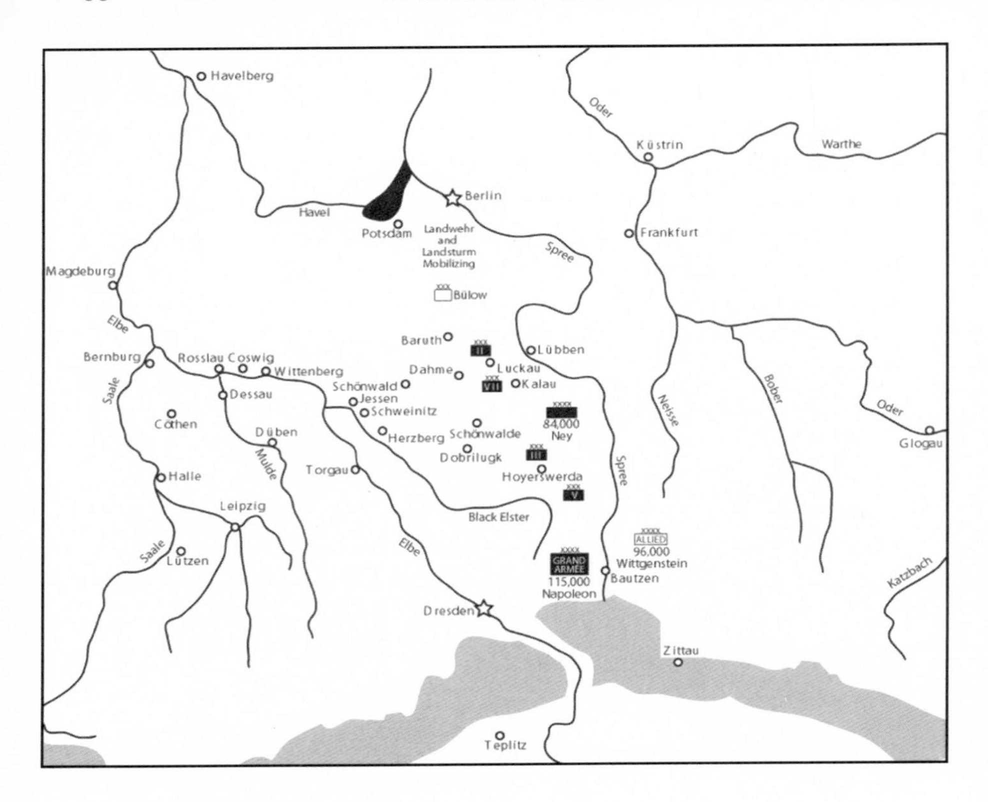

The Situation on 19 May 1813

capital, he had to exercise prudence. The Allied retreat eastward to the Spree facilitated the implementation of Napoleon's "master plan" to take Berlin and relieve the besieged Oder fortresses. With Saxony's renewed adherence to the Napoleonic system, French armies could cross the Elbe at Wittenberg and Torgau. Bülow would not have been able to stop a concerted French operation against Berlin. Two distinct shortages—manpower and water—marred the Prussian defense plans. Labor shortages delayed construction of the fortifications needed to defend the passes through the flood zone. Although the plan to flood the countryside appeared feasible in view of the region's numerous water courses, a drought lowered the water table. As a result of the inadequate water level, the value of the six main passes that led through the flood zone likewise diminished. Due to the insufficient floodwaters a French army could evade the posts and isolate their defenders. Since the Prussians had no control over the success or failure of this natural phenomenon, the entire project depended on fate rather than on competent leadership and hard work. A shortage of manpower can hardly justify basing a military operation on chance. Consequently, Bülow's aversion to the flood plans was warranted according to sound military principles. He understood the dangers of hinging the success of a military operation on luck.

4

LUCKAU

Following the defeat at Lützen the Allied army retreated to Bautzen to confront Napoleon for a second time. Possession of Torgau, Wittenberg, and Magdeburg now provided Napoleon with three bases from which to launch operations against Berlin. Bülow's task of holding the Elbe from Magdeburg to Torgau—with his left exposed between Torgau and the Spree—would have challenged the skills of any general. Doubts over the effectiveness of the Nuthe-Notte defense line and the slow progress of the Landwehr increased his concerns. Without a reserve any operation would be risky. His troops formed the heart of the Prussian army in the Kurmark; to sacrifice them would be to sacrifice the capital.

In the event of another Allied defeat, Bülow believed that Wittgenstein would be forced to retreat to Silesia. He assumed that Napoleon would then attempt to relieve the besieged Oder fortresses and threaten the Russian army's lines of communication to force them out of Central Europe. By 19 May Bülow's corps had grown to 25,000 men and extended from the Trebbin-Mittenwalde line to Baruth. He was convinced that Ney had made a sudden turn toward Bautzen; since no French forces threatened Berlin from the lower Elbe, Bülow decided to follow the French columns with the hope of threatening Napoleon's left flank and rear.[1]

Boyen left the Prussian capital and arrived at Bülow's headquarters in Baruth on 19 May. Acting on the authority of the Military Government, he proposed to form a brigade from the reserves, convalescents, and available Landwehr units quartered around the capital. He suggested that the brigade could cover Bülow's right flank and allow him to advance deeper into Saxony. Bülow agreed and pledged to support Boyen with Cossacks and a Russian battery. On the twenty-first the industrious staff officer assembled his 3,800 men at Luckenwalde. From there his scouts scoured the right bank of the Elbe between Torgau and Wittenberg but found only enemy patrols. For this reason, he urged Bülow to press the rear of the Grande Armée.[2] Bülow, however, reconsidered the situation. He lost his appetite for the counteroffensive and concluded that further pursuit of Ney would be futile, especially since Victor's Second Corps had a two-day head start. Moreover, an advance to Bautzen would limit his ability to hold a front that now consisted of the entire right bank of the Elbe from the North Sea to Dresden. Some of his subordinates complained that he had squandered a great opportunity.[3] Borstell implored him to pursue the French or at least to allow his brigade to march on Bautzen.[4] Bülow refused to divide his forces until he learned the fate of Wittgenstein's army. He also believed that Borstell's troops would needlessly suffer from supply shortages along the 105 miles between Berlin and Bautzen. More importantly, he did not think Borstell could arrive in time to participate in a general battle.

Supply problems also hindered the pursuit of Ney's army. The mobilization of the Landwehr and considerable portions of the Landsturm had exhausted the Kurmark's resources. French garrisons in Küstrin and Stettin blocked the flow of grain from Pomerania and Posen up the Oder and Warthe to Berlin.[5] With little food and even less to be found in the depleted countryside, Bülow's corps did not resume the advance to the Black Elster until 23 May. In a report to Wittgenstein dated the twentieth, Bülow explained that "it would be futile to pursue the enemy any farther since the last enemy corps, that of Victor, reached Sonnenwalde on 19 May just as I arrived at Baruth and thus has an advantage of two days. Moreover, further pursuit would draw me too far away from my purpose: the coverage of Berlin. I believe that it would be more feasible to advance toward the [Black] Elster and to observe Torgau and Wittenberg with all the troops that I can spare." Not knowing of the events at Bautzen, Bülow assured Wittgenstein that he would cross the Elbe and disrupt Napoleon's communications between Dresden and Magdeburg.[6] As a preliminary step, raiding parties and patrols moved deep into the region between the Black Elster and the Spree.[7] Early on the twenty-fourth he finally learned of the Allied defeat at Bautzen from a captured French courier.[8] Napoleon had again defeated the Allied army after two days of hard fighting that resulted in 20,000 casualties on each side. Although the Allies retreated eastward toward Silesia, the emperor could not exploit his victory with a devastating pursuit.

Certain that another French offensive against Berlin would follow, Bülow retreated northeast to block an enemy advance. That evening his main body reached Dahme, Borstell's brigade camped in Kalau, and an advance guard under Gen. Adolf Friedrich von Oppen held Sonnenwalde.[9] Patrols moved as far east as the Neisse River in search of the defeated Allied army.[10] None of the couriers dispatched to Allied headquarters returned, and farmers spread rumors of an Allied disaster. Borstell's scouts confirmed that the Allied army had withdrawn toward Silesia. When orders finally arrived, the king merely instructed Bülow to defend the Kurmark, especially Berlin and Potsdam. Frederick William's letter dismissed the rumors of a disaster and assured Bülow that the Allied army remained in good condition despite the defeat. Moreover, both he and the tsar believed that Austria would soon join the coalition.[11]

Bülow believed that Napoleon would probably resume his operations against the Kurmark. Since Ney and Victor had commanded at least 50,000 men for the invasion prior to Bautzen, Bülow told L'Estoq to expect similar numbers or perhaps more.[12] The Grande Armée could certainly spare such a force. With the Allied army in full retreat to Silesia, a French force could take the direct route north to the Oder. After liberating their besieged garrisons in Glogau, Küstrin, and Stettin, the French would only be a few short marches from Berlin. A French drive down the Oder would easily flank Bülow's position in the Kurmark.

As for support, the Kurmark militia still could not assist Bülow. The Landwehr commanders informed him of the militia's problems. On 11 May one brigade commander portrayed his men as "cripples, farmers, and children who possess no military virtues." He protested that one of his battalions had only one officer who could lead the exercises. "The lances are made of caterpillar-damaged wood and break as soon as they are thrown in the air. This battalion has no mess gear, no haversacks, no shoes, and is still not ready to march," he wrote. He added that defective firearms caused the most problems.[13] Hirschfeld himself aloofly maintained that his men lacked what it took to be real soldiers. He claimed that their muskets were still in the hands of the smiths and their uniforms still in the hands of the weavers. Most of his companies lacked experienced officers. "I would be guilty of treason," he insisted, "if I considered them fit for duty."[14] On 18 May he again complained of the shortage of experienced officers, adding that his "raw recruits" lacked uniforms and weapons.[15] Equipment shortages prompted him to describe his cavalry squadron as nothing more than "peasants on bare-back horses."[16] President Bassewitz informed the Military Government that as of 20 May all of the Kurmark Landwehr units had left their districts, but the battalion commanders had only reported to their posts shortly before the deployment. He also noted that two battalions still lacked commanders and many companies needed chiefs. On the brigade level, some of the brigadiers had not yet reported for duty. When a copy of this letter reached Bülow, it convinced him that he could not depend on the Kurmark militia to assist him in the field. The Landwehr needed to finish mobilizing without being disturbed by the war.[17] Bülow knew that time was still the key.

Bülow now made arrangements to secure his flanks and utilize the interior lines afforded by his central position. He remained at Luckau with the bulk of his infantry, but his cavalry continued to disrupt French communications between Dresden and Bautzen. Borstell, longing for an independent command, once again sought permission to operate against the French. He suggested that his brigade advance against the rear of Napoleon's Grande Armée in order to cut communications. Bülow refused for a second time, especially since this task could more easily be accomplished by light cavalry rather than by a brigade.[18] For the time being Bülow could do little more than wait. He assumed that the French would come, but the direction of the onslaught remained the question.

According to intelligence, Victor had already reached Rothenburg on the Neisse with 9,000 men. Since this indicated a possible French advance to the Oder, Bülow asserted more authority over the defense measures east of the Oder in the neighboring Neumark. In conjunction with the Military Government between the Oder and the Vistula in Stargard, Bülow concentrated the available Neumark Landwehr battalions and squadrons along the right bank of the Oder.[19] Similar to the situation in the Kurmark, most of the Neumark militia units lacked officers and weapons; they too had been hastily assembled and had received minimal training. On 22 May Gen. Johann von Hinrichs's four battalions and three squadrons of the Neumark Landwehr reached Crossen. Situated at the Bober River's junction with the Oder, Crossen's natural bridgehead guarded the passages to Silesia and formed the extreme left wing of the Prussian defense network.[20] To support Hinrichs the king ordered Col. Leopold Wilhelm von Dobschütz to Crossen with completed units of the Silesian Landwehr.[21] Bülow instructed Dobschütz to entrench Crossen and send one of the three Neumark Landwehr brigades to Müllrose.[22] Bülow hoped that this important position on the Frederick William Canal could be defended by a Landwehr force of at least 5,000 men. Further north, between Küstrin and Stettin, a Landwehr brigade of six battalions and six squadrons held the Oder crossings at Königsberg-im-Neumark and Schwedt.[23]

On Berlin's eastern flank the Spree, the Frederick William Canal, and the Oder from Frankfurt to Crossen had not figured prominently in the defense plans until this point. Only a few entrenchments had been constructed in this sector. A defense of the region primarily depended on the destruction of the bridges over the Frederick William Canal at Müllrose and Lindow as well as those spanning the Spree at Neubrück and Fürstenwalde. Of the four crossings, only Fürstenwalde maintained a degree of strategic importance due to its position between Berlin and Küstrin. Fortifications were planned for this city, but nothing had been done.

Following his victory at Bautzen, Napoleon ordered Marshal Nicolas Oudinot to continue the operation against Berlin with the three divisions of his Twelfth Corps. The emperor instructed Oudinot to drive Bülow across the Oder and take the Prussian capital.[24] On 25 May the vanguard of the Twelfth Corps began the march from Bautzen toward Berlin, followed by the main body on the next day. By no means could Oudinot's force be compared to the impressive army that Ney had led against the Prussian capital only one week earlier. Oudinot's corps had dwindled during the campaign to a mere 20,000 men. Although equal in numbers to Bülow's mobile troops, Oudinot's men possessed one advantage: experience. They had fought at both Lützen and Bautzen. Oudinot himself may have been the weak link. By 1813 the forty-six-year-old marshal, who was brave and fearless to a fault, had received the majority of the thirty-six wounds that marked his career. Oudinot's

Marshal Nicolas Charles Oudinot (1767–1847). Oudinot was one of the French commissioners who negotiated an armistice with the Allies after Napoleon abdicated on 6 April 1814; he refused to rally to Napoleon in 1815 during the Hundred Days.

real skill lay in commanding a division rather than a corps or an army. Like most of Napoleon's senior generals, he lacked a true grasp of strategy and did not understand his master's art of war. When the emperor was not present, Oudinot succumbed to indecision and melted into mediocrity. While in exile on Saint Helena Napoleon once commented that although Oudinot was "a decent fellow, he was not very bright."[25] Had he realized this in 1813, the campaign in North Germany—and the war itself—might have taken a completely different turn.

Bülow contemplated shifting his forces eastward to the Oder, but events drew his attention back to Saxony.[26] On 26 May the French drove his Cossack outpost from Hoyerswerda.[27] The French force that attacked Hoyerswerda was Oudinot's advance guard: the Thirteenth Division under Gen. Michel-Marie Pacthod. This northward thrust both concerned and puzzled Bülow. He still placed Victor at Rothenburg, poised to advance down the Oder. His spies around Wittenberg discovered that French troops had recently entered the fortress.[28] These movements made it difficult for Bülow to predict the road or roads the French might take to Berlin. He decided that since Borstell's and Oppen's brigades probably equaled the French force at Hoyerswerda, he would have them probe southward but hold his main body in reserve. Borstell received orders to attack the French force at Hoyerswerda by 28 May.[29]

Borstell believed that the French force in Hoyerswerda numbered no more than 7,000 men and 20 guns. He began the advance on the night of 27 May and united with Oppen on the left bank of the Black Elster. During the march Borstell dispatched Colonel von Krafft to create a diversion on the right bank of the Black Elster with 1,800 men and 4 guns. Borstell planned to lead his main force of five and one-half battalions, six squadrons, one and one-half Cossack regiments, and twelve guns on the open terrain along the river's left bank.

Around 9:00 A.M. two separate combats commenced when the Prussians converged on Hoyerswerda. On the right bank Krafft's force surprised Pacthod's eight battalions and eight guns between Neuwiese, Bergen, and the Wasserburg Mill. Borstell's plan appeared to work perfectly. A surprised Pacthod retreated to Seydenwinkel, chased by Prussian skirmishers. Krafft stormed Seydenwinkel and prepared for Pacthod's inevitable counterattack. After a Bavarian division arrived, Pacthod recovered from the initial confusion and used his superior numbers to drive the Prussians from Seydenwinkel shortly after 12:00 P.M. Krafft learned that Borstell's attack had failed and so ordered a retreat; Pacthod only pursued to Bergen.

Meanwhile Borstell had led his 4,500 men to Hoyerswerda. While on the march he received word that an additional 7,000 French troops and 20 guns had moved north through Königswartha on the way to Hoyerswerda during the previous day. Although much exaggerated, this news took some of the fight out of Borstell. As the Prussians neared Hoyerswerda they found an estimated 8,000 French soldiers arranged in battle order on the plain northwest of the village. Borstell unlimbered his artillery on the hills north of the town and ordered a cavalry charge to slow the advance of the French infantry. The Prussian gunners opened fire and found their mark thanks to the charging cavalry

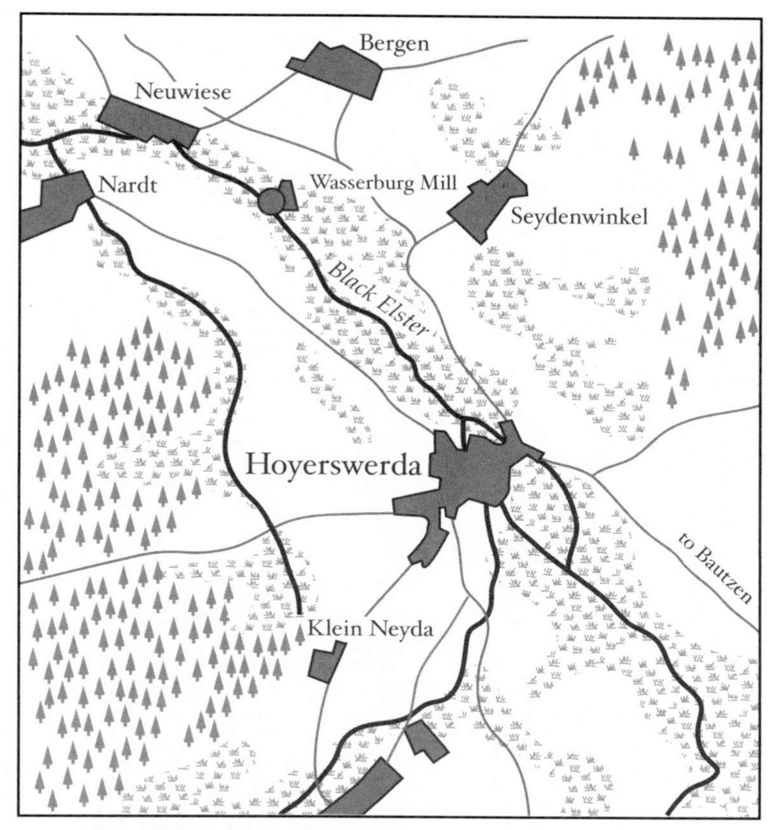

Hoyerswerda and the Surrounding Area

that forced the French into squares. According to Oudinot's chief of staff, Louis-François Lejeune, the Prussians "poured a murderous fire upon us, which mowed down our ranks, and soon compelled Marshal Oudinot himself to take refuge in one of the many squares into which he hastily formed his troops, and in which the grapeshot was working terrible havoc."[30]

Oudinot had left Lejeune at Hoyerswerda's southern gate with two battalions, a Hessian cavalry brigade, and all of his artillery, while he led the infantry through the narrow streets to deploy on a wide meadow northwest of the town. Leading his infantry from the front, Oudinot found himself pinned down by Borstell's artillery. A few staff officers reached Lejeune, who released the reserve. He directed eight twelve-pounders and two battalions to move west around Hoyerswerda and attack the Prussian right wing; a Hessian cavalry brigade covered the advance.

Concerned by the estimates of French strength, Borstell convinced himself that this small force was in fact the French reinforcements. He feared that a fresh enemy force of 7,000 infantry was advancing from Klein Neyda to envelop his right wing. Although Borstell was wrong, Oudinot's corps still doubled the number of Prussians on the field. Oudinot's heavy artillery had just unlimbered when Borstell ordered a retreat. The two Prussian detachments withdrew northward, but Oudinot did not pursue because he thought that Bülow's entire corps was present. In the combat the Prussians lost 360 men, while French losses were slightly higher at 450.[31]

On the eve of Borstell's operation Bülow had shifted his attention back to the Oder and decided to march to Cottbus so he would be closer to Silesia. The fate of the Allied army—as well as the need to secure the Oder—weighed heavily on him. He still believed that Napoleon would detach a significant army to take Berlin, but from which direction? Bülow ordered an eastward flank march toward the Oder to gain a more central position so that he could react to a threat on Berlin from any direction. On 28 May he instructed Boyen to form a forty-mile cordon between Treuenbrietzen and Lübben to shield Berlin.[32] Boyen complained when Bülow restrained him from conducting more aggressive operations, but the security of the province and the Kurmark Landwehr's ongoing mobilization demanded prudence.[33] The completion of the militia depended on Bülow's success. At this point only eight battalions of the projected twenty-eight could take the field, and only one cavalry regiment was fully equipped. Not one of the seven Kurmark Landwehr brigades had been formed yet. The Kurmark authorities reported that the Landwehr infantry and cavalry would not be combat-ready before 12 June.[34]

Although reports claimed that Victor had crossed the Bober at Sagan and advanced north toward Crossen, the combat at Hoyerswerda forced Bülow to reconsider his plans to march to the Oder. Now confronted by Oudinot's force, which he hardly expected to remain idle, he remained in Kalau, while Oudinot lingered twenty-five miles away in Hoyerswerda. Bülow had to determine if Oudinot or Victor posed the true threat to Berlin or if the two marshals would jointly operate against the Prussian capital. Oudinot's delay in Hoyerswerda actually helped the French cause. With Victor's advance toward the Oder,

Bülow revived his earlier plan of moving closer to Silesia and the upper Oder.[35] On the thirtieth the corps marched eastward as a Cossack screen covered Bülow's right flank.[36] These terrifying Russian horsemen raided the wide region between the Black Elster, Spree, and Bober Rivers.[37] The information they returned confirmed that after crossing the Bober at Sagan Victor had turned east toward the fortress of Glogau rather than continuing west toward the Kurmark.[38] Letters from Allied Headquarters also provided encouraging news. Bülow learned that the Allies expected Austria to declare war on France in the immediate future. Wittgenstein assured him that Austria's entry into the war would prevent Napoleon from detaching considerable forces against Berlin.[39]

Although Allied Headquarters seemed confident of Austria's accession to the Alliance, Bülow hoped to secure Swedish support on his own. Bülow soon learned that the crown prince of Sweden refused to move from Stralsund and support the Prussians due to a diplomatic tiff. The prince-royal had recently received the infuriating report that Tsar Alexander had allegedly vowed to preserve Norway for Denmark on the condition that King Frederick VII abandon Napoleon and join the Allies. Moreover, according to the Russo-Swedish Convention of Abo, Bernadotte had been promised command of a Russian corps for use against the Danes. Alexander, who could not spare any manpower, now informed Bernadotte that when his army reached the front—in Germany—it would be reinforced by a Russian corps.[40] Bülow's representative in Swedish headquarters, Kalkreuth, gained an audience with a recalcitrant Bernadotte on 29 May. He soon realized that Bernadotte placed little value on protecting Berlin. Personal and political motives drove the crown prince rather than military considerations. When Kalkreuth suggested a joint operation, Bernadotte declined on the grounds that the original Russo-Swedish alliance treaty of 5 April 1812, which predated the Abo Convention, only required Swedish military activity in North Germany *after* Bernadotte had taken Norway from Denmark.[41] Bernadotte had not yet conquered Norway, and this remained his obsession. Kalkreuth's report also sheds light on a concern that eventually became a skeleton in the Allied closet. "It appears to me," recalled Kalkreuth, "that his regret for not having kept the French throne for himself in the year 1799—which he has claimed he could have done and does not appear to be a fantasy to him—is his secret ambition."[42] For this reason Bernadotte strove to separate the Allied struggle against Napoleon from a war against the French nation.

Although Bülow could not depend on Swedish assistance, news that Oudinot had apparently retreated in the direction of Dresden, perhaps to defend the Saxon capital against an Austrian attack, provided some relief. He had planned to continue the march east on 31 May, but these new circumstances convinced him to give the corps a day of rest; only Borstell moved down the Neisse to Guben.[43] Bülow also granted permission for Boyen to besiege Wittenberg. The ambitious staff officer had sent numerous requests for such an attack or at least a raid into Saxony. After initially opposing both ideas, Bülow agreed to an operation against Wittenberg and also ordered Boyen to verify rumors of a French supply depot in Herzberg.[44] Boyen delegated this mission to Capt. Ludwig von der Marwitz's Landwehr detachment of two battalions and four squadrons, marking the first time in the war that a Kurmark militia unit conducted an independent operation. Marwitz raided Herzberg on 2 June and collected 1,368 bushels of grain, 150 horses, and 59 oxen—not bad for "peasants on bare-back horses."[45]

Bülow's brigades maintained their positions on 1 June. Northeast of his corps the Military Government in Stargard moved the other two brigades of the Neumark Landwehr to the left bank of the Oder.[46] The Military Government in Berlin reciprocated by occupying the line between Trebbin and Müllrose with ten battalions and two and one-half squadrons of the Kurmark Landwehr.[47] Although pleased with the militia's growing strength, Bülow received a disturbing message from a Cossack patrol west of Hoyerswerda. According to the Russians, Oudinot's corps had marched through the town and appeared to be headed for Torgau.[48] Bülow grew concerned that the marshal would attempt to slip around his right flank and take the open road to Berlin. A letter from the new Allied commander-in-chief, Mikhail Bogdanovich Barclay de Tolly, however, minimized the threat of a French operation against Berlin. Although his orders urged Bülow to remain cautious and always maintain his communications with Berlin, Barclay requested "rapid movements and decisive operations" on the French rear between Bunzlau and Dresden. Ironically, the letter authorized the very operations that Borstell and Boyen had been demanding.[49] Barclay explained that the speed of Bülow's movements could "cause a complete change in the overall situation . . . for if you seize the enemy's line between Dresden and Bautzen, you would place his army in the greatest predicament." He urged Bülow to begin his operation as soon as possible and stressed that Berlin would not be attacked.[50] The new commander could not have been more wrong.

Reports placed Oudinot's corps at Ruhland near the left bank of the Black Elster. To shadow his movements Bülow ordered the corps to retrace its steps and countermarch westward.[51] This earned sharp criticism, since the frequent marches and countermarches exhausted his men. L'Estoq complained of "constant marches, forward and backward, here and there, without a set goal, without a robust attack; he needlessly tires the troops and does not use them."[52] On the afternoon of 2 June Cossacks spotted French forces marching north through Finsterwalde to Sonnenwalde on the great highway from Dresden to Berlin.[53] Oudinot's corps had not continued westward toward Torgau; nor had it turned south for Dresden. Instead the marshal had pivoted north and struck the highway to Berlin. No further questions remained: Oudinot's objective had to be Berlin.

In one of those typical occurrences in military history that defies explanation, the news of Oudinot's advance to Sonnenwalde did not reach Bülow until the morning of the third—after his brigades had already set in march. Once he received this information Bülow resolved to stop Oudinot at Luckau on the Berlin-Dresden highway rather than withdraw behind the suspect Nuthe-Notte defense line. Getting to Luckau, however, proved to be quite a task for the Prussians. It took considerable time and effort to redirect their columns. French forces were only four miles south of Luckau, while the Prussians had to march seven miles west. To close the gap Bülow divided his corps into five columns that marched to Luckau on two roads.

Oudinot had planned to crush Bülow and then proceed to Berlin. His march route on 3 June brought him very close to Kalau and Bülow's approaching columns. Lejeune recalled that Oudinot squandered an opportunity to take "grand revenge for his suffering outside of Hoyerswerda. He had halted at the village of Protha, and his three divisions were marching in front of him. I was going round the outposts of the advanced guard when I discovered that General Bülow, in his turn, was marching in columns half a league in advance of our divisions, also on the way to Velau [Luckau], and that his flank was exposed to us in a very unfortunate manner for him." This was Oppen's brigade, which led the Prussian advance and approached Kalau around noon. Oudinot's vanguard had already entered the town and occupied the eastern edge.

A brief skirmish erupted in the village. Behind Oppen General Thümen's East Prussian brigade arrived, followed by Harpe's Russians; the head of another Prussian brigade, commanded by Prince Ludwig of Hessen-Homburg, reached Vetschau to the north. Although Bülow possessed superior numbers, he did not want to engage the French while his columns were strung out on the march. He thus ordered Oppen to abandon Kalau and move north to Vetschau; Thümen's column followed. According to Lejeune's account, Oudinot's divisional commanders asked permission to attack the Prussian columns, but "the Marshal, always brave enough himself, now hesitated to give the word." After Oudinot "climbed into a belfry to see for himself," he shouted down orders for Lejeune to have his divisions attack, but Oppen and Thümen had already withdrawn. Lejeune lamented that "to act now would be as useless as dividing water with a sword."[54]

Late in the afternoon Bülow's entire corps assembled on the Vetschau-Luckau road. His forward units did not arrive in Luckau until 11:00 P.M. on the third. Since Oudinot remained in Kalau, the Prussians easily took possession of Luckau. The troops had completed a forced march of almost sixteen hours in unseasonably high heat and thick dust from the dry roads. An unusually warm day had taken its toll; scores of men suffered from heat exhaustion. Hessen-Homburg's brigade marched through the city and camped on the hills to the north, while Oppen's brigade occupied Cahnsdorf. Harpe's Russians arrived in the morning and moved onto the hills next to Hessen-Homburg's troops. Thümen came up later with only two-thirds of his men; the rest had dropped from heat exhaustion. To the west Boyen rushed from Jüterbog, while to the east Borstell drove his men from Cottbus in the hopes of reaching the battlefield on the fourth.[55]

Encircled by a medieval wall, Luckau offered the Prussians an excellent defensive position. A small stream, the Börste, flowed through the town and emptied into a large marsh to the south. Swampy lowlands protected the northern and southern approaches. Heavy rains fell on the morning of 4 June to deepen the quagmire. At dawn Bülow surveyed the area and situated his troops. He took his main position on three hills that commanded the terrain west of the town. Bülow placed Harpe's Russian brigade on the extreme right wing in the area of Wittmannsdorf. Thümen's brigade occupied Luckau, the Sando suburb, and the village of Sando. Hessen-Homburg formed the left wing with positions on the hills north of the city. Two battalions from his

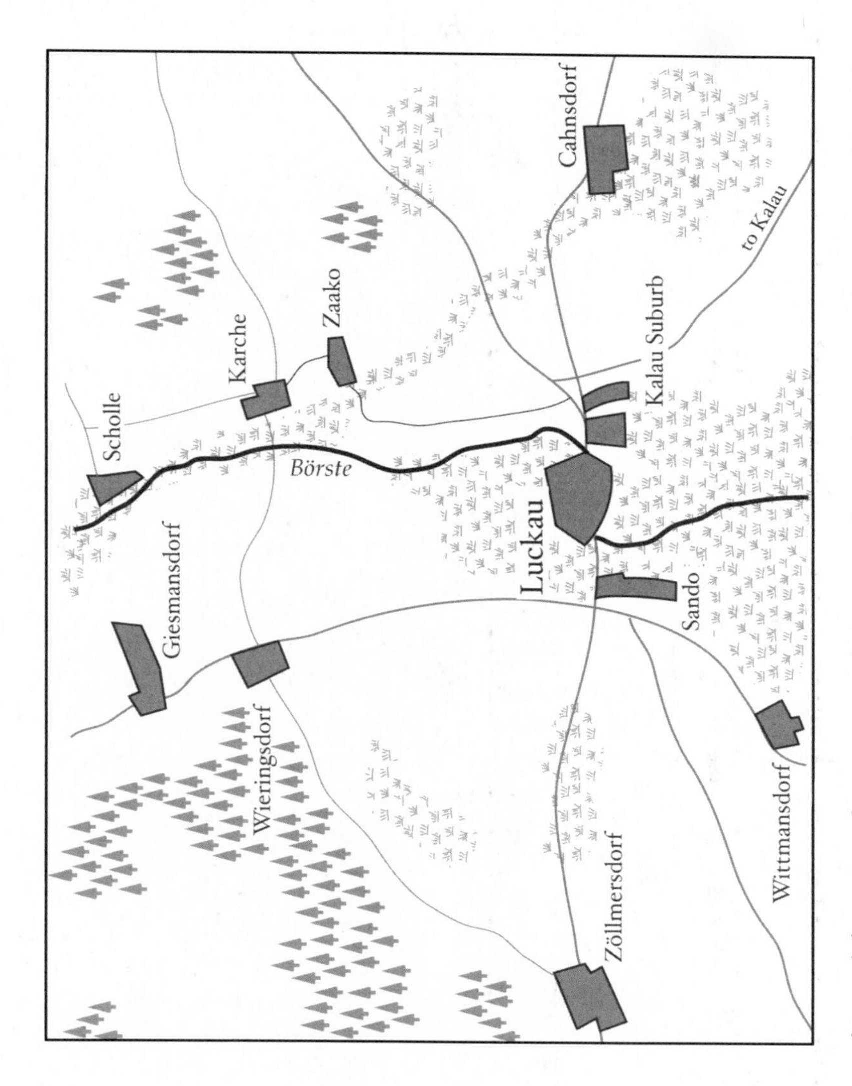

Luckau and the Surrounding Area

brigade defended the gardens to the north. Bülow positioned the reserve cavalry and artillery by Hessen-Homburg. From Oppen's rearguard a fusilier battalion and two Jäger companies occupied the Kalau suburb. Bülow distributed the remaining troops of the rearguard to the right and the left of Luckau. Oppen himself took command of two battalions and two squadrons sent to Wieringsdorf. Borstell would reinforce the left wing if he could arrive in time.[56]

Bülow's headquarters issued the orders of the day later than usual since the general had gone personally to reconnoiter the terrain. As a result the French arrived from the east and attacked Cahnsdorf between 9:00 and 10:00 A.M. The French assault occurred just as Bülow's orders to occupy the Kalau suburb arrived, but the French overran the area and routed Oppen's battalions. French skirmishers also advanced deep into the gardens north of Luckau. Oudinot's troops continued to advance toward the city gates but hesitated at the Börste. Although it was not a very good start for the Prussians, a few of their squadrons, followed by some light infantry and Jäger, harassed the French right. Skirmishing broke out in the fields and gardens east of Luckau. At the city gates soldiers of a Prussian company used their bayonets to fend off a French attack. Bülow did not waste time and committed troops from his center to recapture the Kalau suburb. Oppen also advanced with one and one-half battalions in unison with the battalions from the Prussian center. The counterattack failed to dislodge the French, but a second assault drove them from the suburb.

While this occurred, Oudinot brought up several batteries. Unaffected by Bülow's artillery, the French bombarded the Prussians and prepared for a new assault. Pacthod's division led the attack, which left the French in possession of the majority of the suburb's wooden structures. The Prussians finally held the French at the edge of Luckau, where a Jäger company stubbornly defended a cemetery on the town's eastern edge. Both sides fought tenaciously. Flames soon engulfed the Kalau suburb and consumed the seriously wounded men of both sides. Lejeune described the smoke as the "thickest and blackest" he had ever seen.[57]

Meanwhile a lively skirmish ensued in the gardens on Luckau's northern side. French battalions crossed the Börste and navigated through the marshes northwest of the city. This activity drew forth the Prussian force from Sando as well as two Russian battalions. While the French engaged the Allies northwest of Luckau, Oudinot shifted his attention and ordered a simultaneous advance against the city from the south. Bülow noticed that this opened a gap in Oudinot's line. To exploit it he ordered a cavalry attack near the Kalau suburb, but the blaze prevented the Prussian horsemen from executing the maneuver.

Up to that point Oudinot had only committed Pacthod's division; Gen. Antoine Gruyer's Fourteenth Division and a Bavarian division remained in reserve. Aware of the French reserves, Bülow feared that they would block Borstell's approach and possibly ambush him. Hoping to open the road for Borstell, Bülow gave Oppen six squadrons and half of a horse battery to cross the Börste and attack Oudinot's right flank. After fording the shallow Börste, Oppen led his men south along the right bank toward the foot of a small hill chain that rose northeast of Luckau. Turning toward Cahnsdorf, his lead dragoon squadron found three French cavalry squadrons. Oppen soon arrived with the remaining five squadrons and compelled the French to withdraw. Rather than pursue the enemy cavalry, Oppen led his men past Cahnsdorf to attack Oudinot's infantry, which hastily formed four squares that were guarded by artillery and a Bavarian cavalry regiment. A drainage trench with steep banks separated the Prussian cavalry from the French infantry. Oppen's cavalry negotiated the trench and scattered the Bavarians. Although the Prussians captured one howitzer and two guns, the French infantry remained unperturbed. Quickly and effectively, the French soldiers fired massed volleys into the ranks of the Prussian horsemen as soon as they came within range. Repeated charges failed to break the French squares. Oudinot's forward batteries swung around and fired over the heads of the infantry. The French artillery found its mark and prompted Oppen to pull his men out of the fire. He withdrew to the right bank of the Börste and took a position north of Luckau to observe Oudinot.

As night fell, Oudinot received incorrect news that enemy reinforcements had arrived, so the marshal decided to retire around 9:00 P.M. Owing to the physical exhaustion of his troops, Bülow did not order a pursuit. Allied losses amounted to 737 men, while Oudinot lost approximately 181 dead and 1,286 wounded.[58] Bülow's efforts to meet the French offensive in the open field had accomplished his objective. Had he failed, the road to Berlin would have been opened and the capital would have fallen into French hands irretrievably. For his victory Bülow received the new symbol of service to the Fatherland: the Iron Cross, first class. Tsar Alexander also recognized his efforts and awarded him the Russian Order of Saint Anne, first class. Bülow himself awarded ninety-five Iron Crosses to his men. The Prussian infantry had shouldered the brunt of the combat and performed well under fire. Oppen's cavalry also displayed courage in attacking the enemy artillery and especially the vaunted French squares. Both sides fought bitterly, and many wounded perished in the flames of the Kalau suburb. Maj. Friedrich Jacob von Rüchel-Kleist, who rushed from Lübben to inform Bülow of Borstell's arrival, noted: "In riding through the Kalau suburb, the condition of the burnt corpses lying there, and the general destruction of the place, made such an impression on me that when I returned to my brigade, everyone was astonished by my pale complexion. I have witnessed many similar scenes such as the battlefield of Leipzig and the starving prisoners in that city, as well as the bivouac on the battlefield of Belle-Alliance, but the memories all of these scenes are pushed aside by the horrible vision of the Kalau suburb."[59]

Oudinot withdrew to Sonnenwalde during the night of 4–5 June and remained there for twenty-four hours before marching southwest to Übigau, where he crossed the Black Elster. Four Prussian squadrons and some Cossacks pursued his corps. In Luckau food was scarce, and the weary troops had no energy to forage. To make matters worse, Borstell arrived around 3:00 A.M. on the morning of the fifth. Bülow had to order Boyen to halt his march since the area could not sustain the troops.[60] On the fifth Prussian cavalry patrols reached Übigau only to find that the French had crossed the Black Elster. Oudinot then turned northwest again and advanced down the Black Elster from Übigau toward Herzberg, apparently to resume his operations regardless of the rebuff at Luckau. Bülow's cavalry observed French movements and helped themselves to some of their supplies. One detachment surprised a column of wagons coming from Dresden and captured a captain and sixty-four men.

Two more days passed while Bülow chased Oudinot. Shortly after 12:00 A.M. on 8 June Russian, Prussian, and French officers arrived in Bülow's quarters to inform him that an armistice had been negotiated at Pläswitz. A letter from the king also arrived to clarify the situation.[61] During the main Allied army's retreat to Silesia after Bautzen, Austria had finally acted. Instead of entering the war, however, Metternich had proposed an armistice. The armistice had actually been signed on 4 June—as Bülow and Oudinot were engaged at Luckau! The armistice was initially scheduled to expire on 20 July, but negotiations later extended it to 10 August with a further six-day suspension of hostilities. Napoleon hoped the respite would allow him to rebuild his cavalry and rest his exhausted army, which included a sick list of 90,000 men. He also sought a diplomatic coup either by splitting the coalition or possibly by convincing his father-in-law, Emperor Francis, to support the French cause. The Allies also needed time for the exhausted Russians to rest, to secure more subsidies from Great Britain, and to court the Austrians. In the interests of resting, reorganizing, and reinforcing, both sides accepted Metternich's proposal.[62] According to the truce, the Allies conceded all of Saxony, while the French surrendered territory along the Oder.[63] A surprised Bülow had no other choice than to lead his corps back to Berlin.

Bülow's operations and the signing of the Armistice of Pläswitz proved crucial for the mobilization of the Landwehr. Of the projected twenty-eight battalions and twenty-eight squadrons of the Kurmark Landwehr, only two battalions and four squadrons under Marwitz's command were combat-ready by 1 June. All other Landwehr battalions were still not ready for field service. The significance of Bülow's operations for the completion of the mobilization remains paramount. Proof emerges from Bassewitz's letter of 27 May, which claimed that neither any of the seven Landwehr brigades nor the Landwehr cavalry could march before 12 June. Bassewitz concluded that it would be best for the Landwehr units to remain in their cantons for another two weeks.[64] Bülow's operations in May and June thus earned crucial time for both the organization of the Landwehr and the construction of the entrenchments.

Due to the lack of progress on the flood and entrenchment lines, Bülow realized the importance of his troops. His men formed the only reliable corps in a theater replete with suspect forces. Without his corps the Landwehr and Landsturm could not defend the capital. Consequently, the idea of conserving his troops characterized Bülow's actions. The major responsibility for protecting Berlin with limited resources hampered his ability to conduct offensive operations. This provoked ill-feelings among his own officers and the Berlin authorities. Regardless of this criticism, Bülow realized that with limited reserves he had to use his troops with caution. A defeat in the field would have forced him to retreat to the incomplete defenses along the Nuthe-Notte line, where only a few inexperienced Landwehr battalions could support what remained of his corps. In the beginning of June, however, Bülow disregarded these considerations. He chose to concentrate his corps and meet the French in the open field rather than disperse his men along the Nuthe-Notte line. Bülow understood that the salvation of the capital lay in an energetic, offensive-oriented defense of the province. Despite the lack of reinforcements, he marched to meet Oudinot's advance rather than withdraw to the incomplete defense line. His strategy worked, and he returned to Berlin in mid-June with increasing prestige and confidence.

Muskets, Saddles, and Shoes

The signing of the armistice produced immediate changes in the Kurmark Landwehr. When Bülow returned to Berlin on 12 June, he found a royal order that placed all defense measures exclusively under his jurisdiction. Dissatisfied with the progress of the Military Governments in Berlin and Stargard, the king vested Bülow with sole authority to complete the mobilization of both the Kurmark and Neumark Landwehr.[1] Frederick William's instructions reflected the armistice's original 20 July expiration date as well as the army's new interest in the militia. Bülow had to have the Landwehr combat-ready within one month.[2] Field service marked a significant change in the militia's role. Initial plans called for the Landwehr to provide provincial defense and support duty: conduct sieges, form garrisons, and guard communications. The spring campaign showed that the Landwehr could not be raised and trained in time even to fulfill this auxiliary role—not to mention confronting the French on the field of battle. Despite these problems the pressing issues that confronted the Prussians after the spring campaign forced Frederick William to depend on the Landwehr. Treaty negotiations with Great Britain, Russian demands for a larger Prussian army, and Prussia's future geo-political position pressured the king to double his forces in a short period. The need to replenish battlefield losses also provided a practical reason to reconsider the role of the

Landwehr. Thus the Prussians now viewed the Landwehr as a means to expand their combat power rapidly. The army debated several methods of combining the Landwehr with the line: forming mixed battalions, adding a Landwehr battalion to each regiment, or adding a Landwehr regiment to each brigade.[3] Merging the Landwehr with the line according to the French *amalmage* of 1793 received little support from the king, who feared the collapse of the line's discipline and morale.[4] These issues still had to be clarified, but by early June it became clear that the militia had shed its auxiliary role.[5]

Although the army now assumed direct control over the Landwehr, finishing the mobilization would not be easy. March and April had been spent recruiting and drafting able-bodied men and forming companies and squadrons. During the first week of May battalions formed, followed later in the month by brigades, consisting of four battalions and one cavalry regiment. The seven brigades of the Kurmark Landwehr were organized into two divisions. On 5 May the king appointed two division and seven brigade commanders.[6] These veterans found that their units suffered from shortages of manpower, experienced junior officers, weapons, equipment, and supplies. Lack of funds and lethargic civilian officials only made matters worse.

Throughout the spring campaign the mobilization of the Kurmark Landwehr had fallen under the jurisdiction of the Military Government in Berlin, the Kurmark General-Commission for Landwehr and Landsturm, the district mayors, and local district commissions.[7] The district commissions played a central role in the decentralized mobilization process.[8] Officers below the rank of company and squadron commander were chosen by the district commissions, approved by the Military Government, and commissioned by the king. The army's thorough recruiting of veterans meant that the civilian officials and professionals who served as the Landwehr's junior officers had little military experience.[9] Too consumed with learning their own duties, these junior officers were hardly qualified to train recruits. Although most company and battalion commanders did possess some experience, they have been characterized as "ignorant, incompetent, or superannuated."[10] These shortcomings proved critical since the brigades now needed to be trained for field service.

The district commissions also attempted to provide funds for uniforms and equipment. Prussia's repressed economy hindered their success. The Randow District, for example, raised four infantry companies that had received neither weapons and uniforms nor pay, and the officers went on foot since their mounts lacked bridles and saddles. The Randow District Commission did accept responsibility for equipping the companies but planned to have the Landwehr men uniform themselves. If a man could not afford the cost, the community would assume the expense. To pay for the mobilization, the commission levied a contribution of 15,000 thalers from the populace. Of the 3,000 thalers due from the village of Jasenitz, authorities could only collect 25 thalers and 17 pfennigs. Threats of execution, reprisals, sanctions, and coercive measures still failed to provide the necessary funds. The police intervened to collect a further 1,100 thalers. The remaining 1,900 thalers simply could not be collected due to the region's poverty.[11] Throughout May the same shortages of equipment and arms rendered useless several units from other districts.[12]

Bülow certainly had a long road ahead of him. In addition to his responsibilities with the Landwehr, he also had to prepare his corps for the resumption of hostilities. Moreover, the king ordered him to take command of the defense plans for the Kurmark. For this reason, Boyen—a staunch proponent of the militia—was assigned to assist Bülow with the completion of the Kurmark militia. The two tackled this task by first reviewing the voluminous amount of reports forwarded to Bülow's headquarters by both provincial and municipal authorities.[13] According to L'Estoq and Sack, at least seventy-five percent of the Kurmark Landwehr had received basic training on the battalion and squadron level. The Military Government estimated that each Landwehr battalion lacked at least one-third of its required officers. Available weapons only armed two-thirds of the men; the remainder drilled with pikes. Bülow found the Second, Third, and Sixth Kurmark Landwehr Brigades fairly well organized, but the First, Fourth, Fifth, and Seventh Brigades remained in disarray. According to the battalion reports, the men lacked muskets, rucksacks, tunics, and cartridge pouches. Cavalry squadrons needed saddles, pistols, sabers, and experienced officers. Three companies from one district had no weapons.[14] Manpower shortages also existed, especially in the battalions raised from the depopulated districts near the Saxon border.[15] It was more surprising to Bülow that the city of Berlin had mobilized few recruits to meet its quota of four battalions. Reports from the Berlin Commission for Landwehr and Landsturm convinced him that the mobilized units of the Landsturm offered the most expedient means to collect manpower for the Landwehr battalions. The commission had already taken steps to provide more recruits and decreed on 6 June that the responsibility of serving in the Landwehr fell on all males in the city's 102 districts.[16] Getting the men into the ranks became Bülow's task.

Bülow also discovered deplorable conditions in the Neumark Landwehr's three brigades.[17] According to reports from divisional headquarters, the Neumark brigades lacked organization, and only a handful of men possessed muskets. A partially mounted cavalry had to share saddles. Experienced officers, ammunition, and provisions remained limited. Very few men had ever fired a musket![18] Alarmed by such an unflattering description, Bülow appointed Krafft to assist with the Neumark Landwehr.[19] Krafft immediately set out for the Neumark on a fact-finding mission. On 22 June the colonel reported that he could not even find the brigades. After a few days of searching, he finally observed the exercises of the Second Brigade and noted deficiencies in open-order tactics, skirmishing, and outpost duty. He informed Bülow that the brigade needed at least three straight weeks of "uninterrupted diligence and continuous effort" before its battalions could be considered fit for service. Fortunately for Bülow, the shortage of weapons in the Neumark infantry had been exaggerated; two-thirds of the men carried muskets, while one-third, or the whole first line, drilled with pikes. Nevertheless, limited ammunition reserves did not permit more than six shots per man for target practice. Besides ammunition, the brigade lacked support personnel, especially surgeons and gunsmiths, as well as the necessary horses for the staff officers, company commanders, and adjutants. In addition, neither cooking dishes nor canteens had been supplied; 2,406 rucksacks remained on back order. The Second Brigade lacked fourteen drums, and the entire supply of frock coats had still not arrived.

Conversely, Krafft found the battalions of the First and Third Brigades to be superior in training and equipment. He assured Bülow that they would be ready for field duty by 15 July.[20] The men possessed muskets and equipment, but the brigades lacked ammunition reserves, baggage wagons, draft horses, surgeons, and a gunsmith forge. Krafft requested that the Military Government in Stargard fill these needs by 10 July. Despite his efforts, the colonel doubted that the material would be supplied unless Bülow personally intervened. On a more critical note, he urged Bülow to influence the Military Government in Stargard to pay the men and reimburse the company commanders for the costs of musket repairs. Since the battalions lacked gunsmiths, the company commanders had been forced to pay for repair costs out of their own pockets.[21]

Before concluding his inspection, Krafft instructed the officers of the Neumark Landwehr to stress "the main and essential points: advancing, retiring, forming columns, movement in columns, forming squares, deploying, rallying, and charging." He also suggested allocating the limited ammunition to the skirmishers for target practice. Overall, the "professionalism of the brigadiers, battalion commanders, and all of the officers" impressed Krafft. Although he did not observe the Neumark Landwehr cavalry, reports indicated that it had likewise progressed.[22] He also advised Bülow to fill the Neumark Landwehr's officer vacancies with at least one veteran per battalion so that the militia would benefit from experienced leadership. With the exception of the battalion commanders and a few company commanders, the officers of the Second Brigade had no military experience, and Krafft criticized the civilian authorities for not exercising more prudence in their selection of officers. Finally, he suggested that Bülow attach each Neumark Landwehr battalion to a line battalion for maneuvers. Once they had received joint training with the line, Krafft believed the Landwehr would match the army's proficiency.[23]

Although the joint training of line and Landwehr had not been popular with the architects of the militia, the king left the decision to the army officers who now directed the mobilization. In his instructions of 8 June Frederick William mentioned Gneisenau's measures: "Here in Silesia, I have ordered that two companies of the most serviceable units detach from each Landwehr battalion. These companies will then be reassembled into field battalions completely armed with muskets. The remnant, of which few are fit for field service, will be appointed to remain behind as garrison crews. To what extent you hold this arrangement applicable there, I leave wholly to your judgment."[24] Krafft rejected the Silesian model out of concern that separating the companies would lower morale, and Bülow accepted his argument.[25] While Bülow and Boyen struggled to complete the Kurmark Landwehr, the mobilization of the Neumark militia progressed during the latter half of June. Neumark Landwehr battalions exercised with line units that drilled in the region. In early July the civilian officials of the Neumark General-Commission for Landwehr and Landsturm proudly announced the successful mobilization of the militia. With only individual points such as officer vacancies to be settled, the Neumark General-Commission had fulfilled its responsibilities. In comparison with the troubles that Bülow encountered with the Kurmark Landwehr, the Neumark's achievement remains noteworthy.[26]

As for the Kurmark Landwehr, after familiarizing himself with its problems Bülow had to confront his first major obstacle: opposition from the Military Government in Berlin. Since the inception of the Landwehr, the four Military Governments had exercised complete control over the mobilization and use of the militia. According to the Landwehr Decrees, the militia of each province was to serve its respective Military Government as an auxiliary defense force.[27] Both the raising and training of the Landwehr had been delegated to the Military Governments, the provincial authorities, and the district commissions. Thus the king conferred complete control of the mobilization process on regional and local authorities. After he agreed to incorporate the Landwehr with the army, however, the decentralized nature of the mobilization became a detriment to achieving the level of organization and effectiveness suitable for the militia's use in the field. The Military Governments simply lacked the resources to prepare the Landwehr for more than a support role.[28] Thus the Military Governments lost control over the Landwehr after the army took greater interest in the militia's development. Army commanders now took charge of the mobilization in order to prepare the Landwehr to fight alongside the line.

Despite the king's orders, the Military Government in Berlin struggled to retain its authority over the Landwehr. Only three days after Bülow received command of the Kurmark Landwehr the Military Government attempted to reassert its control. It informed Bülow that the Military Government reserved the right to assign the officers and corporals to the Landwehr battalions and squadrons. Bülow flatly refused to concede this right.[29] To expedite training he and Boyen then rearranged the Landwehr battalions in new quarters that reflected their varying degrees of combat-readiness.[30] Prior to Bülow's arrival in Berlin, the Military Government had scattered the units throughout the province.[31] Their arrangements sought to spare the farmlands that would bear the burden of supply when the war resumed. Bülow, however, wanted the battalions of each brigade kept close together for exercises. He had Boyen rearrange the Landwehr camps without notifying the Military Government.[32] On 16 June the Berlin authorities protested.

Writing to Bülow, an outraged L'Estoq insisted that the new camps would ruin the province. He suggested alternative quarters on the grounds that the Kurmark was completely exhausted and added that the Military Government had no funds to purchase supplies. L'Estoq noted that the Military Government "had to protect the unripe grain and the meadows of the province from the ensuing damages of independent foraging, which, in our opinion, could be averted by arranging quarters in conjunction with the authorities, yet we were not consulted." He concluded by accepting "the responsibility of *intending* to quarter and provision both the manpower and the horses," but promised nothing.[33]

As commanding general, Bülow had more important considerations. He explained that with French camps near the border it would be "totally irresponsible" if he kept the troops rearward. He had rearranged the quarters so that his corps and the militia troops fit for duty faced the French while the incomplete Landwehr units formed a second line. "Regarding the question of what I can do for the relief of the land," Bülow concluded, "I already explained myself extensively to the Civil-Governor yesterday: I would like to do more, but any more and I might as well surrender myself to the enemy."[34]

This silenced the Military Government for a while and allowed Bülow to proceed with the task at hand. On 18 June he informed the king of the "very disparate progress" of the Kurmark and Neumark brigades. He hoped that they would be combat-ready in three or four weeks but noted that many of the battalions still lacked sufficient manpower. As a result only three of the seven brigades could participate in maneuvers.[35] Several reasons accounted for the shortage of manpower. Although Landwehr service had been decreed compulsory for every male aged seventeen to forty, recruiting was initially limited to volunteers. Except in East Prussia, where anti-French sentiment had been magnified by the Grande Armée's excesses prior to the 1812 Campaign, many peasants had migrated or fled to the forests following the announcement of universal conscription. In fact, that announcement, combined with the Landwehr decree, sparked an exodus across the frontier into Russian Poland. Only 18,038 recruits volunteered for the line and Landwehr between 1813 and 1815—a period when 300,000 men served in the army.[36] Thus the Military Governments, the district commissions, and royal officials throughout the kingdom all competed for recruits during the spring of 1813. Civilian supervision of the Landwehr had led to assorted recruiting practices that produced varying results. The conscription of men into the regular army mainly caused the Kurmark's manpower shortage. In February and March the army drafted all veterans and reservists. Conscription to replace losses in the line units followed. Estate-owners and the urban bourgeoisie also thwarted recruitment by opposing the reduction of their respective labor forces. Middle-class conscripts requested exemption from Landwehr service on the grounds that their careers would be ruined. The Military Government's investigations into their complaints caused further delays and exemptions.[37] Finally, various *Freikorps* and Jäger units quartered near Berlin also reduced the number of Landwehr recruits since upper-class youths preferred to serve with these special volunteer units.[38]

The state's miserable financial status was another reason for the shortage of manpower. Landwehr units were not paid, and the men had to get by as best they could. This ultimately led to desertions and sometimes worse, as in the case of the Cottbus District, which raised three poorly supplied companies totaling 400 men. During the armistice the district commission sparked widespread desertions by suspending all financial assistance. Two of the three companies mutinied on 21 June; the officers renounced their duty and led the men toward Müllrose. The Landsturm of the Upper-Barnim and Lebus Districts eventually captured the rebels at Müncheberg. The men were arrested and brought to Berlin. According to the Historical Section of the Prussian General Staff, the wives of the Landwehr men had instigated the mutiny![39]

To solve the Kurmark's manpower problems, Bülow and Boyen diligently enforced the conscription laws. But getting recruits into the ranks of the Landwehr was only half the battle. Over one-third of the men lacked muskets—a number that increased as the ranks filled. To remedy the equipment shortages, Bülow petitioned the Military Government in Stargard to distribute the British weapons, ammunition, and uniforms that had arrived in the Baltic port of Kolberg.[40] Following Great Britain's 15 June agreement to subsidize the Prussians, large quantities of arms and supplies became available.[41] Despite Bülow's repeated requests, British stores went to the army, which refused to share the arms and equipment with the Landwehr until its own needs had been met.[42]

While negotiations with Stargard continued, Bülow ordered a comprehensive review of all Kurmark Landwehr units in late June. By 3 July Boyen had rendered an extensive description of the brigades. Manpower shortages, lack of uniforms, and poor equipment reduced the number of Kurmark Landwehr battalions from the projected twenty-eight to nineteen. Boyen reported that numerous problems still afflicted the Kurmark militia. Of the three battalions that the Military Government in Stargard had to contribute to the Kurmark's First Brigade, Boyen found only two companies of barefooted and "half-naked" recruits. A battalion raised in the Second Jerichow District still lacked 800 frock coats, 504 pairs of boots, 380 pairs of trousers, 147 caps, and mess gear. He inspected three other battalions that could not exercise due to the lack of uniforms and equipment, two that were understaffed, and one that had not yet received a commander.[43] To compensate for the undermanned and ill-clad Kurmark companies, Bülow accepted Boyen's suggestion to reorganize the best companies into nine and one-half field battalions. This certainly did not provide a long-term solution, and only the extension of the armistice from 20 July to 10 August enabled them to raise the Kurmark's full contingent.

Despite the problems of men and material, Boyen described the morale of the officers and soldiers as "thoroughly excellent" and "unusually good."[44] Although conscription never received popular support, men who accepted their new roles out of duty, regional loyalties, and patriotism—rather than coercion and harsh discipline—filled the ranks of the Landwehr.[45] They endured the various privations of military life with few complaints. Due to their enthusiasm, Boyen expected positive results when the Kurmark militia took the field. He interviewed each brigade and battalion commander as well as the two divisional commanders, Hirschfeld and Gen. Friedrich Wilhelm von Putlitz. Both generals had worked diligently to prepare their respective commands, but Hirschfeld resented his position with the Landwehr. Putlitz, however, supported the idea of a national war effort and the need for the army to break with its tradition of mindless discipline and ferocious punishment. Although times had changed in the army, the old military reform party did not want the Landwehr trained in the same rigorous tradition as the line. Scharnhorst feared that the army's basic training would destroy the Landwehr's patriotism and willingness to serve. Putlitz reflected these sentiments in his instructions to the brigade commanders:

> We must constantly increase the knowledge of the militia-man, but also conserve his strength. Therefore, make everything easy for him so that he does not grow to hate his service. He is to be

> made accustomed to the rigors gradually. His appearance must not be neglected; the grace of his movements as well as the cleanliness of his body, clothing, and weapons are to be maintained. Through helpful and respectful treatment his self-respect is to be increased as much as possible. Subordination is the soul of service; it fits very well with the proscribed self-respect that the true militia-man must possess. Officers must never be allowed to forget that they have to deal with people of whom several have volunteered for the defense of the Fatherland. In this regard, one must also use self-respect. Some degenerates might have to be treated sternly, but the dignity of the men must never be compromised.[46]

Boyen commended Putlitz and described him as a "respectable, experienced officer" who understood the needs of the militia. As for Hirschfeld, Boyen described him as a "highly respectable officer whose actions and good intentions are truly admirable." Despite this positive evaluation, Boyen rebuked him for using excessive force to discipline the men when they made mistakes. A disciple of Scharnhorst, Boyen abhorred the harsh discipline of the pre-Jena army, yet many of the Landwehr's senior officers were veterans of this tradition. In contrast to Hirschfeld's harshness, Boyen praised the commander of the Second Battalion of the Six Brigade, Major von Streit, whose most severe punishment was to have his men turn their caps around in shame during the exercises.[47]

Boyen reported that the brigade and battalion commanders with no prior military experience had adapted well to their new occupations. The commander of the Fifth Brigade, Colonel von Bredow, had dramatically improved the status of his four battalions since the beginning of the armistice. Prior to joining the Landwehr, Bredow had worked for the Kurmark province as a *Landrat* (county commissioner). Major von Grolman particularly caught Boyen's attention. Commander of the First Battalion of the Fourth Brigade, Grolman had resigned from his civil post as *Regierungsrat* (privy councillor) and volunteered for militia duty. Boyen noted that the major led his men quite well, despite his complete lack of experience.[48] Several newly commissioned company and squadron commanders also earned Boyen's praise during the exercises. Others, however, did not escape the colonel's scrutiny. The meticulous Boyen found that Major von Teschen's six cavalry squadrons lacked cohesion. He attributed this to the major's hoarse voice, which hampered his ability to issue clear commands. He criticized another battalion commander, Major von Treskow, for talking too much during the maneuvers. Boyen reported that another officer, Major von Dieczielsky, should have been embarrassed by the way his battalion exercised. Surprisingly, veterans who had served in the pre-Jena army and had been discharged in 1807 and 1808 committed most of the infractions. Nonetheless, their combat experience remained invaluable to the militia. Beyond these relics and undesirables that the army did not want, the Kurmark Landwehr still needed experienced men to fill seventy-six officer slots. Boyen warned Bülow of the improbability of finding suitable candidates in the province.[49]

Boyen believed that twenty-four undermanned squadrons of the Kurmark Landwehr cavalry could be combat-ready by the end of the armistice if sabers could be supplied. When he made his inspection, four squadrons had to remain in their depots due to the lack of uniforms and saddles. Manpower shortages also plagued the Kurmark cavalry. Most squadrons barely numbered ninety-six men—which Boyen considered too low for field duty when considering attrition rates. One squadron consisted of only nine men, while the horses of another proved so unfit that Boyen ordered a special investigation into the matter. As with the infantry, Bülow accepted Boyen's suggestion to combine the best cavalry units into field squadrons.

After receiving Boyen's comprehensive reports, Bülow solved some of the problems. He dispatched his adjutants to the Military Government in Stargard to demand the necessary muskets and sabers from the reserves in Kolberg. Additional officers and corporals from his line battalions drilled the militia.[50] He doubled the conscription efforts to bring the battalions to full strength. Under his supervision the level of conscription for the Landwehr paralleled the vigorous recruiting of native subjects during the Seven Years' War.[51]

Before filling the seventy-six officer vacancies in the Kurmark Landwehr, Bülow attempted to solve a similar problem in his own corps. An order of 7 May 1813 had instructed him to fill line vacancies with volunteer Jäger "who possess the characteristics of an officer" and had received a "quality" education. The order emphasized the need to recruit men from the Jäger who had combat experience and whose behavior had been "flawless."[52] After filling the line vacancies according to these guidelines, Bülow and Boyen nominated suitable officer candidates for the Kurmark Landwehr. They based their selection on the 7 May instructions for the line, supplemented by their own desire to use a system of merit. Bülow's stipulations did not specifically mention the Jäger. Instead any soldier from his corps who had served with distinction would be eligible for a commission in the Landwehr.[53] If this selection process failed to fill the Landwehr's vacancies, Bülow planned to select the remainder from the Jäger.[54]

In developing these principles, Bülow and Boyen took full advantage of two great victories of the reform party that had revolutionized Prussia's military establishment. The first, issued on 6 August 1808 and entitled "Regulations for Making Appointments to Vacancies among Ensigns and for the Selection of Officers for the Infantry, Cavalry, and Artillery," stated that

> officer commissions shall henceforth be awarded in peacetime only for knowledge and education, and in wartime for outstanding bravery and quickness of perception. From the whole nation, therefore, all individuals who possess these qualities can lay title to the highest positions of honor in the military establishment. Any Prussian who possesses these qualifications can aspire to the highest military posts of honor. All advantages hitherto enjoyed by the [noble] Estate in the Army are hereby abolished and all men, regardless of their origins, shall have the same duties and rights.[55]

According to historian Karl Demeter, this decree "breathes the unmistakable spirit of Scharnhorst and Gneisenau."[56] The second decree—also the work of Scharnhorst—was issued on 9 February 1813. It established universal conscription and abolished exemptions from military service; any man serving one month became eligible for a commission. Boyen naturally subscribed to the beliefs of his great mentor, but Bülow's willingness to commission non-nobles is indicative of not only his liberal tendencies but also the militia's dire need for capable officers.

On 16 July Bülow submitted to the king a list of the ensigns, corporals, sergeants, and Jäger personnel suited to be Landwehr officers.[57] Some of Bülow's subordinates, however, did not share the army's confidence in the Jäger. Hirschfeld rendered a typical conservative opinion on this subject, claiming that the Landwehr could not be effective unless it was led by "officers who understand military duty." With few exceptions the Landwehr officers under his command had been recruited or elected by their men. These officers simply did not have the expertise or the desire to imitate the army's strict discipline. Much to Hirschfeld's horror, he noticed that the officers designated for his division were "mostly volunteer Jäger and almost equally as ignorant of military service as the local [Landwehr] officers." Hirschfeld frankly concluded that such men "can be of no help to me."[58] Regardless of this reactionary attitude, Bülow and Boyen valued the Jäger. Reflecting their emphasis on merit and experience, they believed that the seniority of any Jäger personnel commissioned should be calculated from the date they volunteered rather than the date they received their commissions. In his report to the king Bülow acknowledged that the Jäger had been "animated by zeal and patriotism" and had "hurried to the flag and volunteered." He argued that it would be unjust "if they now had to step behind several people, who had not fixed their sight on the great cause, had initially remained in their homes, and only when the Landwehr was formed were chosen as the only suitable candidates to fill the officer slots." Bülow felt that the Jäger who had combat experience could not be classified behind officers who had none. Therefore, he submitted suggestions for the establishment of seniority based on combat experience.[59]

Six days later the king confirmed all of the Jäger and line candidates that Bülow had recommended for promotion to the rank of second lieutenant.[60] Frederick William did not accept Bülow's plan for establishing seniority, however.[61] As in the case of the Landwehr, the role of the Jäger also posed problems. The king provided no explanation for rejecting Bülow's suggestion, but it can be assumed that the uncertainty over how the Jäger fit into the Prussian military establishment influenced his decision.[62] Moreover, the decree that regulated the formation of the Jäger conveniently stated that volunteers could not apply for commissions until they had completed their training.[63]

At the end of July Bülow classified the Kurmark Landwehr as combat-ready. Enforcement of the conscription laws for six weeks had produced enough recruits. On 27 July he reported that twenty-six battalions and twenty-eight squadrons of Kurmark Landwehr could take the field. The Kurmark provided the second largest Landwehr contingent of the Prussian provinces, surpassed only by Silesia's sixty-eight battalions and forty squadrons. For its part the Neumark contributed a noteworthy twelve battalions and eight squadrons.[64] Except for a few officer slots that still needed to be filled and a shortage of mounts for the officers, the Kurmark Landwehr appeared to be combat-ready. The majority of the infantry possessed muskets, while the cavalry had received pistols, lances, and sabers from the stores at Kolberg. Uniformed and equipped battalions only lacked the cooking gear that remained on order. In the Neumark some units still needed frock coats and mess gear, but the district committees had negotiated contracts with a supplier in Stargard. Regardless of the minor deficiencies, the development of the Neumark Landwehr satisfied Bülow; he rated its cavalry as superb. Despite heavy recruitment by the army and the agrarian character of the region, the Kurmark and Neumark provided over 30,000 armed, uniformed, and trained men.

On 27 July a royal decree reorganized the militia. No longer grouped in divisions and brigades, the Landwehr was henceforth designated as regiments. The king also endorsed a plan to merge the Landwehr regiments into the brigades of the field army. Each army brigade would consist of three regiments: one line, one reserve, and one Landwehr.[65] Bülow reorganized the Kurmark and Neumark Landwehr units in accordance with the new regulations and distributed the regiments under his command to the army brigades in early August. No longer divisional generals in the Kurmark Landwehr, Putlitz and Hirschfeld became brigadiers under Gen. Bogislaw Friedrich Count von Tauentzien. Tauentzien received command of the newly formed Fourth Corps, which consisted mainly of militia units. Putlitz now commanded a brigade consisting of the Third and Fourth Kurmark Landwehr Regiments and the Third Kurmark Landwehr Cavalry Regiment—6,400 infantry and 450 cavalry.[66] Hirschfeld's brigade included the Sixth and Seventh Kurmark Landwehr Regiments—8,650 men—and their corresponding cavalry regiments with 1,000 men.[67] Bülow divided the entire Neumark Landwehr, as well as the First and Second Regiments of the Kurmark Landwehr, among his Third Corps and the other brigades of Tauentzien's Fourth Corps.

Due to the king's opposition to universal conscription during the Reform Era, Prussian mobilization plans originally intended to use the canton system to conscript the lower classes into the regular army. Napoleon's great disaster in 1812 and the example provided by the East Prussian Landwehr finally gave Frederick William the courage to accept Scharnhorst's advice and declare all able-bodied males eligible to serve the colors.[68] Thus on 9 February 1813 the king abolished all exemptions from military service.[69] To minimize the widespread opposition sparked by this decree, the Prussians created Landwehr and Jäger units for subjects previously exempted from military service.[70] Recruiting for these new branches of service was supposed to occur on a volunteer basis, in the hopes that an appeal to defend the Fatherland would be more palatable than a demand to serve the king. Although this was a temporary setback for Scharnhorst, who wanted Frederick William to make national defense the *equal* obligation of every subject, one month later, on 17 March 1813, he succeeded in convincing the king to base the national Landwehr on universal conscription.[71] Service in the Landwehr thus became compulsory for all landed peasants and middle-class males aged seventeen to forty.[72] Since the conscription of the lower class had not produced the rapid expansion of combat power needed to secure and satisfy allies—not to mention liberate the state from French control—the Prussians used their militia to increase the size of the army. When hostilities resumed, the combined Prussian army totaled 279,000 men, including 120,504 Landwehr troops—one-quarter of which came from the Kurmark and Neumark.[73]

6

Axes, Spades, and Water

Problems on the defense line started prior to the signing of the armistice. Not only did the water level remain insufficient, but work on the fortifications hardly progressed. Both civil and military engineers complained repeatedly to the Military Government about the lack of skilled workers, laborers, and material. On 2 June only 25 workers out of 250 reported for work at Trebbin. Without the necessary workers and equipment, the construction dragged during the last few weeks of the spring campaign. French operations in May and June appear to have provided little motivation for district, provincial, and municipal officials to provide a civilian labor force to work at the various construction sites. With the harvest only one month away, either the construction had to be accelerated or the defense plans had to be completely revised. Despite the engineers' efforts, they received little cooperation. One exasperated officer noted:

> The Mayors of the Teltow, Zauch, and Luckenwalde Districts have explained to me that it is impossible for them to provide the requested number of workers. I have also requested, but not received, wagons to transport the palisades—I need fifteen daily. Carpenters and masons are needed daily for the construction, the maintenance of the dams, and the palisading. I seek

> permission to allow these poor people to at least receive provisions from the military magazine, since no funds are available to pay them. For the barricades, I need a considerable amount of wrought iron. I need an order that will force the local magistrate to produce this material; otherwise I can hardly expect to receive it due to the lack of funds.[1]

In the flood zone the drought, heat, and wind had completely drained the lowlands between Zossen and Königs-Wusterhausen, an area that had been impassable just three weeks earlier.[2] Evaporation and the lack of rainfall rendered some zones of the floodplain worthless. Although deep flooding remained in some areas, others were completely dry. On 8 June the Military Government in Berlin informed Bülow that the drought had reduced the effectiveness of the floodplain and that the water alone could not prevent an enemy army from reaching the capital.[3] Four days later he arrived in Berlin and received the royal order that placed the whole defense network under his jurisdiction. As with the Landwehr, the army now assumed full control over the defense projects during an armistice that could not have come at a more fortuitous time for the Prussians.

Owing to the incomplete status of the defense line and the lack of cooperation from civilian officials, Bülow did indeed revise the plans. His ideas for defending both the province and the capital varied greatly from those of the Military Government. Bülow only placed importance on fortifying Berlin and the Nuthe-Notte line. The content of his instructions left little doubt that he disagreed with the Military Government's defensive strategy. He did not want the French to reach the defense line unopposed. Instead he planned to confront them on the Saxon frontier. Rather than being outposts for a corps or army that stood north of the line awaiting the enemy, the entrenchments along the Nuthe-Notte line would serve as rallying points for Allied forces should they be driven back from Saxony. Bülow believed the fate of Berlin should be decided in the open plain south of the capital rather than behind entrenchments. He reserved the decision to initiate the floods but ordered the civilian authorities to continue their work on the dams. Bülow's ideas for the defense of the Kurmark and Berlin reflected his experiences during the spring campaign, when his small corps had shouldered this tremendous responsibility. He still believed that the best means of defense would be offensive strikes in the open field. Should his forces be defeated, however, they could then withdraw to the Nuthe-Notte defense line. There he could rally his forces and hold the crossings through the floodplain in conjunction with the Landwehr and Landsturm. With any luck, the floodwaters would be deep enough to prevent the French from advancing. At this early stage of the armistice Bülow had to be mindful of the initial four-week length of the truce and take only the most expedient measures. Moreover, his own manpower remained a concern. Austria and Sweden had still not committed to the coalition. For Bülow, this meant that his corps would probably face superior French numbers once hostilities resumed. Consequently, he continued the Nuthe-Notte flood and entrenchment projects in order to create a last line of defense for the capital.

Eastern Defenses: The Spree, the Frederick William Canal, and the Oder

Work on the fortifications in the Kurmark continued according to the blueprint outlined in May. As the spring campaign had shown, a French operation against Berlin could come from any direction: west from the lower Elbe, southwest from Magdeburg, south from Wittenberg and Torgau, or east from a French force attempting to liberate the Oder garrisons. The Oder scenario had particularly troubled Bülow at the end of the campaign. He now wanted to extend the Spree line and reinforce the Frederick William Canal that linked the Spree with the Oder. In early July he instructed the engineer, Lieut. Johann Meyer, to inspect the terrain around Müllrose to determine the defensibility of the Frederick William Canal.[4] If he found the area suitable, Bülow wanted a defense plan drafted as soon as possible. Müllrose's strategic position on the canal and in the left flank of any Allied force defending Berlin warranted concern. L'Estoq also urged Bülow to take measures at this point, because his spies in Saxony informed him that the French intended to relieve the Oder garrisons as soon as the armistice expired.[5]

Meyer reported that the narrow and shallow Frederick William Canal could be bridged at many points, which thus reduced Müllrose's importance. His opinion of Frankfurt-am-Oder, a major point of passage over the Oder directly east of Berlin, appeared even less encouraging. Meyer did not believe the town, which was located in a valley surrounded by steep hills, could be held. He suggested that the importance of the Frederick William Canal, as well as the surrounding region, be based on the French positions and their presumed intentions. Meyer found evidence of French activity near the Oder and along the Prusso-Saxon frontier. According to a preacher who had just arrived from Saxony, Marshal Victor had 9,000 men camped around Friedland. Other locals reported that an estimated 3,000 men had already moved into Fürstenberg, where a camp for 15,000 had been prepared. In addition, the cantons of Oudinot's 20,000 men extended from Luckau over Lübben to Lieberose. According to this information, Meyer expressed his belief that the French would attempt to relieve the Oder fortresses once hostilities resumed. He predicted the enemy's success unless an Allied corps defended the canal.[6] Bülow did not have the authority—not to mention the manpower—to allocate another corps southeast of the capital. Meyer's report, however, with its estimates and positions of French forces, later influenced Allied planning. After the army decided to incorporate the Landwehr, a brigade of mostly West Prussian militia units observed the Oder.

The reports of another subordinate, Borstell, shaped Bülow's views of the Spree sector and the southeastern district of Beeskow-Storkow. Borstell reported that no defensive measures had been taken in Beeskow-Storkow, and nothing had been done to destroy the numerous bridges across the Spree. The terrain itself would not hinder the approach of a French army. From their suspected positions Oudinot and Victor could initiate operations against the Kurmark, Silesia, or West Prussia. Borstell's scouts also found French camps at Fürstenberg, Guben, Friedland, Lübben, and Luckau. Since the Beeskow-Storkow District provided a vital military position for the observation of these points, he advised posting a flying column there to ascertain French movements and block any attempt to cross the Spree. Borstell also wanted permission to destroy the bridges over the Spree.[7] Bülow did not share his concern over this sector and continued to believe that Berlin's fate would be decided directly south of Berlin and the Nuthe-Notte line. He also believed that it would be "highly unlikely" for the Allied forces around Berlin to remain on the defensive when hostilities resumed and that they would need the passages over the Spree to conduct an offensive.[8] On this point Bülow would eventually be proven wrong—not by the French, but by the man who would supersede him as the chief defender of Berlin.

Western Defenses: The Havel and the Elbe

On the opposite side of the Kurmark, Magdeburg remained in enemy hands, and the presence of French troops along the lower Elbe as far as Hamburg posed a considerable threat to Berlin. In early June the Military Government had asked Eytelwein to formulate a defense plan for this sector.[9] He reported that a defense of the Elbe south of Havelberg seemed impractical on account of the enemy's ability to cross the river at Magdeburg, Rosslau, Wittenberg, and Torgau. Instead he proposed fortifying the entire right bank of the lower Elbe with redoubts between Quitzöbel and Dömitz.[10] Since this matter now fell under Bülow's supervision, L'Estoq forwarded Eytelwein's proposals to him.[11]

Eytelwein's suggestion impressed Bülow, who ordered Markhoff to conduct a feasibility inspection. Due to the major's many commitments, the results did not reach Bülow for almost three weeks. Markhoff rejected Eytelwein's proposal to defend the right bank of the lower Elbe directly. Instead he suggested utilizing the terrain east of the Elbe, claiming that it suited the irregular forces that would initially confront the French.[12] Markhoff suggested building fortifications at Rathenow, Havelberg, Quitzöbel, Wittenberge, Lenzen, and Dömitz. Bülow turned his attention to these points, especially Havelberg, and at the end of July ordered Meyer to draft a plan to fortify Havelberg. On 1 August Meyer proposed the construction of ten redoubts, each requiring a workforce of 200 men for fourteen days of work. This overambitious plan far exceeded the Kurmark's resources and would have diverted valuable manpower and material from work along the Nuthe-Notte line, where Bülow believed the French would attack. He rejected Meyer's proposal, and nothing further could be done since the end of the armistice approached.[13] Once hostilities reconvened, Allied field units successfully defended the lower Elbe from the French and Danish forces under Marshal Davout.

Southern Defenses: The Nuthe, the Nuthe Canal, and the Notte

By minimizing the work on the outer defenses (namely along the Havel, Spree, and Oder) Bülow concentrated the Kurmark's limited resources on the Nuthe-Notte line directly south of the capital, but problems continued. Since the signing of the armistice, the Military Government in

Berlin had been flooded not with water but with complaints. Mill owners and farmers in the Nuthe-Notte sectors that remained under water protested against the continued damming. On 11 June Günther explained to Civil Governor Sack that the dams along the Nuthe had flooded a large portion of the adjacent lowlands so that the landowners suffered considerable loss of their pastures. Günther suggested that this problem could be alleviated by opening some of the dams and allowing the water to flow along its normal course.[14] He claimed that the floodwaters could be restored within forty-eight hours by closing the dams. Bülow authorized the civil engineers to open some of the dams and partially release the floodwaters.[15] This still did not solve the problem, which only worsened despite the lack of rain. By the end of July the damming of the water in the lowlands between Trebbin and Zossen, at the very edge of the Nuthe-Notte line, caused hardships for the local residents. Since large tracts of their land remained flooded, they would be deprived of much of their winter crop. The smaller villages particularly suffered from the loss of their pastures. One of Borstell's subordinates wrote that the peasants "do not know where they should take their livestock and are in the greatest predicament."[16]

Aside from the deep flooding achieved at the edge of the sector between Trebbin and Zossen, water levels in most sectors along the Nuthe dropped in July. On the Notte the water level remained so low at some points that the mills between Zossen and Königs-Wusterhausen could not operate. The rains that fell sporadically did not compensate for the high level of evaporation. Cochius viewed the decreasing water level as a losing battle against nature. He explained that "since all tributaries flowing into the Notte valley are low, it would be completely impossible to replenish the floodwaters since the influx would seep into the dry terrain and frustrate the whole plan."[17]

Besides nature's unwillingness to cooperate, Bülow's engineers faced multiple complications on the entrenchments in the flood zone. At Trebbin the engineer Lieutenant von Rhaden complained to the Military Government that the mayors of Teltow and Zauche-Luckenwalde ignored his requests for laborers. On Rhaden's behalf, Günther attempted to convince the magistrates to provide a workforce but had no success. One civil official informed Rhaden that "he would not be surprised if the people were not provided, since too much was already demanded of them." Rhaden requested "stern orders" that would force them to supply more workers and wagons.[18]

In response to Rhaden's difficulties, Bülow ordered a complete inspection of the central defense line between Potsdam and Königs-Wusterhausen. Mittenwalde concerned him most since construction there remained far behind due to the lack of workers. Up to that point the Teltow District had provided 120 workers, the majority being "children and old men," while the Beeskow-Storkow District had contributed very few workers at all. Bülow informed the Military Government that hardy workers had to be found. He reminded the governors that he could not provide any more military personnel for the work since they had insisted on quartering only a minimum number of troops in that area. For logistical reasons the bulk of his corps camped over six miles away from the Nuthe-Notte line. He instructed L'Estoq to order the mayor of Beeskow-Storkow to furnish 200 workers daily at Mittenwalde. As for the approaching harvest, Bülow suggested a "rigorous pursuit of the construction" in order to complete the work before it began.[19] The usually uncooperative L'Estoq agreed and ordered the mayor of Beeskow-Storkow to provide the necessary workers at Mittenwalde. Although the workers reported in unprecedented numbers, another problem delayed construction at both Mittenwalde and Trebbin: Rhaden and his pioneer company were transferred to Yorck's corps in Silesia![20]

Bülow also learned that little had been completed on the main east-west defense line between Trebbin and Zossen. Redoubts still needed to be constructed at the main passages over the Nuthe and the Nuthe Canal. Bülow sent Markhoff to inspect the entrenchments and supervise the construction. On 31 July Markhoff reported that the left-wing fortifications on the Notte required an additional ten to twelve days for completion, but he assured Bülow that the work at Trebbin would be concluded the following week. He had already completed the work at Saarmund, further north on the Nuthe. On the Nuthe Canal he planned to construct a redoubt at Jühnsdorf and one or two redoubts on the hills of Wietstock, north of Wilmersdorf.[21]

Bülow continued to receive discouraging reports about the water levels on the Nuthe-Notte floodplain throughout July. The extension of the armistice from 20 July to 10 August provided additional time during which the Prussians hoped that nature would bolster their efforts. In the meantime nature did summon the farmers to their fields, and the harvest required a workforce. This need conflicted with the construction on the Nuthe-Notte line. To spare the rural labor force,

L'Estoq asked Bülow for a temporary increase of military laborers. Bülow sternly replied: "So, with the extension of the armistice, the farmers believe they can begin the harvest while military personnel finish the work? This is quite impossible." Undaunted, the Military Government reiterated its request for military labor. With construction lagging due to the absence of workers, Bülow had no other choice than to order Borstell, whose brigade occupied the line between Trebbin, Zossen, and Mittenwalde, to place his troops at the disposal of the various engineer officers.[22]

Central Defenses: Spandau and Berlin

In accordance with a royal order, construction had already begun on an entrenched camp at Spandau prior to Bülow's return to Berlin in early June. The Military Government in Berlin authorized Maj. August von Reiche to direct the project and planned to employ four Landwehr battalions as his labor force in order to spare the farmers.[23] Although all four battalions were scheduled to arrive at Spandau on 13 June, only one reported. Two days later Bülow, who now assumed jurisdiction over the project, met with Reiche to discuss the delays and problems. The project's urgency, no doubt based on its royal origins, convinced Bülow that the construction could not be delayed, and he authorized Reiche to impress civilian workers.[24] With the harvest approaching, he could only collect 300 workers; this number did not suffice. Reiche lodged complaints with the Military Government, which in turn informed Bülow that "the countryside can not provide the workers since so many people have been recruited, and we request that you appropriate Landwehr and line troops for this purpose."[25] Bülow conceded and added three line battalions to the workforce at Spandau but instructed Reiche to continue requisitioning civilian laborers. As of 25 June 500 civilian workers were laboring at Spandau, an accomplishment that would not be matched anywhere else in the Kurmark. By mid-July the military and civilian workforce at Spandau completed the entrenchments; only the palisading and construction on the blockhouses still needed to be finished.[26] The cooperation between the military and civilian officials remains noteworthy, yet unique to the construction at Spandau.

Bülow soon found that blurred lines of authority and bureaucratic confusion eclipsed military expediency. Aside from the work at Spandau, the implementation of the defense plan around Berlin proved chaotic. Boyen's ambitious plans to build several redoubts along the southern rim of the capital concerned Bülow. He inspected the works, found that little progress had been made, and reevaluated the entire project. As a result he had one of his engineers, Lieutenant von Heune, draft a plan for the construction of fortifications only on the hill chains at Berlin's Halle and Cottbus Gates. Heune's plan included a detailed calculation of worker requirements and building materials. He suggested the construction of five redoubts, each capable of holding 200 men and two guns with a blockhouse for the whole garrison. Heune requested 200 workers per redoubt for a total of 1,000 men for the initial stage of construction. For the second phase he wanted to increase this number to 800 per redoubt for a total of 4,000 workers. According to his calculations, this manpower could complete the construction in fourteen days, while the carpentry work on the blockhouses would take eight days. For material, Heune's project required 3,505 wooden beams forty feet long and ten inches thick as well as forty-seven planks each twenty feet long and several inches thick.[27]

On 21 June Bülow and Boyen inspected the terrain around the Halle and Cottbus Gates to determine the feasibility of Heune's plan. Convinced that the proposed redoubts could protect Berlin against a French force that penetrated the Nuthe-Notte line, they submitted Heune's plan to the Military Government for completion. Once again Bülow emphasized that these redoubts would only serve as rallying points "if the mobile army is forced to make a retrograde movement to the city." As long as the Spree and the Havel could be held, he assured L'Estoq that the redoubts would stop the French. Bülow also promised to support the construction with a significant number of military pioneers. He expected L'Estoq's full cooperation as well as the assurance that the military-governor would "procure the necessary resources . . . without delay."[28]

Two days later L'Estoq and Sack rejected Heune's plan for several reasons. The Military Government did not agree that the French would advance against Berlin through the Nuthe-Notte line. Instead they believed the French would attempt to avoid the flood zone directly south of the capital and use the wooded banks of the Spree to conceal their movements. The Spree, neither deep nor wide, offered more chances for a successful crossing than the Havel. The Military Government maintained that an attempt to cross the Spree would be made near

Müllrose. A second point of contention concerned Heune's proposal for a blockhouse. L'Estoq claimed that blockhouses were "really only required near fortresses and mountain positions." The exorbitant cost of their construction and the vast quantities of wood required simply made the project unfeasible. He reminded Bülow that funds neared exhaustion and questioned the expense of Heune's project, claiming "that the advantage of having redoubts before Berlin might be outweighed by the costs." Due to the price of lumber, the Military Government only approved construction of a bomb-proof powder magazine, gun platforms, and barricaded entrances for each redoubt. Only sixty beams would be needed per redoubt, and the lumber requisite for all five entrenchments would be reduced to a manageable figure of 300 beams. The Military Government also flatly rejected the estimated time-frame of fourteen days to finish construction because the approaching harvest would make it difficult to find the necessary workers. Although the governors implored Bülow "to consider what is to be expected of us," their protests did not dissuade him from pursuing Heune's plan, which he considered vital from a military viewpoint.[29] Accompanied by the engineer Captain von Loos, Bülow again inspected the area on 25 June and ordered Loos to begin work on the redoubts immediately.[30] Bülow would deal with the Military Government himself.

Despite Bülow's efforts, complications slowed the redoubt construction on the Halle and Cottbus Gates. Shortages of tools and resources proved to be the biggest problem. On 27 June the construction at the Cottbus Gate alone required 1,020 spades, 120 axes, and 102 wagons to haul dirt; only 474 spades, 51 axes, and 38 wagons could be collected. The Berlin magistrate, Oberbürgermeister Johann Büsching, ordered each of the city's 102 district managers to requisition one horse-cart, one ax, and ten spades from their respective districts. Owners received written guarantees that their property would be returned. Berlin's police chief, Paul Ludwig Lecocq, promised to assist by having his men deliver the borrowed equipment to city hall. Büsching's subordinates only partially obeyed his instructions. Rather than collecting the requisitioned material themselves, they issued a general call for donations. As a result contributions arrived sporadically, and it became impossible to determine which districts had fulfilled their obligations. The persisting tool shortage forced the engineers to file multiple complaints with anyone who would listen.[31]

Securing a workforce to use the tools became an even bigger dilemma. Manpower shortages existed, despite the employment of 800 pioneers from Bülow's corps. He instructed the Military Government to increase the number of workers at the Halle and Cottbus Gates by 400 to 500 rural laborers in order to complete the work within eight to ten days. Bülow based this time-frame on the labor of peasants—people he considered to be "more accustomed to the work" and who would "perform the same amount of work as twice the number of urban workers."[32] L'Estoq and Sack rejected Bülow's request. In view of the harvest, they felt that this measure did not serve the interests of the state. Since the Military Government lacked the means to fill Bülow's needs, the governors asked him to employ more of his troops, particularly the two brigades quartered in Berlin.[33] They warned Bülow that "it would be disgraceful to demand any more from the inhabitants." The Military Government felt that the peasants could not be spared during the harvest. According to their estimates, much of the beet crop had already spoiled in the fields because the depleted rural labor force could not harvest it in time. L'Estoq and Sack urged Bülow to encourage his troops "to lend a helping hand with the field work." At this impasse the Military Government turned the matter of additional manpower over to the city's Committee for Landwehr and Landsturm.[34]

Because of the blurred lines of authority and the basic manpower shortage, neither the military nor the civil authorities could produce the necessary workers. Loos complained that he still did not have an adequate workforce. The total number of workers provided by the city for the redoubt construction barely numbered 700; Loos had requested a minimum of 1,200.[35] Exemptions that spared the Berlin Civic Guard from work on the entrenchments proved to be the cause of his problems. The Military Government, by now quite annoyed with Bülow and his engineers, provided Loos with an early-nineteenth-century version of red tape. To solve the problem Loos first had to obtain an order from Bülow stating the amount of manpower to be supplied by the city. Then he had to submit his request to the Berlin Committee for Landwehr and Landsturm, which would provide the specified number of workers.[36] Although this superfluous paperwork aggravated the situation, the Military Government did attempt to solve the labor shortages by exercising more authority over the Berlin Committee for Landwehr and Landsturm. The committee received instructions to end the exemptions from manual labor enjoyed by the Landsturm who served in the Berlin Civic Guard, since this privilege was "unfair to their fellow citizens."[37] L'Estoq figured that only 450 of the 4,100 guardsmen patrolled the city at any given time, so off-duty members of the guard could supply an additional 3,500 workers.[38] The Military Government also estimated that the Landsturm could provide at least 24,000 men. A further 6,000 men would be provided by "widowers over sixty years of age and old men who can fulfill their civic duty on the entrenchment construction." L'Estoq thus speculated that over 33,000 men could be employed on the construction sites. Relying on the accuracy of their calculations, the Military Government threatened to hold all members of the committee personally responsible if they failed to fill the military's labor needs.[39]

Büsching added to the confusion by insisting that all requisitions for workers and material always be submitted first to the Military Government, probably with the hope that the royal purse would cover the costs. He neglected to make payments for the material and labor.[40] His tactics mainly affected the work at the Halle and Cottbus Gates. Loos in particular continued to experience labor problems due to the fact that the carpenters were not paid. He notified Bülow that the shortage of manpower, tools, and funds again threatened to halt construction. Bülow confronted L'Estoq, who in turn again threatened Büsching and his city council. The Military Government sought the names of all city officials "authorized with this affair so that they can be held accountable by General von Bülow."[41] Büsching steadfastly denied the charges of incompetence and doubled his efforts. Three days later Loos reported that most of his needs had been met.[42]

Loos's satisfaction was short-lived. In less than one week the shortage and quality of urban workers again became acute. An investigation into the matter revealed that not all of the exemptions for the Civic Guard had been abolished. Most of the guardsmen were wealthy enough to purchase exemptions, so the obligation of manual labor almost always fell on the poor.[43] The widespread abuse of the substitution system that allowed citizens to purchase a replacement to take their place at the construction site posed a second problem. Loos complained that lower-class women formed the majority of the substitutes.[44] A third cause emerged as an indirect result of the 17 July ordinance that virtually suspended the Landsturm.[45] In order to disturb trade as little as possible, the king decreed that Landsturm units would only participate in civil defense if absolutely necessary.[46] In Berlin the Military

Government gave the Committee for Landwehr and Landsturm permission to demobilize the city's Landsturm.[47] Since the prospects of digging a trench seemed much less inspiring than fighting a guerrilla war, the demobilized men of the Landsturm did not feel compelled to labor on the fortifications. Confusion again emerged, rendering L'Estoq's paper calculations as useless as the receding floodwaters.

On 21 July only 95 workers reported instead of the 1,200 that Loos had requested.[48] Construction practically ceased when the crown prince of Sweden arrived in Berlin for a six-day inspection on 24 July. The flamboyant prince-royal, who had recently been named commander of all Allied forces in North Germany, demanded parades and reviews that forced Bülow to pull his men from the construction sites. The Military Government, at this point stymied in its attempts to procure workers, asked Bülow to reduce the number of entrenchments under construction. Reiterating its arguments from June, it claimed that the burden of the construction outweighed the anticipated benefits. Increasing complaints from the inhabitants and the king's own dissatisfaction moved the Military Government to urge moderation.[49] Frederick William, who resided in Charlottenburg from 14 to 23 July, had supposedly been so disgusted with the fortifications at the Halle Gate that he sent the workers home.[50] An equally frustrated Bülow informed the Military Government that the entrenchments at the Halle Gate were the most critical and had to be completed.

By the end of July the Military Government refused to mediate between Bülow and Büsching. It increased its pressure on the Berlin municipal government and again directed Büsching to furnish the workers. He responded by abolishing the remaining exemptions of the Civic Guard and regulating the substitution. Permissible exemptions were restricted to public officials whose posts required their continual presence as well as any career that "conducts trade and industry or anything that concerns the economy." Other exemptions included homeless journeymen, domestic servants, and students who were not residents of Berlin or who could not support themselves. Although substitution remained, children, the elderly, and *weak* women could not be employed. In addition, Sunday was decreed a work day as long as the construction did not interfere with religious services.[51]

Bernadotte's arrival in Berlin actually liberated Bülow from the burden of coordinating the defense plan. The crown prince, as commander of all Allied forces in North Germany, superseded Bülow's authority. While inspecting the defense network on 28 July, Bernadotte became particularly interested in the fortifications on the Tempelhof hill chain near the Halle Gate.[52] There he ordered the construction of a large redoubt—the so-called Citadel of Berlin—that could sustain 2,000 men for fourteen days. Bernadotte's demands required greater resources than the Prussians could provide. His completion deadline of 15 August also appeared impossible. Starting on 2 August, Bülow had to provide 2,000 workers from his two brigades that were quartered in Berlin. He requested 1,300 spades from the commandant of Spandau and ordered 6,000 palisades as well as 400 thick planks for the bomb-proof magazines. Bülow informed the Military Government that when the wood arrived 500 carpenters would be needed. An unhappy L'Estoq had to find both the lumber and the carpenters.[53]

The next day the strained gears of the Prussian bureaucracy ground to a halt under the additional weight of Bernadotte's demands. The Military Government transmitted Bülow's orders to Büsching's municipal government. In case the magistrate could not procure the wood from city land, L'Estoq advised him to contact Bassewitz and the Kurmark provincial government.[54] Büsching responded with a request that the countryside supply the wagons and horses. The Military Government refused on the grounds that the peasants were already "extremely strained by the harvest."[55] Bülow also notified L'Estoq that Spandau could only spare 800 spades and that an additional 800 had to be collected at city hall that evening.[56] Once again the Military Government forwarded this request to Büsching.[57] Unable to fulfill this order, Büsching protested. In response to his complaints the Military Government insisted that the tools be taken from the inhabitants.[58]

As the resumption of hostilities approached, all concerned parties labored to avoid the embarrassment of royal retribution. Büsching requisitioned 1,600 laborers and guaranteed Bülow at least 1,000 workers each day. Bülow demanded an additional 50 carpenters from the Military Government to finish the construction on the Nuthe-Notte line.[59] L'Estoq forwarded this to Büsching with instructions to take "the most emphatic measures" to provide the carpenters, but neither the carpenters nor the lumber ever arrived.[60] A labor dispute kept the carpenters in their homes and proved to be the source of this latest crisis. The city authorities failed to reach a new contract with the guild. Negotiations between Büsching and the guild's master continued, but the situation persisted for several days. Loos complained, and on 11 August the

Military Government again threatened to hold the members of the municipal government personally responsible for the delay.[61]

Disregarding these empty threats, Büsching refused to accept the contract negotiated between Landbaumeister (master builder) Kolberg and the carpenter's guild.[62] The situation caused Bülow to complain to the Military Government on 15 August.[63] Instead of exercising more direct authority, the Military Government again turned to Büsching. Its letter of 16 August simply contained harsher threats.[64] This letter crossed in the courier service with Büsching's proposition of the same day. In his note Büsching asked the Military Government to discontinue the whole defense project. He based his request on the "general welfare" of the "already very pressed citizenry." The matter was then referred back to Bülow, who claimed that since Bernadotte had decreed the additional construction he did not possess the authority to alter the situation.[65] The contract discrepancy persisted between Büsching and the carpenter guild. Regardless of its cause, the situation remained after the outbreak of hostilities and continued long after the theater of war moved away from Berlin.

Assessment

The success of the Prussian defense network cannot be measured. Only a fraction of the fortifications were completed and came into use. Labor problems, combined with the apathy of mid- and low-level civil officials, had already plagued the construction before Bülow assumed direction of the works. These difficulties only increased when the fear of a French invasion faded during the armistice. In addition, the works themselves generally displaced the inhabitants. This is evident from the various complaints received about the floods and the measures of the Military Government to safeguard the economy. Moreover, the harvest demanded the labor of the hard-working rural population, whose livelihood depended on the land they worked rather than on Hohenzollern control of Berlin.

Although the material fruits of these labors appear useless, Bülow's approach displays the qualities that later earned him success on the battlefield. From the start he had been opposed to a localized defense behind the Nuthe-Notte line. He wanted to use this position as a rallying point should his corps be defeated in the field. After the crown prince of Sweden superseded him as Allied commander in North Germany, the defense plans once again took another turn. Bernadotte's plans for the Nuthe-Notte line sharply contrasted not only with Bülow's views, but also with those of the Military Government. Where Bülow sought to operate in the open terrain south of the capital and only use the defense line as a rallying point, the Military Government believed the Nuthe-Notte network should provide the city's main defenses. The crown prince, however, viewed the fortifications on the Nuthe-Notte line as merely forward posts for an army entrenched around Berlin's Halle Gate; thus his interest in the "Citadel of Berlin." By remaining near the capital, Allied forces would be able to escape northward, over the Spree and Havel Rivers. Now subordinated to the crown prince, Bülow had to comply with his new commander's strategy. The events of the fall campaign would eventually prove Bülow correct; but even though the French did advance against the Nuthe-Notte line as Bülow predicted, the crown prince refused to meet the enemy on the open terrain south of the defense line.

Plans and Preparations

Significant events unfolded on the diplomatic front during the course of the armistice. Just as the death of the Empress Elizabeth had effected a change in the Russian government that saved Frederick the Great fifty years earlier, a change in the British government in 1812 had profound implications for the Allied war effort. Robert Stewart Castlereagh emerged as the foreign secretary of Lord Liverpool's new ministry. The moderate Castlereagh possessed essential qualities for the success of any coalition, including "a genuine interest in Europe, and a genuine readiness to listen to others and work with them."[1] Castlereagh pursued a policy bequeathed to him by William Pitt.[2] Pitt's peace plan, stillborn in 1805 but resurrected by Castlereagh in 1813, symbolized Great Britain's commitment to attaining a stable balance of power by reducing France and strengthening Austria and Prussia in order to balance Russian expansion.[3] As proof of London's renewed interest in Central Europe, Britain concluded alliance and subsidy treaties at Reichenbach with Prussia and Russia on 14 and 15 June respectively.[4] The British agreed to subsidize the Russians and Prussians directly with £2,000,000, two-thirds of which would go to the Russians and one-third to the Prussians. This would be augmented by £5,000,000, of federal paper currency, which would be backed by the British government's credit and used by the Russian and Prussian governments for war expenditures.[5] In return, no separate peace would be signed and Hanover would be restored to Great Britain.[6]

The British had also ratified a generous subsidy treaty with Sweden, partly to satisfy the tsar and despite the fact that the Treaties of Kalisch and Breslau had ignored British interests. Moreover, the Swedes had failed to meet Allied expectations. Although logistical and financial problems hindered Swedish operations in the spring campaign, Bernadotte had been less than eager to fulfill his part of the agreements and even delayed his arrival in Stralsund. The tsar retaliated by refusing to transfer command of a Russian corps to the Swedish prince-royal until he appeared in the theater, which prompted Bernadotte to cry foul. With the signing of the armistice, he found himself in a predicament: he had done nothing for the Allied war effort and they owed him nothing in return.[7] Nevertheless, the British believed the balance of forces in Central Europe to be so equal that Sweden's part could be vital. They agreed to a £1,000,000 subsidy for 30,000 Swedes to fight on the Continent and naval support in Sweden's war against Denmark for Norway and held out the possibility of Stockholm's acquisition of the island of Guadeloupe. Little doubt surrounded Sweden's interest in this war; Norway remained Bernadotte's price for participating. Sweden's alliance with Great Britain kept Frederick VII of Denmark firmly in the French camp and made any Allied military action in North Germany a hostage of Bernadotte's ambitions.[8] The former French marshal thus based his politics not on Napoleon's defeat but on the acquisition of Norway. As the war dragged on, it became clear that he would not sacrifice his troops for the coalition. To secure his hold on the Swedish throne and avoid criticism at home, Bernadotte believed he had to protect his Swedes from battlefield losses.

Although the tsar had succeeded in obtaining British aid without having to share the leadership of the coalition with Great Britain, Austria began to stir. Metternich had skillfully secured Austria's neutrality during the chaotic months following Napoleon's debacle in Russia. In late January he concluded a secret military convention with the Russians that detached the Austrian corps from the Grande Armée. The corps moved through the Grand Duchy of Warsaw to Bohemia, where it served as a nucleus for Austria's general mobilization. This coincided with Napoleon's demand for greater Austrian military participation against the Russians in December and January. As in Prussia, Austrian mobilization did not go unnoticed by the French, yet Vienna assured

Napoleon that the Habsburg army would support France. In April, however, Metternich reversed his position, declaring that Austria would mediate between Napoleon and the Allies. Napoleon threatened and demanded, but Metternich held his ground and informed Napoleon that Emperor Francis possessed the armed might to defend his neutrality.[9] During the armistice Metternich employed all his skill to mediate a peace that would favor Austrian interests. With an eye on London, he steadfastly insisted that only Austria could contain the ambitions of both Russia and France.[10] Should the war continue, Metternich feared that France and Russia might conclude another Treaty of Tilsit and divide Europe between them.[11]

Austria's diplomatic initiative posed a dilemma for the Anglo-Russian-Prussian consensus. The separate interests of these three partners were being woven into the general goals of a coalition: Russian domination of Poland, Prussian compensation in Saxony, and a free hand for Great Britain in Iberia, the Low Countries, Sicily, the colonies, and on the high seas.[12] By the end of March Metternich had failed to gain British acceptance of Austrian mediation and so believed that a settlement for Central Europe could only be achieved by removing British interests from the equation. He also began to fear Russia almost as much as France and committed himself to breaking not only French power east of the Rhine but also Russian influence west of the Vistula. The Austrian minister targeted the Treaty of Kalisch—and with it Prussia's dependence on Russia—by offering the Treaty of Prague to King Frederick August of Saxony on 20 April, in which Austria guaranteed Saxony's territorial integrity. Prussian threats also induced Bavaria to enter Metternich's camp in early May. Metternich labored to maximize Austria's mediating power by recruiting a sizable following of Central European states and made overtures to Baden and Württemberg as well. He planned to use Austria's newfound leverage to force the belligerents to negotiate at a peace conference.[13] His scheme collapsed after French victories at Lützen and Bautzen firmly returned Saxony and the South German states to the Napoleonic fold. Despite his failure to create a Central European block, Metternich used the armistice to negotiate a peace.

Although willing to negotiate, the Allies demanded harsh terms. On 16 May Hardenberg and Nesselrode had expanded the Kalisch war aims to include the dissolution of the Rheinbund, the independence of Germany, the independence of the North German trans-Rhine provinces annexed by France and known as the 32nd Military District, and the liberation of Spain, Holland, and Italy.[14] Fresh from two victories over Allied arms, Napoleon would inevitably reject such terms, but Metternich feared that he might exploit Allied intransigence by using the harsh conditions to rally the French people.[15] Metternich agreed in principle with the terms, yet believed that the Allies would have to propose a minimum program in order to attract Napoleon to a peace conference.[16] Moreover, he still sought to undermine one of the cornerstones of the Prusso-Russian alliance—the exchange of Prussian Poland for Saxony, which challenged the traditional Habsburg national security objectives of limiting Prussia's influence in Germany and restraining Russian expansion in Central Europe.[17] Metternich used this opportunity to push his own peace plan, which not only added the perplexing questions of Italy and Illyria but jeopardized the course that Russia, Prussia, and Great Britain pursued.[18] The centerpiece of his scheme called for Russia and France to retire behind the respective frontiers of the Vistula and the Rhine and remain separated by an independent Central Europe "in which Austria, Prussia, and the rest of Germany would be sufficiently strengthened."[19] Metternich envisioned a progressive peace settlement through persuasion and consensus that would produce equilibrium and durable tranquility in Europe.[20] Balance and stability became the pillars of his political theory.[21] The Allied defeat at Bautzen had considerably strengthened his hand, and over the next month he worked diligently to convince the Allies to offer Napoleon a minimum program as the basis for a peace conference.

Metternich's efforts influenced Alexander to "adopt more conciliatory attitudes and tactics toward Austria"; but mutual suspicion still separated the courts of Vienna and St. Petersburg, and the actions of both in the first six months of 1813 had only served to intensify the competitiveness of two traditional rivals.[22] Metternich feared Russia and felt threatened by Russia's patronage of Prussia. Vienna viewed the Treaties of Kalisch and Breslau as Russia's commitment to fight for Prussia's territorial compensation. Alexander, firmly believing that Austria's neutrality had cost the Allies victory in the spring campaign, only offered Francis the restoration of his 1805 status as Austria's reward for joining the coalition.[23] This appeared dubious to Vienna. Although the Russians implied that the Austrians would have a free hand to determine the future of South Germany, Francis desired the restoration of his 1797 status and inferred that the Russians would do little to assist Austria's quest for compensation. Ultimately, diplomatic posturing and bombastic talk set the tone for relations between the eastern powers for the duration of the war with France. Numerous Russo-Prussian designs for a German national uprising threatened Metternich's peace plan and, combined with what appeared to be Russo-Prussian insistence that North Germany was their exclusive sphere, forced Vienna to view Russia as a rival for influence over Germany.[24]

Austrian relations with Prussia also experienced the same uncertain ebb and flow. By the armistice the Prussian king had been firmly, if not forcefully, placed in Alexander's camp. Metternich rejected the Russian-sponsored plans for Prussia to seek compensation in Germany and appeared ready to profit from Prussia's dismemberment should the opportunity present itself.[25] He did not wish for Prussia's destruction but understood that Russia's plan to push Prussia westward was an attempt to "rekindle the Austro-Prussian rivalry, which in turn would limit Vienna's ability to counter Russian schemes in the Balkans."[26] His peace plan focused on an independent Central Europe. Metternich sought to detach the larger Rheinbund states from the war and encourage them to join Austria's neutrality. Although Prussia's salvation could be found in the outlines of Metternich's schemes, Austria's crafty statesman took steps to block Hohenzollern ambitions in Germany by promising to protect Saxony and Bavaria from Prussian expansion. To make matters worse, the Prussians themselves could not reach a consensus regarding Metternich's proposals. Yet they did agree on one significant point that Metternich could never satisfactorily explain: the fact that his peace plans attempted to save Napoleon and prevent the liberation of Europe. As a result the two leading German powers "were like two climbers stranded on separate ledges on a mountain face, each unable to reach the other and afraid of being pulled to his death if he threw the other a rope."[27]

Nevertheless, the necessity of war and the success of future peace demanded that Austria shed its neutrality. By the end of the spring campaign both the Russians and the Prussians accepted this fact, despite British suspicion that Metternich's scheming would benefit Napoleon. As noted, Metternich's British policy had failed early on. He believed that Austria's main goals—containing Russia and preventing future revolutions—could best be achieved by confining Napoleon within his natural frontiers rather than dethroning him.[28] Metternich had no interest in the issues that afflicted Europe west of the Rhine (i.e., the Low Countries and Iberia), and British interests in the Italian peninsula were always a concern.[29] When he produced a peace plan that ignored maritime trading rights, the Low Countries, Iberia, and Sicily, even Castlereagh complained of Metternich's apparent "spirit of submission" to Napoleon.[30] Metternich disregarded British interests to concentrate on peace for Eastern, Central, and Southern Europe.[31] To achieve his goal, he sought to isolate London and exclude the British from negotiations. Castlereagh, however, understood that Metternich feared the consequences of Napoleon's fall and thus preferred a negotiated peace and that he purposefully attempted to bar Great Britain from the decision-making process of the coalition. Castlereagh's immediate objective was to win Austria as a loyal ally and prevent Metternich from negotiating a settlement with Alexander and Frederick William that ignored British interests. Castlereagh failed to do this during July and August. The British pound eventually brought the two powers together, but not until September. Austria needed British funds to wage war; in return for a £1,000,000 subsidy, Metternich agreed not to make a separate peace with Napoleon.[32] Nevertheless, the British could not derail Metternich directly; nor could they limit his ability to mediate during the armistice.

Regardless of Metternich's struggle with the Allies, he understood that only Napoleon's endorsement could validate his peace plan. Metternich possessed one advantage that his peers lacked: he understood Napoleon.[33] With cool savvy, Metternich held a nine-hour tête-à-tête with the French emperor on 26 June in Dresden, where he held out the prospect of preserving Napoleon's crown in return for an independent and neutral Central Europe. Napoleon scoffed at the thought of sacrificing imperial territory, particularly the regions that had been gained during the Revolution: the Low Countries and northern Italy. He reportedly called Metternich a liar and demanded that Austria's minister reveal his master's true aims.[34] "So you want war? Well, you shall have it," screamed Napoleon. "I annihilated the Prussian army at Lützen; I smashed the Russians at Bautzen; now you want to have your turn. Very well—we shall meet at Vienna."[35] Paul Schroeder maintains that "Napoleon refused to make peace because he did not want to, chose not to," and because he lacked the diplomatic skills and mentality to do so.[36] "For Napoleon to make a Continental peace," notes Henry Kissinger, "was psychologically impossible. It would have meant that Napoleon ceased being Napoleon."[37] Despite such critical assessments, Napoleon's own words probably reveal the true reason why he rejected Metternich's offer: he had just defeated the Prussians and Russians twice in the same month and therefore saw no reason to compromise.

Although Metternich's first meeting with Napoleon failed, his efforts were rewarded on the following day, 27 June, when the Austrians, Prussians, and Russians signed the Treaty of Reichenbach. This treaty, a victory for Austria, authorized Metternich to present a minimum program to Napoleon as the Allies' price for a peace conference. The stipulations demanded the partition of the Grand Duchy of Warsaw, Prussia's expansion in Poland, the return of the Adriatic coast (Illyria) to Austria, and the independence of only Hamburg and Lübeck in North Germany rather than the entire 32nd Military District.[38] Should Napoleon refuse these terms, Austria would join the Sixth Coalition with at least 150,000 men and fight for the harsher Allied peace terms as formulated by Hardenberg and Nesselrode on 16 May. All appeared to be in place for Metternich; if Napoleon rejected the peace plan, then Austria would enter the conflict as arguably the leading power. Metternich succeeded in spinning quite a web, for Napoleon's rejection of the terms would prove to the cautious Austrian emperor that all prospects of peace with his son-in-law had been exhausted. Napoleon's acceptance, conversely, would have secured him only the dubious *possibility* of negotiating a permanent settlement with the Allies. Yet the chances that Napoleon would accept the Reichenbach stipulations remained slim. "It was out of the question," explains Kissinger, "that the man who had so often identified the fate of his dynasty with the unimpaired existence of his empire would agree to such a confession of weakness."[39] Historian Rory Muir perhaps states it best by asserting that had Napoleon "been the man to accept such a peace, he would never have made the great conquests he had."[40]

On 30 June Metternich presented the Reichenbach protocols—as well as their 20 July deadline—to Napoleon. To the chagrin of the Allies, he managed to convince the emperor to reject the protocols but accept Austria's mediation—and with it Vienna's continued neutrality—at a general peace conference to be held at Prague on 5 July.[41] To allow sufficient time, the Austrian chancellor took it upon himself to arrange for the extension of the armistice to 10 August.[42] He explained to the irate Russians and Prussians that his offer to mediate between the two sides was mainly to gain time for the Austrian army to mobilize.[43] Neither side believed peace would result from the ensuing discussions, and they considered the armistice itself to be "a breathing space, a brief interval between rounds in a life or death contest."[44] The Prague Congress began on 5 July, but the chief French representative, Armand de Caulaincourt, did not arrive until the twenty-eighth and even then lacked full authority to negotiate.[45] Under strict orders from Napoleon, Caulaincourt's actions rendered the conference nothing more than a "charade." In the end the congress dissolved in failure. Although Napoleon had no intention of making any major concessions for peace, he did, on 9 August, offer to restore Prussia to its 1806 status as well as surrender the Grand Duchy of Warsaw and Illyria, but insisted on retaining Danzig, Trieste, and Istria.[46] Austria rejected his offer and, as the unchallenged leader of the coalition, declared war on France three days later.[47]

Although the coalition members resigned themselves to settling the great issues of the day through war, much confusion still existed in the Allied camp simply because they failed to establish clear war aims. Generals, diplomats, and even monarchs "were never quite certain whether their final objective was the complete elimination of Bonapartism, or whether, under certain safeguards, Napoleon should be allowed to retain his throne."[48] What did become increasingly clear was that Metternich remained determined to direct the war in a manner to establish a peace that suited Austria's needs. To quote Nipperdey, Metternich's war "would not be a people's war, not a revolutionary nationalist war of patriots and emancipators," and certainly not a Prussian crusade against the French.[49] Ultimately supported by the Austrian emperor, Metternich successfully transformed the struggle "from a war of national liberation into a cabinet war for the equilibrium" of Europe.[50] As a result strategic planning during the fall campaign "would be hampered by uncertainty of purpose and division of counsel."[51] Even the tsar, the self-styled "Liberator of Europe," was affected by what some historians have called a split personality or schizophrenia, which caused him "to oscillate wildly between a given theory of action and its opposite . . . he often tried, in an almost pathetic confusion, to carry out the recently discarded and the recently adopted theory at one and the same time."[52] Prussia's generals would exploit this confusion to benefit their war of retribution against the French. Despite their king's secondary status at Grand Allied Headquarters, they refused to sacrifice national interests to international needs and, in the case of the crown prince of Sweden, personal ambition.

Unprecedented military preparations coincided with the diplomacy of the Grand Alliance. Frederick William and Alexander met with a disgruntled Bernadotte at Trachenberg on 10 July. There the Allied sovereigns endorsed Austria's proposal to extend the armistice to 10 August. On the evening of the eleventh Bernadotte received their promise for an army commensurate to his status. According to these arrangements, Bernadotte would command 22,000 Russians under Gen. Ferdinand von Wintzingerode, 60,000 Prussians under Bülow and Tauentzien, and Wallmoden's corps, which was increased to 20,000, as well as his own 30,000 Swedes under the seventy-year-old field-marshal Curt Stedingk. In return Bernadotte pledged to concentrate his efforts against the French and postpone his war with Denmark.[53] On the following day the sovereigns adopted a general plan for the upcoming campaign. Several contemporaries claimed authorship of the so-called Trachenberg Plan, but credit belongs to the Austrian Count Radetzky von Radetz. His plan depended on Austrian cooperation and called for the formation of three principal Allied armies.[54]

Metternich insisted on vesting an Austrian general with supreme command. The Habsburg Empire had lost the most during the struggle with France and now had the chance to win the most. Metternich fully understood that for the war to be an Austrian success it would have to be waged in a manner conducive to restoring Habsburg preponderance over Central Europe and limiting Prussian and Russian influence. Vienna had carefully prepared for this hour, and Emperor Francis placed his hopes in the largest army Austria had ever fielded against France: 479,000 officers and men. "The power that puts 300,000 men in the field," argued Metternich, "is the first power, all the others only auxiliaries."[55] Allied defeats at Lützen and Bautzen, resulting from what Metternich believed to be a lack of strategic direction, concerned the Austrians. Prussian impetuosity and carelessness, as well as the tsar's "penchant for superseding his commander-in-chief at critical moments in the battle," also contributed to Metternich's insistence.[56] Tsar Alexander presented his candidate: the Austrian archduke Charles, who was not only the brother of Francis, but the only man ever to beat Napoleon in the field. Metternich refused, knowing that Charles's love for Alexander's sister Caroline would place the archduke squarely under the influence of the tsar and give the Russians "a preponderance of influence" at Grand Allied Headquarters.[57] Thus the forty-two-year-old Prince Karl Philip zu Schwarzenberg received command of all Allied forces, including the main army—the Army of Bohemia—which consisted of 220,000 Austrians, Prussians, and Russians. Blücher received command of the Army of Silesia—75,000 Russians and Prussians. Bernadotte took command of the Combined Army of North Germany—120,000 Prussians, Russians, Swedes, and North Germans. The Allies created these multinational armies both to prevent Napoleon from defeating them piecemeal and to limit politically motivated acts of national self-interest.

According to the Trachenberg Plan, the three Allied armies would form a wide arc around Napoleon's forces in Saxony and only engage detached corps of the Grande Armée; pitched battles with the emperor had to be avoided. Should Napoleon concentrate against any one army, it would retreat, while the other two attacked his flanks and lines of communication. The plan sought to split Napoleon's forces and exhaust them through constant movement. Although Napoleon had the advantage of interior lines, he would be forced to fight against armies advancing simultaneously on his center, flanks, and communications.[58] Schwarzenberg's army would concentrate in the Bohemian mountains and challenge Napoleon in either Saxony or Silesia. Bernadotte's force would assemble south of Berlin, while Wallmoden's corps observed French forces in Hanover. Once hostilities resumed, the crown prince would cross the Elbe and march on Leipzig, while Blücher also advanced into Saxony from Silesia.

The armistice also facilitated the general expansion and reorganization of the Prussian army. The Prussians now had the time to remedy the problems caused by the chaotic nature of the mobilization that had occurred in March. Veteran regiments of the spring campaign were grouped into three separate corps commanded by Yorck, Kleist, and Bülow. Initially Blücher received command of all three, respectively designated the First, Second, and Third Corps. Subsequent negotiations distributed the Prussian corps among the three Allied armies. Each Prussian corps contained four brigades consisting of one line regiment, one reserve regiment, one Landwehr regiment, one cavalry regiment, and one six-pounder battery. Each corps also included a reserve of two cavalry brigades (sixteen to twenty squadrons), three twelve-pounder batteries, and three horse batteries. Like the French division, each Prussian brigade consisted of infantry, cavalry, and artillery, had its own staff, and could operate independently. This allowed one brigade to form the advance guard, two others to follow in support, and the fourth to remain in reserve with the cavalry and artillery.[59] As noted, Tauentzien received command of the Fourth Corps. By explicit order of the king, this corps of mostly Landwehr units would only cover communications, conduct sieges, and mask fortresses.

In July Bülow officially received command of the Third Corps. Some of his veterans from the spring campaign remained with him, but in the general redistribution of the regiments he received several new units, including twelve Landwehr battalions and sixteen Landwehr squadrons.[60] Two Russian twelve-pounder batteries and some Cossack regiments from the spring campaign also remained attached to Bülow's corps. All together his corps totaled 31,480 infantry, 6,550 cavalry, 1,985 gunners with 102 guns, and 2,280 pioneers. The corps consisted of four brigades: the Third, Fourth, Fifth, and Sixth, respectively commanded by the Prince of Hessen-Homburg, Thümen, Borstell, and Krafft. Oppen commanded the reserve cavalry, and Lieut.-Col. Karl Friedrich von Holtzendorf the reserve artillery. Bülow enjoyed cordial working relationships with his senior officers, especially Oppen and Krafft, but Borstell proved to be the exception. Borstell had held a semi-independent command over a Pomeranian brigade throughout the spring campaign. Now assigned to the Third Corps, Borstell resented his subordinate position and complained to the king. To soothe him Frederick William decreed that Borstell's Fifth Brigade should operate independently, an avoidable and unfortunate political measure.

One of Scharnhorst's goals—the creation of an elite corps of well-educated staff officers to lead the new national army—also reached fruition at this time. General Staff officers would provide the Prussian army with an intellectual nerve center that radiated enlightened leadership. This leadership not only would embrace the modern principles of warfare but also would personify the evolving concepts of civic duty, nationalism, and professionalism. Staff officers received vigorous educations, and Scharnhorst instilled in them "a high sense of moral responsibility and glowing idealism." He selected the best of his pupils and trained them to plan and execute military operations.[61] Their function was not to command but to assist their commanders in determining the technical and tactical feasibility of an operation.

Scharnhorst firmly believed that the forces of a national war effort could only be harnessed and directed by a General Staff system. Resistance to his General Staff originated among the army's aristocratic element, which refused to embrace any principle that might endanger its rights and privileges. Scharnhorst's educational emphasis and other "bourgeois notions" intimidated Prussian traditionalists and conservatives. Before reaching an understanding with Scharnhorst in 1809, Yorck had championed the opposition. Although a member of Scharnhorst's Militärische Gesellschaft, he once commented that "there was too much learned talk in the society, more of it, in fact, than an honest Prussian's brains could cope with."[62] Opposition also came from reactionaries who still retained illusions of Frederician invincibility. Such men did not view the Prussian catastrophe of 1806 as the modern refutation of Frederician operational doctrine; nor did they heed the social and organizational implications that accompanied the defeat. Instead they blamed the unfortunate outcome of the war on irresponsible leadership and bad luck.[63]

Bülow had been ranked among Scharnhorst's antagonists prior to 1806. Scharnhorst and his followers felt that Bülow had no place in modern warfare since his military education was "mainly derived from the experiences of the Seven Years' War and our old military regulations."[64] Bülow's aversion to military scientists originated from problems caused by his brother, the controversial author and theorist Heinrich Dietrich von Bülow.[65] Consequently, Bülow could not tolerate Scharnhorst, whom he scornfully referred to as "the schoolmaster."[66] He had sometimes accused his brother Dietrich of being "brain-dead" and applied the same irreverent expression to Scharnhorst and his followers. Although Bülow wanted improvement and progress no less than they did, he was rooted more deeply in the traditions of the Frederician state than the reformers were. According to historian Friedrich Meinecke, Bülow did not want to be associated with the military theorists but "was quite a finely educated and intellectually receptive man, similar to Frederick the Great, in whom the aesthetic and the political-military lives strictly adhered to each other."[67]

Following the Peace of Tilsit in 1807, Bülow had served on the Superior Investigating Commission as well as a subcommittee of the Military Reorganization Committee. The king appointed both bodies to examine the causes of the defeat as well as to resurrect and reform the army.[68] In this capacity Bülow became better acquainted with Scharnhorst and his followers. Although he respected their competence and intelligence, he still disagreed with them on several issues. Bülow generally acknowledged the obsoleteness and insufficiencies of the Frederician system. He also understood that warfare had changed and that new methods were needed to defeat the French. Like the reformers, he too demanded faster mobility, better equipment, and modern tactics. Bülow, however, believed that this evolution would take place once the right commanders led the army and that the army's utter defeat in the War of the Fourth Coalition was due to poor leadership at the top. He detested sweeping innovations, the so-called educated officers, and the theorists and planners, of whom his own brother Dietrich offered a deterring example.[69]

In 1811 Scharnhorst had expressed reservations about Bülow's promotion to general of brigade. He wrote that Bülow's views "reflect our former conditions." In expressing his wish that Bülow retire, Scharnhorst noted that he was "a worthy and sensible man, but still a Bülow. All Bülows are odd, very self-confident, and unsocial."[70] Despite his aversion to the Bülow family—a product of his philosophical differences with Dietrich—Scharnhorst was unable to prevent Bülow's promotion to corps commander in the spring campaign. For the fall campaign, however, each corps and brigade commander received a staff officer to serve as a personal consultant. Through such pairings Scharnhorst believed he could better control the antiquated senior officers who had survived the purges of the reform era. Scharnhorst envisioned a "military marriage" between the commander and his chief staff officer. To assure unity of command on all levels, Scharnhorst's chief assistant, Gneisenau, encouraged all staff officers to influence their commander into complying with directives issued by army headquarters, where the king, chancellor, and chief of the General Staff coordinated policy. Gneisenau thus favored a more assertive role for chief staff officers to guarantee the army's coordination.

During the armistice both Scharnhorst and Gneisenau sought to refine the role of the General Staff. After Scharnhorst died unexpectedly on 28 June from wounds received at the battle of Lützen, Gneisenau succeeded his late colleague as chief of the General Staff of the Prussian Army. His aggressive personality prompted him to execute the measures that would guarantee unity of command. Gneisenau filled all of Scharnhorst's personnel appointments for the upcoming campaign, so that each of Prussia's four army corps received one of Scharnhorst's pupils as chief of staff. He informed chief staff officers that they would share the responsibility of command with their commanders. This system of dual command would guarantee that individual corps commanders pursued objectives that reflected Prussia's interests. Should a commander refuse to comply, his chief of staff was expected to report him directly to Gneisenau, who would then take the matter to the king.[71]

Since treaty obligations dispersed the four Prussian corps among the three Allied field armies, Gneisenau planned to utilize the Prussian General Staff to prevent the subordination of Prussian military goals in a multinational coalition.[72] His position as both chief of the General Staff of the Prussian Army and chief staff officer of Blücher's Silesian Army enabled him to obtain a considerable degree of autonomy from Allied Headquarters, where the sovereigns consistently interfered with Schwarzenberg's plans. Gneisenau intended to direct all Prussian operations through the chief of staff of each corps. He hoped that this unity of command would enable him to fulfill Scharnhorst's conception of seeking and destroying Napoleon's forces regardless of political considerations. Gneisenau instructed each staff officer to coordinate policy with his corps commander in order to maintain pressure on the enemy. The Prussians believed that this would allow them to protect and pursue their national interests, despite the coalition's multinational composition. In reality Gneisenau's directive required Prussian corps commanders to adopt an individualistic operational approach that sometimes undermined coalition warfare.

Although Boyen had passionately hoped to command a brigade, and Hardenberg had suggested that he succeed the deceased Scharnhorst as director of the General War Department, Frederick William decided otherwise and appointed Boyen to be Bülow's chief of staff. A shocked Boyen admitted that this assignment "just did not seem right." Their pairing certainly marked the clash of divergent schools of thought within the Prussian army. Boyen had emerged as one of Scharnhorst's closest associates during the reform era. Although Boyen respected Bülow's talents and was currently working closely with him on the Kurmark militia project, he was intimidated by his new commander's "well-known, instantaneous ill-temper" and reputation for demanding total obedience from his subordinates. Boyen was also concerned that his friendship with the late Scharnhorst would be held against him.[73] Boyen assumed his new post with the primary goal of winning the general's confidence. Fortunately, it did not take long for Bülow to refute his fears.[74] According to Boyen, he received a warm welcome from his new commander, who "had very keen understanding and a good memory . . . a brave self-confidence directed his moves, but also placed him in the ranks of opposition against his superiors and made him a difficult subordinate." Bülow's intellectual gifts surprised Boyen, who commented that his new commander "had acquired vast knowledge throughout his life despite never receiving a formal education." Although Bülow was stubborn, defiant, and highly ambitious, he respected Boyen's knowledge and always considered his suggestions. A friendship developed, and the military marriage envisioned by Scharnhorst soon evolved.[75]

On the French side, Napoleon formulated his plans for the upcoming campaign between 11 and 13 August. The armistice had provided crucial time to rest, reinforce, and supply his army. By mid-August he could field 450,000 men to face an estimated 512,000 Allied soldiers.[76] The results he expected from an operation in North Germany again influenced his strategic planning. Although Austria joined the coalition, Napoleon still believed that a successful offensive in North Germany would have a decisive impact on his operations in Saxony. He hoped that a drive through Berlin to at least the Oder, and perhaps as far as the Vistula, would pull the Russians eastward and away from the Austrians. The aggressive move toward Berlin in the spring had not induced the Prussians to separate from the Russians, but Napoleon continued to allow these calculations to dominate his planning in August. He still believed that a coup de théâtre in North Germany would force the Russians back on their lines of communication and test the coalition's strength. Other advantages that a successful operation against Berlin offered included the demoralizing psychological effect the city's fall would have on the Prussians. Reality would also beset the wavering courts of Napoleon's German allies—Berlin's fall would certainly send a message to any Rheinbund prince who considered breaking his ties with France. Also, Allied numerical superiority could be erased by a decisive, morale-breaking victory over the Army of North Germany. Lastly, Napoleon still wanted to relieve the besieged garrisons on the Oder and Vistula.

Personal considerations may also have swayed Napoleon to revive his "master plan" in August. He undervalued the troops of the Army of North Germany due in part to the large contingents of raw, hastily trained, and poorly equipped Landwehr regiments. Moreover, the emperor harbored little respect for Bernadotte. Inflicting a crippling defeat on the army of his former marshal certainly would be pleasing. Contemporaries also claim that a vindictive Napoleon determined to open the campaign by taking the capital of his former Prussian ally. According to Marshal Auguste-Frederic Marmont: "Passion prompted him to act quickly against Prussia. He desired the first cannon shots to be fired against Berlin, and that a startling and terrible vengeance should immediately follow the renewal of hostilities."[77] Although Napoleon's strategic considerations regarding Berlin and North Germany were rooted in his "master plan of 1813," such personal vendettas no doubt made the Berlin project more appealing.

Napoleon initially decided to take a defensive position between Dresden and Bautzen with his main army of 300,000 men while a second French army marched on Berlin.[78] He united the Fourth, Seventh, and Twelfth Corps and Third Cavalry Corps under the command of Marshal Oudinot for another offensive against Berlin.[79] To support Oudinot, Marshal Davout would advance from Hamburg against Berlin with the 37,500 men and 94 guns of his Thirteenth Corps.[80] An auxiliary force of 9,000 men commanded by Gen. Jean-Baptiste Girard would operate from Magdeburg in conjunction with 5,000 Poles under Gen. Jean Dombrowski from Wittenberg.[81] Both generals would facilitate Oudinot's offensive by uniting, advancing, and forming a link between Oudinot and Davout.[82]

On 12 August Oudinot officially received command of the Army of Berlin's 54,191 infantry, 9,008 cavalry, 4,243 gunners and pioneers, and 216 guns.[83] Napoleon's orders made it clear that he wanted the marshal to have his army concentrated at Baruth between the eighteenth and nineteenth. The emperor expected him to be master of Berlin by the twenty-second and authorized him to use his heavy artillery to bomb the Prussian capital into submission if necessary. Oudinot would then push the Allies over the Oder and relieve Küstrin and Stettin in the process. Napoleon also firmly instructed Oudinot to drive the Swedes from the Continent.[84] An overwhelmed Oudinot expressed his sincerest appreciation for the emperor's confidence but claimed poor health and requested that the command be given to someone else.[85] Napoleon certainly did not select one of his top subordinates to command the Army of Berlin. Although more able commanders such as Davout and Gouvion St.-Cyr were available, Napoleon, always conscious of political repercussions, based the success of this operation on Oudinot's fierce loyalty.[86] He refused to entertain Oudinot's excuses, and the marshal retained command of the army.

Oudinot perhaps had reasons to complain other than failing health. His army contained more foreign infantry units than French divisions. Saxon, Bavarian, Württemberger, and Italian regiments made this army a true multinational force.[87] Since most of Napoleon's satellites had lost large contingents in Russia the previous year, numerous conscripts filled Oudinot's ranks. Napoleon planned to unleash the Army of Berlin and the auxiliaries—by far the largest French commitment in North Germany up to that point—against the Prussian capital. He believed that Oudinot's army, Davout's corps, and the divisions under Girard and Dombrowski would be able to simulate the cohesion and coordination that past French armies had perfected under his own diligent command. The difference in August 1813 was that Oudinot was not Napoleon and the Army of Berlin was not the Grande Armée.

Napoleon did revise his plans on 13 August. Rather than hold 300,000 men around Dresden, he created another army to facilitate Oudinot's operations and pressure the Allied army in Silesia. Later christened the "Army of the Bober," this force consisted of four infantry and one cavalry corps, or 130,000 men and 408 guns.[88] Situated in two lines on the Katzbach and Bober Rivers, it would shield Oudinot's right flank while he advanced against the Prussian capital. As for Napoleon's remaining forces, the small Eighth Corps of 8,000 men and Fourth Cavalry Corps held the passes over the Erzgebirge Mountains at Zittau. North of Zittau at Görlitz were the 100,000 men and 330 guns of the Imperial Guard, Second Corps, and First Cavalry Corps. The First Corps and Fifth Cavalry Corps—37,000 men and 88 guns—camped at Bautzen. To the east, in and around Dresden, were the 35,000 men and 198 guns of the Fourteenth Corps, one cavalry division, and various garrisons.[89] When Napoleon asked his marshals to comment on his strategy, Marmont warned: "I fear greatly that on the day that you are victorious and believe that you have won a decisive battle, you will learn that you have lost two." Marmont believed that dividing the army for operations against Berlin and Blücher would deprive Napoleon of the manpower needed for a decisive victory over the main Allied host, be it the army in Silesia or in Bohemia.[90] An unperturbed Napoleon declared that he had "allowed for everything; the rest depends on Fortune."[91] Believing that half of the Silesian Army had marched to unite

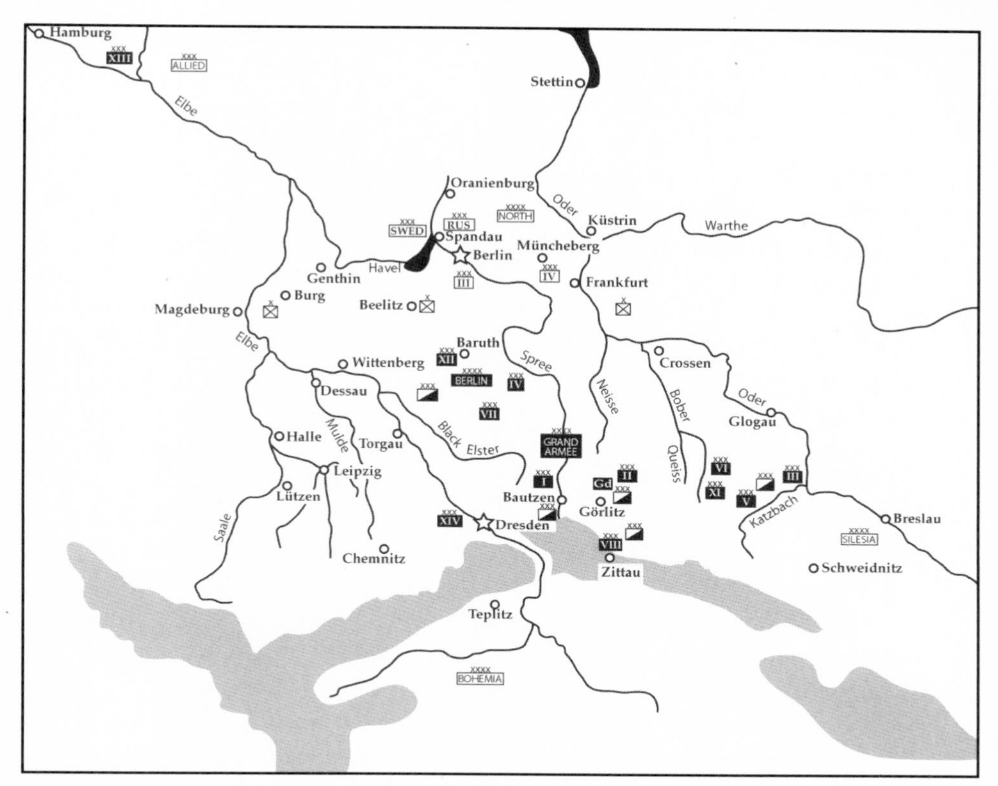

The Situation at the End of the Armistice

with the Army of Bohemia, the emperor planned to destroy the remainder of Blücher's forces, which he estimated to be 50,000.[92] Shortly after the armistice expired, he led the Guard, Third, Fifth, Sixth, and Eleventh Corps east to confront Blücher.[93] Unfortunately for the emperor, Marmont's prophecy became a dreadful reality within the first ten days of the campaign.

As the end of the armistice approached, both sides prepared for an epic struggle. Few believed that diplomacy could bring peace: war would settle the issue. In Prussia Bernadotte assembled his Army of North Germany in and around Berlin.[94] Allied Headquarters expected all army commanders to operate within the guidelines of the Trachenberg Plan, but Bernadotte had other ideas. During a meeting with Bülow and Tauentzien on 13 August he explained that the Army of North Germany consisted of too many inexperienced troops stretched over too large a territory. Davout's force at Hamburg threatened his right wing on the lower Elbe. Enemy strongholds at Wittenberg, Torgau, and Magdeburg menaced his front; the enemy garrison at Stettin remained a threat to his rear. He placed little faith in the reliability and timely assistance of the other Allied commanders. The crown prince predicted that a vengeful Napoleon would open the campaign with an offensive against him to take Berlin. Thus he planned simply to watch and wait.

Bülow expressed his desire to confront the French in the open region south of the Nuthe-Notte line. Bernadotte disliked the terrain and ambiguously retorted that it did not provide a firm position. Discussion then focused on positioning the army on the Nuthe-Notte line. The crown prince once again rejected this idea, claiming that the numerous streams and wide marshes would impede the movement of large forces. In many places artillery and cavalry could only pass along the narrow dikes. The Prussians interjected that such problems would also plague an advancing enemy army. Nevertheless, Bernadotte believed that a significant military force could break through at any point and defeat the isolated defenders. The low water level of the flood zone also concerned the crown prince. Although heavy rains fell during the next two weeks, the influx was not enough to raise the water level in all sectors along the line. Moreover, construction at some points remained incomplete. Due to these conditions Bernadotte drew some shocking conclusions that flabbergasted the Prussians. The flood line would only be observed; no attempts would be made to contest an enemy passage.[95] Instead the entire army would remain north of Berlin behind the Havel-Spree line. Not only would the completed works along the Nuthe-Notte line be abandoned, but Berlin would be conceded without a battle.[96]

Bülow refused to accept the crown prince's decision and protested vehemently. He pointed to the advantages of positioning the army on the open plain south of the capital. Reports claimed that the Army of North Germany had twice the manpower of the French forces camped along the Prusso-Saxon frontier. Bernadotte acquiesced, probably for political reasons. Had he abandoned Berlin that early in the campaign, a conflict with the Allied sovereigns would certainly have arisen. The crown prince did not want to earn the mistrust of his allies and jeopardize his political ambitions. Therefore, he compromised by allowing Bülow's corps and a Russian brigade to remain south of the Havel-Spree line between Berlin and Brandenburg, while the Swedes and Wintzingerode's main body remained north of the capital at Oranienburg and Spandau. As for Tauentzien and Hirschfeld, Bernadotte overextended their Landwehr units on his wings. Tauentzien's troops marched far to the east of Berlin, while to the west Hirschfeld received orders to mask Magdeburg with 5,000 men and echelon his remaining 10,000 between Burg and Genthin.[97] Although Bülow was relieved that at least his corps and a Russian brigade would remain south of Berlin, Bernadotte's strategy shocked him. The Prussian promptly informed his king and requested that measures be taken to change Bernadotte's attitude.[98]

Unlike Bülow, Tauentzien realized that flattery might help him attain his own goals. Not designated for field operations, his Fourth Corps was to serve as a reserve, conduct sieges, and cover communications. Tauentzien's brigade commanders, Putlitz, Hirschfeld, Dobschütz, and Karl Georg von Wobeser, thus received a greater degree of independence than their counterparts in Bülow's corps. For the most part they fell under Bernadotte's direct command and conducted independent operations. Tauentzien resented his support role and wanted to participate in offensive operations. To gain a greater degree of responsibility, he courted the crown prince and lobbied for Bülow's corps to share the auxiliary duties. This offended Bülow, who thought that fielding two weak corps rather than one complete unit was absurd. Tauentzien's persistence only added to the growing tension between Bülow and Bernadotte over the latter's passive strategy and willingness to sacrifice Berlin without firing a shot.[99]

According to treaty obligations, Bernadotte had to take an active part in the war to attain Norway. This meant risking his position in Sweden, for if the French destroyed his army Norway's conquest would be impossible. To avoid this he planned to spare his Swedes and the troops of his dubious patron, Tsar Alexander, while using the Prussians to fight his former countrymen. As a confrontation with the French grew imminent, politics curbed his appetite for military glory. Not receiving command over all of the Allied armies had also disgruntled the vain prince-royal. Finally, from the moment he confronted his former countrymen, self-doubt besieged him. As early as June the Prussian representative in Bernadotte's headquarters predicted this duplicity: "If you could see him, you would undoubtedly find that he cannot act against his native country. He might do something with words."[100]

Bernadotte had indeed acquired vast military experience. As a subordinate he had obediently executed orders but lacked initiative, the essential characteristic of any successful field commander. During Napoleon's early campaigns his opponents proved that no amount of experience could replace this vital trait. A commander who lacked initiative only saw the risks of a military operation. This often led to defensive measures that devolved to inactivity. For Sweden's crown prince, lack of initiative would be the signature of his leadership throughout the fall campaign and the seed of his problems with the Prussians.

Opening Moves

The crown prince addressed his multinational army a few days before the resumption of hostilities:

Proclamation
The Royal Prince, Generalissimo, to the Army:

Soldiers! Called by the confidence of my King and of the sovereigns of his allies to lead you in the campaign that is going to reopen, I rely for the success of our arms on the divine protection, on the justice of our cause, on your valor and your perseverance.

Had it not been for the extraordinary concurrence of events that have provided the last twelve years with a dreadful celebrity, you would not be united on German soil; but your sovereigns feel that Europe is a great family and that none of the states that compose it can remain indifferent to the evils imposed upon any one of its members by a conquering power. They have also recognized that when such a power threatens to attack and subjugate every other, there has to exist only one will among those that are determined to escape from shame and slavery.

From that moment you were called from the banks of the Volga and the Don, from the shores of Britain and the mountains of the North, to unite with the German warriors who defend the cause of Europe.

This then is the moment when rivalry, national prejudices, and hatreds have to disappear before the great purpose of the independence of nations.

The Emperor Napoleon can not live in peace with Europe, unless Europe be his slave. His audacity has carried 400,000 brave men seven hundred miles from their country; misfortunes, against which he did not deign to caution them, fell upon them, and 300,000 Frenchmen have perished on the territory of a great empire, whose sovereign had made every effort to remain at peace with France.

It would be expected that this great disaster, the effect of the Divine anger, would have inclined the Emperor of France to a less murderous system, and that, instructed by the example of the North and of Spain, he would renounce the idea of subjugating the Continent and would consent to let the world be at peace; but this hope has been disappointed, and that peace, which all governments desire and which every government has proposed, has been rejected by the Emperor Napoleon.

Soldiers! We must resort to arms to win tranquility and independence. The same sentiments that guided the French in 1792 and that prompted them to assemble and to combat the armies that entered their territory should now animate your valor against those who, after having invaded the land that gave you birth, still hold in chains your brethren, your wives, and your children.

Soldiers! What a noble opportunity has opened for you! The liberty of Europe, the reestablishment of its equilibrium, the end of that convulsive state that has had twenty years' duration, and, finally, the peace of the world will be the result of your efforts. Render yourselves worthy, by your union, by your discipline and your courage, of the high destiny that awaits you.

From my Headquarters in Oranienburg, 15 August 1813.

CHARLES JOHN[1]

Not only did Bernadotte crank up his propaganda machine, but he also had his subordinates attentively observe French movements. Bülow's forward posts discovered French camps stretched along the Prusso-Saxon frontier at Fürstenberg on the left bank of the Oder; by Friedland west of the Oder; and by Lieberose, Lübben, and Lübbenau on the Spree. Spies claimed that the French also had camps at Guben, Cottbus, and Luckau. Marshal Victor commanded the troops near the Oder, and Oudinot commanded those on the Spree; together the Allies estimated they had 50,000 men. From Trebbin and Mittenwalde on the Nuthe-Notte line, Borstell and Thümen scoured the region between Beeskow and Luckenwalde. On 13 August they reported a general movement along the Prussian frontier. From their camps at Fürstenberg, Friedland, and Lieberose, the French marched southwest toward Guben. Borstell reported on 14 August that the French had retracted their forward posts from the frontier. It now appeared that Oudinot and Victor had concentrated their corps between Luckau and Baruth. Borstell further speculated that these movements could signal the preliminaries of an attack but could also serve to mask a retreat.[2]

From these reports Bülow incorrectly concluded that the French would either invade Silesia or assist Napoleon's main army around Dresden.[3] For these reasons he suggested that the Army of North Germany cross the Saxon frontier when the armistice expired at 12:00 A.M. on the seventeenth. Tauentzien agreed, but Bernadotte remained skeptical and particularly doubted the claims of a French withdrawal. He insisted that Napoleon would lead an offensive to destroy him. On the sixteenth Bülow finally realized that he had misinterpreted the intelligence and that a large French force appeared poised to advance against Berlin. His incorrect assumption probably lowered his stock in Bernadotte's opinion.[4]

Bernadotte knew the French would come, but from which direction? Regardless of the sizable cavalry forces at his disposal, Bernadotte's outposts failed to collect the news he needed. Although the inhabitants could be considered "friendly," their reports of French marches and countermarches further clouded the situation. To clarify these contradictory reports, the prince-royal ordered a general reconnaissance for the night of 16–17 August. By the evening of the sixteenth Bülow's corps stretched in front of Berlin and along the Nuthe-Notte line to form the center of Bernadotte's army. Hessen-Homburg's and Krafft's brigades garrisoned the city. Thümen's brigade held the passes over the

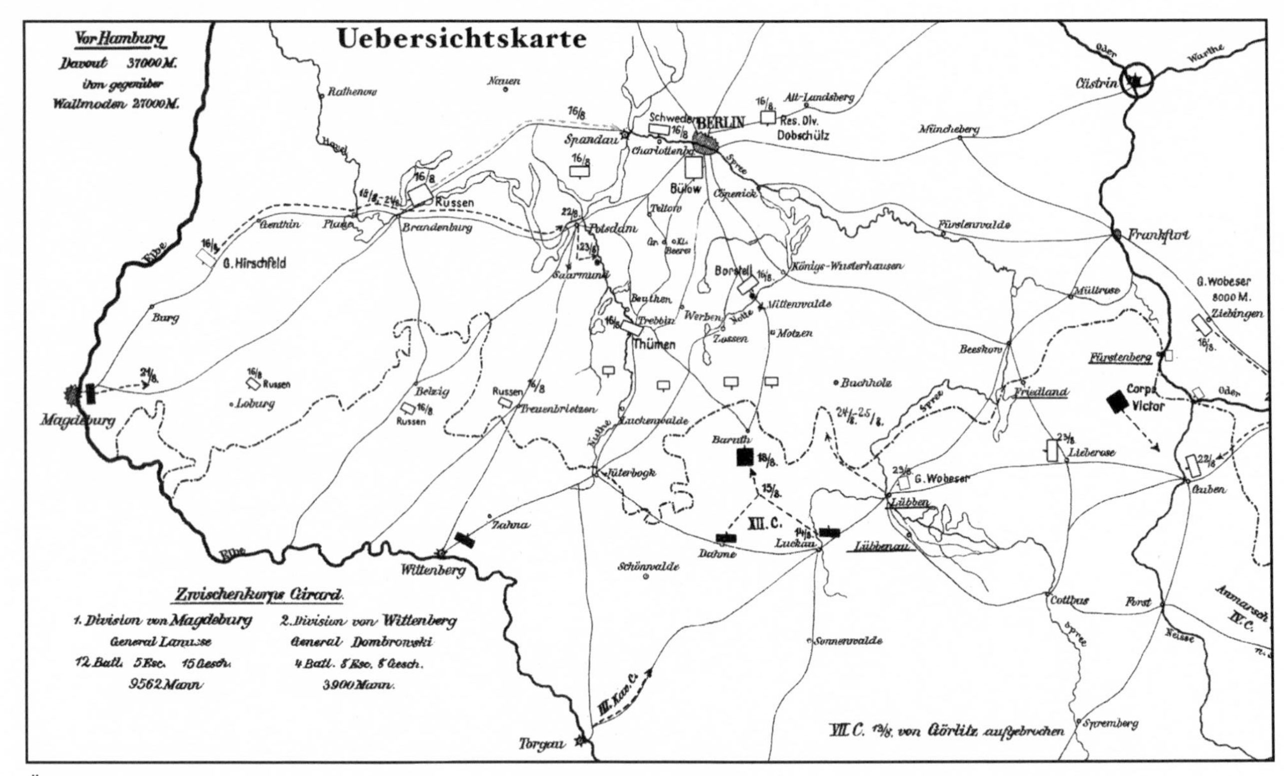

Übersichtskarte

Nuthe Canal, while Borstell's brigade covered the Notte sector from Zossen to the Saxon frontier. Far to the east of the Prussian capital Tauentzien reached Müncheberg with Dobschütz's brigade, and Wobeser patrolled the Oder between Frankfurt and Crossen. On the right wing the Swedes moved into Charlottenburg, while the Russian corps extended from Spandau through Beelitz to Treuenbrietzen.[5]

From these positions the Russians and Prussians launched surprise attacks along Oudinot's perimeter during the night of 16–17 August.[6] From Zerbst the Russians and Prussians swept southwest of Berlin through Jüterbog and Baruth to Lieberose on the extreme southeast.[7] Allied scouting parties crossed the Saxon frontier to collect reports from Belzig to the Spree. They captured approximately 500 prisoners, including four captains and one colonel. The captives reported that 30,000 men under Oudinot occupied Baruth, while an equal number of French troops stood in Luckau.[8] Additional reports placed Oudinot's army near 70,000 and claimed that Napoleon had left Dresden for Silesia.[9]

With the armistice officially expired, the war resumed. Bernadotte responded by concentrating his army around Berlin on the seventeenth. Thümen and Borstell occupied the Nuthe-Notte entrenchments, and Bülow assembled his other brigades on the Tempelhof hills near Bernadotte's incomplete "Citadel." Tauentzien's corps marched west to the capital, the Swedes remained in Charlottenburg, and the Russians took a position between Charlottenburg and Spandau.[10] Cossacks patrolled the region between Beelitz, Treuenbrietzen, and Jüterbog. Bernadotte revealed his true concern in his instructions to the Russian generals: "Napoleon is moving to Baruth escorted by two cavalry regiments; he marches at the rear of his army. The Crown Prince will award 500,000 rubles to the Cossack regiment that can capture him, and in proportion for his staff."[11] Despite the reports of Napoleon's march to Silesia, the thought that the French emperor would open the campaign against him drove Bernadotte to the point of paranoia.

Early on the morning of the seventeenth Bülow moved his Third and Sixth Brigades into position on the Tempelhof hill chain, where Bernadotte joined him to review the troops. In an attempt to remain on good terms with his Prussian subordinate, the crown prince invited Bülow to voice his opinion freely, especially when it involved military operations. Bernadotte added that since the war particularly concerned the Prussians he felt obligated to consider Bülow's opinion.[12] This was vintage Bernadotte: flattery and verbose promises. He probably meant little of what he said but had no idea that Bülow would take this invitation quite literally and exercise his right to be honest throughout the entire campaign.

To decipher the numerous reports that his raiding parties had collected the previous night, Bernadotte held a council of war in Charlottenburg later that afternoon. After reviewing them, the crown prince declared that Napoleon himself would advance over Mittenwalde and Zossen. He based his judgment on a 15 August report that Napoleon had crossed the Elbe at Dresden and proceeded north.[13] After sharing this report with his subordinates, Bernadotte concluded that Napoleon had 100,000 men at Baruth ready to advance on Berlin.[14] Bülow, however, did not share his concern over Napoleon's supposed approach. He reminded the prince-royal that according to the Trachenberg Plan Oudinot's apparent isolation at Baruth warranted an offensive. He suggested moving the army into the open plain south of the Nuthe-Notte defenses. Bernadotte, however, refused to take the initiative. Although the crown prince conceded the next move to the French, he did ask Boyen if the Nuthe-Notte line could be held. Boyen perceived a deeper meaning to this question and embarked on a dangerous game of verbal chess with the crown prince, a master orator. He had just witnessed Bülow's failure to convince Bernadotte that the open plain south of the Nuthe-Notte line would offer an excellent position to strike Oudinot. Knowing that Bernadotte wanted to abandon Berlin by withdrawing north, over the Havel-Spree line, Boyen somehow had to convince him to keep the army south of the capital. He feared that if he gave the defense line a glowing review the crown prince would have Bülow's corps occupy the fortifications while the rest of the army retreated north. Notwithstanding his personal share in the line's construction, Boyen downplayed the strength of the line. Concluding a description of the defense network, he made a final attempt to prevent the army from retreating northward. Boyen suggested that Tauentzien's corps occupy the line as an advanced guard, while the rest of the army concentrated between Groß Ziethen and Heinersdorf, a few marches south of Berlin.[15] This position, although not as good as the open plain south of the defense line, could at least protect Berlin by allowing the army to strike an enemy force that penetrated the Nuthe-Notte line.

When Boyen finished, Bernadotte asked Bülow to confer with the chief of staff of the Army of North Germany, Gen. Karl Johann von Adlercreutz, and the army quartermaster-general, Karl Emil von Löwenhielm. After a short discussion Bülow suggested two plans. According to the first, his corps and Wintzingerode's corps would advance in four columns toward Baruth. To double-envelop Oudinot, Bülow's corps would form two columns and converge on Baruth from the east and north, while Wintzingerode's two columns would approach from the west. Bülow's alternate plan required the entire army to wheel southwestward to strike Oudinot's left flank and rear, while a pinning force approached from the north. Both plans appeared sound, and the second promised decisive results. Bernadotte, however, rejected both on the grounds that Napoleon's presence would completely alter the circumstances. Wintzingerode, the Russian commander, then advised treating Berlin like Moscow. By retreating and abandoning the Prussian capital, he argued, the army would actually draw the French away from the Bohemian Army. Not at all pleased with his Russian counterpart's solution, Bülow loudly reiterated his original suggestion for the army to advance against Oudinot. In a fit of indecision Bernadotte shifted his support to Boyen's advice. Although concentrating the army between Groß Ziethen and Heinersdorf ruled out a strategic offensive, the possibility for tactical strikes remained. More debate followed, but the council ended without Bernadotte rendering a final judgment. To all involved, it appeared that the Army of North Germany would not slow Oudinot's march to Berlin.[16]

After the meeting Bülow and Boyen rode back to Berlin, discussing the talks with Bernadotte over the past four days. A disillusioned Bülow vowed that his corps would attack the enemy and avoid evasive maneuvers. This proved to be a decisive moment in the relationship between Bülow and his chief of staff. Bülow's "decision was very significant for Prussia, and the morale of our troops," recalled Boyen. "Several times when I was away from him, I knew what to do to act in accordance with his wishes."[17] Both men committed themselves to attacking an advancing enemy, despite the Swedish prince-royal. Bülow also unintentionally adhered to Gneisenau's plan to free the Prussian army from the lethargy of a multinational coalition.[18] During this opening period of the fall campaign Bülow and Boyen established the principles that would enable them to save Berlin on two occasions. They also sowed the seeds of discord in the Army of North Germany.

After returning to his headquarters, Bülow received the discouraging order to build two bridges across the Spree between Berlin and Charlottenburg. Construction had to begin immediately and proceed "with the greatest activity, by night and day," so that the bridges could be finished as soon as possible.[19] This signaled Bernadotte's desire to retreat and convinced the Prussians that he would not keep his army south of the Havel-Spree line to defend Berlin. Reports that a large French force had reached Jüterbog prompted Bernadotte's decision to build these additional bridges to facilitate a retreat across the Spree.[20]

Since it appeared that the Army of North Germany would not challenge the French, Bülow shifted his attention to the incomplete fortifications around Berlin. Disgruntled carpenters, who cited contractual differences with the city government, continued to delay construction. To save money Büsching had classified them as temporary laborers and adjusted their pay accordingly. This proved unacceptable to the guild, which told the carpenters to go home. Büsching now wanted to use capital punishment against the leaders![21] Regardless of the dispute, Bülow pressured Büsching and L'Estoq to finish the construction of Bernadotte's "Citadel." Since his troops had to remain under arms, he could not provide laborers. Instead, starting on 19 August he wanted 2,600 laborers working on the entrenchments at the Halle Gate. Büsching had to furnish these workers, who in turn had to supply their own tools. Bülow instructed him to use force if necessary to impress the workers.[22]

Meanwhile Bülow's pioneers began work on the bridges. A subsequent order from Bernadotte decreed the construction of bridgeheads to protect the bridges. Bülow turned this construction over to Loos and Büsching. The latter promised to provide 2,500 workers daily, but only 1,300 reported on the twentieth and less than 1,900 on the twenty-first. Loos complained about the quantity and quality. He explained that even with 1,900 capable workers he could have accomplished much, but children and old women composed the majority of his workforce; men numbered less than 200.[23] Consequently, the entrenchment construction on the Nuthe-Notte had to be suspended so that all manpower could be used on Bernadotte's bridgeheads and the fortifications around Berlin.

As the Prussians toiled with the construction, the crown prince brooded. Believing the French army would advance north from Baruth, he planned to take the army westward to threaten its flank. On the eighteenth and nineteenth the Russian corps moved south toward the Nuthe. Wintzingerode's main body marched from Spandau to Saarmund, while his advance guard reached Trebbin. Russian patrols and Cossacks probed as far south as Wittenberg and eastward to Lynow, only a few miles from Baruth. Of Bülow's corps, only Thümen's brigade dispatched patrols to Luckenwalde; the others remained in their positions throughout the eighteenth.[24] On the following day Bernadotte ordered Hessen-Homburg and Krafft from the bivouacs on the Tempelhof hills to their quarters in the city. Thümen and Borstell remained on the Nuthe-Notte line. Bülow's patrols extended southeast as far as Lübben and Friedland in search of the French army. Tauentzien placed Wobeser's brigade at Müllrose to cover Frankfurt-am-Oder.[25] The Swedes remained by Charlottenburg and the Russians at Saarmund.

While the Army of North Germany searched for the French southeast of Berlin, Oudinot concentrated his forces to the southwest. On 17 August his own Twelfth Corps, Bertrand's Fourth Corps, and Arrighi's Third Cavalry Corps united at Baruth, only three marches from Berlin. Reynier's Seventh Corps marched north from Luckau to join the rest of the army on the following day. Oudinot's army then moved northwest in three columns across Bernadotte's front on the nineteenth. From Baruth he led his corps and the cavalry to Luckenwalde on the Nuthe. Reynier's columns followed later in the day, marching to Schönefelde and Schöneweide. Bertrand's corps remained in Baruth to shield Oudinot's right flank during the upcoming march to the Prussian capital. During the ensuing march Arrighi's cavalry reached Luckenwalde first and expelled some Cossacks.[26] Oudinot now possessed the hub where two of the three major highways leading to Berlin converged. One ran through Groß Beeren, the other through Blankenfelde. Oudinot's army would utilize these roads to advance on Berlin.

From Trebbin, Thümen reported Oudinot's march to Bülow at 7:00 P.M. on the nineteenth. It appeared the French would either remain at Luckenwalde or attack Trebbin the following morning.[27] Neither the Prussians nor the Cossacks spotted Reynier's columns.[28] At 10:00 P.M. Borstell reported that a French force from Baruth had attacked his posts south of Zossen. Bülow forwarded this information to army headquarters, hoping in vain that it would influence the crown prince.[29] Bernadotte, however, had already drafted orders for 20 August that reflected his concern over a French advance due north from Baruth against his left. The army's southwestward shift thus continued on the twentieth. Bülow again led his two brigades out of Berlin to Klein Ziethen, while Borstell's Fifth Brigade and Thümen's Fourth Brigade maintained their positions on the Nuthe-Notte line. Tauentzien's corps

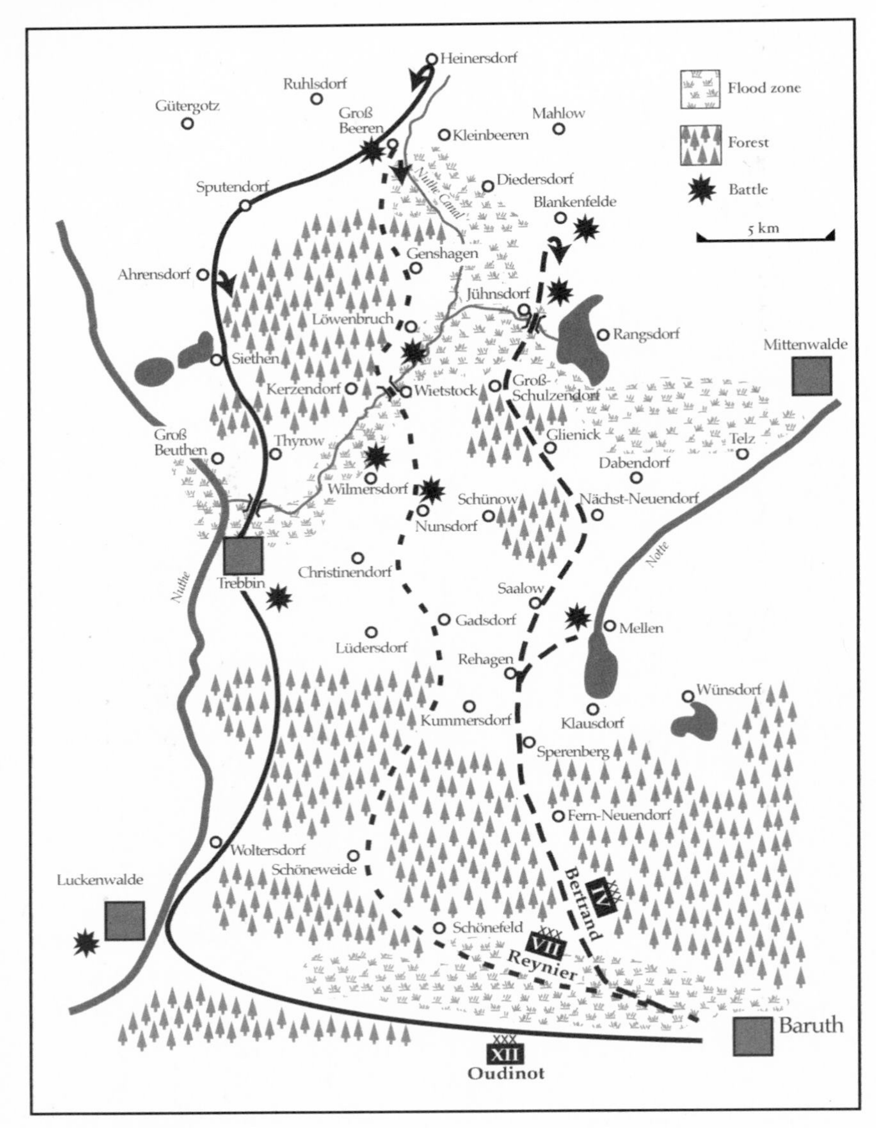

Oudinot's Advance

moved into Berlin and Köpenick, while Wintzingerode's Russians marched to Beelitz on the right flank.[30] Allied cavalry patrolled between Mittenwalde and Trebbin and as far east as the Oder River but failed to provide the information that would reveal Oudinot's intentions.[31] Conflicting intelligence continued to undermine the situation.

As the crown prince of Sweden moved his lieutenants like chess pieces, Bülow made several attempts to influence his decisions. Gen. Friedrich Wilhelm von Krusemarck, Prussia's envoy in Bernadotte's camp, failed to convince Bernadotte of the need to attack Oudinot. His counterparts in army headquarters, Karl Andreas, Count Pozzo di Borgo, from Russia, Ferdinand von Vincent from Austria, and Edward Thornton from Britain likewise proved ineffective. Frustrated, Bülow wrote the king to request that "an officer of high rank equipped with the necessary diplomatic abilities and military knowledge to protect royal interests" replace Krusemarck. Since Bernadotte was more inclined to accept verbal suggestions rather than written proposals, he hoped Frederick William could appoint an envoy more forceful than Krusemarck.[32] The request went unfulfilled.

When Oudinot reached Luckenwalde on 19 August, his entire army faced the flood and entrenchments of the Nuthe-Notte line. He realized that the defense line would present difficulties. Recent rains had deepened the floodwaters. An apprehensive Oudinot decided to advance on the twentieth, but inaccurate intelligence and the Prussian defenses compelled him to change his mind. Bertrand's incorrect report that Bülow had reached Mittenwalde with 30,000 men probably accounted for Oudinot's discretion. Other exaggerated reports claimed that an Allied army of 50,000 men had united between Trebbin and Mittenwalde. Moreover, French engineers informed Oudinot that the entrenchments and floodwaters rendered the road to Trebbin impassable. This convinced the marshal that the floodwaters would prevent him from reaching Berlin.[33] As a result the Army of Berlin remained idle throughout the twentieth—a small victory for the Prussians who had labored on the Nuthe-Notte defense line. After his subordinates became restless, Oudinot finally ordered an advance for 21 August. That morning Bertrand marched to Sperenberg and Saalow, Reynier to Nunsdorf, and Oudinot and the cavalry to Trebbin.[34]

From their base in Mittenwalde Borstell's scouts remained active. On 20 August they captured a French captain and brought him to Borstell at 6:30 P.M.[35] After a brief interrogation Borstell sent the captured officer to Bülow, along with a note stating that the enemy would probably advance between the Nuthe-Notte on the following day. The prisoner arrived in Bülow's headquarters at 1:30 A.M. on the twenty-first. After further questioning he revealed that the entire Twelfth Corps had been at Luckenwalde since the nineteenth; Bertrand's Fourth Corps

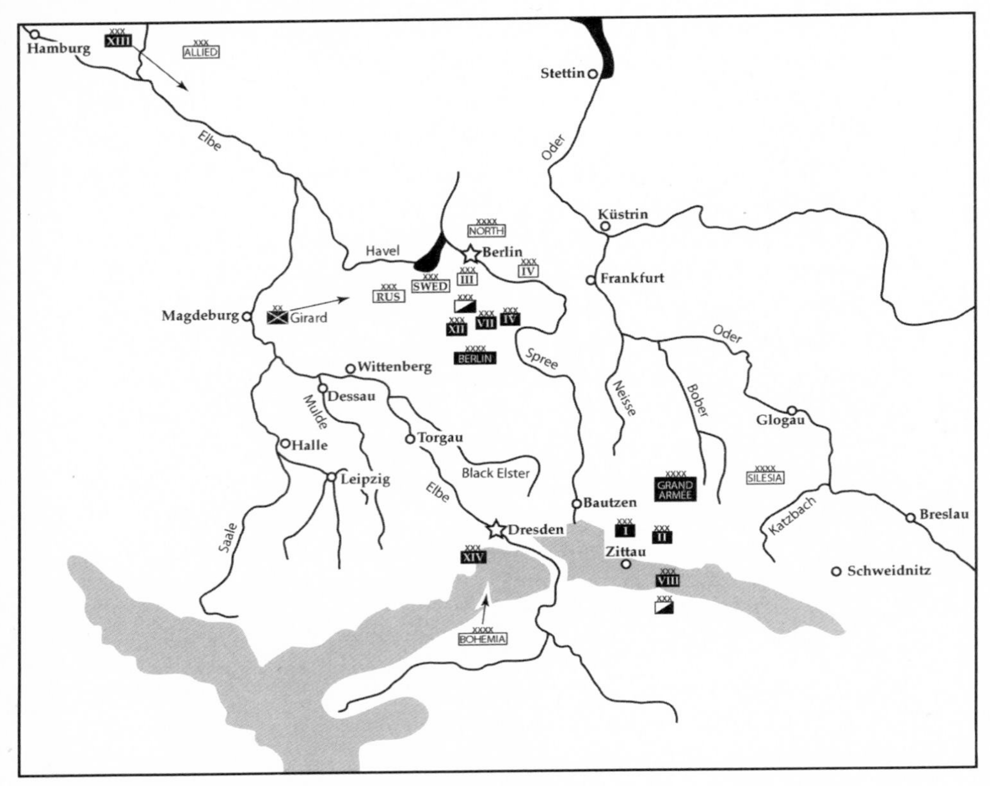

The Situation on 21 August 1813

stood at Baruth; and Reynier's Seventh Corps formed the center. This information reached Bernadotte at 4:00 A.M. on 21 August, but once again the orders of the day already had been distributed. According to these orders, the Army of North Germany marched westward and away from Oudinot's path. The Russians and Swedes moved to Beelitz and Potsdam, too far west to have any influence on the Nuthe-Notte line. A reluctant Bülow led his Third and Sixth Brigades farther west to a position between Philippstal and Sputendorf, while Borstell and Thümen remained isolated in their posts on the Nuthe-Notte line.[36] From his new position Bülow could no longer support Borstell's Fifth Brigade at Mittenwalde. To the Prussians it seemed as if the entire army was moving west, away from the fortifications, entrenchments, and floodplain, but most of all away from the French army. This movement also created a gap between Tauentzien and Bülow that opened the southern approaches to Berlin.[37]

Bernadotte's westward shift had no effect on Oudinot, who attacked Trebbin at 1:00 P.M. on 21 August. After a four-hour skirmish the outnumbered Prussian garrison evacuated the village as well as the pass through the floodplain. East of Oudinot, Reynier's Second Saxon Division took Nunsdorf, while Bertrand drove the Prussians from Mellensee. That evening Oudinot's Twelfth Corps camped at Trebbin and Reynier's at Christinendorf; Bertrand's men crossed the lowlands north of Saalow to bivouac in the wooded terrain around Schünow. The French army had successfully penetrated the Nuthe-Notte line. Encamped between Trebbin, Nunsdorf, and Schünow, it could now separate Thümen from Borstell, exploit the gap between Bülow and Tauentzien, and march unopposed to Berlin.[38]

Aware of the gap between Bülow and Tauentzien, Bernadotte drew his wings closer to his center. He ordered Tauentzien's corps to unite with Oppen's cavalry at Klein Beeren on 22 August. Bülow's Third and Sixth Brigades would march farther westward to Saarmund. From Trebbin, Thümen had to attack the flank of any French force that appeared to his left at Zossen. Borstell, supported by Tauentzien and Oppen, had to hold Mittenwalde at all cost. Wintzingerode's infantry would countermarch to Saarmund, while the Russian cavalry remained at Beelitz. From Jüterbog and Treuenbrietzen, 3,000 Cossacks would harass Oudinot's rear. Stedingk also received orders to have his Swedish corps at Saarmund by 6:00 A.M. on 22 August. Bernadotte hoped to have Hirschfeld's 8,000 men at Potsdam by 10:00 A.M. on the twenty-second.[39] Although aggressive, these orders did not reflect the events on the Nuthe-Notte line. The crown prince refused to believe that Oudinot had advanced west from Baruth to Luckenwalde and then turned north. Instead he based his orders on the statements of a prisoner who claimed that at least 60,000 men still stood in the region of Baruth and would march against Berlin on the twenty-second.[40] The orders for Borstell to hold Mittenwalde and for Thümen to march from Trebbin to Zossen reflect this incorrect report. With Oudinot's army between the Nuthe and the Notte rather than east of the Notte, Bernadotte's dispositions would have led to the destruction of Thümen and Borstell.

The direction of Oudinot's advance required a drastic modification of Bernadotte's orders. Not only did the combats of 21 August breach

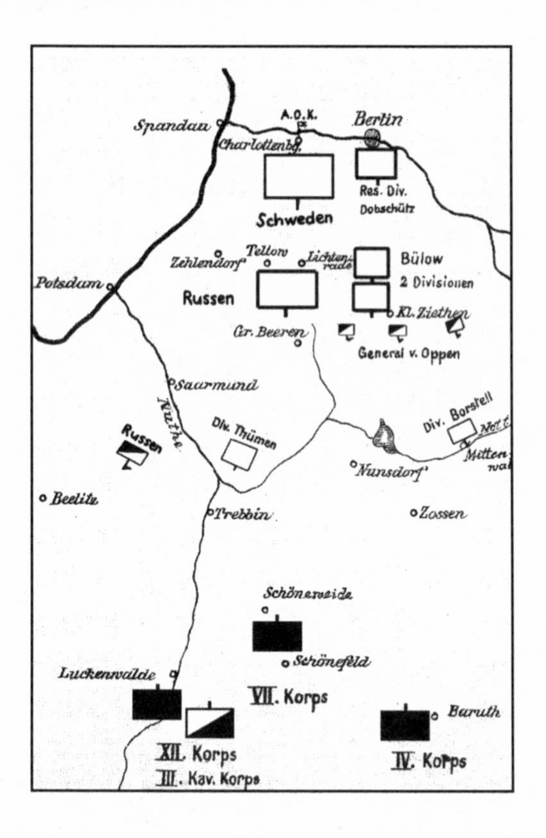

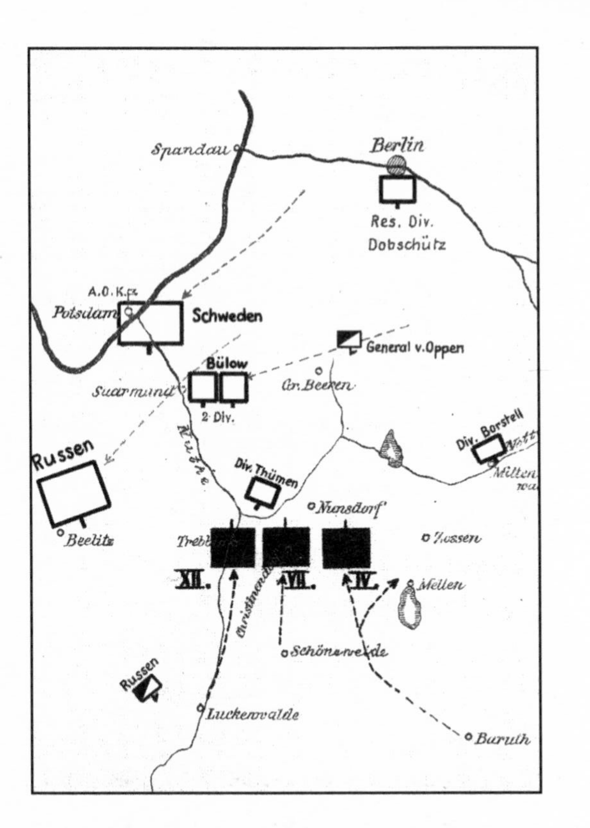

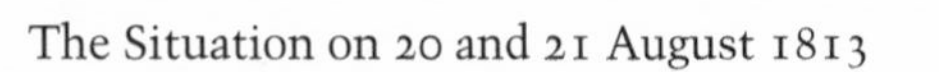
The Situation on 20 and 21 August 1813

the defense line, but the French were in position to exploit the gap between Bülow and Tauentzien. Reports clarifying the true state of affairs reached the prince-royal during the night of 21–22 August. As a result he held a council of war in Philippstal on the morning of the twenty-second. Bernadotte insisted that Napoleon himself was approaching and repeated his desire to withdraw over the Spree.[41] He based this assumption on a letter from Blücher that he had received on 19 August. It stated that according to the recently defected French staff officer Antoine de Jomini Napoleon himself would attack Bernadotte's army. Moreover, the crown prince had little confidence in his own troops, especially the Landwehr, who would confront the French for the first time. Bülow objected, explaining that he would not abandon Berlin without firing a shot. Although his words may be apocryphal, Bülow rejected the decision to retreat, stating: "Our bones shall bleach before Berlin, not behind it."[42] After debating the pros and cons of defending the Prussian capital, he announced his refusal to follow the crown prince over the Spree. Bernadotte again conceded and agreed to keep the army south of Berlin until he could prove that Napoleon himself commanded the approaching French army. He dismissed his generals and ordered them to prepare their men for combat.[43]

A few hours later the crown prince issued orders to move his army east to block Oudinot's advance. Bülow was ordered to march his Third and Sixth Brigades northeast from Saarmund to Heinersdorf. The Swedes and Russians moved into positions at Ruhlsdorf and Gütergotz. From Potsdam, Hirschfeld raced toward Saarmund. The crown prince instructed the Swedes, Russians, Bülow, and Thümen to retire to the hills of Stegelitz if forced to retreat; Tauentzien and Borstell would retreat to the Tempelhof fortifications.[44] Strategic necessity justified this countermarch, but it did not improve troop morale, which had plummeted over the past few days due to the lack of provisions. Despite their nearness to the capital, supply had already become a problem.[45]

As Bernadotte's army retraced its steps eastward, Oudinot's army crossed the floodplain between the Nuthe and Notte. The swamp lying between the two streams practically connected the waters and would have afforded the Allies a fairly effective defense line had Bernadotte occupied the positions with sufficient numbers. To continue his march Oudinot had to secure the passes over the Nuthe Canal at Thyrow, Wilmersdorf, Wietstock, and Jühnsdorf. He found the defenses at Thyrow to be the strongest and decided to attack Wietstock and Jühnsdorf first, hoping to force the Prussians to retreat from Thyrow. Oudinot ordered Reynier to attack Wietstock on 22 August. His own Twelfth Corps would assault Wilmersdorf, while one division remained on the outskirts of Thyrow to pin Thümen's forces. On the right Bertrand's Fourth Corps would push north through Jühnsdorf.[46]

At Thyrow, Thümen believed that at least 25,000 men had attacked Trebbin on the twenty-first and that the French would renew their offensive at daybreak, turn his left, and take the open road to Berlin.[47] He also assumed that Oudinot would attack Wilmersdorf rather than Thyrow. Only four battalions held Wilmersdorf, while two battalions stood in Wietstock, and on the far left wing a Kurmark Landwehr battalion occupied Jühnsdorf. Thümen placed his remaining troops at Kerzendorf, Thyrow, and Groß Beuthen. He asked Bülow for support, assuring his commander that he could not "make the impossible possible."[48] Bülow could not directly assist his subordinate but sought Tauentzien's help. During the night of 21–22 August he suggested that Tauentzien take a position at Blankenfelde and occupy the pass at Jühnsdorf to free Oppen, who could then move to support Thümen.[49] Tauentzien received Bülow's letter while on the march to Klein Beeren in accordance with Bernadotte's orders. He accepted the advice and continued to Blankenfelde. Oppen left a dragoon regiment and two guns in Blankenfelde to observe Jühnsdorf until Tauentzien arrived, and he led the remainder of the reserve cavalry to posts on the Nuthe Canal. Tauentzien's decision to accept Bülow's advice and march to Blankenfelde changed the course of operations north of the Elbe and perhaps the entire war itself. Although Tauentzien lost the pass at Jühnsdorf on the twenty-second, his position at Blankenfelde proved far more decisive on the twenty-third.

Early on the morning of 22 August it appeared that Napoleon's plans were about to achieve fruition. To the south the emperor himself was pursuing Blücher's Army of Silesia. In the north the French Army of Berlin began its final drive to the Prussian capital. Oudinot approached Wilmersdorf with a French division supported by a Saxon brigade from Reynier's corps. Some unfinished entrenchments on the windmill hill probably appeared very threatening from a distance. The French expected fierce resistance and spent the entire morning planning their attack. In the afternoon combat began with artillery fire from two twelve-pounder Saxon batteries. While Saxon gunners pounded the Prussian position, the French infantry formed seven attack columns.

No match for such superiority, the Prussians withdrew. The French stormed the hills, only to find the Prussians marching away.

From Reynier's corps, Gen. Pierre François Durutte's division took Wietstock, but an East Prussian battalion and two guns held firm at the dam west of the village. Oppen arrived with five cavalry regiments and two horse batteries. One battery reinforced the fire against the French and Saxons in the village, while the other remained in reserve. Saxon artillery unlimbered and bombarded the Prussians. At 6:00 P.M. French infantry used planks to cross a trench that separated them from the Prussians, formed a column, and charged the enemy entrenchments. The second Prussian horse battery opened fire and thwarted this attack with a blast of case-shot. Before the French could fully recover, Oppen ordered his five cavalry regiments to charge over a narrow strip of solid ground. The attack failed due to the coolness of the French infantry, which quickly formed squares and leveled their muskets at the Prussian troopers. Oppen's Kurmark and Pomeranian Landwehr squadrons received their first taste of combat and fell back in disorder. Saxon reinforcements soon crossed. Oppen realized that nothing more could be done and ordered a retreat. His withdrawal from Wietstock prompted Thümen to evacuate Thyrow and order a general retreat to Groß Beeren. Oudinot's plan had worked brilliantly, and it seemed like nothing except Thümen's shaken brigade stood between the Army of Berlin and its prize.

Northeast of Thümen's sector, Tauentzien's corps had reached Blankenfelde early on 22 August. Despite the recent heavy rains the floodplain around Jühnsdorf remained dry enough for the passage of infantry. Tauentzien reinforced Jühnsdorf with two Landwehr battalions, two guns, and one squadron. Later that morning Bertrand's skirmishers approached the village. As the sound of gunfire increased from the direction of Jühnsdorf, Tauentzien led five battalions, four squadrons, and two guns to reinforce his post. What should have been a short march inexplicably turned into a long ordeal, and he did not arrive until 6:00 P.M. By that time Bertrand had already forced the Prussians out of Jühnsdorf. Tauentzien ordered a counterattack, and the Third Battalion of the Second Neumark Landwehr Regiment stormed and recaptured the village. Unsure of his adversary's strength, however, Tauentzien ordered a retreat to Blankenfelde. Both sides were quiet throughout the night of 22–23 August. Bertrand's corps camped at Jühnsdorf; Reynier's at Wietstock; and the Twelfth Corps remained with the

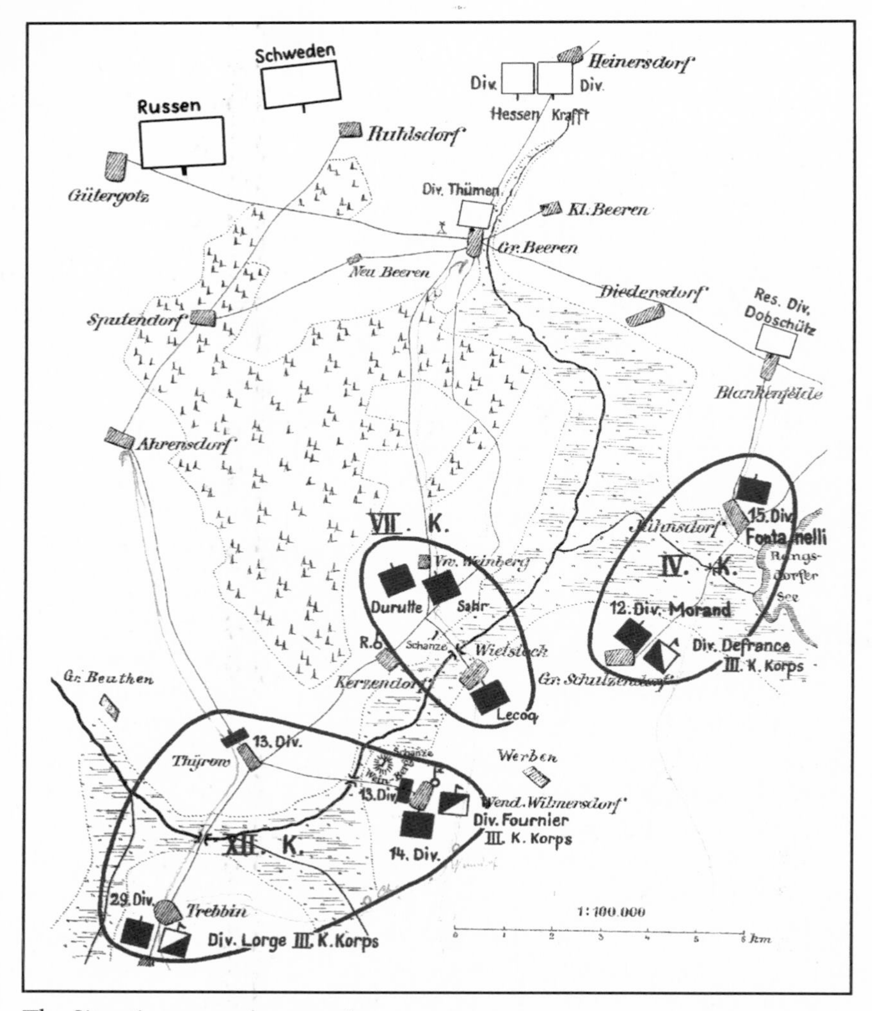

The Situation on 22 August 1813

cavalry at Thyrow. Oudinot spent the night preparing for his conquest of Berlin on the following day.[50]

While Oudinot engaged Bülow's outposts on the twenty-second, the Army of North Germany had moved into a position with the Swedes in the center at Ruhlsdorf, Wintzingerode's corps at Gütergotz on the right, and Bülow on the left wing between Ruhlsdorf and Heinersdorf. That evening Bernadotte issued dispositions for the following day. Bülow's corps again had to march farther west to link with the Swedes at Ruhlsdorf, while Tauentzien was supposed to move into Heinersdorf. If Borstell and Thümen were forced from their positions, they were to withdraw on Ruhlsdorf and form Bülow's advance guard. On the army's far left Wobeser's brigade was to advance from Buchholz to Baruth, while Hirschfeld continued his advance to Saarmund on the far right.[51]

Bülow believed that Oudinot would advance from Wietstock to Berlin on the direct highway that ran through Groß Beeren and so modified Bernadotte's instructions.[52] Rather than position Borstell and Thümen south of Ruhlsdorf, he summoned Thümen to Heinersdorf.[53] With the exception of a cavalry detachment that would remain in Mittenwalde, Bülow ordered Borstell to move his entire brigade north along the Mittenwalde-Berlin highway to Birckholz.[54] This modification proved crucial. From Birkholz, Borstell could attack the flank of a French force that debouched onto the plain between Heinersdorf and Blankenfelde. The adjustments made by Bülow and Tauentzien on 22 and 23 August mark the beginning of a series of events that sparked subsequent debate in Germany, France, and Sweden. On the morning of the twenty-third Bernadotte did not know the whereabouts of either Borstell or Tauentzien. He later accused the Prussians of disobeying his orders and ruining his plans to destroy the Army of Berlin. The fact remains that Bülow's suggestions for Tauentzien to take a position at Blankenfelde and his order for Borstell to march to Birkholz saved Berlin on 23 August.

At 1:00 A.M. on 23 August a letter from army headquarters advised Bülow to be prepared to attack the French if they advanced on Heinersdorf. The crown prince expected "the Prussians to recall the glory of their Great Frederick and avenge all the insults that the Emperor Napoleon has made for ten years."[55] The stage was set for a struggle before the gates of Berlin.

Groß Beeren

As dawn broke on 23 August Bertrand's corps marched out of Jühnsdorf on the highway to Blankenfelde, while Reynier took the main road from Wietstock to Groß Beeren. On the French army's left wing, Oudinot left Trebbin and advanced on the road to Ahrensdorf. Although all three roads converged on Berlin, the thick, swampy forest south of the Prussian capital denied the French corps mutual support. A chain of dunelike sandy hills separated Reynier from Bertrand, while a forest belt limited communication between Oudinot and Reynier.[1] Nevertheless, morale remained high in the Army of Berlin. Oudinot's French and German soldiers encouraged each other with promises of reuniting in Berlin. The Saxons in particular boasted that their attack on the Prussian capital would leave no stone standing.[2]

As for the Army of North Germany, Chernyshov's cavalry held Beelitz, and Hirschfeld's brigade occupied Saarmund on the right wing. Wintzingerode's Russians stood at Gütergotz, Stedingk's Swedes at Ruhlsdorf, and Bülow's Third and Sixth Brigades formed the center between Ruhlsdorf and Heinersdorf. Most of Thümen's brigade had reached Groß Beeren, but Borstell's brigade remained on the march to Birkholz. Tauentzien anchored the left wing at Blankenfelde. Bernadotte decided to constrict his line and ordered Bülow to proceed further west to Ruhlsdorf. This not only reopened the gap between the two

Prussian corps, but signaled the preliminaries of a retreat over the Spree and the abandonment of Berlin. Boyen informed Bülow that the purely defensive position at Ruhlsdorf would prevent the army from launching an effective counterattack.[3] At Ruhlsdorf the Army of North Germany could only be attacked. An inquiry from army headquarters about the status of the bridges at Charlottenburg convinced Bülow that Bernadotte intended to retreat and sacrifice Berlin. That morning he hastily scribbled a note to his wife, Pauline, that instructed her to pack their belongings and prepare to flee the capital. Convinced that the army would either retreat or be defeated, Bülow had orderlies bring post horses to the stalls of the palace where Pauline and his two children awaited news.[4]

Bülow complied with Bernadotte's orders despite his reservations. At daybreak on the twenty-third the Third Corps shifted westward, reaching Ruhlsdorf at 7:00 a.m. Three hours later, firing could be heard to the east. Bülow knew that after negotiating the forest and swamp belt Oudinot would break through to the plain between Blankenfelde and Heinersdorf, exploit the gap between the two Prussian corps, and march to Berlin. In desperation he sent Boyen to army headquarters to seek permission for the Third Corps to fill the gap between Blankenfelde and Heinersdorf. Reports of Bertrand's attack on Tauentzien arrived in Ruhlsdorf around the same time as Boyen. He found Bernadotte in the Ruhlsdorf windmill and stressed the need for Bülow to support Tauentzien by moving into the sector between Heinersdorf and Blankenfelde. After a long, heated conversation Boyen received permission for the Third Corps to return to Heinersdorf. He headed for the stairwell; when he reached the ground floor, the crown prince yelled down to him: "How will you fight?" Boyen clambered back up the stairs to describe the good morale of the troops. After he excused himself and reached the ground floor a second time, Bernadotte repeated his question. Again Boyen lumbered up the windmill's narrow stairwell to promise success. Bernadotte repeated this scene so many times that Boyen "dripped with sweat as if I was in a Russian bath." After he lost count of how many times the crown prince mockingly recalled him, Boyen shouted from the ground floor: "We will fight as brave men and win you a victory!" He left the mill and returned to Bülow. He later noted that "whether I was called once more, I do not know. In fact, I had decided to ignore it, and as soon as I could, I ran to my horse. Up to now, the crown prince had treated me very kindly, even with reverence. It appeared that due to this meeting, in which I might have become too animated, a change occurred. This became increasingly pronounced due to the quantity of difficult assignments that I had to debate with the crown prince on Bülow's behalf."[5]

Boyen left Ruhlsdorf with an apparent victory for the Prussians, but Bernadotte would have the last word. Without informing Boyen or Bülow, he ordered Hessen-Homburg's Third Brigade to remain at Ruhlsdorf. News of a French advance on Ahrensdorf, just a few miles south of Ruhlsdorf, alarmed the prince-royal. Rather than risk his Swedes, he withheld Hessen-Homburg's brigade. A surprised and infuriated Bülow arrived at Heinersdorf without his Third Brigade.[6] He dispatched aides to Ruhlsdorf to demand that Hessen-Homburg be allowed to rejoin the corps. Incoming reports of the combat at Blankenfelde helped Bülow's case. Although Tauentzien reportedly held his position, the crown prince now feared that Oudinot would turn his left. Strong Russian cavalry forces west of the Nuthe and Hirschfeld's brigade at Saarmund shielded the army's right wing, but Bernadotte's concern over his left mounted. As a result he ordered Hessen-Homburg to rejoin Bülow's corps. By late afternoon Bülow's three brigades, including the reserve cavalry and artillery, bivouacked around Heinersdorf, while Borstell's brigade marched from Birkholz to Klein Beeren.[7]

At Blankenfelde Bertrand's corps had attacked Tauentzien's 13,000 men earlier that morning. Combat began in the Genshagen Forest just south of the village, where Prussian skirmishers and a light infantry battalion engaged their French and Italian counterparts. As the skirmishing continued in the forest, Bertrand's Fifteenth Division steadily advanced against Tauentzien's left wing of Kurmark and Neumark Landwehr units. The tips of Bertrand's infantry columns could soon be discerned on a bald hill southeast of the village. Two French batteries unlimbered and opened fire. The Landwehr battalions in Tauentzien's first wave recoiled and fell back in disorder. Bertrand continued the bombardment rather than exploit his success. Hoping that maneuver would win his objective, he withdrew without unleashing his infantry on the Prussian militia, many of whom would have experienced combat for the first time. Bertrand believed that Reynier's advance through Groß Beeren on Tauentzien's right flank would eventually force the Prussians to retreat from Blankenfelde. Had Tauentzien's two brigades not consisted of inexperienced militia, he might have engaged Bertrand's columns as they withdrew. Unsure of his raw Landwehr, Tauentzien

Gen. Henri-Gatien Bertrand (1773–1844). Loyal to the end, in 1815 Bertrand and his entire family followed the emperor into exile on St. Helena, where the general endured personal servitude to a demanding Napoleon, who was rumored to be having an affair with his wife.

only pursued the French half the distance to Jühnsdorf but still managed to take 211 prisoners. All combat ceased around 2:00 P.M., and both sides resumed their former positions. Later in the afternoon heavy firing could be heard to the west in the direction of Groß Beeren. After a few hours the dull rumble faded into an uneasy silence. Night broke, rain fell in torrents, and nothing else remained than to await the news from Groß Beeren.[8]

Eleven miles south of Berlin the village of Groß Beeren formed a hub where several roads converged, particularly a main north-south thoroughfare to the capital. Nestled at the edge of the Genshagen Forest on the Berlin highway, Groß Beeren stood on a gentle hill. A plain north of the village gradually rose slightly northeast toward Heinersdorf. A swampy, impassable canal separated Groß Beeren from Klein Beeren.[9] Bülow recognized the importance of this position and occupied Groß Beeren with three battalions, one cavalry regiment, and four guns.[10] In his headquarters at Heinersdorf he and his staff had just sat down to a late lunch when gunfire erupted in the distance. Tired and hungry, they pulled themselves away from the table as reports arrived of a French attack on Groß Beeren. Boyen, who immediately left to scout the French position, observed Reynier's troops debouch from the forest and take a position between Groß Beeren and Neu Beeren.

Reynier had also heard the same gunfire from the direction of Blankenfelde earlier that day. When it grew weaker and ceased altogether, he believed that Bertrand had advanced and so ordered his Seventh Corps to march around noon. He took the main highway from Wietstock to Berlin and advanced to Groß Beeren as Oudinot's corps marched on Ahrensdorf. Around 3:15 P.M. Reynier's vanguard debouched from the forest and assaulted the Prussian outposts in Groß Beeren.[11] A Saxon division advanced from the forest edge in four columns, and two batteries bombarded the village, sparking multiple fires. The Saxons drove the Prussians from the burning village back to Heinersdorf.[12] Rather than pursue, Reynier took his headquarters in Groß Beeren after his men had extinguished the flames. Very uncharacteristically for such an efficient officer, he neglected to dispatch scouting parties to the surrounding region. His subordinates failed to establish outposts or even a perimeter of pickets, perhaps a sign of the growing inadequacy of the French command structure. Weary from the march, and believing the day's toils had ended, Reynier's men slumped down to prepare a late afternoon meal. Gen. Sahrer von Sahr's Twenty-fifth Saxon Division camped between the windmill hill on the left and Groß Beeren on the right. In the center General Durutte echeloned his Thirty-second Division rearward on the road between Groß Beeren and Neu Beeren, while Gen. Karl von Lecoq's Twenty-fourth Division held the rear farther down the road by Neu Beeren.[13]

Boyen observed the enemy position and found its weakness. He knew that Borstell would soon reach Klein Beeren and be in a position to attack Reynier's right flank. The open plain on Reynier's left would accommodate the Prussian cavalry. Boyen advised Bülow to attack the vulnerable French corps. Bülow agreed and ordered the battle to begin with an assault on Reynier's center and right with Groß Beeren as the

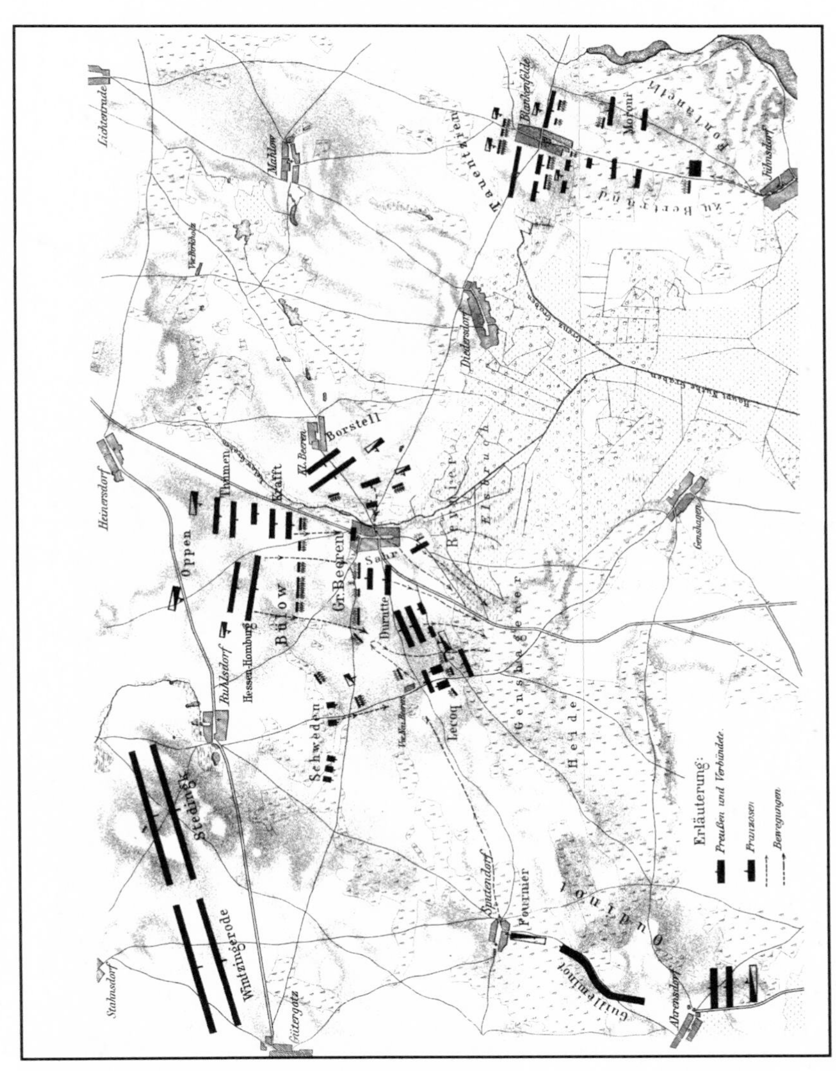

The Battle of Groß Beeren, 23 August 1813. From Friederich, *Die Befreiungskriege*, vol. 2.

objective. According to the orders of battle, Bülow's batteries would open the struggle from the right wing of the Prussian battle line. On the left Krafft's Sixth Brigade would advance on Groß Beeren; Hessen-Homburg's Third Brigade would form the right wing. As the reserve, Thümen's Fourth Brigade would follow Hessen-Homburg and steadily slide left to support Krafft's attack on Groß Beeren. As soon as Borstell arrived, his Fifth Brigade would proceed from Klein Beeren and attack Reynier's extreme right.[14]

Once the Prussian deployment began, Bülow dispatched Major von Reiche to army headquarters with a request for a diversion on Reynier's left flank. He told Reiche that by the time he reached Bernadotte the crown prince would already have heard the Prussian artillery. Bülow wanted him to present the issue as a fait accompli. After a short ride to Ruhlsdorf, Reiche found Bernadotte lounging under the windmill. His message enraged Bernadotte, who did not feel obligated to support Bülow. Reiche insisted that cooperation would only lead to victory. In verbal sparring, however, the loquacious crown prince outclassed the Prussian major. After repeated requests Bernadotte refused to assist Bülow, shrieking, "[T]he enemy is before me, each must defend his front!" Ultimately he dictated an order to Löwenhielm for Bülow to retake Groß Beeren—a mere formality since Bülow had already engaged Reynier.[15]

At Groß Beeren Hessen-Homburg's brigade led the advance of the Third Corps by debouching from Heinersdorf around 5:00 P.M. Six line battalions formed the first wave, followed by four Landwehr battalions and a light battalion. The brigade's cavalry covered the right flank. On the left Krafft's brigade deployed three line battalions in the first wave, supported by three line and three Landwehr battalions. Bülow arranged Thümen's reserve in three waves. An aid from Borstell's staff arrived to inform Bülow that the Fifth Brigade had reached Klein Beeren. All of the pieces were now in place. As Bülow's first wave of battalion columns approached the Saxons, a summer storm poured rain onto the combatants.

Taking shelter from the storm, Reynier's men finished their meals, believing that the soggy day would end quietly. Suddenly the sound of drumming and horns broke the calm of the French camp. Although the downpour limited visibility, the clamor made it clear that battle was sought. Reynier remained unmoved, thinking that Bertrand had already advanced through Blankenfelde and would be able to support

Gen. Jean-Louis-Ebénézer Reynier (1771–1814). After being captured at Leipzig, Reynier returned to France during the 1814 Campaign but died of gout on 27 February.

his right. Oudinot had also assured him that the Twelfth Corps and Third Cavalry Corps would be within supporting distance. Not unaccustomed to independent command, Reynier had found himself in a similar situation two years earlier when he held the Duke of Wellington at the battle of Sabugul in Portugal. The Calvinist heritage of Reynier, who was described as "silent, aloof, and taciturn," perhaps accounted for his unemotional, austere command style. A rocky relationship with Napoleon during the Consulate probably prevented Reynier from ever winning the coveted marshal's baton. Reynier was both a stolid leader and a quarrelsome subordinate, yet the emperor never failed to recognize his penchant for military discipline, order, and protocol.[16]

Before Bülow's artillery opened fire, a few tense moments passed between the Prussian and Russian artillery officers. Lieutenant-Colonel von Holtzendorf commanded Bülow's reserve artillery, which included two Russian twelve-pounder batteries commanded by Colonel Dietrichs, who had not yet resigned himself to obeying a junior officer. Just prior to the commencement of the cannonade Holtzendorf rode up to Dietrichs and requested that his two batteries move into the firing line. The Russian officer hesitated, and the two stared at each other for a few awkward seconds. Without wasting another moment Holtzendorf led the Prussian reserve batteries a few hundred yards forward and unlimbered. Dietrichs watched for some time before deciding to move into the Prussian battle line. Although Boyen claimed that after that moment the Russians became their "true, honorable comrades throughout the campaign," relations between the Russians and Prussians, especially the officers, were sometimes strained.[17]

Once the Russian artillery moved into line, Bülow opened the combat with a bombardment from 1,800 yards by eighteen twelve-pounders and twenty-eight six-pounders. Reynier answered with forty-four guns. After several minutes ten additional twelve-pounders from Bülow's second Russian battery as well as four more six-pounders advanced to within 1,200 yards and opened fire—Reynier's front now came under the fire of sixty-two Allied guns.[18] To the right a Prussian horse battery pushed too far forward and attracted fire from two Saxon batteries, which destroyed four guns and disabled a fifth. During the cannonade Borstell's advance units reached Klein Beeren. Finding it already occupied by Prussian light infantry, Borstell advanced his entire brigade through the village. He deployed his infantry southwest of Klein Beeren on the road to Groß Beeren and perpendicular to Reynier's right flank, while his cavalry filled the gap between the infantry and the Genshagen Forest. One foot battery and some horse artillery opened fire on a Saxon battalion that emerged from Groß Beeren. After forcing this battalion to retreat, Borstell directed his fire against two battalions posted at the forest's edge.

Bülow's infantry continued to advance under the fire of the Saxon batteries. To protect his infantry from the impact of the shells, Bülow ordered the battalions of the first wave to form long, thin lines. This proved to be a disaster since the mass column formation preserved morale. Only the rapid reorganization of the battalions into columns averted the destruction of Bülow's front line.[19] By 6:00 P.M. eighty-two

Allied guns finally overpowered Reynier's fire. Once the Saxon fire weakened, Bülow ordered a general attack with the bayonet since small arms could not be fired in the wet conditions. Oppen's cavalry also bore down on Reynier's left. Thümen's Fourth Brigade advanced from the rear of the battle line to fill a gap that had opened between Krafft and Hessen-Homburg. Bülow had little concern for his own right flank. If Oudinot advanced in force on this side, the Swedes, according to Bernadotte's own words, would be obliged to defend their front. For this reason Hessen-Homburg received orders to move out of the range of Reynier's artillery so that his men could recover from the shelling. Bülow now turned the whole weight of his attack against Reynier's right and advanced in an oblique order. Echeloned in battalion columns, 16,000 Prussians assailed Reynier's right wing of 7,000 Saxons. As the Kolberg Infantry Regiment of Krafft's brigade advanced on Groß Beeren, Bülow yelled to the lead battalion: "Swedes and Russians look to us, behind us lies Berlin: do not forget that you are Pomeranians."[20]

The stoic Reynier anchored his left wing by forming Lecoq's division into a large square with eight guns before the front and four on the left. A few moments later Prussian columns crashed into the Saxon line like waves on a beach. Bayonets slashed and musket butts swung; Allied artillery moved into range to fire on Reynier's reserves. On the far left of the Prussian line Borstell sent two battalions and two guns over the canal and into Groß Beeren, while two hussar squadrons swept south of the village. At the same time Krafft's First Kolberg Battalion attacked the front of Groß Beeren. The Saxons provided desperate resistance both in the village and along Sahr's front. Reynier redirected two Saxon battalions and a half battery from his left to slow Borstell, but Prussian artillery dispersed the Saxon reinforcements. Borstell's infantry then entered Groß Beeren from the east.

Reynier remained calm and ordered Sahr to counterattack Krafft. A Saxon regiment advanced in two battalion columns and overran a Landwehr battalion from Krafft's brigade. Two line battalions countered and held the Saxons. At this time Hessen-Homburg's lead battalions also came into line. Shouting insults at the Saxons, the Prussians charged with a fury.[21] With the prince personally leading the Third Battalion of the Fourth Reserve Regiment, the Prussians smashed into the Saxon front. Hessen-Homburg's pressure gradually broke Sahr's division, beginning with the regiment anchored to Groß Beeren. Prussian battalions rolled up Reynier's line and stormed his batteries. Moving through Groß Beeren, one Prussian company captured two guns. Farther south of the village two battalions captured a six-pounder foot battery. Only six shaken battalions from Sahr's division remained around the Groß Beeren windmill hill. Led by Sahr himself, the Saxons stubbornly defended the windmill against their hated neighbors. Sahr received three wounds while leading a bayonet attack. After vicious fighting the Saxons broke, yielding 330 prisoners. Despite the bloodshed, Sahr had achieved his purpose by providing time for some of his battalions to reach the safety of the forest. Only four disabled six-pounders remained on the windmill hill.

South of Groß Beeren Prussian cavalry fell on some of Sahr's retreating infantry that could not reach the forest. Borstell's Third Pomeranian Hussar Squadron cut through a battalion square and took several prisoners. Saxon Uhlans countered, freed a majority of their comrades, and forced the Prussians to seek protection behind their own infantry. The First Kolberg Battalion formed a large square with two other battalions from the Fifth Reserve Regiment. Thümen's First Pomeranian Landwehr Cavalry Regiment came up, attacked the Saxon Uhlans, captured their commander, and pursued them to the swamp.

With the collapse of his right wing, Reynier moved Durutte's division into line. Borstell, however, had already won the southern exit of the village and greeted Durutte's troops with case-shot. His battalions then engaged Durutte's infantry. After a brief clash the French receded. Inexplicable panic seized the division, which, up to that point, had stood behind the Saxons and out of the range of Bülow's artillery. Seeing the Saxons retreat only accelerated the collapse of discipline and order in the French ranks. The majority of Durutte's men threw down their guns and fled into the forest—leaving a wounded Durutte in their wake.[22] Two battalions retained their composure long enough to cover the retreat. Under their protection the division melted into the woods. After the Frenchmen disgraced themselves, Reynier turned to his other Saxon division and ordered General von Lecoq to retake the windmill hill in order to cover the retreat to Wietstock. The Saxons ferociously stormed the hill and stunned the disorganized Prussians. Lecoq's men dispersed Hessen-Homburg's lead battalions, but his second wave charged up the hill. After savage combat the Prussians drove Lecoq's Saxons from the windmill. Hessen-Homburg's battalions pursued, followed by twenty six-pounders and twelve Russian twelve-pounders. Darkness fell, and Reynier had no reserve left to commit. He instructed Lecoq to withdraw, form a square at the entrance of the forest, and cover the retreat down the Neu Beeren road. The battle ended with Reynier's corps in full retreat.[23]

A bottleneck at Wietstock slowed Reynier's retreat and forced Lecoq's Saxons to fight a desperate battle against superior Prussian numbers. Bülow's skirmishers penetrated the wood south of Neu Beeren and spread panic among the retreating French and Saxons. Just as the Prussian cavalry prepared to capture a twelve-pounder battery, a strong cavalry force appeared on the right. Although darkness and smoke limited vision, French cavalry could be seen moving southwest of Neu Beeren at Sputendorf; they belonged to Gen. François Fournier's division of Arrighi's Third Cavalry Corps. Arrighi and Oudinot had led their corps on the highway to Ahrensdorf when they heard the cannonade from Groß Beeren. Oudinot released Fournier's cavalry and Gen. Armand-Charles Guilleminot's infantry division to march to the sound of the guns. Moving through the thick forest, they hoped to assist the Seventh Corps but did not arrive until the combat had ended. Fournier's cavalry deployed onto the plain, while the infantry remained concealed in the forest.

The appearance of this new foe prevented the Prussian cavalry from routing Reynier's corps. Alarmed, Bülow sent an aide to army headquarters with a request for Swedish cavalry and artillery support at Neu Beeren.[24] He also directed two reserve cavalry regiments to Neu Beeren, where they encountered the French cavalry. The Prussian cavalry charged Fournier's 2,000 troopers. Surprised by the night assault, the French were pressed against the forest and scattered in several directions. A portion fled into the forest, while others surrendered to the Prussians.[25] The majority galloped onto the plain between Groß Beeren and Heinersdorf, where they were either captured or ridden down by the pursuing Prussian cavalry. In the confusion a group rode right through Bülow's staff and past the general, who mistook them for celebrating Prussians![26] Guilleminot withdrew his infantry after observing Fournier's debacle.

The French cavalry did distract the Prussians long enough to allow the last Saxon troops of Reynier's corps to recede into the forest. A Swedish horse battery escorted by some cavalry finally appeared on the field, but it was too late to make any significant contribution. Nothing more could be accomplished except dispersing the fugitives with a few shots. By 9:00 P.M. darkness covered the field. With exhausted

Gen. Jean-Toussaint Arrighi (1778–1853). Napoleon's cousin through marriage, Arrighi became governor of Corsica during the first Bourbon restoration.

troops and fresh enemy forces in the vicinity, pursuit was out of the question. Prussian losses at the battle of Groß Beeren numbered 159 dead, 662 wounded, 228 missing, and 6 guns destroyed. Bülow's men captured 14 guns and 52 filled ammunition carts.[27] Reynier's two Saxon divisions lost 20 officers and 1,918 soldiers, while the French division lost 1,138 men.[28] Saxon prisoners received brutal treatment at the hands of their Prussian captors, who tauntingly assured them that they would now be going to Berlin. Saxons who begged for mercy on the grounds that they were German and not French only received harsher beatings. Saxon officers, after being stripped of their valuables, were thrown into the mud.[29] The demoralizing effects of defeat, however, proved far worse than Reynier's modest losses. The Seventh Corps needed a few days to reorganize. Reynier's reverse at Groß Beeren also completely disheartened Oudinot, who ordered the entire Army of Berlin to retreat to the safety of Wittenberg.[30]

As the Army of Berlin withdrew to the Elbe, the French commanders fired salvos not at the Allies but at each other in an attempt to defray the guilt. Oudinot blamed Reynier for rashly advancing. Reynier felt that he had been abandoned by Oudinot and Bertrand.[31] Moreover, Davout and the other supporting units also failed to achieve their objectives. Confronted by Wallmoden's Landwehr force of 18,463 infantry, 7,096 cavalry, and 60 guns, an uncharacteristically cautious Davout did not press his advance but halted at Schwerin. Reynier's repulse at Groß Beeren and Oudinot's subsequent retreat exposed Davout's right. This news prompted the "Iron Marshal" to end his offensive and eventually withdraw to Hamburg.[32] To the right of Bernadotte's army Hirschfeld left Saarmund to block Girard's advance from Magdeburg.

As disruptive as the defeat at Groß Beeren proved to be for French strategy, the combat itself served as a defining moment for the architects of the new Prussian army. Although historian F. L. Petre wrote that Groß Beeren was "of no real importance to either side," all of the key ingredients were present to either substantiate or refute five years of reform in Prussia.[33] Without a doubt, the victory silenced critics who still questioned the combat-efficiency of the Prussian troops, especially the Landwehr. In this battle, which took place only a short march south of Berlin, the Prussian soldiers truly fought for hearth and home. Fighting before the gates of their national capital certainly provided a poetic setting to test the resolve of the line troops, the reliability of the Landwehr, and the patriotism of both. By no means, however, can Oudinot's Army of Berlin be compared to the Grande Armée that overran Prussia in 1806 under Napoleon's personal command. Although the conscripts in the ranks of the Grande Armée of 1813 lacked the same quality, tactical skill, and vital élan that had given the French army vast superiority in 1805, 1806, and 1807, they proved reliable and tenacious during the spring campaign. Reynier's Saxons, in garrison during the battles of Lützen and Bautzen, harbored no love for the Prussians; nor could the slightest hint of pan-German nationalism be detected.

The excellent relationship between Bülow and Boyen exemplified the military marriage between senior commanders and their chief staff officers. Their close cooperation symbolized the harmony between the old and new elements in the Prussian army. They based their opposition to a withdrawal behind the Havel-Spree line on sound military judgment as well as patriotic sentiments for the Prussian capital. Bülow and Boyen correctly assessed the need to accept battle south of the city in order to avoid the demoralizing effects of losing the capital.[34] Their commitment to offensive operations exemplified the new aggressive leadership of the Prussian army of 1813. Had the Prussians been defeated at Groß Beeren, Bernadotte's remaining corps would have been enveloped or forced to retreat behind the Havel-Spree line. Conversely, had Bülow retreated before Reynier, both Tauentzien and Bernadotte would have been threatened by Reynier's advance. Either way, the loss of the capital would have disheartened the Prussian army and people at a moment when national expectations and sacrifices demanded decisive action.

On the day after the battle Bülow wrote a modest report to the king that described the battle as "an artillery combat," where the Russian and Prussian gunners distinguished themselves. He emphasized that he rather than the crown prince had decided to attack the enemy. Bülow's report also praised the performance of his troops. "I must congratulate the entire corps, including the Landwehr," he noted. "Many enemy squares were attacked and dispersed with the bayonet. Without exaggerating, I believe that if it were not for the darkness and the exceedingly bad weather, the corps of General Reynier would have been destroyed. With the exception of the Russian artillery and Cossacks assigned to me, the troops of Your Royal Majesty fought alone. Only four Swedish guns supported by some infantry and cavalry crossed the distance, but took no decisive part."[35]

Groß Beeren provided much needed confidence for the recruits as well as the veterans. Even Bülow, an officer in the Prussian army for over thirty years, could not contain his pride. In a letter to his wife he compared Reynier's retreat "to that of Auerstädt—the whole road was strewn with full ammunition wagons left behind!" He assured Pauline that the war "goes badly for Napoleon."[36] Weather conditions did ease the horrors of combat for the inexperienced Prussian soldiers. Due to the constant downpour, small arms could not fire, and the Prussians received only a limited taste of the enemy's musketry. Nevertheless, the rigorous and terrifying ordeal of hand-to-hand combat demanded bravery and determination. The Landwehr fought alongside the line throughout the battle, and Bülow issued a very complimentary order of the day that recognized the militia's efforts. "The Landwehr of the corps has earned a glorious distinction," wrote Bülow. "On this day, they have proved their love for King and Fatherland for the first time. No greater praise could they acquire than to be compared to their veteran comrades."[37] A report from the staff of the Third Brigade also praised the Landwehr for "advancing with great calm and determination under the heaviest cannon fire and likewise for the numerous bayonet attacks."[38]

Although Bülow was the victor at Groß Beeren, some historians have accused him of insubordination.[39] The arguments behind these charges stem from his modification of Bernadotte's instructions yet fail to consider the consequences had Bülow strictly obeyed orders. His modification of Bernadotte's orders to Borstell on the night of 22–23 August enabled the Fifth Brigade to flank Reynier's corps. Bülow's opposition to the Ruhlsdorf position on the twenty-third enabled him to be in a position to repulse Reynier at Groß Beeren. His suggestion that Tauentzien take a position at Blankenfelde rather than Klein Beeren also proved crucial in stopping Bertrand's advance on the twenty-third. Had Bertrand proceeded through this village, he would have enveloped Bülow at Groß Beeren. Bülow probably would have been defeated, Bernadotte probably would have retreated over the Spree, and Berlin probably would have fallen. The Allies did fail to execute a proper pursuit on the night of 23 August, and Bülow shares some of the blame. Bernadotte, however, had the opportunity to close the Neu Beeren road with either the Russians or Swedes. Instead of pursuing, the crown prince remained idle, as he had throughout the day. Had the Russians advanced down the highway from Gütergotz to Ahrensdorf, and Bülow's entire corps pursued, both Reynier and Oudinot could have been destroyed. Reynier's only line of retreat would have been over the small dam at Wietstock. With the Russians attacking the flank and front, and Bülow pressing the rear, both corps might have been routed. Such a victory would have crippled Napoleon's ability to execute the "master plan" and would have forced him to divert valuable manpower from the Grande Armée to hold the Elbe against the Army of North Germany. Nevertheless, neither Bülow's victory at Groß Beeren nor Oudinot's subsequent retreat induced the crown prince to launch an offensive. Instead the Army of Berlin lived to fight another day.

10

The Politics of Dissension

Bülow's victory at Groß Beeren certainly boosted the morale of the Prussian capital. Reports of the French advance on 22 August had placed the population in perpetual fear. According to the journal of Bülow's sister-in-law, Friederike von Auer, "it started to rain heavily in the afternoon. It was Sunday, August 22. Bülow's troops fought upon various points, yet despite their bravery, they had to retreat due to the enemy's superiority. One heard the intermittent cannon fire in the distance; it was an unusually anxious day. The population of Berlin was terrified. Messengers reported that the enemy was only three miles from Berlin; we all went to bed in inexpressible excitement and apprehension." During the battle itself the Berliners could clearly hear the artillery. Auer noted that "the rain fell in torrents, and in its midst the thunder of the guns grew louder; our fear became indescribable! It may have been 2:00 P.M. when I walked out upon the balcony facing the street in order to look at the wagons filled with wounded men that came from the Potsdam Gate along the Wilhelmstraße to take the road to the hospital. The cannonade became louder and louder. The large crystal chandeliers in the hall trembled and clinked throughout it." That night Bülow's messengers delivered news of the victory, and word spread quickly. "On the morning of the twenty-fourth all of Berlin celebrated," recalled Auer. "Bülow sent the captured enemy guns and prisoners to the city. This was a new sight for the inhabitants."[1] The victory not only boosted the spirits of the Berliners but provided an opportunity for civilians to express their gratitude and patriotism. Despite the rain, crowds streamed to Groß Beeren on the twenty-fourth, bringing carts loaded with food and wagons for the wounded. Auer fondly recorded that "a crowd of people hurried to the battlefield. The thankful citizens brought a long line of wagons filled with food and drink; they transported the wounded to the city hospital, where warm-hearted women took care of them."[2]

Pleased with the victory, the crown prince also rode out to inspect the battlefield on the twenty-fourth. Bülow, who was angry over Bernadotte's inactivity during the battle, avoided him. Rather than report to the crown prince personally, he submitted his account in writing. To make matters worse, the Berlin magistrate, Büsching, also sent a deputation to thank the victor. Perhaps due to the tense relationship between Bülow and their chief, Büsching's representatives ignored Bülow and only praised the crown prince. Boyen felt that the gesture to thank Bernadotte was appropriate, but he criticized the delegation, who drove "through the middle of Bülow's quarters and the bivouacs of his troops, seeing their wounded countrymen who had really fought to save the Fatherland, and on their return from headquarters said nothing, but passed by rather snobbishly." Reiche wrote: "Inexplicable and shocking were the actions of the Berlin magistrate, who sent a delegation that passed by Bülow, hardly acknowledging him, in order to visit the crown prince of Sweden to thank him for saving Berlin."[3]

Since landing in Stralsund on 18 May Bernadotte had won the adoration of the Prussian public. In her memoirs Friederike von Auer described the excitement that Bernadotte's arrival in Berlin had caused: "The Berliners, who thrive on sensation, were delighted. The former French Marshal, Bernadotte, named the Prince of Ponte Corvo by Napoleon and afterward adopted by the old, childless King of Sweden to be the crown prince, certainly had to know how to defeat the French. A cheering crowd of citizens greeted his arrival in Berlin. The ladies wore round Swedish hats with yellow and blue feathers, the national colors of Sweden. . . . I took the opportunity to listen to exalted speeches at a great parade in the Tiergarten where I observed this hero."[4] Now, on the day after Prussia's response to the French cannonade at Valmy twenty-one years earlier, Bernadotte received the city's deputation and presented an inaccurate account of the battle, implying that it had been won by him and the entire army. He took the liberty to state Bülow's losses, while exaggerating the casualties suffered by the Swedes and Russians. This provoked deep indignation among the Prussians. Boyen recalled how this adversely affected relations with the crown prince: "There are no roses without thorns, and this victory proved to be no exception; tension between Bernadotte and Bülow considerably increased. . . . This day of rest, hardly fitting after a victory, only added to Bülow's despondence."[5]

Oudinot believed that his operation against Berlin had failed and so began his retreat to Wittenberg on the twenty-fourth, but he had little to fear from the Army of North Germany. On that day the Prussian Third Corps rested, and the crown prince rejected Bülow's request for a general advance. Bülow had to be content with forwarding cavalry patrols to the passes over the Nuthe Canal.[6] Only Cossacks pursued Oudinot's army, but at least Berlin was safe for the moment. A portion of the Army of North Germany finally began the pursuit on 25 August. Reports stated that Oudinot had vacated the Nuthe-Notte line and continued his march south to the Elbe.[7] The two Prussian corps advanced to the southern edge of the defense line, and their vanguards pushed as far as Baruth and Kummersdorf. A Russian advance unit also reached Beelitz.[8] Not only did Wintzingerode's main body and the entire Swedish corps remain in their camps, but Bernadotte transferred his headquarters rearward to Teltow, thereby renewing Bülow's suspicions of a retreat over the Havel-Spree line.

In the midst of these movements the corps commanders received the *Fifth Bulletin* of the Army of North Germany, which contained the crown prince's account of Groß Beeren. Bernadotte mixed flattery with statements that Bülow called absolute lies. According to the crown prince, after Reynier had occupied Groß Beeren, "General Bülow received orders to attack; he executed it with the determination of a skilled general. The troops marched with the calmness that distinguished the soldiers of the Great Frederick in the Seven Years' War."[9] Except for a brief reference to a Prussian bayonet charge, Bernadotte attributed the victory to the Swedes and Russians, who had supposedly repulsed Oudinot's corps and then forced Reynier to retreat. Bülow called the crown prince's version of the battle a "miserable concoction." Writing to his wife, he claimed to have "asked the crown prince several times to commit the Swedes, since he could cut off the enemy's retreat, but he did nothing. It pleases me that we did everything on our own."[10] Such propaganda was not new to Bernadotte. He had been embarrassed and condemned by Napoleon for issuing a bulletin to his Saxon Corps after the battle of Wagram on 5–6 July 1809, which praised their victory although they had panicked and fled.[11]

Like most generals, Bülow was concerned about public opinion, and he became enraged when the Military Government in Berlin published the Bulletin in the city newspapers.[12] Bernadotte's apparent attempt to take credit for what he believed to be his victory prompted Bülow to draft a simple description of the battle and submit it to the Military Government for publication in the city press. His story made it clear that he had decided to attack Reynier and had then reported his decision to the crown prince.[13] Bülow learned that the Military Government refused to publish his story. According to Civil Governor Sack, the two censors (the chief of police, Lecocq, and his boss, the minister of police, Prince Wilhelm von Sayn-Wittgenstein) rejected Bülow's article because the crown prince wanted only his accounts published. The Prussian censors also refused to publish Bülow's version, since Bernadotte's account stated that Bülow had received the order to attack Groß Beeren.[14] A long and heated correspondence ensued between Bülow and Wittgenstein. This flabbergasted Bülow, who could not understand why Wittgenstein and Lecocq were so "willing to obey the orders of a foreigner." Instead he suggested that it would "be better to insure that no ridiculous news is printed in the newspapers that would offend the German character. The crown prince has command over the army but no right to suppress publications in the Prussian state, and even less to lie about the Prussian troops in his bulletins. The people have a right to know about their soldiers, and the Prussian commander has the duty to publish" this news.[15]

As much as Bülow claimed to be the victor of Groß Beeren, Grand Allied Headquarters showered the crown prince of Sweden with the rewards. Bernadotte received the coveted Grand Cross of the Iron Cross of 1813—the most prestigious decoration of the Prussian army; only seven were ever awarded.[16] Not to be outdone, Tsar Alexander awarded him the Grand Cross of the Order of St. George, while the Austrians reciprocated with the Grand Cross of the Order of Maria Theresa. Bülow only received the oak leaves for his *pour le mérite* decoration that he had won during the siege of Mainz in 1793; Oppen received the same award. Since the sovereigns did not acknowledge the importance of Bülow's contribution by awarding him a higher distinction, his men felt that Grand Allied Headquarters did not appreciate their efforts.[17]

Aside from the fallout caused by the victory at Groß Beeren, the Army of North Germany still had to confront Oudinot's Army of Berlin. On 26 August the Allies pursued Oudinot slowly and cautiously. West of the Nuthe the Swedes and Russians moved south, while both Prussian corps debouched from the Nuthe-Notte line. Russian cavalry patrolled the region north of Wittenberg in a wide arc. Bernadotte also recommended the completion and expansion of the entrenchments on the Nuthe-Notte line.[18] Bülow's headquarters viewed this order with suspicion, since it implied that the crown prince might be content with Groß Beeren and refrain from pursuing his former countrymen.

On 27 and 28 August the army remained idle; only the advance guards and wing detachments moved south. On the army's right flank, however, Hirschfeld defeated Girard at Hagelberg on the twenty-seventh. Hirschfeld had been ordered to cover the right wing of the army and observe Girard's division. He had positioned his main body at Brandenburg, while a vanguard of six battalions, three squadrons, and three guns under Putlitz observed Magdeburg. Between 21 and 23 August Girard's force of 8,000 infantry, 900 cavalry, and 23 guns chased Putlitz back to Brandenburg. As Putlitz retreated, Hirschfeld moved his main body closer to Berlin. In accordance with Bernadotte's orders, he left two Landwehr battalions in the entrenchments at Potsdam and marched to Saarmund. On the twenty-third, as the Army of North Germany faced the Army of Berlin before the gates of the Prussian capital, Hirschfeld arranged his battalions in battle-order at Saarmund but never received orders to march to the sound of the guns. On the following day he led his brigade back to Brandenburg, where he reunited with Putlitz on the twenty-fifth.

Girard continued his march to Ziesar and pushed an advance guard to within a few marches of Brandenburg. Lacking accurate information about Girard's strength and intentions, Hirschfeld ordered Marwitz to conduct reconnaissance with four Landwehr battalions and four Landwehr squadrons. Marwitz returned to Brandenburg that evening and provided the necessary details: Girard's infantry stood in Ziesar, his cavalry slightly to the northeast.[19] At dawn on the twenty-fifth Putlitz's advance guard marched directly south to Golzow. After allowing his troops some rest, Hirschfeld followed that night with the whole corps. At Golzow the Prussians learned that Girard had turned southeast and marched toward Belzig to cover Oudinot's retreat. Hirschfeld now made great use of interior lines to execute a brilliant maneuver on the twenty-sixth. First he marched west from Golzow to Ziesar. From there the Prussians turned southeast toward Görzke. That night his troops camped in the region between Görzke and Ziesar, west of Girard's position at Lübnitz. Before sunrise on the twenty-seventh Hirschfeld assembled his troops in the vicinity of Görzke and began the march east to Benken in two columns. Reports convinced Hirschfeld that Girard's attention remained fixed on Belzig. Unknown to Hirschfeld, Chernyshov had led five Cossack regiments west from Belzig and harassed the French throughout the previous day. At Benken, Hirschfeld's corps stood just northwest of Girard's position at Lübnitz. To prevent him from reaching Oudinot, Hirschfeld decided to attack the French position with his 10,350 infantry, 960 cavalry, and 11 guns. With the exception of four line battalions, Hirschfeld's brigade consisted of thirteen Kurmark Landwehr battalions and twelve squadrons of Kurmark Landwehr cavalry. Only ten days after the expiration of the armistice the Kurmark Landwehr faced its first real test in the field against Girard's French division.[20]

Combat lasted for five hours and culminated with Hirschfeld's order for a general attack on Hagelberg. One French battalion barricaded itself behind the village's garden walls. A bloody melee ensued, where the musket-butt proved more effective than the bayonet. Girard was seriously wounded during this fighting, and a large gap opened between his left and center: the rout was on. Eight Russian guns unlimbered on the windmill at Hagelberg to fire on the withdrawing French battalions. Girard's rearguard held Klein Glein, before withdrawing to Groß Glein as night fell. Under the cover of darkness the French withdrew in two columns, one west to Magdeburg, the other south to Wittenberg. Cossacks pursued, but Hirschfeld led the majority of his brigade to camp in Lübnitz. The French lost 3,000 casualties, 3,000 prisoners, 6,000 muskets, 20 powder wagons, 8 guns, and Girard's baggage. According to reports, only 1,700 men returned to Magdeburg. Hirschfeld's losses totaled 37 officers and 1,722 men.[21] Hagelberg provided a great victory for the Kurmark Landwehr and rewarded Bülow's hard work during the armistice. The battle also provides another glaring example of the failures of independent command by Napoleon's lieutenants.

Coming only four days after Groß Beeren, Hagelberg certainly bolstered the increasing confidence of the Prussians. After removing Girard's

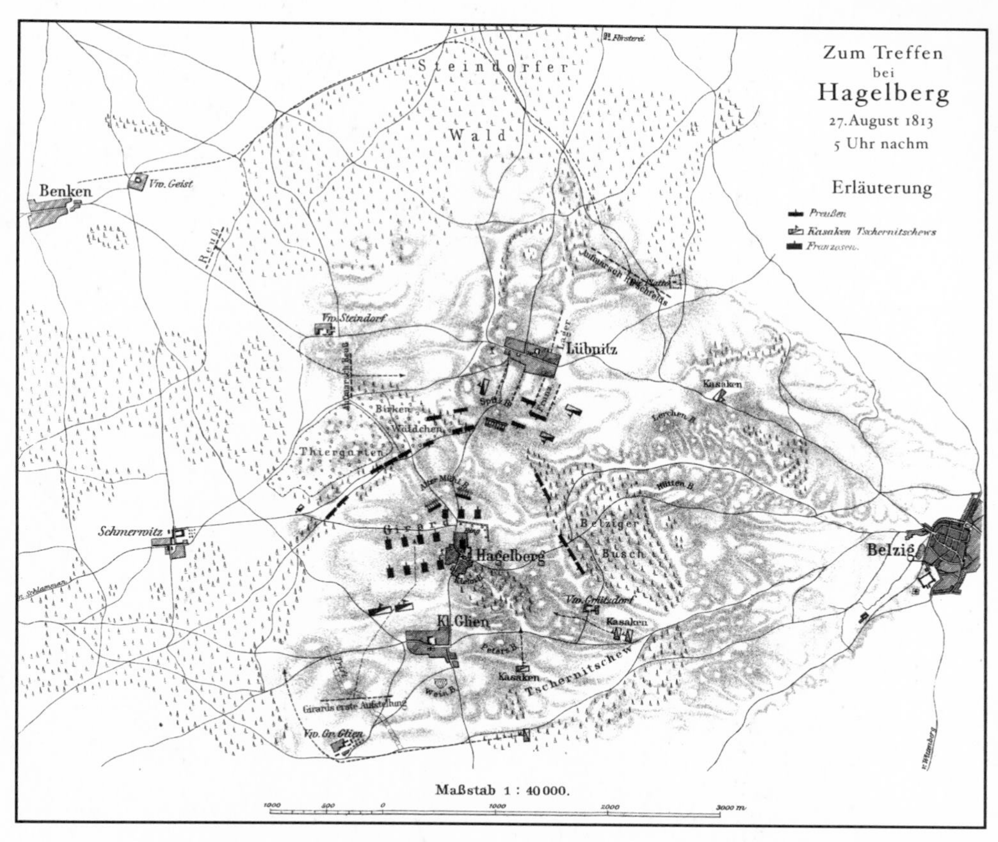

The Battle of Hagelberg, 27 August 1813. From Friederich, *Die Befreiungskriege*, vol. 2.

threat, Bernadotte could have used Hirschfeld to sweep around the right flank and rear of Oudinot's retreating army. Despite another victory, the Army of North Germany continued to creep forward, much to Bülow's chagrin. He compared the army's march to a "snail's-pace" and explained to his wife that Bernadotte's passivity had allowed the French to escape to the Elbe. "I have never experienced anything more pitiful than this," he grumbled. "Today I will make a short, completely useless march to Beelitz." In addition to feeling ill and having a nasty cough—the consequences of getting drenched during the heavy rains of the twenty-third—he described the supply situation as horrible. "You cannot get anything [to eat]," he lamented.[22] If a Prussian general had reason to complain, the misery of the troops must have been indescribable. Bülow also described to his pregnant wife the hardships of campaigning and being away from his two children:

> The weather is already so bad that it seems like the month of November—please send me one or two warm camisoles . . . they must be long and wide. Also send me some wine from Herr Maire; I will send him the money for it at once. I wish I could be with you for a few hours to see your new furniture and to see how my little Albert walks all by himself. I will not be happy until I can return to my family. Tell Marianne to learn how to write so she can send me a letter. Choose a doctor; the time of delivery must be soon. Kiss the children for me. The local region has been spared by the enemy, but very hard hit by the Russians. . . . Send me a few bottles of cognac also. I will try to force the crown prince of Sweden to move forward, but it is difficult. Today is another lost day.[23]

On 29 August outpost fighting erupted along the entire front. Tauentzien's vanguard surprised a French force at Luckau, capturing 9 guns and 1,000 prisoners.[24] At Jüterbog, however, the French proved more resilient and repulsed a combined Prusso-Russian force.[25] Although Oudinot continued his retreat to Wittenberg, he had little knowledge of Bernadotte's movements. According to Baron Lejeune:

> [W]e were quite ignorant of the very names of the generals opposed to us, of the number of their troops, or the positions they occupied. There is no doubt that the Emperor provided ample means for organizing an efficient system of espionage and paying for secret service of various kinds, but the avarice of many of those in command of French forces led them to appropriate the money to their own use, when they ought to have expended it lavishly in obtaining information about the enemy. We really did not know whether we were about to fight Russians, Prussians, or Austrians. We therefore had to maneuver altogether in the dark.[26]

Cossacks swarmed the perimeter of Oudinot's army; their persistence hampered French reconnaissance.

Although the Allied army did move south, Bülow's frustration increased. "Today, during our snail's-pace pursuit, I have advanced to Treuenbrietzen," he complained to his wife:

> The enemy is in full retreat to Wittenberg. I have sent Borstell and Oppen to pursue him; perhaps we can achieve something further, but we could have destroyed him. Hopefully we will advance tomorrow, but not much will remain on this side of the Elbe. Our country is now cleansed and hopefully safe from this war. The Berlin residents can rejoice. My passionate wish is that the war will be conducted with all vivacity so that it ends soon, and I can return to my family. Hopefully the peace will last for a long time and the state will be restored to its former strength; I do not doubt this will occur. My only wish is that I soon receive news of your successful delivery.[27]

Not only did the pace of the pursuit aggravate Bülow, but the crown prince followed up his 26 August recommendation to continue construction on the Nuthe-Notte line with a direct order to resume work on the fortifications. The various combats prior to Groß Beeren had partially destroyed the entrenchments along the Nuthe-Notte line, and Bernadotte realized that they might still be useful. He instructed Bülow to have the Military Government repair the fortifications from Trebbin to Wietstock in the shortest possible time.[28] The thought of retreating back to the line rather than pursuing the enemy did not please Bülow. Frederick William's refusal to replace Krusemarck prompted Bülow to dispatch Major von Kalkreuth from his own staff to army headquarters. Although more persuasive than Krusemarck, Kalkreuth also failed to spur Bernadotte. Tension between the Prussians and the crown prince increased with each day. The inactivity agitated Bülow for both personal and professional reasons. He simply wanted the war to end quickly and victoriously so that he could return to his wife and children. On his behalf, Boyen made daily visits to army headquarters to urge Bernadotte forward and to recite Bülow's two main requests: a rapid pursuit of Oudinot's army and an operation against Napoleon's communications. Both adhered to the Trachenberg Plan and would have supported the Bohemian and Silesian Armies. Despite the soundness of his proposals, Boyen's missions proved fruitless. In fact he described his visits with the crown prince as "painful business" and compared them to threshing empty wheat.[29]

Bernadotte's procrastination continued on the thirtieth, when he declared a day of rest for the entire army.[30] The slow pursuit caused the Allied forward posts to lose track of the French. On the following day Bülow had to conduct a general reconnaissance with his reserve cavalry to find Oudinot's army.[31] After a relatively short ride the Prussians debouched from a wood and found themselves facing the right flank and rear of a French camp near Marzahna, much farther north than reports had indicated. Oppen urged a surprise attack, but Bülow did not want to risk his small force. Their presence did not go unnoticed, and the French quickly wheeled some artillery against the interlopers. Bülow retreated, hurried along by case-shot.[32]

Intimidated by Bülow's appearance, as well as the Cossacks that continuously harassed his flanks and rear, Oudinot left a rearguard in the woods by Thießen and Kropstädt and withdrew to Wittenberg. Bülow, Tauentzien, and Wintzingerode urged Bernadotte to engage the French before they reached the safety of Wittenberg's guns.[33] The crown prince responded by giving the entire army another day of rest on 2 September. Bülow dispatched Boyen to army headquarters with a plan to attack the French on the open terrain west of Wittenberg.[34] Bernadotte appeared to accept this suggestion. A satisfied Boyen returned to Bülow with the great news, but orders to implement the plan never came. Instead Bülow's corps moved into a position between Kropstädt and Thießen. Bülow again sent Boyen to army headquarters to explain to Bernadotte the folly of dispersing the army around a concentrated enemy. Boyen experienced the first of several heated confrontations with Bernadotte that he endured on Bülow's behalf. Boyen recalled:

> It is always difficult to conduct a hypothetical argument against a superior, moreover in a foreign language, and I will not deny that now and then I became too animated to be able to select the most appropriate words. For my part, this did no good, and the crown prince appeared to believe that I was the real source of Bülow's opposition toward him. This, however, was not really the case, and although I chiefly agreed with Bülow's military views, and he with my suggestions, I had never encouraged his disrespectful remarks; on the contrary, I always tried to calm him as much as possible.[35]

While Boyen presented his case at army headquarters, Bülow attacked the French positions south of Thießen. Combat took place in the woods, and Borstell's brigade did not fare well. Reinforcements had to be brought up to drive the French deeper into the wood. After sustaining 200 casualties, Bülow withdrew his men and established an outpost perimeter. The French withdrew to Trajuhn and the protection of Wittenberg's guns. That night the Army of North Germany formed a wide arc around the fortress. To the right Wintzingerode's Russians camped on the heights around Dobien. North of them the Swedes bivouacked at Rabenstein. Borstell's brigade, camped around Köpnick, held Bernadotte's center. Krafft's Sixth Brigade stood at Kropstädt, while Bülow took his headquarters farther to the north at Marzahna with the Third and Fourth Brigades. Due to the region's scarce water supply, Oppen's reserve cavalry bivouacked east of Werkzahna, where the small Zahna River could sustain his horses.[36] Dobschütz, temporarily under Bülow's command, posted his brigade of mostly Landwehr regiments to the left at Zahna.[37] Tauentzien's corps, now reduced to one brigade of 12,000 men and 24 guns, received orders to march from Luckau to rejoin the army.[38] He reached Seyda on the afternoon of 4 September to fill the large gap between the army's left and the Elbe.[39]

Although the Army of North Germany had gradually moved forward, the French army—should it suddenly be spurred into action—could break out at any point, brush aside Tauentzien's weak corps, and take the open roads to Berlin or Torgau in order to unite with reinforcements coming from Dresden. Oudinot's retreat did indicate that he did not wish to fight, but a change in command or the arrival of Napoleon himself could alter the situation completely. Bülow continued to urge the crown prince to be more aggressive, but his suggestions went unheeded. He tried one last time and wrote a long letter to the crown prince on the fourth. He began by stating the obvious: during the twelve days since Groß Beeren Oudinot had only retreated. All reports confirmed that the Allied army outnumbered Oudinot's forces, a portion of which had purportedly withdrawn over the Elbe. Prisoners claimed that Oudinot's supply had steadily dwindled and that despair—the natural consequence of a lost battle and accompanying retreat—had weakened morale. Logistical problems also mounted, as the burden of supplying the army fell on Prussia's dwindling resources. He warned that if the army maintained its current position much longer, "the meager resources still offered by the land will be exhausted, and the siege and blockade of Wittenberg, as well as any operation on this side of the Elbe, if misfortune necessitates it, will be much more difficult. The means by which a soldier is forced to exist in an area devastated by the enemy—combined with inactivity—make him very recalcitrant."[40]

From a strategic viewpoint Bülow also expressed concern over allowing Oudinot to remain at Wittenberg in communication with Napoleon. He reminded Bernadotte that Napoleon could "arrive in Wittenberg at any time to encourage his troops, bring reinforcements, begin an offensive, and seize the initiative." Oudinot had to be attacked, and Bülow assured the crown prince that the troops desired to fight. "This moment is full of advantages for us, and we must use it," he concluded.[41] Bülow's letter failed to change Bernadotte's mind. For political reasons that became increasingly clear to the Prussians, he refused to go on the offensive.[42] A second French operation against Berlin soon exploited Bernadotte's lethargy.

11

DENNEWITZ

As noted, Napoleon marched against Blücher after the expiration of the armistice. In accordance with the Trachenberg Plan, Blücher had retreated. While pursuing Blücher, Napoleon learned on 23 August that Schwarzenberg was advancing on Dresden. Not wanting to lose his base, the emperor left Macdonald in command of the Army of the Bober and raced back to the Saxon capital. Before departing he instructed Macdonald to hold the Bober and continue to shield Oudinot's operation from a possible flank attack by Blücher.[1] Despite Napoleon's orders, Macdonald continued the offensive. In a driving rain Blücher attacked Macdonald's army as it attempted to cross the swollen Katzbach River on the twenty-sixth. Not only did Macdonald lose 15,000 men, but the Army of the Bober collapsed.

Meanwhile at Dresden Napoleon defeated Schwarzenberg's Army of Bohemia during two days of heavy fighting on the twenty-sixth and twenty-seventh that cost the Allies 35,000 casualties.[2] A subsequent disaster, however, marred the emperor's victory. Schwarzenberg's army retreated into Bohemia during the night of 30 August, and Napoleon dispatched Gen. Dominique Vandamme's First Corps in pursuit. As Vandamme engaged the Russians, Kleist's Prussian corps caught the rear of the French force near Kulm. Vandamme, himself taken prisoner, lost approximately 15,000 men. The successive failures of Napoleon's

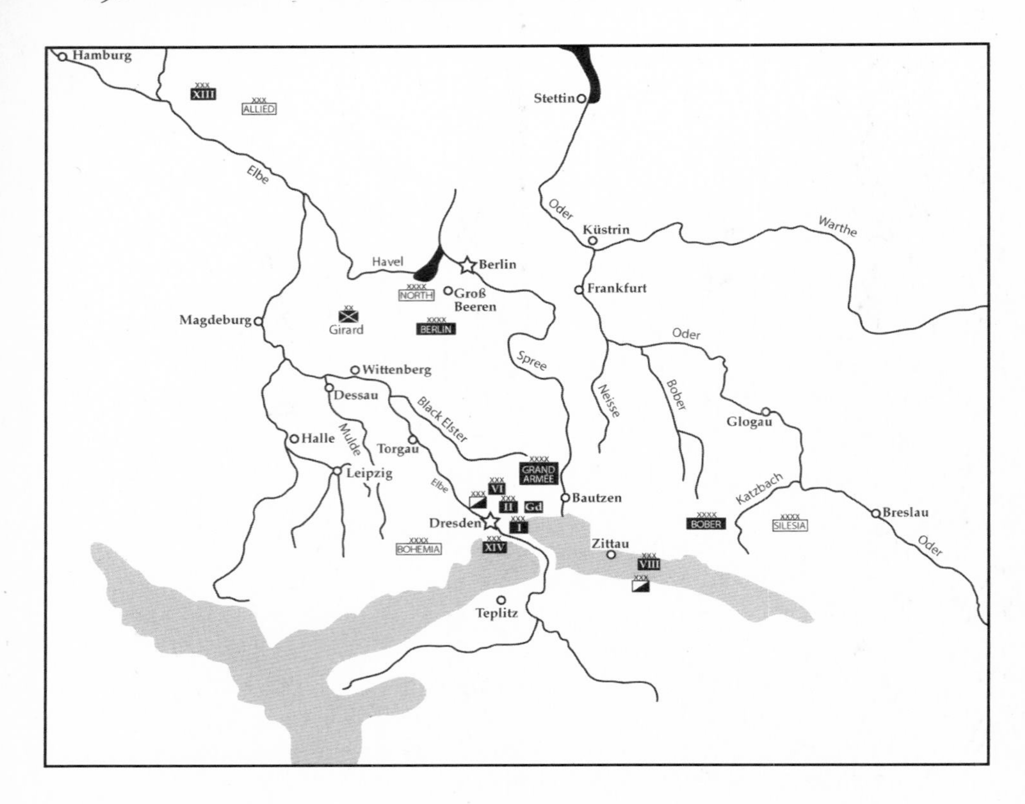

The Situation on 26 August 1813

lieutenants at Groß Beeren, the Katzbach, Hagelberg, and Kulm counterbalanced his great achievement at Dresden, which proved to be his last major victory on German soil.

By the end of August—just two weeks into the campaign—Napoleon had to revise his plans. Despite Oudinot's rebuff, the emperor remained determined to see the French tricolor flying above the Brandenburg Gate. He still believed in the strategic advantages of an operation in North Germany. Consequently the emperor opted personally to lead another advance against Berlin rather than Prague.[3] Napoleon planned to lead a part of his Grande Armée from Dresden to unite with Oudinot's army. He decided to leave four corps at Dresden under Murat to detain Schwarzenberg, who, after his drubbing at Dresden, would need time to reorganize. Despite Macdonald's defeat, the emperor had faith

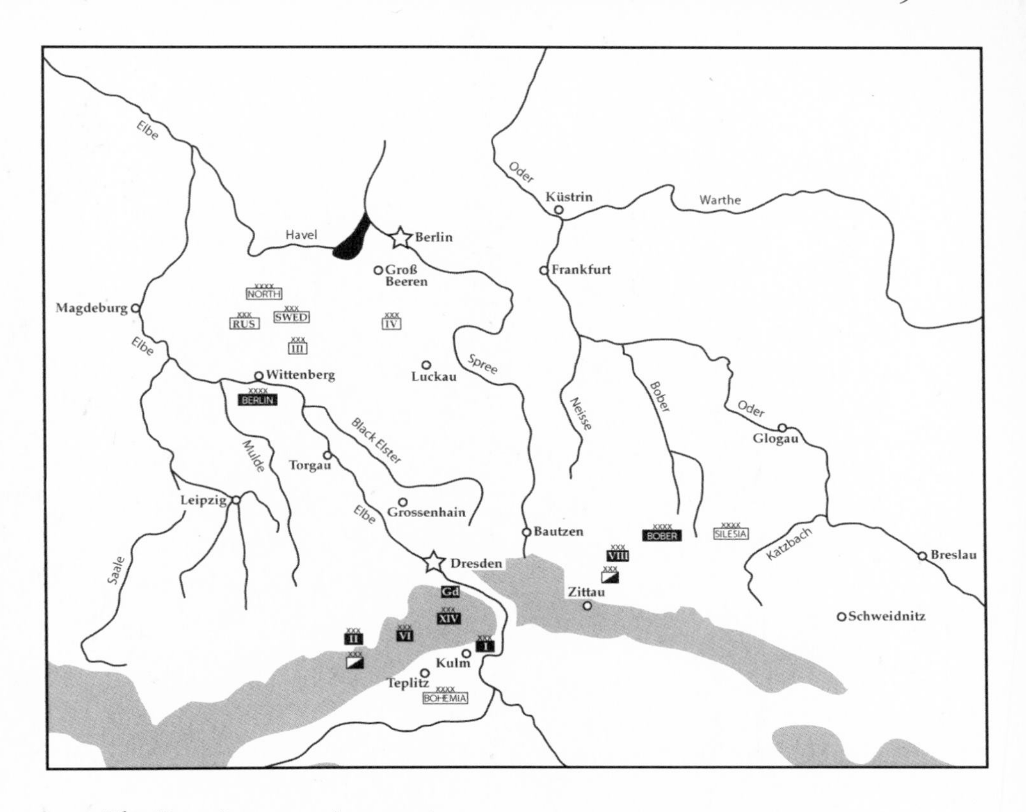

The Situation on 30 August 1813

in the marshal's ability to regroup and hold Blücher east of Bautzen. With the Imperial Guard, the Eighth Corps, and a portion of the First Cavalry Corps, Napoleon planned to march almost sixty miles north to Luckau. From Luckau Napoleon would be able to support either Oudinot or Macdonald, and once he began the operation against Berlin both Murat and Macdonald would cover his rear. The execution of this plan commenced on the afternoon of the thirtieth, when several guard units marched through Dresden toward Grossenhain. By 31 August Napoleon planned to have 18,000 infantry and 7,000 cavalry at Grossenhain; from there they would continue the march to Luckau. Despite his plans, Napoleon recalled these troops on the thirty-first after he received reports of Vandamme's defeat.[4]

Unfortunately for Oudinot, his humiliation did not end once the Army of Berlin reached the protection of Wittenberg. The retreat to the Elbe fortress, rather than to Luckau, exposed Macdonald's communications. It also limited Napoleon's ability to pursue Schwarzenberg, since Bernadotte could have threatened the rear of the Grande Armée by advancing to the Elbe. As Napoleon's chances of personally commanding the Army of Berlin became uncertain, he punished Oudinot for his incompetence and placed the army in the hands of a lieutenant who would doggedly execute his orders. Disgusted with his luckless subordinate, whose actions prompted Napoleon to comment that few could be as stupid as Oudinot, the emperor appointed Ney to be the new commander of the Army of Berlin.[5] The change took place on 2 September; an embittered Oudinot retained command of his Twelfth Corps.[6] Napoleon's chief of staff, Marshal Berthier, informed Ney that the emperor would be at Hoyerswerda on 4 September. Napoleon wanted Ney to march northeast to reach Baruth by the sixth.[7] On that day Napoleon planned to be thirteen miles to the southeast at Luckau, ready to support the advance on Berlin. Berthier instructed Ney to cross the thirty-five miles that separated Baruth from the Prussian capital and attack Berlin on the ninth or tenth.

Doubting the resolve of the Army of North Germany, the emperor had Berthier assure Ney that "all this swarm of Cossacks and pack of bad Landwehr infantry will retreat to Berlin if your march is determined." Berthier also warned Ney not to repeat Oudinot's mistakes. "You understand the necessity to maneuver quickly in order to exploit the confusion in the Bohemian Army, which will set in motion once it recognizes that the Emperor has done so," explained Berthier. He relayed Napoleon's frustration with Oudinot for failing to attack the enemy. "[Oudinot] was so clever that he allowed one of his corps to be isolated and defeated," wrote Berthier, who no doubt had this point impressed upon him by the emperor. "If he would have boldly attacked the enemy, he would have defeated him everywhere."[8] Such was the nature of Ney's instructions—a veritable directive for the fiery marshal to seek out and destroy the Army of North Germany. For Ney there would be no alternative: he would either steamroll Bernadotte's army or destroy himself in the process.

Necessity once again forced Napoleon to alter his plans on the morning of 3 September after he received a report describing the chaos in the Army of the Bober. Macdonald begged him to restore order personally. To make matters worse, Blücher pressed his demoralized foe. Napoleon grudgingly canceled his intended advance to Luckau and recalled the troops that had already set out to reinforce Ney. The emperor ordered a new offensive to chase Blücher from Bautzen, where Macdonald attempted to rally his battered army. Napoleon did entertain thoughts of dashing north once he eliminated Blücher's threat. On the third he notified Ney of his intention to attack Blücher on the following day, after which he would march on Berlin "with great haste."[9] Although Napoleon repulsed Blücher's advance guard on the fourth, he did not order the march to Berlin. Instead he monitored Blücher's movements throughout the fifth. For his part, Blücher realized that Napoleon himself had commanded the attack on the previous day and therefore withdrew his army eastward in compliance with the Trachenberg Plan. Finally, early on the sixth, Napoleon ordered the Sixth Corps and First Cavalry Corps to march for Brandenburg. This plan, as well as Napoleon's dream of personally leading the offensive against Berlin, had to be scrapped for good just hours later when reports arrived that Schwarzenberg was again advancing on Dresden. Napoleon recalled the two corps and sped back to Dresden, arriving in the evening. The Trachenberg Plan again spared Bernadotte from a confrontation with his former master.

Ney's subsequent instructions for the Army of Berlin suggest that he never received a dispatch on the fourth or fifth informing him that Napoleon would not support his operation against Berlin. Thus the marshal coordinated his movements, believing that he first had to advance eastward to link with Napoleon. He planned to move the army to Dahme, where it would turn north and march ten miles along the main Luckau-Berlin highway to Baruth. On 5 September he intended to take a position between Zahna and Jüterbog along the Wittenberg-Berlin highway. Early that morning Oudinot's corps debouched from Wittenberg and led the advance to Zahna. Reynier followed and marched through Bülzig, while Bertrand moved to Euper.[10]

On the clear afternoon Dobschütz noticed dust clouds approaching Zahna. Knowing that Tauentzien's Fourth Corps had reached Seyda and could support him, he did not want to retreat without offering battle. Utilizing the few available minutes, Dobschütz arranged his twelve battalions into two lines supported by cavalry and artillery. As the Prussians formed their lines, Oudinot's artillery unlimbered and blasted them with at least twenty-five guns. Dobschütz held his position until

Oudinot's artillery finally forced him to withdraw to Zallmsdorf. Earlier that morning Tauentzien had left for Rabenstein to confer with Bernadotte. Despite the corps commander's absence, his chief of staff, Maj. Karl Wilhelm von Rottenburg, marched to the sound of the guns. Rottenburg led the Fourth Corps west from Seyda to Gadegast, where it contested the French advance. Showing the resolve he had lacked only a few weeks earlier, Oudinot drove the Prussians northeast to Mellnitz before he disengaged.[11] In another example of excellent staff work, Rottenburg withdrew northeast to Jüterbog in order to close the Wittenberg-Berlin highway. Although Ney had no intention of taking this route to Berlin, he still planned to march through Jüterbog to utilize the fine east-west road that ran to Dahme. Just as Tauentzien's corps had blocked Bertrand's path on the morning of Groß Beeren, it would do the same on the morning of Dennewitz.

Once again, as at Groß Beeren, Bülow and his staff had just sat down to lunch when they heard the sound of artillery in the distance. Reports arrived that a strong enemy force had advanced against Dobschütz. Boyen and a few staff officers immediately left for Woltersdorf, just west of Zahna.[12] Bülow's outposts from Euper to Rahnsdorf also reported French activity in their sectors. Oppen dispatched patrols toward Zahna and Bülzig to investigate thick dust clouds. The dust from the dry roads allowed Prussian scouts to move very close to the French columns. Bülow joined Oppen to observe Ney's movements. Despite the veil of dust, he correctly perceived that Ney's main body had marched through Zahna, but he could not explain the simultaneous advance toward Seyda. Bülow could not determine if this movement implied an offensive against Berlin or a march to Torgau.[13] In either case he wanted to remain on Ney's left, to support Tauentzien or to harass Ney's march to Torgau.

Bülow informed Bernadotte that the French had driven Dobschütz from Zahna. According to previously issued instructions, the crown prince wanted Bülow to concentrate his corps at Kropstädt if the French debouched from Wittenberg. Since the Swedes and Russians could not reach Kropstädt in time to participate in a general battle, Bülow planned to withdraw Borstell's advance guard and attack Ney by Marzahna.[14] Bülow reported his intentions to army headquarters, and Adlercreutz responded with encouraging news. If the French attacked Tauentzien's corps, Adlercreutz assured Bülow that Bernadotte intended "to resume the offensive if the enemy advances." An order to Wintzingerode instructed the Russians to assist Bülow if necessary.[15] Much to the satisfaction of his Prussian subordinates, the crown prince of Sweden finally appeared ready to accept battle.

After observing Ney's movements, Boyen returned and explained to Bülow that Tauentzien would be crushed on the following morning unless the Third Corps marched east to Jüterbog. According to Boyen, Ney could easily smash through Tauentzien's corps at Jüterbog and take the open road to Berlin.[16] Bülow agreed with Boyen's assessment and ordered the Third Corps to assemble at Werkzahna.[17] He planned to remain on Ney's left flank by marching parallel to the French army. By twilight his corps had united at Werkzahna, except for the Fifth Brigade. Borstell reported that he had to remain at Kropstädt under Bernadotte's direct command. In a move reminiscent of his detaining of Hessen-Homburg's brigade on the morning of Groß Beeren, Bernadotte ordered Borstell's brigade to hold the passes at Köpnick, Woltersdorf, Werkzahna, and Kropstädt. Boyen recalled that "this order was even more inexplicable, for while the crown prince stood with two corps and faced no enemy forces, he deprived the 3rd Corps of a quarter of its strength as it marched against the enemy."[18] With no other choice, Bülow led the rest of his corps directly east from Werkzahna to Kurzlipsdorf, southwest of Jüterbog. Eluding French patrols, the Prussian cavalry reached Kurzlipsdorf at dusk; the infantry arrived around 2:00 A.M. The reserve artillery and Hessen-Homburg's Third Brigade marched through the night to reach Kurzlipsdorf by daybreak. Patrols reported French bivouacs less than one mile away at Seehausen and Naundorf.[19]

Before leaving Werkzahna, Bülow reported his measures to Bernadotte and requested that Borstell's brigade be permitted to rejoin the corps. Bülow also petitioned the prince-royal to support him with the Swedes and Russians. Bernadotte only partially complied.[20] He ordered the Swedes and Russians to unite at Lobbese on the army's right wing, but instructed Bülow and Tauentzien to await their arrival before engaging the French.[21] Moreover, Borstell had to remain at Kropstädt. Although pleased that the Swedes and Russians would at least unite, Bülow could not understand why Bernadotte chose to concentrate them far to the west at Lobbese. Even more puzzling was the decision to keep Borstell at Kropstädt. At this point it mattered little whether Bernadotte released Borstell—Bülow had promised Tauentzien his full support if Ney advanced against Jüterbog.[22] Bülow would march to the

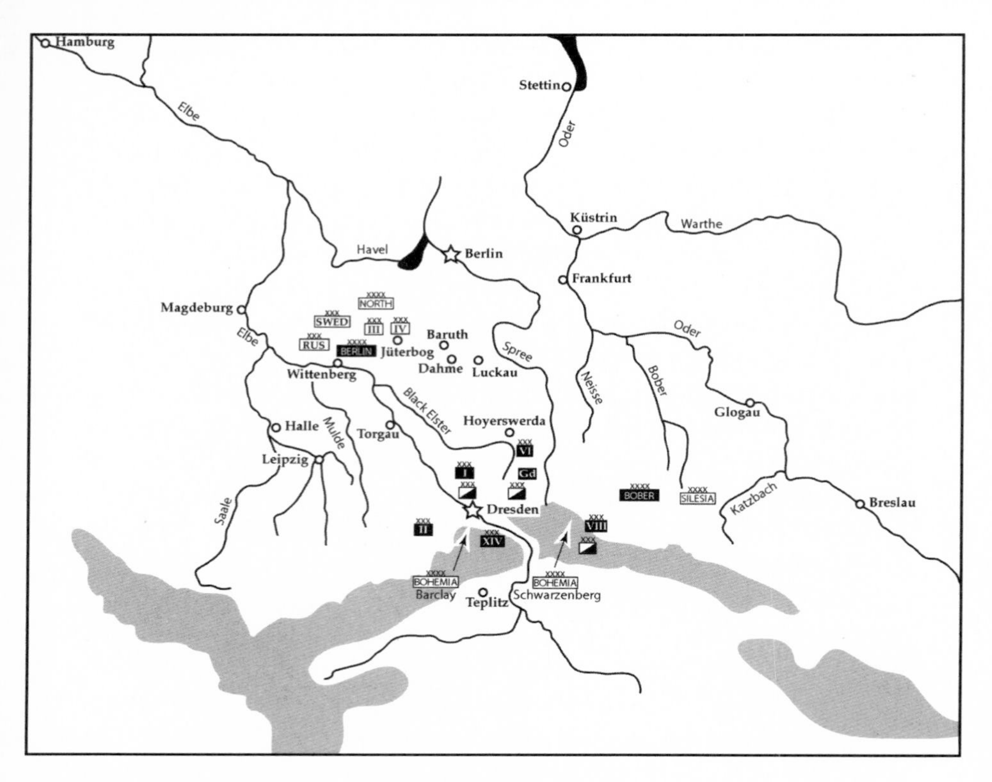

The Situation on 6 September 1813

sound of the guns with his available forces, regardless of what Bernadotte did with the Swedes and Russians.

Ney's army had bivouacked at Leetza, Zallmsdorf, and Seyda during the night of 5–6 September. His orders for the sixth continued the army's march to Dahme.[23] Reynier's Seventh Corps would make for Rohrbeck via Gadegast. On Reynier's left Bertrand would march through Dennewitz and reach Jüterbog first. Oudinot's Twelfth Corps would remain in position at Seyda until Reynier passed Gadegast and then march northeast to Öhna. Bertrand's corps reached Dennewitz without incident. Reynier, however, cut cross-country rather than take the road through Gadegast. As a result, his corps emerged at Gölsdorf, two miles southwest of Dennewitz. Not only did Reynier leave late and take the wrong roads, but Oudinot, who had to wait until the Seventh Corps passed through Gadegast before beginning his march, did not move until Ney finally summoned him between 1:00 and 2:00 P.M.[24]

By sunrise on the sixth the Prussians were still puzzled by Ney's dispositions. As dust clouds rolled toward the Third Corps at 8:00 A.M., Bülow climbed the church steeple at Kurzlipsdorf and watched Bertrand's Fourth Corps advance on the main highway toward Jüterbog. Since the terrain around Kurzlipsdorf offered no advantages for a flank attack, Bülow ordered the corps to march north to Eckmannsdorf, where a chain of hills commanded the region.[25] Before departing he sent Maj. Christian von Märtens to army headquarters to report Ney's movements and repeat the request to release Borstell's brigade.[26] After reaching Eckmannsdorf, Bülow moved the Fourth and Sixth Brigades into a front line, with the Third in reserve. Each brigade formed two waves with the right wing at Danna and the left south of Eckmannsdorf on the road to Dalichow. The twelve-pounder Prussian and Russian batteries took a position on the hills before the front, while the light batteries remained with the brigades; Oppen's reserve cavalry moved to Dalichow.[27] Orderlies dispensed bread, along with the encouraging news of Blücher's victory on the Katzbach.[28]

For his part, Tauentzien planned to close the gap between himself and Bülow by marching west to Maltershausen. Around 9:00 A.M. on the sixth, just as his corps debouched from Jüterbog, he could see the tips of Bertrand's columns on the hill chain south of the village of Dennewitz. Bertrand's advance threatened to sever Tauentzien's communications with Bülow and forced him to alter his march route. At 9:15 Tauentzien ordered his eleven battalions, sixteen squadrons, and nineteen guns to march to Kaltenborn, where they could unite with Bülow and attack the left flank of the French army.[29] The head of his corps had just reached the thick forest north of Dennewitz when Bertrand's artillery opened fire. Several French columns deployed in wide intervals north of Dennewitz.[30] Additional batteries followed by cavalry filed onto the open plain northeast of Dennewitz. Tauentzien had to make front or risk having his corps cut to pieces by Bertrand's superior numbers.

Bülow could now hear the dull rumble of artillery from the direction of Jüterbog. He assumed that Tauentzien would not reach Kaltenborn and ordered his 25,000 men to advance at 11:00 A.M.[31] To shield his right flank Bülow executed the movement by brigades, echeloned from the left to the right. Thümen's brigade formed the left echelon, and Krafft's the right. Hessen-Homburg followed Thümen, and the reserve artillery remained in the rear. Oppen's cavalry covered the right flank from a position south of Wölmsdorf. The infantry marched southeast past Kaltenborn to Niedergörsdorf, where Thümen's Fourth Brigade deployed between the village and the pine forest north of Dennewitz. Krafft, who echeloned his Sixth Brigade between Niedergörsdorf and Wölmsdorf, had to support Thümen's attack or proceed against the French columns on the road to Dennewitz should they attempt to turn Bülow's right. Hessen-Homburg remained in reserve. By 12:45 Bülow's corps was ready to finish the business it had started at Groß Beeren.

The plain around Dennewitz gradually descends southward from Treuenbrietzen to Gölsdorf and is encompassed by flat, embanked ridges. In 1813 the four small villages of Rohrbeck, Dennewitz, Gölsdorf, and Niedergörsdorf—all situated on the main roads—lacked strong enclosures and provided little cover. Farmers planted their crops on gentle, rolling hills between the villages.[32] At Niedergörsdorf arose a marshy stream, the Ahebach, which divided the field into a northern and southern sector and flowed across the entire battlefield. Infantry could only ford it with difficulty; horses could cross over a wooden bridge in Dennewitz or on a narrow stone bridge at Rohrbeck.[33] In the northern sector a prominent hill north of Dennewitz and northeast of Niedergörsdorf—subsequently named the Denkmalsberg (Monument Hill)—commands the region. Along with the forest north of Dennewitz, the Denkmalsberg separated the two Prussian corps. In the southern sector the struggle would center around the village of Gölsdorf, as well as two low-lying hill chains that extended north-south between Dennewitz and Gölsdorf. Although topography played a role, the timely arrival and engagement of fresh units became the deciding factor. On 6 September a strong southeast wind also spawned dust clouds that occasionally limited vision to 100 yards.[34]

As Bülow prepared for battle, the crown prince concentrated the Russians and Swedes at Lobbese, but typically remained one step behind the flow of events. According to Bernadotte's orders for 6 September, Tauentzien had to hold the French as long as possible, and Bülow had to remain at Kurzlipsdorf until he received further orders.[35] Märtens arrived at army headquarters around 10:00 A.M. with Bülow's report and request for support. The crown prince discovered that his impetuous Prussian subordinate had advanced against the enemy rather than remaining in Kurzlipsdorf. In a rage, Bernadotte scornfully replied to Märtens's request for support. "It does not surprise me that the enemy will attack you," shouted the prince-royal. "I expected this; now show what Prussian bravery is all about. It is only fair that you fight in the first line since it means that your own capital and your Fatherland are at stake. Here you see that the Swedish and Russian armies are ready. I know Prussian courage, and today it is no less. To prove it, I have given you the place of honor. Return to your General and say to him that I will come to support him."[36] As at Groß Beeren, the bombastic crown prince spoke of assisting but promised nothing.

By noon Tauentzien and Bertrand were engaged between Dennewitz and Rohrbeck. Tauentzien's infantry—one reserve and four Landwehr regiments—had been driven back by Bertrand's superior numbers, and Ney pounded the Landwehr with heavy artillery.[37] Before Bülow could arrive, Tauentzien's left wing of Kurmark Landwehr units broke. To gain time he ordered the nine Landwehr cavalry squadrons of his right wing to charge the left flank of Gen. Appiani Fontanelli's Italian division. In another noteworthy achievement for the Landwehr, the militia troopers broke the Italians. French cavalry support could not stop the Landwehr, which routed Gen. Jean-Thomas-Guillaume Lorge's counterattack. French infantry from Gen. Charles Morand's Twelfth Division finally repulsed the Prussian cavalry, but the psychological effect of the rout proved critical. The majority of Lorge's cavalry fled, some directly through the infantry.[38] The panic spread south of Dennewitz and triggered the flight of Bertrand's baggage. Ney had no other choice than to take defensive measures. Tauentzien's desperate cavalry charge gained enough time for Bülow's corps to deploy from Niedergörsdorf around 12:45. Outnumbered by the arrival of a second Prussian corps, Ney constricted his front. Fontanelli pulled his Italians back to Dennewitz, while Gen. Friedrich von Franquemont's Württemberger division faced Tauentzien northeast of Dennewitz. Morand's division moved toward Niedergörsdorf as French artillery on the Denkmalsberg opened fire on Thümen's advancing battalions.

Four battalions formed Thümen's first line; behind them marched a second wave of three battalions. Eight twelve-pounders advanced with his infantry and unlimbered on the hills north of Niedergörsdorf. Despite the artillery support, order collapsed when the Prussians debouched on the hilly terrain north of Niedergörsdorf. Thümen's right wing slowed to a halt, and the left wing received flanking fire from three of Morand's battalions. At the same time, a French twelve-pounder battery opened fire from the Denkmalsberg. This unexpected greeting broke the lead battalions on Thümen's left wing. Two battalions from this wing's second line managed to maintain their composure and ascend the long slope toward the commanding Denkmalsberg. A few minutes later the heads of their columns were likewise smashed. Morand's skirmishers pressed the flank and rear of Thümen's line at close range as French infantry crossed the distance between the Denkmalsberg and Niedergörsdorf. Under these circumstances Thümen could do nothing but retreat and reorganize his lines. He withdrew his right wing in good order, but the left-wing battalions could not regain their composure for almost one hour. Although one and one-half Allied batteries vainly sought to repulse the French infantry, the Prussian artillery had to retreat after the loss of two guns and several horses—a very inauspicious start for the victors of Groß Beeren!

Farther south, Bülow directed Krafft's Sixth Brigade to advance between Wölmsdorf and Niedergörsdorf as soon as Thümen's brigade engaged Bertrand's left wing. Krafft dispatched one and one-half batteries with one Landwehr squadron to flank the French artillery on the Denkmalsberg. The rest of Krafft's guns took a position on the southern end of Niedergörsdorf. After Thümen's debacle Boyen brought up Dietrichs's twelve-pounder battery from the reserve artillery. As soon as the battery arrived, Bülow personally led it onto the hills of Niedergörsdorf until it was in range of the advancing enemy's left flank. Dietrichs began a very effective bombardment, which, combined with Krafft's fire, forced the French to abandon the Niedergörsdorf windmill hill and fall back to the protection of their guns on the Denkmalsberg. This saved Thümen's shaken battalions from utter destruction.[39]

At this early but critical point in the battle Bülow committed some of his reserves. The Fourth Reserve Regiment from Hessen-Homburg's brigade marched past Thümen's shaken battalions to confront the Denkmalsberg and its twenty-eight guns. To support this assault Bülow ordered Dietrichs's twelve-pounders to take a position on the Niedergörsdorf windmill. An artillery duel then commenced at a distance of 900 yards. Covered by this fire and the support of Krafft's guns, the Fourth Reserve Regiment proceeded forward. Despite considerable losses, the battalions maintained their formation. Prussian skirmishers repelled the French marksmen but were thrust aside by Morand's advancing infantry. Once in range, the Prussian battalions opened fire. After advancing a few more paces the French battalions halted, and a disorderly melee erupted as Krafft's guns bombarded Morand's left

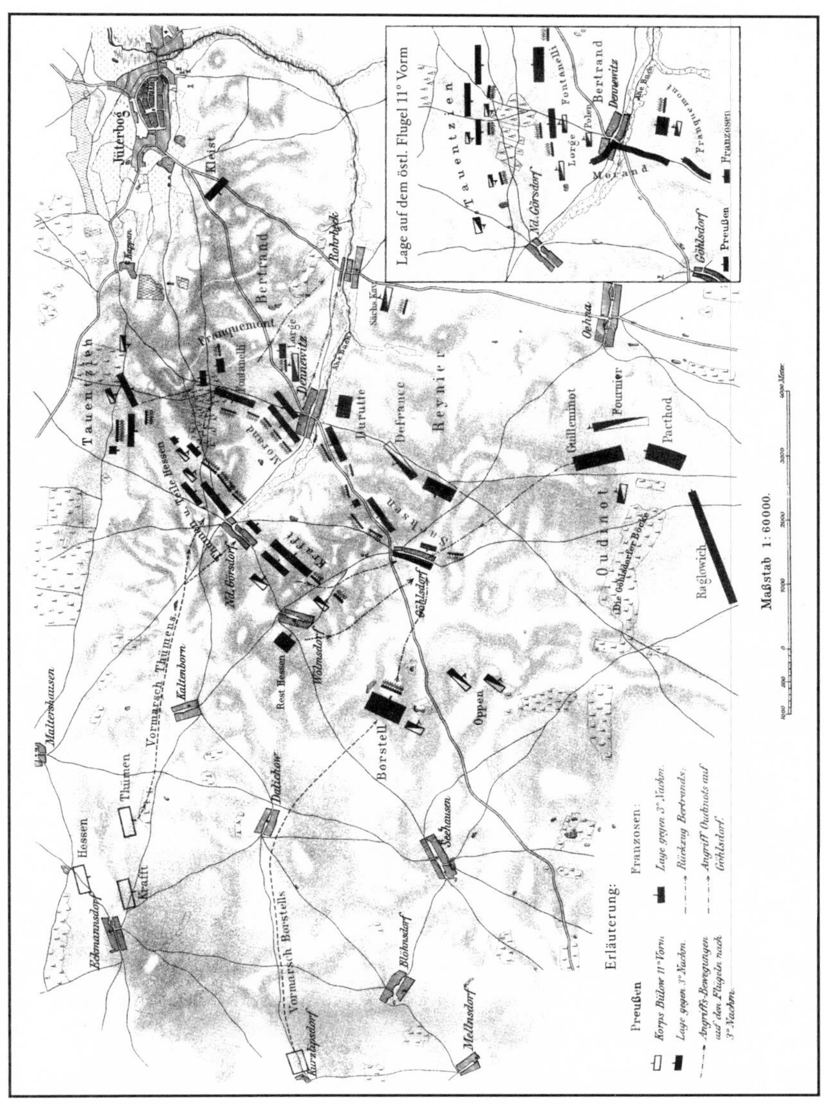

The Battle of Dennewitz, 6 September 1813. From Friederich, *Die Befreiungskriege*, vol. 2.

flank from a distance of 500 yards. Under this barrage the French infantry withdrew and abandoned the Denkmalsberg. Covered by skirmishers, Morand's units retreated in good order to Dennewitz. A Prussian dragoon squadron pursued, but superb musket fire claimed all but nineteen of its men. Nevertheless, the Prussians had won the most commanding position on the northern sector of the battlefield.

Bülow's heavy artillery followed the Fourth Reserve Regiment onto the Denkmalsberg, where the Prussians erected a battery of thirty-four cannon. Horse artillery on the right bank of the Ahebach also harassed the retreating Frenchmen. Two howitzers shelled the French position around Dennewitz in unison with the fire coming from the Denkmalsberg. Shielded by this artillery, Thümen reorganized his broken battalions. He prepared thirteen battalions to storm Dennewitz, including Hessen-Homburg's Fourth Reserve Regiment.

After withdrawing from the Denkmalsberg, Morand's division took a position between the Dennewitz windmill hill and the pine thicket. The terrain offered no advantage to Morand, who was situated at the base of a steep slope descending from the Denkmalsberg to the Dennewitz windmill. He could only hope that the Prussians would overextend themselves and offer the Italians and Württembergers, who remained near the pine thicket, an opportunity to attack Thümen's exposed flank.

Bülow observed the situation from the Niedergörsdorf church and decided to utilize his artillery to pound Morand's front before Thümen advanced any farther. He also ordered some of Thümen's battalions to clear the pine thicket on his left and link with Tauentzien's corps. By 3:00 P.M. the Prussians had driven the Württembergers and Italians from the western portion of the thickets. After eliminating this threat to his left flank, Bülow finally signaled Thümen to advance. Morand's division, reinforced by the arrival of Durutte's division from Reynier's corps, held the Dennewitz windmill hill until the Prussian artillery on the Denkmalsberg forced the French to abandon the position. Tauentzien's troops emerged from the thicket and united with Thümen's battalions as they threatened to envelop Morand's right. Bertrand now committed his last reserve of two battalions and four horse guns from a Württemberger brigade. Several horses were shot, and the stationary artillery was demolished before the guns could even unlimber. Personally leading the two battalions, the Württemberger General Franquemont refused to allow his troops to be killed for no reason and withdrew south over the Ahebach. Around 3:30 Morand and Fontanelli retreated toward Rohrbeck. Ney, however, refused to abandon the ground north of the Ahebach. He knew the arrival of Reynier and Oudinot would give him numerical superiority and a chance to resume the offensive.

As noted, Durutte's division had already reached the battlefield and moved into line to support Bertrand's left wing at the Dennewitz windmill. As the other units of the Seventh Corps arrived, they deployed between Dennewitz and Gölsdorf. After Durutte's division had advanced to support Morand, Reynier moved the rest of his corps toward Gölsdorf. The two Saxon divisions and Arrighi's heavy cavalry slowly rolled northwest toward Gölsdorf with sixteen battalions, thirty-three squadrons, and forty-two guns to face Krafft's eleven battalions, twenty-four squadrons, and thirty-four guns. The Second Brigade of Lecoq's Twenty-fourth Division led the advance. Around 2:30 Reynier's left wing of five battalions from Lecoq's Second Brigade approached Gölsdorf and formed a line. A Prussian light battalion assigned to occupy the village rushed to reach it before the Saxons. The Prussians just barely reached Gölsdorf when a Saxon battalion penetrated the village. A bayonet attack momentarily slowed the Saxons, but reinforcements soon arrived to drive the Prussians from Gölsdorf. After securing Gölsdorf, Reynier positioned Lecoq's First Brigade and a six-pounder battery north of the village. A twelve-pounder battery escorted by one battalion and a French horse battery unlimbered on the village windmill hill. Sahr, whose Twenty-fifth Division formed the second line between Gölsdorf and Dennewitz, placed a battery to the right of the twelve-pounders and a second south of Gölsdorf. Instead of attacking Bülow's center and right, Reynier held his infantry in place for over thirty minutes while he awaited Oudinot's arrival.

From their commanding position the Saxon gunners silenced the artillery that the Prussians brought to bear against them. Since Reynier's corps enjoyed a slight numerical advantage, Bülow ordered Krafft to move his right wing toward Wölmsdorf to await the reinforcements that the Prussians hoped would arrive. Boyen, who commanded the right wing, realized that Reynier's advance from Gölsdorf could decide the battle. To make matters worse, dust clouds to the southeast signaled Oudinot's approach. The Swedes and Russians, just barely visible on the horizon, could not arrive in time to stop Reynier. Boyen immediately threw the last reserves—three battalions from Hessen-Homburg's brigade and six twelve-pounders—onto the Prussian right wing.

Hessen-Homburg's three battalions, supported by three from Krafft's brigade, advanced to retake Gölsdorf. Krafft's remaining battalions followed in left echelon to cover against any counterattacks from the Saxons between Gölsdorf and Dennewitz. The Prussian battalions slowly approached Gölsdorf as steady fire from the Gölsdorf windmill hill depleted their ranks. Prussian skirmishers reached the gardens and perimeter of the village, where a standing combat ensued until their columns penetrated the small village. Thirty minutes of bloody street fighting erupted between four Prussian and five Saxon battalions before the Prussians took Gölsdorf. By 3:45 P.M. Prussian artillery forced Lecoq's Second Brigade to withdraw.

As for reinforcements, Borstell reached the battlefield with his staff around 3:00. Earlier that morning, around 9:00, Bülow had again ordered him to Kurzlipsdorf. A stubborn Borstell refused unless the crown prince approved. Permission finally arrived at 11:15, along with the news that Bernadotte planned to lead the rest of the army to support the Prussians. Arriving at Kurzlipsdorf at 12:45, Borstell used the mounting columns of smoke to orient his advance. While he marched to Dalichow, the Russians and Swedes moved on a parallel road to Eckmannsdorf. Observing Borstell's march, Bernadotte ordered him to unite with the army at Eckmannsdorf. This time Borstell had the good sense to refuse. He had a staff officer inform the crown prince that since "General Bülow stands in lively fire, it is General Borstell's duty to hurry forward to his support. He directs his march on the enemy's left flank and has already informed General Bülow of his arrival."[40] Borstell learned that Bülow had stabilized the left wing, but Oudinot's approach jeopardized the right. He then watched the struggle around Gölsdorf and observed the dust clouds that announced Oudinot's arrival. After spending thirty minutes distributing food, Borstell resumed his march around 3:30. He ordered his lead battalions to make for Gölsdorf, but the village was retaken shortly after 4:00 by the combined forces of Reynier and Oudinot before his men could arrive. For the moment all that Borstell could do was direct his batteries at the French reserves while his infantry deployed west of Gölsdorf.

At 4:00 P.M. Bülow received word that the Russo-Swedish troops had reached Eckmannsdorf. Bernadotte deployed both corps on the hills southwest of the village but did nothing more. Incensed, Bülow ordered Reiche to ask the crown prince to join the battle. Finding Bernadotte, Reiche relayed the request. "I have arrived with masses whose sight alone will suffice to decide the battle," announced the prince-royal. "Tell General Bülow to withdraw into the second line. The affair will not last ten minutes before the enemy gives the signal to retreat." Reiche thought better of relaying Bernadotte's order and reported instead that the crown prince planned to advance with forty battalions.[41] Bernadotte delayed the advance for so long that only a small portion of artillery and cavalry arrived to participate in the pursuit.

In the meantime Oudinot's troops arrived and deployed under the cover of the Saxon batteries near Gölsdorf. The marshal directed a battery south of Reynier's troops as his infantry filed behind the Saxons. Two fresh divisions took positions on the hills east of Gölsdorf, and a third headed directly for Gölsdorf.[42] Lecoq's Second Saxon Brigade also regrouped and turned to storm the village. The counterattack swept the Prussians—who had failed to reorganize their units after the earlier street fighting—from Gölsdorf. By retaking the village Reynier established a solid base for Ney's left wing. Furthermore, Oudinot threatened to envelop Bülow's right since the Swedes and Russians remained too far away to support.

Unfortunately for the Army of Berlin, Ney sought to regain the northern sector of the battlefield. After Morand's defeat he ordered Durutte's Second Brigade, commanded by Gen. Antoine Jarry, to retake the Dennewitz windmill hill. Jarry's men stormed the hill under murderous fire from the Prussian batteries on the Denkmalsberg. Three Prussian battalions under Maj. Friedrich von Clausewitz counterattacked the Dennewitz windmill before all of Jarry's battalions had arrived.[43] Charging up the slope, the First Battalion of the Fourth East Prussian Infantry Regiment received small-arms fire, wavered, and halted. Although this battalion sustained the second highest casualty rate in Bülow's corps while executing this attack, it held long enough to allow Thümen's troops to hasten from the pine thicket, flank Jarry's position, and force him to withdraw to Dennewitz.[44] Prussian artillery then moved down the road from the Denkmalsberg to the Dennewitz windmill hill, which offered an unobstructed view of the plain between Dennewitz and Rohrbeck.

As the artillery moved onto this commanding position, Prussian battalions continued across the northern sector of the battlefield and forced Durutte's First Brigade from a knoll slightly northeast of Dennewitz. By 4:30 Durutte's division had been pushed over the Ahebach, and Ney's attempt to reclaim the terrain north of Dennewitz had failed.

Most of Morand's and Fontanelli's men had withdrawn toward Rohrbeck in fairly good order. Franquemont's Württembergers also attempted to escape over the Ahebach. Undaunted, Ney ordered Bertrand to assemble as many battalions as possible for one last counterattack. Ney's determination to reach Jüterbog became his undoing. He looked to Oudinot's corps to restore the situation north of the Ahebach. Although Oudinot had already moved into line at Gölsdorf, Ney imprudently ordered the Twelfth Corps to march north to support Bertrand's counterattack. Compliance with this order placed Reynier's Seventh Corps in a precarious position. Refusing Reynier's request to leave him at least one division, the recalcitrant Oudinot led the entire Twelfth Corps to Dennewitz. His withdrawal had an immediate effect on the Saxons, who saw Bülow's battalions massing in the distance. Unfortunately for Ney, his obsession with the northern sector of the battlefield kept him from observing the actual threat to his army. Oudinot's march to Dennewitz deprived Reynier of the forces to hold the Prussians.

Bülow hurried from the Denkmalsberg toward Gölsdorf. He realized that the fate of the battle would be determined at this small village south of Dennewitz. While riding through Dennewitz, he ran into a group of French stragglers and barely escaped being captured. As he oriented himself on the right wing and his staff reassembled around him, they found themselves situated not far from the Saxon batteries; a ball almost decapitated Holtzendorf.[45] After the fall of Gölsdorf, Bülow surveyed the growing peril of his own right and the panic that began to spread among his troops. To restore the situation, he ordered a general advance of his entire right wing. Coinciding with Ney's decision to move Oudinot's corps north, this bold advance ultimately decided the battle.

Borstell and Krafft received the task of taking Gölsdorf. Only seven and one-half battalions could be assembled to assault the village—the remainder still needed to be reorganized after the hard fighting. Boyen directed eight twelve-pounders and sixteen other pieces at the hills north of Gölsdorf. Fourteen additional guns from Borstell's brigade unlimbered southwest of the village to join the ensuing artillery duel. On the fields west of Gölsdorf the Prussian battalions advanced under the steady pressure of Saxon skirmishers. A Pomeranian battalion, which was expelled from the village twice, finally penetrated Gölsdorf at two points. An East Prussian battalion of 300 men led by Bülow's nephew, Maj. Friedrich von Bülow, likewise entered the village. After losing 100 men in the fire-fight, the East Prussians forced the Saxons from the town, the younger Bülow being seriously wounded in the process. Possession of Gölsdorf hinged on a struggle in the small but enclosed village cemetery. A Saxon battalion defended the walls and the individual headstones until the Prussians eventually gained the upper hand. The First Battalion of the First Neumark Landwehr Infantry Regiment lost 12 officers and 222 men in the fighting at the Gölsdorf cemetery. The six other Prussian battalions engaged at Gölsdorf lost 28 officers and 1,006 men; the Saxons sustained 1,500 casualties.

As Borstell engaged the Saxons at Gölsdorf, Krafft's seven battalions stormed the batteries on the hills north of the village. His Second Kolberg Battalion suffered the highest casualty rate of the battle—11 officers and 349 men—while attacking the Saxon twelve-pounder battery on the Gölsdorf windmill hill. The battalion eventually broke 150 yards from the battery, and the survivors receded to the second line, carrying with them a battalion of Neumark Landwehr. An East Prussian Landwehr battalion suffered a similar fate before two battalions from the Ninth Reserve Regiment overran the right side of the Saxon position. Although French dragoons charged and forced the Prussians to form squares, the contest was over. Krafft's second line and the West Prussian Dragoons arrived; the French cavalry withdrew without attacking. The Prussian battalions that attacked the Saxon artillery position lost a total of 49 officers and 1,318 men.

Bülow ordered Krafft to pursue Reynier with six battalions. The retreating Saxons sporadically turned on their pursuers, but thick dust clouds obstructed Reynier's view of the advancing Prussians. As the Saxon and French artillery withdrew from the Gölsdorf hills, panic seized Reynier's second line—the Twenty-fifth Saxon Division. Prussian case-shot, combined with the demoralizing retreat of their own artillery, induced the Saxon infantry to flee. Arrighi's dragoons finally stemmed the Prussian advance and allowed the Saxons to reform. A regiment from Lecoq's division counterattacked, but two brash West Prussian dragoon squadrons charged into the Saxons, inflicted numerous casualties, and forced the disheartened regiment to withdraw. A Westphalian squadron also took flight and stampeded several Saxon skirmishers. Saxon officers reformed their battalions and retreated under the cover of the remaining skirmishers. Numerous damaged and unlimbered guns remained on the Gölsdorf hills. Reynier positioned his few remaining guns southeast of Gölsdorf to slow the pursuing

Prussians. Borstell's staff gradually increased the number of Allied guns by redirecting batteries from other parts of the field. The Prussians assembled forty-four guns, including six Swedish six-pounders, and both sides exchanged deadly artillery rounds during the final stage of the battle. Allied artillery eventually overcame the Saxon guns and forced them to withdraw. Around 5:00 Reynier abandoned his last position.

Borstell's battalions pursued the Saxons toward Öhna. On the extreme right of the Prussian line Oppen's reserve cavalry advanced with one and one-half batteries. At this time Bernadotte finally released the Russians; two cavalry regiments and two infantry battalions from Wintzingerode's corps rushed eastward to take part in the pursuit. Two other Russian cavalry regiments and three Cossack regiments swept southeast of Gölsdorf. Reynier's defeat and the appearance of the Russian cavalry triggered panic throughout Oudinot's columns. Pacthod's division withdrew in battalion squares, while the other two divisional commanders did their best to maintain order. At Öhna hysteria seized the escorts and drivers of Ney's baggage train. This rearward confusion prevented any organized movement and forced Reynier to halt on the hill north of Öhna with the survivors of Durutte's division. Oudinot's Bavarians appeared north of Reynier. Steady attacks by Russian cavalry foiled efforts to restore order and rally the three corps. Allied horsemen circumvented Reynier and closed the road to Torgau. Reynier bravely directed his remaining columns to cover the retreat to Öhna, but Allied horse artillery turned the retreat into a rout. Arrighi's cavalry broke under the weight of Allied shelling. The French troopers galloped through their own columns with the Russian cavalry close behind. Guns and wagons overturned, battalions split apart, and frightened horses stampeded stragglers. Russian dragoons routed Oudinot's cavalry and captured eight twelve-pounders before being stopped by Bavarian infantry. Since Ney's army still offered resistance, thirty-six Russian and Swedish guns harassed the French rear to prevent Reynier from rallying his men.[46]

Prior to Reynier's collapse, Bertrand had rallied some infantry and cavalry units and then ordered a general advance in accordance with Ney's order to counterattack. Bertrand achieved initial success, but Tauentzien's reinvigorated corps tipped the scales. Tauentzien's artillery opened fire on Bertrand's columns before they could engage Bülow's troops. Infantry from the Fourth Corps then pursued Bertrand's troops to Rohrbeck. Without artillery the Prussians made little progress against the French at Rohrbeck. While awaiting the arrival of Bülow's guns, his left wing linked with Tauentzien's Landwehr. Around 5:00 P.M. Dietrichs finally arrived with his Russian twelve-pounders, and case-shot decided the affair. Although Bertrand gave the order to withdraw to the windmill hill east of Rohrbeck, a mass of fleeing French and Italian troops rolled through the village seeking protection behind the Ahebach. The Württembergers covered the retreat and suffered numerous casualties. One Württemberger regiment held Rohrbeck until flames engulfed the village. Five Prussian battalions forded the Ahebach and pursued—Bertrand's corps disintegrated.

Farther south, Bülow's skirmishers drove the remaining enemy troops from Öhna and supported the cavalry on the south side of the village, but his exhausted infantry needed hours to reorganize. The long march on the previous day, the restless morning, and the struggle under an unusually parching sun had fatigued the troops; not even the thrill of pursuing a vanquished foe could stir them. Water had been scarce throughout the battle. Exhaustion and darkness meant that instructions could not be effectively communicated to the disorganized battalions. The majority of the two Prussian corps camped between Bocho, Öhna, and Langenlipsdorf, while the Swedes and Russians bivouacked at Jüterbog.[47]

Bülow and Tauentzien commanded approximately 45,000 men and defeated three French corps commanded by one of the period's most charismatic leaders. The victory cost the Third Corps 200 officers and approximately 6,500 men. Tauentzien's losses totaled 3,000 men. Ney's losses amounted to 8,000 dead and wounded, 13,500 prisoners, 53 guns, and 412 supply wagons. Large quantities of material and small arms were left on the battlefield and used to fill the shortages in the Prussian Landwehr.[48] Ney lost over one-third of his army, and the demoralizing effect of the rout proved considerable.

No outstanding individual genius or superior tactical employment of the troops made this victory possible. Devastating artillery fire dominated the fighting. The engagement of fresh forces at crucial moments proved to be the most important factor in the Allied victory. Tauentzien, Ney, and Bülow all made bold decisions at critical junctures of the battle. Tauentzien's cavalry attack stunned Bertrand's corps and gained time for Bülow to arrive. Bülow's decision for a general advance enabled the Prussians to overcome the numerical superiority on their right flank after Oudinot arrived. This attack achieved fruition due to Ney's pivotal decision to summon Oudinot to Dennewitz.

Ney's conduct in this short campaign was certainly fraught with mistakes. The marshal expected Tauentzien to continue his retreat and thus carelessly marched toward Jüterbog. Ney also failed to detect Bülow's flank march. Due to the easy victory on the fifth, the French neglected security measures. Despite this reproach, Ney's conduct at the beginning of the battle was practical. Attacked on his left flank by Bülow, he continued his operation against Tauentzien and stopped Thümen's first assault with Morand's division. Later Durutte's division again stopped Bülow's Prussians. Ney also effectively placed the Seventh Corps between Dennewitz and Gölsdorf, where Reynier utilized the village and hill chain to establish a strong position bolstered by artillery placed on commanding heights. After making expedient decisions throughout the first two-thirds of the battle, Ney succumbed to his fiery personality. Overseeing the struggle north of the Ahebach, the marshal lost sight of the overall situation and made the fatal mistake of summoning Oudinot from Gölsdorf. The late arrival of the Twelfth Corps also complicated Ney's task. Had Oudinot arrived earlier, Bülow's right wing could have been turned before Borstell arrived. Once Oudinot arrived, Ney's orders put the Twelfth Corps in march at the decisive point of the battle. Both the Prussians and the Saxons interpreted Oudinot's maneuver as the preliminary of a retreat. Both sides acted accordingly: the Prussians regained their confidence and the Saxons panicked. Even if Oudinot did not recognize the folly of Ney's orders, a horrified Reynier certainly made every effort to enlighten him. Reynier's pleas had no effect on Oudinot, who, embittered over being superseded by Ney, strictly obeyed his commander's orders.

The casualty lists suggest that the Prussian battalions, both line and Landwehr, willingly sacrificed themselves. Although the columns that bore the brunt of the attacks consisted mainly of line troops, the performance of the Landwehr remains noteworthy, especially in Tauentzien's corps. According to the journal of the Fourth Reserve Regiment, the Prussian soldiers had not eaten a full meal since the previous noon and had marched almost the entire night.[49] By the evening of the sixth not even bread and water could be found. Even Bernadotte was deeply moved by the conduct of the Prussians. On the following day he informed Bülow that he had witnessed the courage of his troops and the talents of his generals. He urged Bülow to "continue to provide them the excellent and honorable example that they have received since the beginning of the war." He added that the king of Prussia would be advised that he owed everything to Bülow's "performance and steadfast persistence."[50] Regardless of his sentiments, Bernadotte should have appeared on the battlefield earlier. Had he actually engaged his "forty battalions," the results would have been decisive. Rather than reconciling the deep conflict between the Prussians and Bernadotte, the victory only accentuated the problems. Later Bernadotte's pretentious Bulletins would minimize the Prussian achievement. Once again, as after Groß Beeren, Bülow felt slighted and despondent. This tension only increased during the next month, when further disagreements completely destroyed their relationship.

12

At the Rubicon

Ney directed his army east to Dahme, but the total breakdown of command and control ruled out any chance of an orderly retreat. Due to the demoralized condition of his corps, Reynier simply sought a safe haven. Oudinot's two French divisions also moved south on the highway from Öhna to Torgau. Although these units had seen limited combat at Dennewitz, they too had succumbed to the panic and collapse associated with a crushing defeat. Reynier eventually reunited with Oudinot, who suggested a retreat to Torgau. As a result, both corps commanders herded their units toward Torgau, while Ney led Bertrand's and Arrighi's corps, as well as Oudinot's Bavarian division, to Dahme.[1] By daybreak on 7 September Reynier and Oudinot had moved the main mass of the Army of Berlin over the Black Elster River. Four miles separated this portion of the French army from the pursuing Allied units. By that evening the French further distanced themselves by reaching the safety of Torgau.[2] Consequently, the Allied pursuit achieved no further success against this portion of the French army.

As for the ill-fated Ney, after darkness and confusion caused several delays, his march continued throughout the night of the sixth and into the morning of the seventh without incident. His units continued to dissolve along the way as groups of exhausted men melted into the darkness. Fontanelli's Italian division completely disintegrated;

whole battalions discarded their muskets. Around 1:30 A.M. on the seventh Ney's lead units reached Dahme and ejected its Landwehr garrison.[3] The marshal then ordered the retreat to continue to Herzberg at 3:00. By the time Ney and the vanguard departed for Herzberg, the remnants of Bertrand's and Arrighi's corps had reached Dahme. Bertrand allowed the troops a few hours' rest before continuing.[4]

On the previous morning Tauentzien had ordered Wobeser's Landwehr brigade to march from Luckau to Dahme to threaten Ney's right flank. This order arrived in Luckau late in the evening, and Wobeser did not depart until after midnight on the seventh.[5] On the way he met the Landwehr detachment that Ney had driven from Dahme, and its captain informed him of the Allied victory at Dennewitz. Locals added that the French appeared very uneasy and disgruntled. The Prussians continued their march with confidence and reached Dahme just after daybreak to find Bertrand's columns in full retreat on the highway to Herzberg. Concealed by a thick mist, Wobeser surprised Bertrand's demoralized rearguard and took 3,225 prisoners, while sustaining less than 200 casualties. Although this was another successful combat for the Prussian Landwehr, the French held Dahme long enough to allow the last of Bertrand's units to escape.[6]

Except for reports of a French corps moving from Dahme to Herzberg, the Allies did not know the whereabouts of Ney's army. Early on the morning of 7 September Oppen assembled a flying column to scour the right bank of the Black Elster as far as the main highway that ran between Herzberg and Torgau. A Swedish detachment was ordered to assist Oppen; irrespective of Bernadotte's order to be ready to march at 4:00 A.M. the Swedes did not leave their bivouac until late that morning. Forced to wait for his Swedish comrades, Oppen did not depart until noon. When he reached Jessen, the frustrated commander learned that his prey had eluded him; locals reported that a French column had already crossed the Black Elster.[7]

Although an opportunity to inflict further damage on the demoralized French army had slipped from Oppen's hands, Borstell's men had better luck. Bülow divided Borstell's brigade into three flying columns. Two made for Dahme and arrived after Wobeser's combat. The third column, which consisted solely of cavalry, found the highway to Schönewalde covered with baggage, but only captured 150 stragglers. The Prussian commander, Maj. Karl von Lottum, learned that the French had passed through Schönewalde on their way to Herzberg. He gave chase and found Morand's rearguard attempting to cross the Black Elster. The Prussians brought up four guns and surprised the weary Frenchmen. Still far from the bridge, the French infantry hastened to the nearest village, losing 600 men and part of Bertrand's baggage. Once the French took refuge behind the village walls, Lottum could do nothing more without infantry. The French eventually crossed the river and torched the bridge.[8]

Back in Dennewitz, Bülow reflected on the largest battle of his career. In a letter to his wife he described the victory as "one of the most remarkable and most gleaming days in Prussian military history. Our troops worked miracles. They stormed enemy batteries with the bayonet just like the old Prussians of Prague and Leuthen." Bülow certainly expressed the hopes of the Prussian monarchy when he assured Pauline that "through our victories, we will soon be masters of Germany." He also shed light on Bernadotte's inactivity during the battle—a truth that the crown prince could not conceal or easily explain. "The Allies did nothing," griped Bülow, "until we had already driven the enemy from his positions." There was much truth to his claim that his three brigades had "held a superior enemy force for five hours." Many of the army's commanders and senior officers knew this all too well and were embarrassed by Bernadotte's lack of fortitude. Bülow certainly displayed the initiative and mettle that Bernadotte lacked, but he attributed his victory to fate. Although several of his battalions had been cut in half, he firmly believed that "the hand of providence" had protected him and his staff. Never forgetting the finer things in life, he requested that his wife send him more wine as soon as possible since someone had stolen the bottles she had already sent.[9] Bülow would need the wine to help him celebrate, for unlike the battle of Groß Beeren, the king recognized his role at Dennewitz by awarding him the Grand Cross of the Iron Cross of 1813—only Bernadotte and Blücher had thus far received this coveted decoration. Bernadotte also sent him the Grand Cross of the Swedish Order of the Sword, but this hardly impressed the Prussian.[10]

As the Prussians reveled in their retribution for Jena-Auerstädt, Ney sought the remainder of his army. On 8 September he intended to echelon the Fourth Corps from Herzberg to Torgau and position the Twelfth and Seventh Corps along the right bank of the Elbe. At the risk of being captured, the marshal hurried to Torgau. He arrived on the evening of the seventh to find the remainder of his army "gathered under the guns of the fortress" and not at all prepared to counterattack the pursuing enemy.[11] Ney accused Reynier and Oudinot of being insubordinate. "I must say," complained Ney to Napoleon, "that the command of an army similar to that which you have confided in me can produce no good results, and when each chief wants to conduct operations according to his views, the commander-in-chief can gain nothing but dishonor."[12] With no other choice, he ordered Bertrand to Torgau.[13] Bertrand continued the retreat with the remnant of Fontanelli's Italian division in the lead, the Württembergers in the center, and Morand's division as rear guard. Soon after the march began, 500 Cossacks ambushed Fontanelli's foremost battalions. The Italians escaped after case-shot scattered the Russian horsemen. One hour later the Cossacks returned, supported by a few thousand Allied horsemen and three horse batteries. Although Morand's artillery contained them, a column of Prussian infantry appeared in the distance. "At this sight," according to Franquemont, "fear seized the army; it considered itself cut off, which again triggered a general retreat. Cavalry, infantry, and artillery all sought to reach the fortress as quickly as possible."[14] Ney blamed Reynier and Oudinot for the ensuing rout of Bertrand's corps. The marshal complained that, instead of supporting, the Seventh and Twelfth Corps fled across the Elbe "at the sight of several regiments of [enemy] cavalry that were accompanied by a horse battery."[15]

The disintegration of the Fourth Corps forced the Army of Berlin to retreat over the Elbe.[16] Fearing that the Allied army would cross the river north of Wittenberg and march on Leipzig, Ney ordered the entire army to fall back to the Mulde River on the ninth. Such fears were unwarranted. The commandant of Wittenberg, Jean-François La Poype, reported that thus far only 300 Cossacks had been spotted crossing the Elbe.[17] After being reproached by Imperial Headquarters for imprudently abandoning the right bank of the Elbe, and with La Poype's assurance that Bernadotte's army remained idle, Ney returned to the Elbe on the eleventh.[18] While on his way to Torgau, he received orders to cross to the right bank.[19] Upon reaching the fortress, Ney learned that the Allies not only held the Black Elster in force but also occupied all of the Elbe's crossings around Torgau.[20] Moreover, local inhabitants claimed that the Allies planned to build a bridge farther downstream near the village of Elster. Due to this information, Ney felt that he could not order his shaken army to recross the Elbe. He kept his army on the left bank, blaming "the poor morale of the troops" for not allowing him to follow the emperor's instructions.[21]

Despite having only 32,000 effectives and 90 guns, Ney began organizing a counteroffensive to comply with Napoleon's orders. Not knowing the whereabouts of Bernadotte's army made this task particularly difficult. "Some claim the enemy will take a position between Jüterbog and Baruth to cover Berlin; others report that he marches on Berlin," wrote a baffled Ney. Saxon peasants spoke of a large force of infantry camped at Herzberg, while both infantry and cavalry reportedly occupied Jessen. Others reiterated the rumor that the Allies would attempt to cross the Elbe between Wittenberg and Elster.[22] Owing to the Allied presence on the Black Elster, Ney ultimately realized that he could not take the offensive without Napoleon's support. Except for Oudinot's corps, which moved into Torgau, his entire army remained idle on the thirteenth, fourteenth, and fifteenth. The Army of Berlin teetered on the verge of collapse, and this respite could not have come at a more precipitous time.

Ney's army had suffered considerable losses to attrition and desertion during his eleven-day operation. According to Bülow's tally, 13,500 enemy soldiers had been captured at Dennewitz. On 7 September Reynier noted that "one can not estimate the losses. Half of the infantry and artillery of Durutte's division are missing, as well as a third of the Saxons."[23] One week later Reynier reported that the Seventh Corps had been reduced by 5,800 men.[24] By 14 September Bertrand assessed the losses of his Fourth Corps at 8,849 men.[25] Losses for the Twelfth Corps reached 8,566 men, despite its limited role at Dennewitz.[26] The total loss of Ney's army numbered 23,215 men, 53 guns, 412 wagons, and 4 flags.[27] Ney's offensive—as well as Napoleon's "master plan"—had ended in disaster.

The psychological repercussions of defeat proved more decisive than the loss of men and material. As early as the eighth a tired Oudinot requested that the emperor relieve him of his command. Ney lamented that he could no longer lead his army and that it refused to obey him. Like Macdonald only one week earlier, he begged for Napoleon's personal intervention to prevent the army from dissolving. On 13 September Ney again requested the emperor's presence, stating that only he could inspire the troops and renew their courage. Bertrand added that if Napoleon merely reviewed the troops, the resulting psychological boost would double the fighting value of the army.[28]

The French commanders also began squabbling among themselves and exchanging the blame for Dennewitz. Ney distributed the guilt to all three of his corps commanders. In addition to the fact that the two men had hated each other since the invasion of Portugal in 1810, Ney condemned Reynier for modifying his march route and cited the general's alleged insubordination as grounds for a request to have him removed.[29] He accused Bertrand of imprudently beginning an unexpected and unwanted battle. As for Oudinot, Ney charged that he had absolutely no excuse for his ridiculously late arrival.[30] "Currently," grumbled Ney, "it is impossible to use the 4th, 7th, and 12th Corps. Each corps commander does what he wishes to guarantee his own safety. I have lost control! The morale of the generals and officers has been shaken and I cannot lead them. I would rather be a grenadier! Please obtain a statement from the Emperor that names me the commander-in-chief with only generals of division under my orders. If this is not possible, transfer me from this hell! I do not think I need to mention my devotion: I am ready to spill my blood, but I desire that it is not in vain!"[31] Ney's retreat to the Mulde and the accompanying countermarches likewise aggravated his corps commanders. Oudinot reminded him that the Twelfth Corps only numbered 5,000 men and that he did not even have the equipment to arm some hundred invalids![32] Bertrand noted that his "remaining 9,000 infantry would eventually be combat-ready if they could just have a little rest."[33]

The defeat of the multinational Army of Berlin also shook Central Europe, particularly the Rheinbund. Dissatisfaction with the French system mounted, and the demoralization of the Army of Berlin after Dennewitz had immediate political repercussions. On 9 September the Bavarian general Clemens von Raglowich reported to his king that he would attempt to maintain his division for as long as possible but that the slightest shock would break it apart. "The mood of the French army becomes increasingly detrimental; it appears certain to me that we can no longer execute any large undertaking and are incapable of any offensive operations," observed Raglowich.[34] On the following day Franquemont reported to the king of Württemberg that the retreat on the sixth "had degenerated into a shameful flight" and that the rout of Bertrand's corps before the gates of Torgau had further demoralized the army. An embarrassed Franquemont noted that three army corps had fled "before 5,000–6,000 cavalry and one horse battery. . . . It appears to me that the French generals and officers are weary of the wars, and the soldiers can only be animated by the presence of the Emperor himself."[35] Consequently, one last casualty that must be attributed to the "master plan" was the alliance Napoleon had forged with the German princes. News of Dennewitz induced the Tyrol to support Austria's efforts against the French. In addition, the king of Bavaria, Maximilian-Josef, finally summoned the courage to break his alliance with Napoleon. Following Dennewitz, Bavaria made overtures to the Allies and eventually joined the Sixth Coalition as Austria's ally after concluding the Convention of Ried on 8 October.[36]

The victory at Dennewitz also crowned a long succession of Allied victories that the Prussians could claim as their own. Groß Beeren, the Katzbach, Hagelberg, Kulm, and Dennewitz not only restored the army's confidence but also helped strengthen Hardenberg's plans for postwar Germany. He envisioned a Germany divided into two spheres: Prussia would control the North German states and Austria those of the South. The creation of a federal system that unified all of the German states would guarantee the hegemony of both powers in their respective spheres on the basis of a regional division of authority, rather than joint Austro-Prussian administration of the whole.[37] Hardenberg appeared to be one step closer to his goal when the three eastern powers signed bilateral pacts at Teplitz on 7 September. The general terms called for the material restoration of Austria and Prussia to their pre-1805 status; the restoration of the states of northwestern Europe to their 1803 status; the abolition of the Rheinbund and the independence of the German states between the Rhine and the western frontiers of Austria and Prussia; and the partition of the Grand Duchy of Warsaw along lines that would be negotiated at a later date.[38] All three vowed not to make a separate peace with Napoleon, and each agreed to keep an army of 150,000 men in the field until the end of the war.[39]

Although something could be found in the Teplitz agreements that satisfied each eastern power, Metternich achieved another victory in his quest to guarantee that the war not be fought in the name of nationalism.[40] Once again the goal of the alliance was not the ultimate destruction of France. Metternich needed to retain a powerful (and preferably) Napoleonic France to limit Russian expansion. He also undercut the points of the Reichenbach Treaty by not mentioning Italy, Holland, and Spain; these would be used later to coerce the British into accepting his designs on Central Europe. Moreover, Metternich left a loophole by writing into the treaties the stipulation that the German states would achieve "entire and absolute independence."[41] On the surface it appeared that the language of the Teplitz agreements endorsed Hardenberg's plan for dualism in Germany.[42] Technically the agreement to maintain the independence of the German states—rather than create a unified federal structure—ensured that Metternich could limit Hardenberg's designs for reshaping Germany.[43] The Convention of Reid between Bavaria and Austria, for example, was Metternich's version of a Kaunitz-like diplomatic revolution that proved to be a setback for Prussia. King Maximilian-Josef joined the coalition after Austria guaranteed Bavarian sovereignty and a place at the peace table. This, according to Paul Schroeder, set the pattern for other Napoleonic satellites to defect, which did not benefit the Prussians, who hoped to exact revenge on the Rheinbund princes. Nevertheless, Teplitz was not a total victory for the Austrians, and Tsar Alexander recovered some of the diplomatic initiative he had lost to Metternich during the armistice. Both Prussia and Austria remained dependent on Russian assistance to secure their postwar prizes. The very uncertainty of Germany's future meant that Russia would be guaranteed a say in the matter.[44] It appeared that as long as Frederick William remained loyal to the tsar Prussian influence on Germany's future would grow, despite Austrian designs.

Far from the intrigue of cabinet diplomacy, Ney had his problems and blamed them on the Saxons. Napoleon's most faithful German allies now became Ney's scapegoats. Despite Reynier's fierce defense of his troops, Ney accused them of cowardice and disloyalty. The Saxon General Lecoq's inaccurate report regarding Russian troop movements provided Ney additional reason to complain about "the morale of the Saxon troops, officers, and soldiers."[45] Torgau's predominantly Saxon garrison also concerned Ney.[46] To eliminate the threat of mutiny he reduced the number of Saxons in the fortress. Ney explained that "these troops have such [poor] morale that I believe it would be imprudent to leave them there in a stronger proportion."[47] To reduce their number Ney had Reynier extract as many men as possible from the garrison to replenish his two divisions.[48] The marshal replaced the Saxons with French reinforcements that had recently arrived; of the 6,000-man garrison, 5,000 were now French.[49] The removal of the Saxon garrison from Torgau irritated Reynier, who complained to Ney that it "evokes the worst impression on the Saxon troops, who, after witnessing our conduct in their country, are already very ill-disposed. I persevere only by showing them confidence, and by reminding them of their honor, obedience to their sovereign, and their devotion to me. But while I do all that is possible to preserve this corps, your demands ruin my efforts, and I can no longer be held accountable."[50] Reynier informed Berthier that Ney's actions had "the worst effect on the morale of the Saxons, who are already devastated by the latest events and the conduct of the troops in their country."[51]

Loyalty to the emperor aside, Reynier correctly identified the true source of Saxon discontent. The French had devastated the countryside in search of food. Even Raglowich noticed that "the [Saxon] farmer, who is robbed of everything, often destroys his own home and surrenders it to the flames and, out of despair, aids the operations of the more humane enemy."[52] Saxon civilians suffered to such an extent that Reynier's Saxon cavalry seized and distributed a portion of the Seventh Corps food supply to the neighboring villages. "Such is the spirit of the Saxon army," noted a callous Ney. Reynier's calls for moderation did not move Ney, who only accused his foreign units of disloyalty. "All of the foreign troops manifest the worst possible morale," complained Ney, adding that his German cavalry did more harm than good. He warned that the Saxons in particular appeared likely to "turn their guns on us when they get the chance."[53] Unfortunately for the French, this prophecy came true in mid-October, when the Saxons abandoned Napoleon and defected to the Allies in the midst of the epic struggle at Leipzig.

As the defeat at Dennewitz threatened to rip the German satellites from the French alliance, the victory at Dennewitz proved equally unsettling for the Army of North Germany. Following Dennewitz, debate over the army's next step increased the friction between Bülow and Bernadotte. Despite the growing list of Allied victories, Napoleon still loomed in the distance. If one of the three Allied armies imprudently ventured forward, it could easily fall prey to the emperor. From his central position at Dresden, Napoleon waited for such an opportunity. Regardless of the risk, Bülow believed that the Army of North Germany had to cross the Elbe. On 7 September he outlined the advantages of crossing the river in a petition to Bernadotte. Tauentzien's corps would mask Wittenberg and Torgau; Wallmoden would hold Davout's corps at Hamburg, while the rest of the army marched to Leipzig in accordance with the Trachenberg Plan. Bernadotte had the opportunity to threaten Napoleon's lines of communication along the Leipzig-Dresden highway and even harass the rear of the Grande Armée. The Prussians also believed that Ney's army posed little threat. The condition of the French army increased the chances of another Allied victory should Ney be forced to accept battle. A reprieve would only allow him to recover and hold the line of the Elbe. Bülow concluded that even if Napoleon approached with reinforcements the Army of North Germany would have enough time to escape over the Elbe.[54]

Such an operation required determination on the part of Bernadotte. Bülow's proposed offensive demanded flexibility and mobility as well as the resolve to overcome minor obstacles in the pursuit of total victory. These prerequisites appeared to be foreign to the crown prince of Sweden in September of 1813. For Bernadotte, the Elbe's dark waters served as his Rubicon; boldly carrying the war across it proved politically and psychologically impossible. For Bülow and the Prussians, however, crossing the Elbe and launching an offensive against their oppressor seemed the only way to liberate the Fatherland for good.

Bernadotte spent the days following Dennewitz collecting statements about the battle. He eagerly asked prisoners if Napoleon himself had been present. The crown prince then published another controversial and politically charged account of the battle in the *Tenth Bulletin*. According to Bernadotte's version, once the Prussians had engaged the French,

> seventy Russian and Swedish battalions, 10,000 horses of both nations, and 150 pieces of artillery advanced in attack columns. . . . Four thousand Russian and Swedish cavalry advanced in full speed to support some points whither the enemy principally directed his attack. Their appearance checked him, and the appearance of the columns did the rest. The fate of the battle was instantly decided. The enemy's army beat a retreat; the cavalry charged with a boldness resembling fury and carried disorder into his columns, which retreated in great haste.[55]

Contemporaries praised Bernadotte for employing a "keen knowledge of psychology" in his propaganda. With the assistance of literary and political figures such as Madame Anne Louis Germaine de Staël, August Schlegel, and Benjamin Constant, Bernadotte's headquarters spewed forth propaganda that at times had a very demoralizing effect on the enemy. He has even been credited with using propaganda "more consciously and more thoroughly" than Napoleon.[56] On this occasion

Bernadotte's propaganda undoubtedly proved demoralizing, but those most affected happened to be the Prussians of his own army.

Bülow took offense at the crown prince's official account of the battle, which the Berlin newspapers also published. He especially objected to Bernadotte's claim that the Swedes and Russians had won the battle; even the numbers defied the truth, for the crown prince only commanded 46 battalions, 40 squadrons, and 118 guns. Despite receiving praise for his troops' courage, Bülow felt that the statements denied him and his men the honor they deserved. The Bulletin attributed the victory to the whole army and diminished the role of the Prussians. Bernadotte implied that the Prussian corps had fought as a vanguard, while the army followed close behind. Of Bernadotte's columns that had caused such fear in the enemy, Bülow had seen nothing except two Swedish horse batteries. An adamant Bülow maintained that the two Prussian corps had fought alone. He attempted to set the record straight with his own account, but Lecocq and Wittgenstein once again refused to publish his version in the Berlin press.[57] "When reading the Berlin newspapers," vented Bülow, "I became thoroughly disgusted by Bernadotte's shameful Bulletins. He is purposely trying to deceive the public into believing that he had participated in the battle of Dennewitz. His Bulletins contain almost nothing but lies; there is not one word of truth."[58] He informed Pauline that the Berlin municipal government had asked the crown prince for permission to mint a commemorative medallion stamped with his portrait as a memorial to him as the savior of Berlin. Bernadotte responded that although they were chiefly indebted to Bülow, they could still stamp the medal with his portrait, but the other side had to contain the names of Bülow and Tauentzien as well as the Swedish generals Stedingk, Adlercreutz, and Tawast and the Russian generals Mikhail Semyonovitch Vorontsov and Wintzingerode. "When I learned of this," noted a seething Bülow, "I informed the Government that they could not stamp my name on this medal."[59]

Although Bülow may have overreacted, others in Bernadotte's headquarters shared his sentiments and reported the events at Dennewitz to their superiors. Tsar Alexander in particular began to question the prince-royal's commitment to the war effort. As early as 12 August he had instructed the Russian envoy in Bernadotte's headquarters, Pozzo di Borgo, to insure that the crown prince's personal considerations did not influence his decisions as an Allied commander. On 7 September Pozzo wrote a lengthy report to the tsar that described the crown prince's actions at Dennewitz.[60] His opening line amply stated the overall dissatisfaction with Bernadotte: "the harshest expressions can be used to describe the actions of the crown prince." According to Pozzo, an army had "never found itself in a more hazardous and desperate situation than that of Marshal Ney." He recalled that when Bülow's report arrived describing Ney's position and the opening moves of the battle, Bernadotte "only turned to his entourage and criticized the actions of this general." Although he did issue orders to assist Bülow, Pozzo felt that the Prussians "were left to their own fate." He insisted that Bernadotte had no intentions other than to "pick up the [Prussian] troops after they had been defeated." Pozzo explained that as the battle escalated, he feared the Prussians would be destroyed, while 40,000 Russians and Swedes watched. The native Corsican even claimed that Bernadotte had disappeared for more than one hour. When he finally reappeared, "everyone explained to him the necessity to march," especially since the French had no idea of Bernadotte's strength. Although the crown prince finally gave the order to advance, Pozzo stressed that the Swedish corps did not reach the battlefield until "after the French had been driven from the field, and the pursuing Prussians could no longer be seen." Pozzo's conclusion posed a dilemma that Alexander had to consider: "My personal opinion, and that of all the generals with whom I spoke, is that the crown prince could have arrived around 3:00 with his 40,000 men and destroyed the French. According to [his] calculations, Bülow, left alone, would have been defeated; only Bülow's intrepidity and that of his troops averted an Allied disaster. I did not refrain from attempting to motivate the prince."[61]

A subsequent letter from Thornton to Castlereagh also rebuked Bernadotte. The British envoy wrote that he had perceived "a great reluctance on the part of the Crown Prince to give the events of the day a decisive character, and ultimately finish the war in this area by the total defeat and destruction of the enemy's army—which was completely in the Crown Prince's power to accomplish." Thornton accused the Swedes of not executing their approach march as fast as possible, despite Bülow's urgent calls for support. He revealed that "when the Russians and Swedes arrived, one had delayed so much in giving the order to advance, and so much doubt and altering views were brought to light, that the Crown Prince soon went here and there so aimlessly that the attack upon the enemy was delayed for three to four costly hours." During this time "the Prussians stood alone against the enemy and suffered large losses." Had Bernadotte managed his time more efficiently, Thornton believed that Ney's army could have been destroyed. Thornton's conclusion provided powerful testimony:

> I believe to have seen in the battle of Groß Beeren on 23 August, as well as in the subsequent movements since then, a reluctance in the movements of the army in order to spare the Swedish corps from a great battle or heavy losses. I remarked to Colonel Pozzo di Borgo that a great contradiction exists between [Bernadotte's] wish to protect the Swedes, and the enduring wish to protect the French, and asked him for his opinion. He answered that in his opinion, both of these wishes had dictated the actions of the Prince, and that whichever of the two motives was stronger, a reluctance to decide and end the struggle [at Dennewitz] had nevertheless been present. He added that similar judgements were shared by all of the other generals. Pozzo di Borgo has already reported this to the Tsar; Vincent and Krusemarck have informed their sovereigns.[62]

Bernadotte's actions at Dennewitz even angered his Swedes, whose losses in the battle amounted to twelve wounded. At a banquet in Coswig, the Swedish commander of Stedingk's First Division, Gen. A. F. Skjöldebrand, told Bernadotte of his embarrassment at receiving an order to halt his cavalry just before it engaged the French. "You wish that I allow the Swedish army to take part in every encounter and dissolve itself through losses, so that I have no army of my own left?" replied Bernadotte. He asked Skjöldebrand if he was certain that the army would not be needed "for Sweden's own affair, when the issue is to take Norway."[63] Thornton also described the low morale of the Swedish officers. "They have taken no part in the military deeds of the day," he noted. "I could clearly see this attitude in Baron von Adlercreutz, who explained to Colonel Pozzo di Borgo that the entire French army could have been destroyed if the Swedes and Russians had acted in time."[64] Pozzo's report to the tsar also confirmed Thornton's story. He added that Bernadotte had "almost continuously stood by the Swedish troops, with whom he made various movements, but many times would stop one mile from the decision. In addition, the instructions to General Wintzingerode were also indecisive and he complained to me more than once."[65]

According to these reports, as well as the crown prince's statements to Reiche on the day of the battle, it appeared that Bernadotte wanted to sacrifice the Prussians and purposely calculated their defeat. After Bülow held his position, Bernadotte saved face by ordering the Swedish and Russian corps to advance. This became obvious to the military envoys, who now openly accused the crown prince of treachery. Nevertheless, Bernadotte's obsessive desire to husband his Swedish manpower became an accepted fact in the Army of North Germany. One year later, at the height of the 1814 campaign to take Norway, Bernadotte finally admitted his policy of safe-guarding the Swedes during the previous campaign. In a letter to Frederick William, the crown prince requested the support of a Prussian detachment, which he promised to utilize in Sweden's cause with as much caution as he had employed his Swedes in Prussia's cause in 1813.[66]

Despite the negative reports that flowed out of Bernadotte's camp, the Allied sovereigns took no steps to remove the prince-royal. Only Alexander urged Bernadotte to undertake offensive operations regardless of the situation or the immobility of his own forces.[67] The tsar's displeasure with Bernadotte remains suspect, since the crown prince eventually succeeded in getting Pozzo replaced. Castlereagh's reply to Thornton also reflects the tedious nature of coalition warfare:

> You must understand how important it is to keep this point a secret. It is one of those cases in which all must be employed in order to allow this impression to sink into oblivion. . . . The accusation of sympathizing with the enemy is so serious that one dare not make it unless it can be proven. His hostility toward Bonaparte is . . . not to be questioned. The weakness exists, as I believe, in the wish to enlist a faction in France and in the French army. His name and his talents as an officer, his success, and his Swedes themselves are of great importance.[68]

Regardless of the diplomatic fallout that occurred after the battle of Dennewitz, the war continued. As in the days following Groß Beeren, the Army of North Germany again crawled forward, and the Prussians increased their demands for an offensive. Except for scouting parties, Bernadotte's army stood idle on the seventh and eighth.[69] Bülow sent Boyen to urge the crown prince forward, but this only increased the tension. During the discussion Boyen learned that the army remained stationary due to reports that Davout had begun an offensive from Hamburg. Bernadotte believed that if Davout crossed the Elbe, it would be "to take command of the garrison at Magdeburg, march on Ziesar and Brandenburg, harass my right flank, and paralyze my operations." According to the crown prince, such an operation would probably foreshadow Napoleon's appearance in the theater.[70] Davout enjoyed a slight numerical superiority over Wallmoden's force, but the Prussian Landsturm and reinforcements from Tauentzien's corps would have been able to slow his advance. Regardless, Bernadotte claimed that he could not distance himself from Berlin. Moreover, the crown prince simply refused to attempt a passage over the Elbe between Wittenberg and Magdeburg without a bridgehead.[71]

Instead of mounting a general offensive Bernadotte spread his army along the highway that ran from Wittenberg through Jüterbog to Dahme, with advanced units posted along the Black Elster. The two Prussian corps advanced southeast toward Torgau.[72] Although he did not issue an explicit order to cross the Elbe, Bernadotte did instruct the Russians to prepare for the crossing of at least 60,000 men at Rosslau, west of Wittenberg and opposite the march route of the two Prussian corps. The Russians also invested Wittenberg, bombarding the fortress on the night of 9 October.[73] That evening Bernadotte's army extended between Rosslau and Luckau—a front of over 80 miles. Another day of rest was granted on the tenth.[74]

Reports placed Ney's army between Torgau and the Mulde. It appeared that the marshal had neglected to occupy the Rosslau-Dessau area west of Wittenberg. Although this provided an excellent opportunity for Bernadotte's army to cross both the Elbe and the Mulde, the bulk of the Army of North Germany stood idle on the eleventh; only the Russian advance guard moved to the Black Elster and the Swedes to Seyda; Hirschfeld's brigade occupied Zahna. Cossacks continued to scour the region between the Black Elster and the Elbe.[75]

Squandering the opportunity to exploit the victory at Dennewitz increased Bülow's indignation.[76] He sought answers from Krusemarck, who replied that both Pozzo di Borgo and Vincent had explained to the crown prince that the situation demanded a general offensive. Krusemarck insisted that the envoys continuously goaded the prince-royal to utilize the precious time. After meeting with Bernadotte on the eleventh, Krusemarck informed Bülow that the crown prince appeared committed to the idea of crossing the Elbe with at least a part of the army. The Prussian envoy did relay his doubts that Bernadotte would adopt Bülow's plan for a bold offensive. He explained that Bernadotte "certainly does not wish for the Prussian corps alone to earn all of the fame and honor" but added that the Elbe crossing might be delayed for some time since Bernadotte complained that he lacked the necessary materials.[77]

By the twelfth mounting pressure finally moved Bernadotte. Probably to increase morale and pacify his disgruntled subordinates, he instructed each corps commander to bring up enough ammunition for a two-day battle. The Russians and the Swedes formed the right wing of the army and marched west in the direction of Coswig. Only Tauentzien's corps continued to march up the Elbe to observe Torgau.[78] Thirty miles to the east Cossacks sought Blücher's army after rumors circulated of its approach from Silesia. Bülow's corps remained idle, but he received orders to bridge the Elbe at Elster. Bernadotte's instructions for 13 September contained an ominous addendum for the victor of Dennewitz: Bülow had to requisition two mortars, two heavy howitzers, and four twelve-pounders from Spandau "to be employed at the siege and bombardment of Wittenberg." Perhaps tired of Bülow's constant meddling, the crown prince dealt with his bothersome subordinate on the following day by assigning him to the siege of Wittenberg. The victor of Hagelberg, Hirschfeld, also found his Prussian brigade assigned to the siege to support Bülow. Adlercreutz explained to a bewildered Bülow that the army could not "cross the Elbe without having a stronghold on one of the banks." To justify the siege, Bernadotte attempted to convince the Prussians that as long as the French controlled Wittenberg and Torgau, Berlin would never be completely safe, and the army destined to cover the capital would never be able to leave its vicinity.[79]

Without a field army, Wittenberg posed no threat to Berlin. A veteran soldier such as Bernadotte should have recognized Wittenberg's minimal value. Bülow agreed that Wittenberg needed to be masked, but felt a formal siege was unnecessary. He interpreted the assignment as punishment. The prospects of leashing the veteran corps to the rock of Wittenberg drove resentment to new heights in Bülow's camp. To add insult to injury, the crown prince wrote that the fall of Wittenberg would be Bülow's crowning achievement. Bülow again protested by reminding headquarters that the king of Prussia had designated Tauentzien's corps for these auxiliary duties.[80] His protests were ignored. Bernadotte shackled Bülow to Wittenberg under the pretense that the Army of North Germany could not cross the Elbe while the fortress remained a French possession. Rather than attempt to alter the course of the war, Bernadotte planned to maneuver the other corps of his army north of the Elbe, while the irksome Bülow conducted a lengthy siege. According to the Trachenberg Plan, the Army of North Germany should have pursued Ney until threatened by Napoleon himself. Fortunately for Bülow, other influential men attached to Bernadotte's headquarters shared these views and communicated them to the Allied sovereigns.

13

Crossing the Rubicon

Napoleon's situation had dramatically worsened after just one month of campaigning. The success of the Trachenberg Plan had depleted the ranks of his Grande Armée; the French had lost 150,000 men and 300 guns since the expiration of the armistice, and an additional 50,000 names filled the sick roles.[1] While French commanders suffered defeats at Groß Beeren, the Katzbach, Hagelberg, Kulm, and Dennewitz, the emperor raced back and forth between the Elbe and the Bober Rivers in futile attempts to achieve the decisive victory that had eluded him thus far. Under normal conditions the constant marches and countermarches would have exhausted his conscripts both mentally and physically. Yet the conditions remained far from normal. Heavy rains washed out roads, and Cossacks menaced the lines of communication. Although Napoleon granted his men plenty of rest, the slow starvation of the army could not be ignored. Supply shortages and the exhaustion of the Saxon countryside prompted Napoleon to write: "The army is no longer fed; to view it in any other way would be mere self-deception."[2]

Politically, Napoleon's hold on Central Europe steadily weakened. The Rheinbund princes observed his setting star and pondered negotiating with the Allied sovereigns. Only Saxony remained the emperor's impressed servant, but even King Frederick Augustus's continued adherence to the French system seemed to be coming to an end as Saxon desertions increased. The crown prince of Sweden formed a Saxon Legion and waged a paper campaign to encourage the Saxons to defect. Although Napoleon's political problems seemed acute, one decisive victory similar to Austerlitz or Jena-Auerstädt would restore his position in Central Europe. Time, however, was running out for the emperor.

Napoleon's failure to destroy either Blücher or Schwarzenberg had contributed to Ney's disaster at Dennewitz. Blücher's steady pressure on Macdonald had forced Napoleon to move against the Silesian Army in early September rather than march north to support Ney. Once Napoleon approached, Blücher withdrew eastward. With Blücher's threat removed, Napoleon again made arrangements to support Ney. Just when it appeared that the emperor would finally confront Bernadotte, he had to race back to Dresden after reports indicated that Schwarzenberg had left his Bohemian lair. These reports turned out to be true; the Bohemian Army crossed the Elbe after Schwarzenberg learned of Napoleon's advance against Blücher. In fact, Schwarzenberg had divided his army. He advanced with 60,000 men against the right flank of the French army that faced Blücher. Barclay led the other half of the Bohemian Army through the mountains toward Dresden. Schwarzenberg hoped this would draw Napoleon to Dresden so that he and Blücher could crush Macdonald.[3] The plan worked, and the emperor returned to Dresden on 8 September. Schwarzenberg, however, lost his nerve and ordered a retreat on all fronts. Two days later a pursuing Napoleon confronted Barclay in the Teplitz Valley. Fortunately for Barclay, the strength of the Allied position—combined with the poor mountain passes that hindered the movement of heavy artillery—prevented the emperor from attacking; the two armies faced each other for the next few days.

Confirmed reports of Ney's disaster at Dennewitz also contributed to Napoleon's hesitation. Although Marmont claims that the emperor received the news "with all the coolness he could have brought to a discussion of events in China," he had to be concerned that Bernadotte might cross the Elbe and march on Leipzig—the Grande Armée's vital communications link with the Rhine.[4] On 10 September Napoleon insisted that Ney remain on the right bank of the Elbe and face the Army of North Germany. He assured Ney that Gen. Samuel-François Lhéritier's Fifth Cavalry Corps at Grossenhain and Macdonald's army just east of Bautzen would cover his exposed right flank.[5] Napoleon perhaps planned to join Ney to revive the "master plan." Even after two failures, the emperor still looked to the advantages of a successful drive through Berlin to the Oder and perhaps as far as the Vistula. Although the men in Bernadotte's army might disagree, the North German plain had more to offer the hungry French soldier than the ravaged Saxon countryside. Strategically, Napoleon hoped that an eastward offensive through Berlin would draw the Russians and Prussians out of Saxony and isolate the Austrians. Moreover, the destruction of Bernadotte's army would counterbalance his subordinates' successive failures. With such thoughts in mind, Napoleon returned to Dresden on 12 September. Renewed advances by both Schwarzenberg and Blücher during the next ten days forced him to leave Ney to his own devices.

Although Allied victories signaled the success of the Trachenberg Plan, desperation had ruled Grand Allied Headquarters since Schwarzenberg's defeat at Dresden on 27 August. Convinced that Napoleon would pursue his battered army and perhaps make for Prague, Schwarzenberg had ordered Blücher to send 50,000 men to reinforce the Bohemian Army.[6] Such a massive concentration of Allied forces in Bohemia, however, did not correspond to the coalition's needs. If Blücher united with Schwarzenberg, Napoleon would be handed another opportunity to maneuver the bulk of his adversaries' forces into a decisive battle. The fall campaign had already proven that Allied forces could match the Grande Armée, but Napoleon's generalship suffered no rival in Central Europe. Despite his inability to capitalize on this very situation at Lützen and Bautzen during the spring campaign, the Allies certainly could not allow themselves to create a situation that might produce another Austerlitz. Moreover, a union of the Bohemian and Silesian Armies would contradict the Trachenberg Plan, hinder its execution, and allow Napoleon to regain the initiative. Nevertheless, Grand Allied Headquarters remained committed to the idea of bringing Blücher's army, or a significant portion of it, westward to support Schwarzenberg. Only Vandamme's defeat at Kulm on 29 August eased the pressure on Schwarzenberg and restored some confidence in Grand Allied Headquarters. Schwarzenberg and the Allied sovereigns spared Blücher from marching to Bohemia, but they did not forget the idea.

By 10 September, as noted, the situation again seemed dire after Napoleon returned from Bautzen to counter the Bohemian Army's advance. Schwarzenberg believed the French emperor would attack Barclay at Teplitz. On the following evening Tsar Alexander once more summoned Blücher to Bohemia. After another day of anxious waiting, the situation again changed to favor the Allies. Napoleon resisted the temptation to attack and returned to Dresden on the twelfth. On 13 September Grand Allied Headquarters received news of the victory at Dennewitz. This proved so encouraging that Schwarzenberg decided to advance. On that same day a response to the tsar's summons arrived from Blücher. In a letter composed by Gneisenau, the Prussians suggested that the Army of Silesia march to Wittenberg rather than Bohemia. They argued that the victory at Dennewitz had completely altered the war. Gneisenau disclosed that Blücher had already summoned the crown prince of Sweden to cross the Elbe and advance on Leipzig. He added that this movement would only be effective if the Silesian Army also crossed the Elbe somewhere between Torgau and Wittenberg. Constantly informed of Bernadotte's dubious actions by the diligent Boyen, Gneisenau concluded that if the Silesian Army marched to Bohemia the crown prince would remain in "a completely unjustified idleness."[7] Throughout that long night the monarchs and officers at Grand Allied Headquarters debated the advantages of having Blücher cross the Elbe with Bernadotte or moving the Silesian Army to Bohemia. Ultimately they could only agree to leave the decision to Blücher's judgment. According to the early-twentieth-century chief of Section II of the Historical Section of the Great German General Staff, Col. Rudolf von Friederich, "one did not dare put what one wished in the form of an order, and so accept the consequences."[8]

While the thirteenth proved to be a day of indecision, the fourteenth did much to shape Allied strategy for the remainder of the war in Germany. A second letter from Blücher arrived that further addressed the tsar's summons to Bohemia. In a more conciliatory tone Blücher announced that he would march to Bohemia but hoped the tsar would change his mind after he received the news of Dennewitz. Blücher wrote to the king's adjutant, Knesebeck, asking him to "avoid forcing me to unite with the Bohemian Army. What can such a huge mass effect on such difficult terrain? Here I will be effective and useful. I will change the crown prince's plans so that he moves forward with determined steps."[9]

More effective than these letters proved to be the verbal report of an aide from Blücher's staff, Maj. Rühle von Lilienstern. He portrayed Blücher's march to the Elbe as the only means to motivate the crown prince of Sweden. The major communicated Blücher's insistence that

Gen. Gebhard Leberecht von Blücher (1742–1819). Blücher was revered by his troops as "Papa Blücher" and "Old Forward"; his greatest victory over Napoleon in head-to-head contests came on 9 March 1814 at Laon.

Bernadotte would do nothing as long as he remained isolated north of the Elbe. Lilienstern reiterated Gneisenau's belief that only the appearance of the Silesian Army would force the crown prince to cross the Elbe. His lecture convinced the monarchs to drop the plan of moving the Silesian Army to Bohemia. To satisfy the Austrians, Alexander transferred the protection of Bohemia to Gen. Leonti Leontjewitch

Bennigsen's 60,000 strong Army of Poland, which was marching southwest through Silesia. According to Friederich, this "was unquestionably one of the most momentous decisions made by Allied Headquarters."[10] Only the need to maintain pressure on Macdonald and mask Bennigsen's approach delayed Blücher for another ten days.

As for the Army of North Germany, Bülow led the bulk of his corps to Wittenberg on 14 September, while his engineers built a bridge at Elster. On the following day Tauentzien destroyed the bridge over the Elbe at Torgau.[11] Northwest of the Prussians the remainder of the army moved west to Rosslau and Zerbst, and Chernyshov crossed the Elbe with 2,000 Cossacks and some artillery. Bernadotte did indeed adopt Bülow's plan to cross the Elbe, but the Third Prussian Corps would not be involved. Wintzingerode received instructions to collect as many boats as possible at Rosslau, while the Swedes fortified Coswig and began work on a bridgehead on the left bank of the Elbe opposite Rosslau.[12] Although Wintzingerode and Stedingk moved the majority of their men to the right bank, only the Cossacks crossed to reconnoiter the region between the Mulde and the Saale.

On the fifteenth Bernadotte responded to a letter from Blücher that urged him to cross the Elbe. Gneisenau, who authored most of Blücher's correspondence, frankly informed the crown prince that a copy of the proposal had already been forwarded to Tsar Alexander. Knowing that the Allied sovereigns would watch these developments closely, the crown prince chose his words carefully. He explained to Blücher that at present he could not cross the Elbe:

> A few days ago I was in a critical situation with 70,000 men facing me, the Oder fortresses behind me, Magdeburg, Wittenberg, and Torgau in front of me, and 10,000 men on my right flank. The day of the 6th has done much to improve our situation. The enemy no longer holds the region of the right bank in front of us and Marshal Davout has withdrawn to the right bank of the Stecknitz. Nevertheless, all of this does not eliminate the difficulties of crossing the Elbe. The line that I have to keep is immense; it spreads from Hamburg to Torgau. The enemy has three outlets on the [Elbe] river. He can march on Berlin from Magdeburg, while I march on Leipzig. I do not attach the fate of monarchies to that of their capitals, but the case of Berlin is an exception; if the French advance there, they

> would find immense resources, and would fully destroy the means to recruit and equip the Prussian army. Nevertheless, I am determined to cross the Elbe, and will make the necessary preparations.[13]

Just as the crown prince finished dictating his reply, he received a report of French activity around Grossenhain. This provided further reason for Bernadotte to delay crossing the Elbe. "I just received a report confirming that Napoleon has advanced his army to Grossenhain," added the crown prince in a postscript to Blücher. "Now do you see how difficult it is for me to cross the Elbe in force with my left flank thus threatened?"[14]

At this point, when Grand Allied Headquarters became particularly interested in the Army of North Germany's next move, the crown prince of Sweden encountered serious opposition from both of his Prussian corps commanders. Bülow, who reluctantly besieged Wittenberg, believed that the entire operation only served to mask Bernadotte's inertia. His lack of heavy artillery made the task virtually impossible. He complained that his veterans had to conduct a siege while the other Allied corps marched to cross the Elbe. Bülow referred to the task as a "cheap reward" for a corps that had lost twenty percent of its manpower since the resumption of hostilities. He reminded Bernadotte that "all other armies operate from the principle that one must destroy the enemy's forces, but here we remain passive and do absolutely nothing to operate in unison with the other armies." Bülow reiterated the need for the Army of North Germany to cross the Elbe and establish communication with Schwarzenberg's army. He insisted that they had to assist Blücher and Schwarzenberg "through a rapid offensive operation." Bülow also warned that if Schwarzenberg and Blücher pressed the Grande Armée while Bernadotte remained idle, Napoleon would be forced to withdraw toward Wittenberg and Torgau—the path of least resistance.[15] Bülow's argument incorporated the same key element—the joint operation of all three armies—that would bring the Allies ultimate success at the battle of Leipzig in mid-October, but would the crown prince recognize this?

Bernadotte responded by explaining that the bridge at Elster would paralyze any French units on the left bank of the Elbe. As for Wittenberg, he wanted the fortress taken immediately "because it threatens the Prussian capital."[16] Apologists have defended Bernadotte's reluctance to cross the Elbe on the grounds of Schwarzenberg's lethargy and Blücher's distance from the Army of North Germany. Some insist that had the crown prince crossed the Elbe and advanced deeper into Saxony he would have opened the road from Dresden to Berlin and might have enabled Napoleon to destroy each Allied army in turn. Others have argued that Bernadotte's keen understanding of Napoleon's art of war, especially the emperor's ability to execute "snake-like movements," warranted his concerns over Wittenberg.[17]

Wittenberg itself, small and equipped with obsolete bastions, did not rank among history's most daunting fortresses. A moat provided its main defense. Although the Prussians harbored little love for the Saxons, Bernadotte's orders to bombard and burn Wittenberg sparked little enthusiasm in Bülow's camp. Shelling the city did not correspond to Prussia's political agenda. Before Napoleon had even lost a battle in 1813, the Prussians had dreams of a post-Napoleonic Europe where Prussia's borders swept south over the Elbe. They wanted the Saxons to view them as liberators rather than murderers. Moreover, incinerating the city posed no threat to the French and provided no military grounds for capitulation. This meant that Bülow would have to conduct a lengthy formal siege to breach the walls and storm the fortress. His corps lacked the necessary equipment for such an operation. Bülow's "siege train" consisted of two mortars, two heavy howitzers, and four twelve-pounders—the ordinance from Spandau. Once these guns arrived, they had to be used sparingly due to the general shortage of munitions. Bülow's smaller-caliber field guns had little effect against Wittenberg's walls, and, on a practical note, he refused to ruin the chassis of his field guns through daily bombardments.[18]

Regardless of Prussian complaints, the crown prince wanted Bülow to open the siege trenches on the night of the sixteenth or on the seventeenth at the latest.[19] While the Prussians prepared their siege, Bernadotte transferred his headquarters farther west to Zerbst, much to Bülow's chagrin. The Prussians interpreted this as further proof of the crown prince's reluctance to begin an offensive. Bülow responded by proposing another offensive in which his corps would cross the Elbe at Elster, while the Swedes and Russians crossed at Dessau. The army would either locate Ney and destroy him or march against the French forces at Grossenhain. Hirschfeld's brigade would invest Wittenberg on both banks of the Elbe, while Tauentzien would cover the army's left wing from Torgau. This plan did not exceed the army's capabilities—and to please the prince-royal it included the siege of Wittenberg. Risk remained minimal: if Napoleon decided to attack Bernadotte, the Army of North Germany would have plenty of time to escape over the Elbe.[20]

Boyen once again received the odious task of delivering the plan to army headquarters. He reached Zerbst on the evening of the fifteenth and secured an audience with the crown prince around 9:00. While rendering his report of the siege, Boyen attempted to slip Bülow's proposal into the conversation. He failed miserably. Disregarding the military situation, Bernadotte immediately launched a tirade of accusations against Bülow. The meeting, which Boyen described as "savage," lasted until 2:30 A.M. Weary of Bülow's meddling, the crown prince accused him of insubordination and sabotage.[21] Bernadotte based his charges on personnel reports that he had received from a Prussian official, allegedly Wittgenstein. Armed with these dubious character profiles, Bernadotte drew an outrageous conclusion regarding Bülow's politics. He considered Bülow's friendship with Prince Louis Ferdinand, the leader and chief agitator of the Prussian war hawks, who had been killed in 1806. In addition, Bernadotte knew of the problems caused by Bülow's brother, the contentious military theorist Heinrich Dietrich. Since Louis Ferdinand had often been on bad terms with his cousin, King Frederick William III, and Bülow's brother had supposedly died in prison as an enemy of the state, the crown prince concluded that Bülow was a subversive revolutionary. He placed Bülow at the head of the controversial *Tugenbund*, a secret organization that Bülow had labored to prevent from spreading in the army prior to 1813.[22] Bernadotte assumed that Bülow pursued a covert and dangerous agenda that threatened the Prussian monarchy. The crown prince even claimed to know that Boyen was actually a police agent sent by the king of Prussia to spy on Bülow!

Despite his efforts, Boyen could not change Bernadotte's mind. In the middle of his rebuttal Bernadotte screamed: "What will you do if I arrest Bülow?" The crown prince used the remainder of the conference to berate Bülow and his staff. Instead of clearing his commander's name, Boyen succeeded in convincing Bernadotte that he was actually Bülow's accomplice rather than the king's secret agent. At this point Boyen lost his composure as well as his ability to voice his opinion in French, the language spoken in Bernadotte's headquarters. When the conversation returned to bombarding Wittenberg, his frustration mounted. In order to avert the pointless murder of the inhabitants, he again pointed out the operation's futility. After his military and political reasoning failed to persuade Bernadotte, Boyen lost all restraint and shrieked, "[S]o, Your Highness wants us to burn the cradle of your Apostle as well?" A puzzled Bernadotte demanded an explanation. "Luther" was Boyen's simple response; Bernadotte had converted from Catholicism to Lutheranism in order to be adopted by the king of Sweden. With this bitter exchange, the meeting adjourned with relations between the crown prince and the Prussians at an all-time low.[23] Coalition warfare certainly had its darker side.

Meanwhile, increased French activity around Grossenhain had alarmed Tauentzien. Wobeser reported the appearance of a large corps allegedly commanded by Murat. Bernadotte did not believe that the presence of a corps at Grossenhain signaled a French offensive on the right bank of the Elbe against Berlin but did authorize Tauentzien to seek support from Blücher and ordered him to burn Luckau if he could not hold it. The crown prince refused to commit any reinforcements to his left flank.[24] Tauentzien's situation became more precarious after his scouts reported that French troops had occupied Mühlberg and Elsterwerda, just south of Torgau. In desperation he requested that Blücher march on Grossenhain. "We lose time and do nothing," explained Tauentzien in a letter to Blücher. "It appears that Napoleon wants to exploit the weakness of our left and send a corps commanded by Murat to Luckau. My great desire is to unite with Your Excellency."[25] Tauentzien informed Blücher and Bernadotte that he planned to withdraw to Luckau if pressed by a superior force.

Although Bernadotte used the enemy force at Grossenhain as another reason to keep his army on the right bank of the Elbe, he did not believe Tauentzien's claims that the French would resume their operations against North Germany. He informed the Prussian corps commander that the French would not move north, since Blücher's army would "be able to come across the rear of the enemy from the second he marches." At this point the relationship between Tauentzien and the crown prince finally soured. Bernadotte inferred that by choosing Luckau as a point of retreat Tauentzien only sought to elude his orders. To counter this he firmly instructed Tauentzien to "withdraw toward General Bülow in the unlikely case that the enemy executes a serious operation against Berlin."[26]

On 16 September Tauentzien reported that additional French forces had reached Grossenhain. Spies claimed that Napoleon himself would lead these troops against Berlin.[27] A concerned Bülow suggested that the Army of North Germany concentrate at either Jüterbog or Dahme to close the roads to Berlin. He explained to Bernadotte that "according to confirmed reports, two enemy corps with a considerable cavalry force are advancing from Dresden through Grossenhain and Marshal Ney is in Torgau."[28] Bernadotte repeated his belief that the activity around Grossenhain did not imply an offensive against Berlin.[29] Although he insisted that Blücher's approach would freeze the French force at Grossenhain, the ever-cautious prince-royal ordered the Military Governments in Berlin and Stargard to "organize a national war effort" and even requested a levée en masse![30]

The Grossenhain affair finally reached its anticlimactic end on the seventeenth. Wobeser reported that the main purpose of the entire French operation had been to protect a supply convoy moving south from Torgau to Dresden.[31] Although committing one corps and a significant amount of cavalry to ensure the safe delivery of flour remained indicative of Napoleon's severe supply problems, the controversy over Grossenhain provided a victory for Bernadotte in his struggle with the Prussians. As is typical of coalition warfare, the resulting bitterness only contributed to the mounting frustration felt by all of the key players in the Army of North Germany. Due to their lack of confidence in Bernadotte, the two Prussian corps commanders gradually undermined the command process. Bülow passively resisted besieging Wittenberg, while Tauentzien surreptitiously pursued a union with Blücher. In fact, on the very next day Tauentzien suggested that Borstell take over the siege of Torgau in order to allow the Fourth Prussian Corps to join Blücher's army at Bautzen.[32] Bernadotte refused and argued that since he planned "to make a great movement against Leipzig" he did not want Tauentzien overextended on the upper Spree. The crown prince patiently reiterated the need to take the bridgehead of Torgau in order to guarantee the security of Berlin.[33]

Meanwhile the siege of Wittenberg continued; Hirschfeld, Thümen, and Krafft invested the portion of the fortress on the right bank of the Elbe. The French garrison occupied houses in the suburbs but did not venture out.[34] Bülow remained ten miles to the east in Seyda with Hessen-Homburg's and Borstell's brigades to oversee the construction

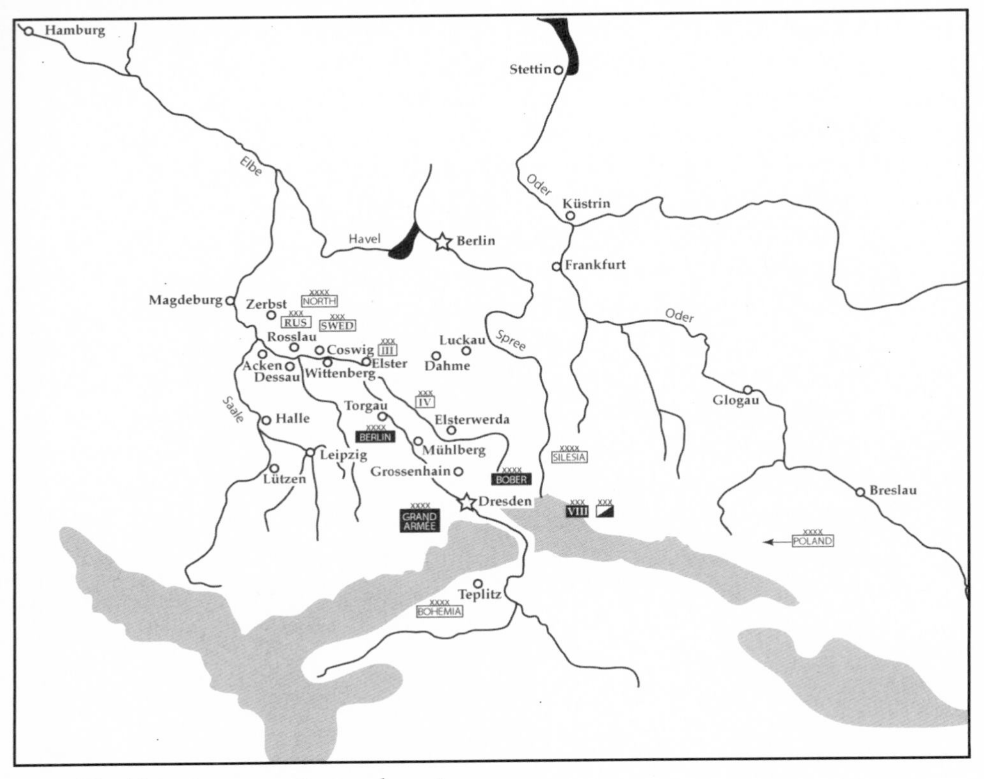

The Situation on 19 September 1813

on the Elster bridge. The Prussian engineers completed construction on 21 September, and Borstell's battalions occupied the bridgehead. Bülow sent a cavalry regiment over the Elbe with orders to raid as far as possible along the left bank.

The French had paid little heed to Bülow's bridge until the twenty-second. From the sixteenth until the twenty-first Ney maneuvered his subordinates between the Elbe and the Mulde in an attempt to discover Bernadotte's next move. Ney's anxiety over an Allied crossing heightened as conflicting reports indicated ever-increasing numbers of Allied troops on the right bank of the Elbe. Although large numbers of Cossacks swarmed over the Elbe, only 100 Swedes had actually crossed by the sixteenth to begin the construction of bridgeheads on the left bank. They entered Dessau on the eighteenth, followed by 500 more on the nineteenth. Swedish engineers finished a bridge over the Mulde on 20 September, and a few regiments crossed the river. Construction on another bridge over the Elbe began at Acken on the twenty-first, just as Bülow's men finished their work at Elster.

Bernadotte's actions might have confounded his Prussian subordinates, but they apparently baffled Ney. Allied construction of two bridges west of Wittenberg (Acken and Rosslau) as well as a third south of Wittenberg (Elster) paralyzed the marshal, just as Bernadotte had predicted. Napoleon's orders finally shook Ney into action by instructing him to march on Dessau.[35] On 21 September he moved the majority of Reynier's corps against Dessau, while Bertrand received orders to destroy the Elster bridge. As for Oudinot, his wish had finally been granted on the nineteenth when Napoleon recalled him to command two divisions of the Imperial Guard. The emperor dissolved the Twelfth Corps and transferred the majority of its manpower to Reynier.

During combats on the twenty-second and twenty-third the Army of North Germany repulsed Ney's attacks on all points. When Bülow allowed a limited pursuit of Bertrand's forces, however, he earned another rebuke from headquarters. Adlercreutz informed him that the crown prince did want the Prussians engaged on the left bank. Should the French follow up their probe, Bülow's troops had to evacuate the left bank and extract the bridge to cover their retreat.[36] As a result the Prussians could not prevent Ney from taking the key village of Wartenburg on the left bank.

Ney's movements had also provided Bülow a pleasant distraction from the siege of Wittenberg. In fact, by 20 September he had still not opened the siege trenches or commenced the bombardment. Bülow reported that fifty-six enemy guns, including four forty-eight-pounders and four twenty-four-pounders, protected the walls of Wittenberg, while an additional eighteen heavy guns guarded the bridgehead. Although Bülow possessed nothing heavier than his twelve-pounder field guns, Bernadotte impatiently urged him to hasten the work.[37] Bülow curtly replied that a siege without siege guns could hardly be effective.[38] Three days later he learned that Bernadotte had completed his preparations to cross the Elbe at Rosslau. The prince-royal boasted that he would reach Leipzig within eight days. He now demanded that Bülow open the trench in front of Wittenberg and use the British rocket battery to incinerate the city. According to his spies, the enemy garrison of 2,000 men would surrender if Bülow either attempted to burn the city or threatened a general attack. The crown prince also lectured Bülow on the importance of taking Wittenberg. He reiterated the need to establish a firm position on the Elbe to cover Berlin and secure the army's operations. Bernadotte assured his Prussian subordinate that Napoleon still desired nothing more than to march against Berlin. Resorting to theatrics, Bernadotte promised that although he and Bülow might die, the agonizing regret of imprudence would not follow them to the grave. He added that as soon as Wittenberg fell Bülow could follow him and perhaps form his reserve.[39] Bernadotte's rhetoric had long ceased to have any effect on the Prussians, and the part about forming the reserve only added insult to injury.

Now that Bernadotte appeared poised to cross the Elbe, Bülow more than ever resented being shackled to Wittenberg. He dispatched Märtens to army headquarters in the hopes of convincing the crown prince to assign the siege of Wittenberg to Tauentzien's corps. Before Märtens said a word, Bernadotte began where he had finished with Boyen a few days earlier. He claimed no longer to have any interest in waging war on the Continent. As for command of the army, the prince-royal declared that Bülow could have it since he obviously wanted it so badly. Bernadotte assured Märtens that he and his Swedes had already contributed more to the Allied cause than was necessary. Noting how the Baltic protected Sweden, Bernadotte then berated the Prussians. "You succumb to your old mistakes," he shouted. "Your arrogance will ruin you! You do not know how to obey and have no discipline. Such arrogance has already ruined the Prussian state and it will happen again if you do not change!" He lamented that he had sacrificed everything for the Prussians but received nothing from them except ingratitude. Bernadotte then unveiled his true exasperation:

> I do not need you or your talents. The field-commander must possess them himself, or he does not deserve to command. I ask for nothing more than respect, courage, and especially obedience. I repeat: I have no need of advice! I have my own plans, which have been ruined by you. Look at the Russians: they do what I ask, they know how to obey. I have always been prudent, and have never lost a gun, a flag, or a regiment. I demand your trust. Tell your General that he can come and talk to me as often as he wishes, but that he will not write me in this tone. I will not stand for these petty annoyances. On a day of battle,

> when I am exhausted and consumed by overexertion, and am surrounded by hills of dead men, when misunderstandings and problems arise, then I will ask him for his advice, then he may whisper in my ear and I will recognize his good intentions. But how can you demand that I change my plans according to the opinion of this general? Bülow may judge his task quite well from his position, but you only have to take the map to see the extension of my line from the Stecknitz to Torgau.[40]

On the same day as Märtens's meeting with Bernadotte—24 September—the military attachés asked Bernadotte if he planned to use Prussian troops against the Danes. In this classic example of poor timing Bernadotte chastised them for their indiscretion. He unleashed a seemingly well-rehearsed diatribe that included phrases and arguments similar to those reported by Märtens. The crown prince insisted that he would lead his army where he pleased. He claimed to owe nothing to the Allied sovereigns but everything to the masses; his own deeds had elevated him to royalty. Bernadotte, who suffered no Prussian criticism, turned on Krusemarck and reminded him of Prussia's destruction in 1806. He added that the Prussians should be grateful that he had not captured Frederick William at the battle of Jena![41] Krusemarck had to fake illness in order to leave the meeting and escape Bernadotte's wrath. A few days later the Prussian envoy conveyed the general feeling shared by all of the foreign attachés in a letter to Knesebeck: "The problems caused by the selection of the crown prince to command the Army of North Germany and assume the leadership of a significant part of the affairs had to be foreseen. It appears certain to me that on every occasion he will only consult his political and personal interests, and we can also assume that he will always subordinate public welfare to his own, and that he will never have the willpower to sacrifice the latter for the former."[42]

After his foray Bernadotte felt compelled to draft a memorandum that described the general situation. He wanted to silence his critics by outlining a strategy that showed the importance of taking Wittenberg and Torgau. Once in possession of these two fortresses, he planned to leave 30,000 men at the Elbe and march to either Leipzig or Magdeburg. The crown prince preferred Magdeburg and described it as the key to Westphalia and Hamburg. He firmly believed that its fall would prompt Denmark to submit to Sweden and induce Holland and Belgium to join the Allies. Bernadotte also insisted that the Allies had to use unorthodox methods to defeat Napoleon. Once again the crown prince's grandiloquent statements did not correspond to the strategic situation. His desire to advance toward the lower Elbe and Magdeburg reflected his obsession with defeating the Danes. A victorious end to the war, however, could only be achieved by defeating the Grande Armée. Despite Napoleon's eventual defeat at Leipzig in October, Denmark, Holland, and Belgium did not defect from the French alliance.[43]

While Bernadotte drafted his views on how to win the war, both Napoleon and the Allies made pivotal changes in their respective strategies. On the night of 23 September Napoleon received Ney's report regarding the completion of Bülow's bridge at Elster as well as Bernadotte's activities at Rosslau and Dessau. Napoleon assumed the Allies would finally breach the Elbe and make a concerted effort to reach Dresden or Leipzig. He also realized that he could no longer shift his starving troops back and forth through the depleted Saxon countryside. The Trachenberg Plan had exasperated Napoleon and robbed him of his usual clear, decisive judgment. According to F. L. Petre, "indecision, such as he showed at this time, was certainly not characteristic of Napoleon in his better days. It looks almost as if, like a tiger surrounded by hunters, he was half bewildered, and unable to make up his mind to do more than make short dashes, first on one part, then on another, of the circle that was steadily closing in on him."[44] Historian Donald Horward adds that "his troops marched and counter-marched across Saxony, exhausting their meager resources. Napoleon was so busy reacting to Allied maneuvers that he had no time to implement his own strategy."[45] With only 260,000 men left, the emperor decided to contract his front to conserve manpower. The main withdrawal of all mobile French forces behind the left bank of the upper Elbe began on the twenty-fourth.[46]

Although he adopted this purely defensive measure, Napoleon explained that "in this position I shall watch the enemy closely, and if they engage in any offensive operation, I shall fall upon them, so that they cannot avoid a battle."[47] The use of interior lines would allow him to mass superior numbers against any one of the Allied armies.[48] Napoleon now sought to profit from the enemy's mistakes rather than permit them to exploit the errors of his subordinates. Had he adopted this course at the beginning of the campaign, Groß Beeren, the Katzbach, Hagelberg, and Dennewitz would have never occurred and Schwarzenberg might have been destroyed at Dresden. This would have freed the Grande Armée to deal with secondary objectives such as Berlin, the Army of North Germany, and the Silesian Army.

As for Blücher, he finally began his march down the right bank of the Elbe to cross the river at Elster and drag the crown prince of Sweden with him. The approach of Bennigsen's Army of Poland to reinforce Schwarzenberg, along with Macdonald's withdrawal to the right bank of the upper Elbe, finally liberated Blücher. After leaving 18,000 men to mask Dresden, he began his northwest march on 25 September. Although Russian cavalry protected Blücher's left, the withdrawal of French forces from Grossenhain across the Elbe to Meissen facilitated his march. For his part, Schwarzenberg decided that instead of making another advance on Dresden he would lead his army north toward Leipzig. The Allied commander-in-chief began the march on 1 October. These movements kept Napoleon guessing and off-balance. In fact, the emperor did not become aware of Blücher's disappearance until 4 October.[49]

Bülow finally opened the siege trenches at Wittenberg and drove the French from the suburbs on the afternoon of the twenty-fourth to appease the crown prince. With great sarcasm he assured Adlercreutz that he knew of no regulations that could justify the siege of a fortress that was not completely surrounded and still maintained communication with a mobile corps.[50] Nevertheless, he launched a two-pronged operation. Thümen took the villages northwest of the Elbe, while Hirschfeld reciprocated on the southeast side. The French offered little resistance and withdrew into the fortress. Half of the siege guns, including the British Congreve Rocket Battery, finally arrived from Spandau that day. Bülow moved Borstell into the bridgehead at Elster, and Hessen-Homburg advanced west to reinforce the siege troops. Bülow received disturbing reports that a force of 28,000 men under Ney had taken a position near Kemberg, directly south of Wittenberg on the highway to Leipzig. He suspected that the French would attack his dispersed brigades. His concerns, however, had no effect on the crown prince, who simply replied that Ney's movement had no bearing on the Army of North Germany.[51] With little choice other than blatant insubordination, Bülow continued the siege, conscious that with Ney so close the garrison might attempt a sortie.[52] The French did try in vain to disrupt the work throughout the night, but Ney's troops did not assist.[53]

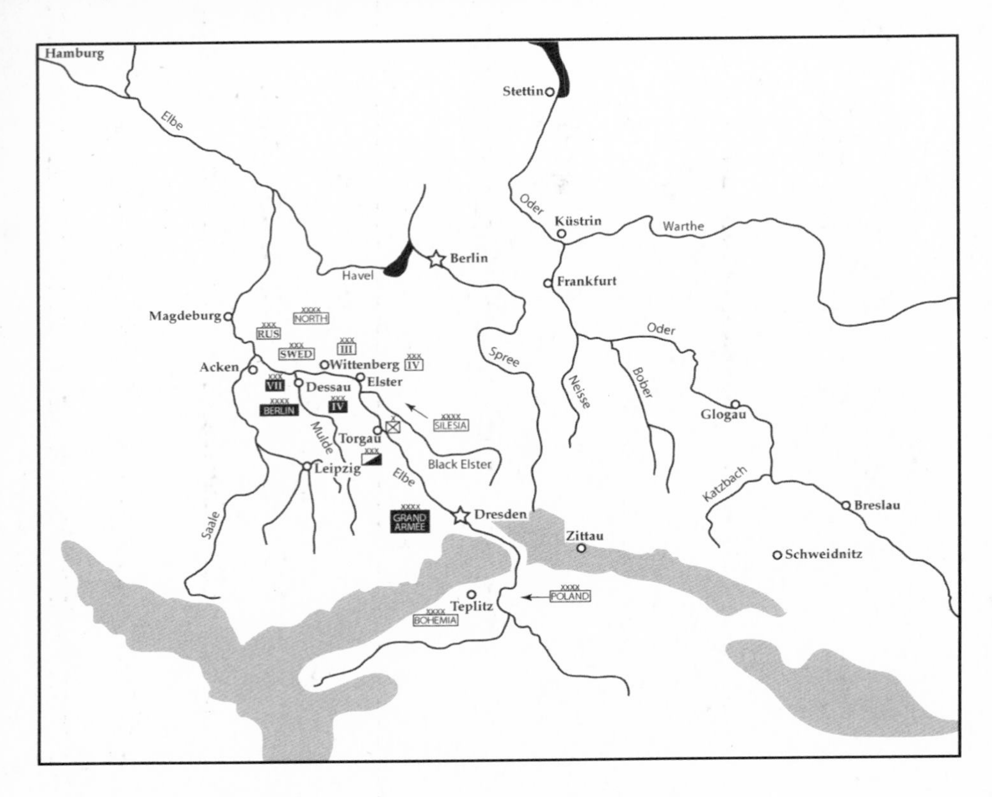

The Situation on 25 September 1813

On the twenty-fifth Bülow continued his bombardment of army headquarters. In a last attempt to move the army forward, he addressed a letter to the military attachés, warning that if Bernadotte continued to remain inactive the Army of North Germany would be forced to resume "a very fatal defensive." Although Bülow conceded a degree of importance to Wittenberg as a staging area to threaten Berlin, he believed that the fortress would lose its importance once the garrison had been tamed by steady shelling and the bridge over the Elbe had been destroyed. Even if the garrison held, the bridgeheads at Rosslau and Elster would allow the Army of North Germany to cross. September had been allowed to slip away with no laudable achievements since Dennewitz, and Bülow reminded them that the ultimate objective had to be the destruction of the enemy army, which could only be achieved by "large, rapid, and bold operations; petty measures have petty results." Bülow again proposed two plans for the army to cross the Elbe and either eliminate Ney or engage the French forces at Grossenhain.[54]

While awaiting a response, Bülow's siege suffered from the whims of the crown prince. On 25 September Bernadotte transferred Hirschfeld's brigade from Wittenberg to Zerbst for no apparent reason.[55] Bülow also received Bernadotte's perplexing order to destroy the bridge over the Elbe at Elster. This not only signaled the definitive rejection of the proposed offensive but also denied Bülow the only means of gathering intelligence along the left bank of the Elbe. The order to destroy the Elster bridge shocked the Prussians. Boyen feared that Bernadotte wanted the bridge destroyed to prevent any portion of his army from crossing the Elbe. "I can discover no other reason for this order," recalled Boyen, "except that by destroying the bridge, the crown prince, who at this time might have already possessed some report of Blücher's approach, wanted to insure that his army did not unexpectedly get carried away in an offensive." Tauentzien also questioned Bernadotte's judgment and warned that if Bernadotte "continues to behave like this, only God can prevent the worst outcome."[56]

A disheartened Bülow wrote a very melancholy letter to his wife on the night of 25 September. In addition to his troubles with Bernadotte, the general deeply resented his current task on humanitarian and religious grounds. He referred to himself as a professional arsonist. "Tonight I begin the bombardment of Wittenberg," he lamented. "Regretfully, I will destroy many monuments that are sacred to us—the room where Luther lived as a monk; the room where he taught as a professor after his conversion; the room where he lived with his wife (the chairs that they sat on are still in it!); and Luther's monument. All this will soon be consumed by flames, and I fear that more innocent, unfortunate inhabitants will probably die. Sitting on a hill, I reflected with sadness on the history of this remarkable city, so distinguished in the history of the Reformation."[57] That night, around 8:00 P.M., Bülow's batteries bombarded the Holy City of Lutheranism.

On the following day Hirschfeld proceeded to Magdeburg in what appeared to be the execution of Bernadotte's Magdeburg Plan. Chernyshov's cavalry reached Cassel and eventually ousted the king of Westphalia, Jérôme Bonaparte. Despite his apparent flirtation with the Magdeburg Plan, Bernadotte still claimed that he wanted to march to Leipzig. This now proved impossible, because Ney returned to the Mulde and attacked Dessau on the twenty-sixth. His advance troops drove the Cossacks and Swedish cavalry back on the village. Bernadotte had waited too long, and Ney now threatened the bridges over the Elbe and the Mulde. Ney's infantry reached Dessau on the twenty-seventh and launched repeated attacks against the Swedes the next day. Bernadotte maintained his composure and ordered Bülow to send a few battalions and some artillery to Elster, as if he intended to rebuild his bridge.[58] Ney took the bait. Fearing that the Prussians would cross the Elbe at Elster and sever his line of retreat, he dispatched Bertrand's corps to hold Bülow as long as possible. Despite the reduction of his manpower, Ney drove the Swedes from Dessau and forced them to burn the bridge over the Mulde. With some loss, Stedingk withdrew to the incomplete bridgehead at Rosslau on the twenty-ninth but held his ground.[59]

As Bernadotte's Swedes contested Ney, the arrival of heavy artillery and ammunition reserves at Wittenberg enabled the Prussians to intensify the bombardment. Bülow's artillery shelled the city continuously on 29 and 30 September. Heavy cannon pounded the walls, while mortars lobbed shells into the city. Fires burned out of control in four parts of the city. The old citadel and adjoining church received severe damage when a magazine exploded and incinerated several homes.[60] Flames also destroyed the door of the university church where Luther had nailed his ninety-five theses on 31 October 1517.[61] Notwithstanding this cosmetic damage, the Prussians could see little change in the fortress itself, and the British rockets proved worthless in siege operations.[62]

At a time when the euphoria of Dennewitz had long since passed and the tedious war of words with Bernadotte had worn both men's nerves, Bülow reached some degree of closure regarding the siege of Wittenberg and his relations with the crown prince. Since intense bombardments of the twenty-ninth and thirtieth exhausted Bülow's ammunition supply, he allowed the corps to stand idle for the next four days. Both sides only fired an occasional shot. After Bülow had burned Wittenberg against his will, he declared that he would do no more. He spoke very openly about what he believed to be a worthless operation; tension increased each day. Well-rewarded spies in both camps reported the bitter, insulting remarks that were expressed among supposed confidants. Finally, on 1 October, Bernadotte harshly scolded Bülow in a general order to the army. He accused the Prussian of paralyzing the army's operations by failing to take Wittenberg.[63] Bülow responded by informing Adlercreutz that he would no longer obey Bernadotte's commands. This proved too much for the proud prince-royal. He decided to inform the king of Prussia of the problem and request Bülow's removal. Märtens, who still remained at army headquarters, played a crucial role in convincing him that his letter would adversely affect Frederick William. He reminded Bernadotte of Bülow's service at Groß Beeren and Dennewitz. Adlercreutz and Löwenhielm also helped soothe the crown prince. As a result, he recalled the courier and destroyed the letter.[64]

The approach of Blücher's army, however, only rekindled the flames. Bülow again called for action and imprudently criticized the crown prince in public. In private he informed Blücher that Bernadotte would probably attempt to use the Silesian Army as a shield to protect his own army, if and when the time came to cross the Elbe. "In the meantime," wrote Bülow, "I hope to God that an opportunity will arise to move away from him. I will no longer allow myself to be hampered by the fears and selfish politics of this foreigner." He assured Blücher that he could count on the support of the Third Corps to cross the Elbe "without delay, and operate on the left bank with all of our forces."[65] A letter of 3 October to his wife reveals both Bülow's excitement at Blücher's approach and his complete disgust with Bernadotte. "General Blücher has reached us with his entire army and wants to cross the Elbe at Elster," scribbled Bülow. "Now the crown prince has no escape, and he will be forced to cross the Elbe. It is a great shame that this charlatan has appeared here; the war would have taken a different turn a long time ago under another commander."[66]

Unfortunately for Bülow, Blücher's approach did not automatically liberate the Third Prussian Corps from Bernadotte's command. Blücher and Gneisenau had requested permission to detach Bülow and Tauentzien from the Army of North Germany and incorporate them into the Silesian Army, but Frederick William denied their request because of his treaty obligations with Sweden.[67] Consequently, Bülow's corps remained part of the Army of North Germany, but his indiscreet public criticism exasperated the crown prince. In addition, mounting pressure to launch an offensive reached Bernadotte from both Grand Allied Headquarters and Blücher's camp. Gneisenau had anticipated just such a scenario—when the paralyzing effects of national self-interest might cripple the coalition's war effort. When possible, Gneisenau, as chief of staff of the Prussian Army, had maintained close communication with his four subordinate chief staff officers. His correspondence best illustrates how the Prussians expected to utilize their General Staff to secure Prussian interests, even after their corps had been distributed among the Allied armies. In a letter to Carl von Clausewitz, Gneisenau discussed plans to wage the war according to Prussia's interests:

> We have now made other plans, and will execute them before receiving the authorization. In Schwarzenberg's army, they always draft new plans that are never executed. After two victories, the crown prince of Sweden loiters between the Nuthe and the Elbe. Therefore, we will break upon the scene and take over the main role since the others do not want it. We will cross the Elbe and draw to us whatever Prussian forces we can. Tauentzien agrees and will cooperate with us. I hope that Bülow will likewise do this without too much trouble from the lethargic crown prince.[68]

There may have been more to the question of Bülow's reliability than Gneisenau realized. Bülow now faced the approach of both Yorck and Blücher. Bülow's rocky relations with Yorck had been bad enough, but they could not compare to the great rift between him and Blücher. The two men had developed a cordial relationship while rallying troops in Swedish Pomerania near the end of the war in 1807. They had agreed on most issues and worked well together. The following year Blücher, the newly appointed governor of Pomerania, fell ill. Since relieving Blücher did not appear advisable and replacing him would have been difficult, Frederick William ordered Bülow to be special adjutant to the sixty-five-year-old warhorse. Throughout the summer of 1808 Bülow's role remained that of a normal adjutant, and Blücher performed his executive duties with only sporadic relapses. On such occasions he willingly conceded his right of command to Bülow. Autumn, however, brought a lapse of Blücher's health. Bülow witnessed the full effects of the older man's agony, which manifested itself in wild and eccentric behavior. Blücher suffered from mental and physical deterioration aggravated by alcohol-induced schizophrenia. He often woke the household in the dead of night by shouting and smashing furniture as he engaged an invisible foe. Claiming that his head was made of stone, he frequently begged his servants to smite it with a hammer. The old hussar appeared insane, but in reality he suffered from venereal disease, alcoholism, and an ulcerated urethra. According to Boyen, Blücher "actually believed that he was pregnant with an elephant . . . he imagined that his servants, bribed by France, had heated the floor of his room to burn

Gen. August Wilhelm Anton von Gneisenau (1760–1831). Gneisenau fell into ill-repute with King Frederick William III and resigned in 1816; his next and final command came in the Polish Insurrection of 1831, during which he died of cholera in his headquarters at Posen on 21 August.

his feet. Therefore, when sitting, he kept his legs raised above the floor, or he would walk on the tips of his toes."[69] Bülow felt little compassion for his commander. The pious Lutheran believed that Blücher was an insane hypochondriac whose frivolous lifestyle caused his problems.

In 1809 the king's refusal to aid the Austrians in their war against France further shattered Blücher's spirits. His health, which had recovered with the prospect of war, now deteriorated. At this time the relationship between Blücher and Bülow ended, due to their divergent views of the war. While Blücher yearned for vengeance, Bülow did not believe Prussia was ready to challenge France. Blücher and Bülow found themselves on opposite sides of an issue that divided the army and the government. Their opinions especially diverged regarding the secret societies that had spread throughout Prussia during the French occupation. Foremost was the Tugenbund (League of Virtue), which had been founded in 1808 by a group of patriotic officers, government officials, and scholars. Although unattainable goals filled the league's constitution, its central purpose was to prepare a national uprising. Despite the league's revolutionary taint, its call for a war of liberation attracted many army officers, who viewed it as an extension of the reform party. In this regard Blücher, Scharnhorst, and Gneisenau supported and cooperated with the league. Army personnel who wished to help plan an insurrection established Tugenbund cells in several garrisons.

Bülow never became a member of the Tugenbund; nor is there any evidence of his involvement with the league. He disagreed with Blücher's decision to allow the league to recruit soldiers as well as with the general's personal involvement with the secret society, which Bülow termed foolish. One evening in 1811 Bülow arrested two junior officers known to be zealous participants in the Tugenbund. He charged them with neglecting to report their arrival to him; but in reality he feared that they might attempt to recruit his men. Bülow had hardly returned to his quarters when somebody began beating on his door. Blücher himself appeared on the doorstep, and a boisterous exchange of words broke the still night. Each contested the other's authority regarding the arrest of the junior officers. Blücher allegedly shouted, "Herr Colonel, you are good at ordering but bad at obeying." He stormed out of Bülow's quarters, thus sealing their final break.[70] Bülow had become accustomed to Blücher's fits. Despite their irreconcilable differences, the two men had been able to cooperate in a professional manner. After this particular tiff, however, they parted as enemies. Although two years had passed, Gneisenau could only hope that the two would put aside their differences for the sake of the Fatherland.

As for Bernadotte, he remained anchored to the right bank of the Elbe despite Blücher's approach. Bülow's defiance provided a distraction that eased his conscience when he could offer no viable excuse for his own inertia. He believed that the Prussians doubted his skills and mocked his authority. To end the unpleasant situation and vindicate himself, he finally reported Bülow to Frederick William. Bernadotte accused Bülow of jeopardizing the army's unity of command through "passive resistance" to his orders and open opposition to the siege of Wittenberg. He charged Bülow with "insubordination and the tendency to pursue his own plans rather than the given orders." Despite these allegations, Bernadotte neither demanded nor wished for Bülow's transfer. Rather, he wanted Frederick William to discipline Bülow and instruct him "to follow the orders of his commander without objection."[71] His complaints achieved immediate success. Bülow received a firm admonishment from the king. Frederick William explained that the crown prince had to be obeyed due to the "the higher political regards" of the Allied sovereigns. The king appealed to Bülow's patriotism and suggested prudence. Bülow had to restrain himself from making emotional remarks concerning Bernadotte and his conduct. Ultimately the king ordered him "to strive to achieve the necessary good harmony."[72] Bernadotte indeed had the last word, and Bülow had no other choice than to obey.

With Blücher's approach, the leaders of the Silesian Army shouldered the burden of stirring Bernadotte. Although Blücher could deal with Bernadotte as an equal, their relationship was one-sided. F. L. Petre notes that "it is difficult to condemn too strongly Bernadotte's conduct in the whole campaign, or to praise too highly Blücher's honesty and devotion to the general cause."[73] The approach of the Silesian Army brought much needed relief to Bülow, who had been exasperated by the mental struggle with the crown prince. He could now concentrate on commanding his corps rather than worry about overall strategy. Although Bernadotte eventually crossed the Elbe, Bülow's role in that affair remained minor compared to his efforts during the months of August and September.

An Allied operation against Ney's army shortly after Dennewitz would have been facilitated by the Army of Berlin's demoralization, the discord among its French commanders, and the discontent of its German troops. Wittenberg posed no threat to Berlin. Instead the real danger lay in the isolated operations of the Allied armies. Berlin would only be safe when all three armies operated within mutual supporting distance. Only then would Napoleon be prevented from reinforcing Ney for an operation in North Germany. Bülow understood that the consequences of a setback by either Blücher or Schwarzenberg could be another French offensive in North Germany. Although the Prussians implored Bernadotte to carry the war across the Elbe, he rejected their arguments, suggestions, and plans.[74] This only convinced Bülow that the prince-royal used the siege of Wittenberg as an excuse to delay offensive operations.

The military and political goal of destroying Napoleon's armed might had been the sole interest of the Prussians since the start of the war. In North Germany they shed their concerns over Berlin for the main objective of destroying Napoleon's ability to wage war. This goal could be attained only through offensive operations. By mid-September the failures of Oudinot, Macdonald, Girard, Vandamme, and Ney had counterbalanced Napoleon's great victory at Dresden. To the Allies, it appeared that the emperor's subordinates had collapsed on all fronts. The Prussians believed that the Grande Armée could be defeated and emphatically supported offensive operations after the pivotal victory at Dennewitz. Rather than coordinate a general offensive, Tsar Alexander and Schwarzenberg summoned Blücher to defend Bohemia. As for the crown prince of Sweden, "we see Bernadotte, after Bülow's victory at Dennewitz, hanging about without making any serious attempt to reap the fruits of his success by crossing the Elbe."[75] Despite their efforts, the Prussians failed to convince Bernadotte to cross the Elbe during September. Once Blücher and Gneisenau exchanged the responsibility of marching to Bohemia for an advance down the Elbe, however, the Prussians at last motivated the crown prince to cross his Rubicon.

Politics governed Bernadotte's decisions at a time when the success of the coalition demanded the subordination of politically motivated acts of national self-interest.[76] His immediate goal of obtaining Norway and defeating the Danes could only be attained by preserving his Swedish troops. To accomplish this, his line of retreat to Sweden had to remain open in order for him to escape Napoleon's attacks, which he firmly believed would be directed at him. His political agenda fooled no one, especially the Prussians. They remained convinced that their commander was an indecisive, incompetent French sympathizer, who pathetically feared his former master. At this time Bernadotte indiscreetly revealed his true aspirations in a conversation with the Count de Rochechouart, a French émigré and aide-de-camp of the tsar. "France does not want an emperor," he declared. "That is not a French title. France wants a King. But the King must be a soldier. The Bourbons are finished and will never rise again. What man would suit the French people better than myself?"[77]

14

LEIPZIG

In early October Napoleon spread the Grande Armée between Wittenberg, Torgau, Leipzig, and Dresden. To the north Ney failed to dislodge the Army of North Germany from its bridgeheads on the left bank of the Elbe. On the southern front Murat's 45,000 men attempted to slow Schwarzenberg's march on Leipzig. Napoleon concentrated his main force of 80,000 men between Dresden, Bautzen, and Meissen. The idea of abandoning Germany crossed the emperor's mind as early as 27 September, when he ordered the French fortresses on the Rhine River prepared for defense.[1]

To the north Blücher's approach caused great excitement among the Prussians in Bernadotte's army. Bülow hoped the fiery Prussian commander would force Bernadotte to act but knew that Blücher faced a difficult task. He warned Blücher that the lethargic prince-royal would refuse to cross the Elbe until the Silesian Army opened a safe path. Blücher knew how to flatter a charlatan and inundated the crown prince with charming letters. His tactic worked, and the crown prince promised that if the Silesian Army crossed the Elbe the Army of North Germany would follow. That was enough to satisfy the seventy-one-year-old Prussian. By 2 October he had 50,000 men between Elster and Jessen with an additional 20,000 expected to arrive the following day. On the third Yorck's First Corps reached Elster; but unfortunately for him, Bülow had destroyed the bridge a few days earlier in accordance with Bernadotte's orders. The Prussians salvaged as much as they could and built two bridges with the Silesian Army's pontoons. Yorck's troops then crossed the Elbe.

Bertrand's 13,000 men held the village of Wartenburg on the left bank of the Elbe opposite Elster. Daily outpost skirmishing with Bülow's pickets had not induced him to surrender his position. Where the crown prince had reprimanded Bülow for conducting offensive operations on the left bank, the aggressive Blücher ordered Yorck to clear Wartenburg on the third. After a sharp contest Yorck's men drove the French from the village and secured the river crossing. Each side lost around 2,000 casualties.[2] After the combat at Wartenburg Ney's Army of Berlin barely numbered 25,000 men. Rather than risk being caught between the two Allied armies, he ordered a retreat south to Delitzsch.

After Blücher's units started crossing the Elbe on the third, Bernadotte had little choice but to act. He ordered Vorontsov to dispatch his Cossacks to Raguhn and Bitterfeld to harass Bertrand's communications, since "Blücher is probably attacking the enemy on the road to Kemberg."[3] Moreover, Bernadotte informed his subordinates that the Army of North Germany would cross the Elbe on the fourth.[4] The crown prince maneuvered the Swedes and Russians across the two rivers, while the Prussians marched to the points of passage on the right bank. Ironically, the two corps of the army that had not contributed to the victories at Groß Beeren and Dennewitz—the Swedes and Russians—received the honor of setting foot upon the left bank of the Elbe before the Prussians. While the Swedes crossed at Rosslau and marched to Dessau, Wintzingerode's main body crossed at Acken. As he had withheld Hessen-Homburg's brigade on the morning of Groß Beeren and Borstell's on the morning of Dennewitz, the prince-royal ordered Thümen's battle-hardened veterans to remain behind on the right bank of the Elbe to continue the siege of Wittenberg. An irritated Bülow moved south with his three remaining brigades and crossed the Elbe at Rosslau on 4 October.[5] Tauentzien marched to Coswig and took a post one mile from Rosslau.[6]

On the fifth Bülow's corps continued to follow the rest of the army south.[7] While they were marching through Dessau, another incident provided fresh fuel for the smoldering relations between Bülow and Bernadotte. Without any advance notice Bülow received word that the crown prince would inspect his corps as it paraded through Dessau.

Bülow's Spartan garb sharply contrasted with the crown prince's flamboyant attire, yet the Prussian refused to change clothes just to satisfy Bernadotte's whim. As the Third Corps marched through Dessau's main square, Bülow rode at the head of his troops wrapped in a weathered frock coat and wearing a dilapidated cap. Aghast and offended by the Prussian's shabby appearance, Bernadotte summoned Boyen as he rode past. In a loud voice heard by all of the bystanders, Bernadotte wove one of his now familiar diatribes of complaints about Bülow. Boyen simply replied that Bülow's uniform corresponded to Prussian regulations—an outright lie that only soured Bernadotte's mood. He abruptly ended the conversation and ordered the colonel to return to his corps.[8]

The incident at Dessau remained indicative of the poor relations between Bernadotte and the Prussians. Nevertheless, after bestowing on the Swedes and Russians the honor of leading the army across the Elbe, the prince-royal now ordered Bülow's corps to lead the march to Leipzig. Bitterness and the simple desire to link with Blücher and carry the war to Napoleon himself eclipsed this symbolic gesture of respect. During the next two days Bülow's corps advanced up the Mulde River and reached Jessnitz. From there his scouts probed Leipzig.[9] By this time the Silesian Army had also reached the Mulde, and Blücher's patrols linked with Bülow's detachments around Leipzig. As for Napoleon, all reports placed him at Dresden on 3 October with 120,000 men echeloned southeast to Pirna. This news encouraged Bernadotte, who still feared that his former master would seek the long-awaited retribution. With Napoleon at Dresden, the crown prince hoped that the combined advance of Bülow and Blücher would induce the French to evacuate Leipzig.[10] Although the situation favored the Allies, Bernadotte refused to endorse an offensive. Blücher suggested that the Army of North Germany take the lead and rapidly advance up the Saale River to Merseburg, west of Leipzig, while the Silesian Army moved south between the Saale and Mulde.[11] This would have covered Blücher's flank attack and completely severed Leipzig's westward communications. Bernadotte flatly refused. Had he accepted this suggestion, the Army of North Germany would have closed the route that Napoleon took to escape from Germany two weeks later.

Bülow's corps received a day of rest on 7 October, but his scouts continued to patrol around Leipzig. Bernadotte maneuvered the Swedes and Russians west toward the Saale River.[12] By that evening his army extended from Dessau to Jessnitz on the Mulde as well as westward to

Zörbig on the highway from Magdeburg to Leipzig. Blücher had two corps at Düben on the Wittenberg-Leipzig highway and a third at Mockrehna on the Torgau-Leipzig road. Only a day's march separated the North German and Silesian Armies.[13] Bernadotte and his corps commanders met with Blücher and his staff at Mühlbeck, halfway between Jessnitz and Düben. Since Napoleon appeared anchored to Dresden, the two commanders agreed that both armies would continue the march to Leipzig. Hardly had the council adjourned when reports arrived that Napoleon had in fact left Dresden and was headed for Leipzig.[14]

News of Blücher's crossing of the Elbe had reached Napoleon on 5 October. A great opportunity now presented itself, and the emperor planned to exploit the apparent change in Allied strategy. The Allies had finally ventured into his lair, and with the Elbe behind them there would be no easy retreat. From his central position at Leipzig Napoleon hoped to destroy at least one Allied army. Murat's 45,000 men would hold Schwarzenberg's 203,000 men for as long as possible south of Leipzig, preferably at Chemnitz.[15] Meanwhile Napoleon would move the remainder of the Grande Armée to Wittenberg and send detachments over the Elbe to march downstream and destroy the bridges at Elster, Rosslau, and Acken. He believed he could annihilate Blücher and Bernadotte before Schwarzenberg could reach Leipzig.[16] The emperor would then turn south and confront the Army of Bohemia. By 8 October Napoleon had 140,000 men concentrated at Wurzen, just south of Blücher's 60,000. On the following day he planned to attack the Silesian Army, raise the siege of Wittenberg, and seize the bridges at Elster, Rosslau, and Acken: the day of reckoning fast approached.[17]

This classic Napoleonic strategy had produced success countless times in the past. After six months and a recent string of defeats, Napoleon finally abandoned his "master plan" of maneuver in favor of a strategy of annihilation. But as he prepared to take advantage of the Allied offensive as only he could, the emperor succumbed to another obsession that would later haunt him. Dresden, the capital of his Saxon ally, played no significant role in the upcoming operation. The approach of Bennigsen's Army of Poland, however, jeopardized its security. Napoleon agonized over the decision to hold or relinquish the city. As in the case of his earlier desire to take Berlin, he allowed this secondary political objective to rob him of the 30,000 men that he left to garrison Dresden. According to historian Yorck von Wartenburg, Napoleon's preoccupation with Dresden was "not so much the mistake of a general

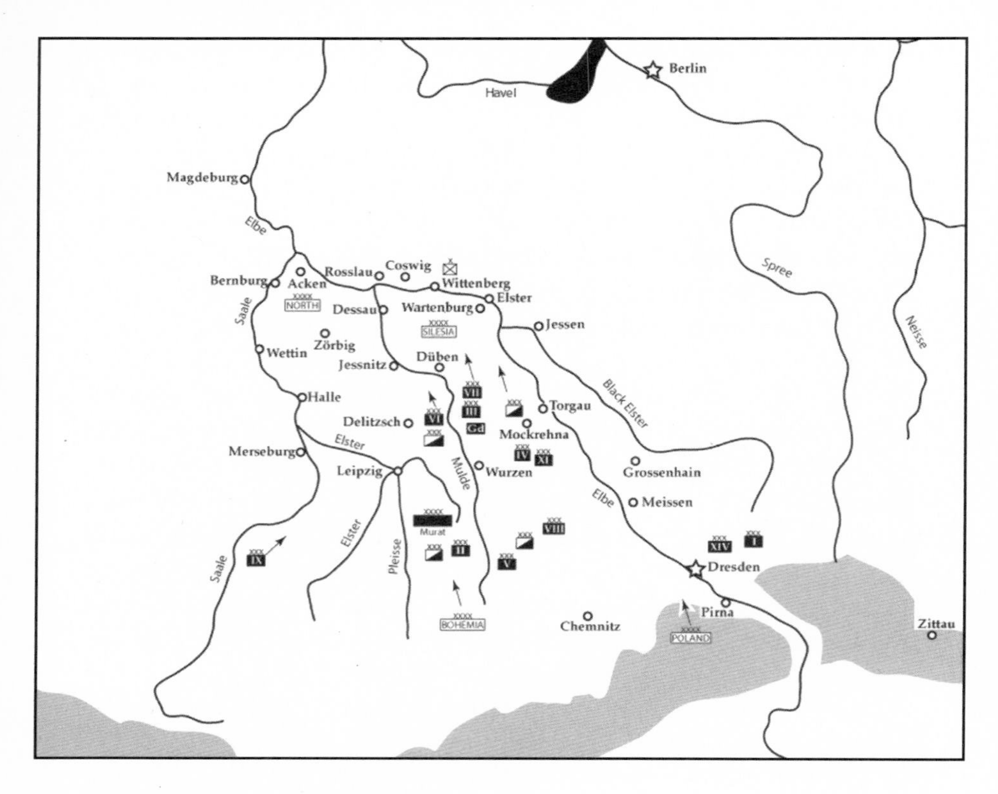

The Situation on 9 October 1813

as the obstinacy of a ruler who will not admit that he can be compelled to relinquish anything."[18] David Chandler notes that "this decision was probably the most fateful one of the campaign," since Napoleon sacrificed his "own principle of concentrating every possible man before battle."[19]

Forewarned of Napoleon's advance, the North German and Silesian Armies had two possible courses of action. The first, which the crown prince supported, called for both armies to retreat northward and cross the Elbe. Had the Allies attempted this, Napoleon probably would have destroyed Blücher's army as it attempted to negotiate the Elbe. The second proposal required both armies to withdraw to the left bank of the Saale until Schwarzenberg arrived. In a meeting with Major Lilienstern of Blücher's staff, Bernadotte argued that the rules of war demanded that both armies immediately retreat over the Elbe. Once again he stressed the need to protect Berlin. Lilienstern replied that Blücher and Gneisenau were not concerned about Berlin. Since the Russians had burnt Moscow, Blücher and his staff felt they could sacrifice their own capital.[20] After much debate Bernadotte agreed to march to the Saale as long as Blücher took a position between the Army of North Germany and Napoleon. Bernadotte also demanded a firm guarantee that nothing stood between him and the safety of the bridges over the Elbe. Blücher agreed, but only to detain Bernadotte's army for the imminent struggle with Napoleon.

Between 8 and 11 October Bernadotte and Blücher moved their armies westward to the left bank of the Saale.[21] Bernadotte's army led the march to the Saale and crossed at Wettin, where the crown prince had promised to build a second pontoon bridge for Blücher's army. When the advance units of the Silesian Army arrived, however, they found a long line of Bernadotte's troops waiting to cross.[22] Not only did the prince-royal fail to construct the second bridge, but nobody seemed to know what had become of the pontoons. An unperturbed Blücher marched further south and crossed the Saale at Halle.[23]

The Allied decision to retreat westward to the Saale proved momentous. Napoleon drove his men with such a fury that by the evening of the ninth French troops had already passed through Düben on their way to Jessnitz. As the Allies crossed the Saale on the eleventh, Napoleon concentrated 70,000 men at Düben with reinforcements on the way. As usual the emperor's appearance sparked new life in his faltering legions and tired commanders. Ney moved in force against Dessau, prompting Tauentzien to retreat over the Elbe. Reynier's corps crossed the Elbe at Wittenberg, where Thümen offered initial resistance before yielding and uniting with Tauentzien. Responsible for Berlin, they withdrew toward the Prussian capital in haste. Bertrand also drove the Prussian garrison from Wartenburg. A strong French force moved up the right bank of the Elbe from Magdeburg to Steutz across from Acken and forced Hirschfeld to destroy the bridge over the Elbe as a precaution. The destruction of the Acken bridge proved fateful for the crown prince of Sweden and the Army of North Germany. With no other escape route, Bernadotte had no choice but to remain south of the Elbe and face Napoleon.

The French counteroffensive along the Elbe fostered the opinion in the Allied camps that Napoleon sought to establish a new base of operations at Magdeburg.[24] Actually, indecision had once again seized the emperor. He spent 10 and 11 October trying to find Blücher and Bernadotte. Reports did not support his belief that they had concentrated between Dessau and Raguhn. At 3:00 A.M. on the twelfth he finally learned that Blücher had marched to Halle two days earlier.[25] Napoleon initially ordered the army to pursue Blücher but then canceled these orders. The emperor's operation on the right bank of the Elbe ended in failure. He could have pursued Bernadotte and Blücher, and probably should have owing to the crown prince's fear of meeting him on the field, but further discouraging news altered the situation. Reports that Bavaria had defected and that the Bohemian Army had accelerated its advance prompted the emperor to leave Düben on the fourteenth and concentrate his army at Leipzig.

Napoleon missed a great opportunity to destroy Blücher and probably Bernadotte as well. Although the Allied retreat to the Saale did open the road to Berlin and North Germany, the time had passed to exploit any of the dubious advantages offered by the "master plan." Moving north over the Elbe would certainly have saved the garrisons in Torgau, Wittenberg, Magdeburg, and Stettin as well as Davout's corps in Hamburg. Murat probably would have been able to escape eastward to Torgau before Schwarzenberg or Bennigsen could catch his army. In a virtual coup de théâtre, Napoleon could have exchanged places with the Allies, stranding the Bohemian, Silesian, and North German Armies in the depleted Saxon countryside and holding the right bank of the Elbe against them from Hamburg to Dresden. The time for running, however, had passed; no maneuver, flank march, or surprise attack could truly alter the course of the war unless it led to the destruction of one or more of the Allied armies. Napoleon's resources in Central Germany neared exhaustion, and a complete withdrawal to North Germany would have exposed his columns to the merciless attacks of partisans and Cossacks. At this late stage of the campaign Napoleon knew that it mattered little if he reached the Vistula; he still had to destroy the enemy's ability to wage war. Mounting war weariness in France meant that a decision had to be reached soon. Instead of wasting his scant resources by evacuating the theater, he decided to draw the Allies to Leipzig for an epic struggle: the Battle of Nations.

The Allies, however, knew little of this. As soon as Bernadotte learned of the proceedings at Wittenberg, Dessau, and Acken, he disregarded his arrangements with Blücher and sought to escape over the

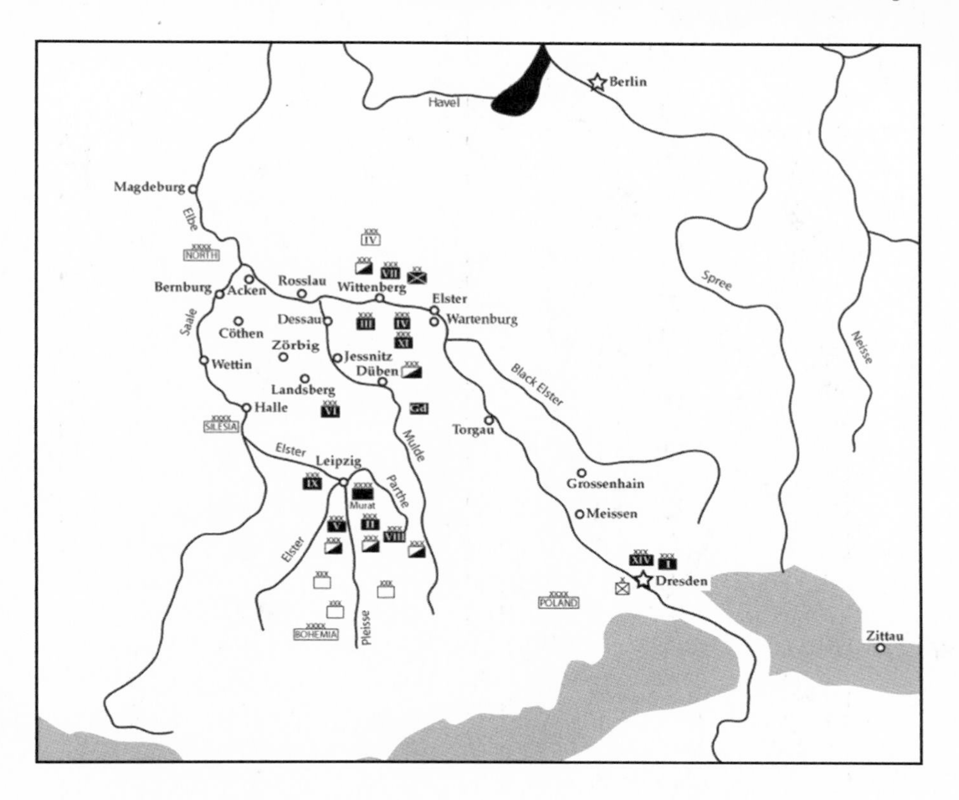

The Situation on 13 October 1813

Elbe. On the thirteenth the Army of North Germany recrossed the Saale and marched north to Cöthen. Hessen-Homburg's brigade continued to Acken in order to rebuild the bridge. Bülow's patrols scoured the Mulde but discovered little French activity. To Bernadotte and Blücher, it appeared that Napoleon had moved his theater of operations to North Germany. The rumors of his departure to Leipzig did not lessen the fear that he would invade North Germany. If he defeated Schwarzenberg quickly and drove him over the mountains into Bohemia, they estimated that Napoleon would have enough strength and time to drive northward through both of their armies. Upon reaching Berlin, the emperor could be reinforced by the garrison at Magdeburg and Davout's Thirteenth Corps in Hamburg. Wallmoden's forces in front of Hamburg would be hard-pressed to contain Davout again. Well aware of Napoleon's mobility, Bernadotte grew increasingly concerned about his lines of communications.

The demoralizing effect of the French counteroffensive—as well as the concern that Napoleon himself would attack—persisted despite reports of his withdrawal to Leipzig. Bernadotte presented his desire to retreat over the Elbe at a council of war on the fourteenth, attended by all corps commanders, their chief staff officers, and the foreign military attachés. Bernadotte opened the discussion by outlining the danger of their current position and the need to protect Berlin by withdrawing over the Elbe as fast as possible. Bülow opposed this plan; in a rare moment of unity, the other corps commanders supported him. He argued that even if a French force appeared on the right bank of the Elbe the Army of North Germany still had to support Blücher and Schwarzenberg. This meant marching to Leipzig and confronting the Grande Armée. Bülow added that a retreat over the Elbe would divide and weaken the army. To counter these arguments the prince-royal changed tactics and appealed to sentimental concerns. "So we should abandon everything that is sacred and dear: communication with the Fatherland, our wives, and children?" asked the crown prince. Stedingk, the commander of the Swedish corps, could not take any more and blurted out that "on certain occasions, one must act out of honor." Coming from the mouth of a Swede, these strong words stunned Bernadotte. He ended his lecture and withdrew to a corner in private conversation with Adlercreutz and Tawast. He finally sent the latter to question Stedingk about the meaning of his words. Although the Swedish field-marshal explained himself and sought forgiveness, this unexpected opposition from his subordinate disturbed Bernadotte. He ended the session without determining the army's next step.[26]

The crown prince also implored Blücher to withdraw over the Elbe with him, but the Prussian commander declined and remained at Halle.[27] On 15 October the Silesian Army actually moved farther away from the Army of North Germany and marched to Leipzig to unite with Schwarzenberg. Finding no support for a retreat over the Elbe, Bernadotte feared being isolated at Cöthen. As a result he decided to hurry after Blücher. He ordered the Army of North Germany to march south in two large columns from Cöthen to Halle.[28] Army headquarters informed all corps commanders that a large battle in the vicinity of Leipzig would probably occur on the following day and told them to be ready to support the other two armies at a moment's notice.[29]

Despite the excitement, the crown prince dragged his feet and his army did little. Bernadotte's hesitation during the next two days ultimately saved Napoleon from total destruction at Leipzig.

As Blücher's army approached Leipzig from the northwest, and Schwarzenberg steadily advanced from the south, Bennigsen marched from the east with 50,000 men. Napoleon concentrated 177,000 men around the Saxon city by the evening of the fourteenth. Planning for the opportunity that had eluded him since his victory at Dresden six weeks earlier, Napoleon no longer worried about keeping the Allied armies apart but welcomed the chance to decide the issue with one great battle. He had no clear idea of how far south Bernadotte and Blücher had advanced, but Schwarzenberg's mammoth army had closed on Murat just south of Leipzig. Both sides spent much of the fifteenth probing and planning for battle on the sixteenth. Napoleon did not intend to fight a defensive battle. Instead he would attack Schwarzenberg's army between the Pleisse and the Parthe Rivers. The Allies also decided to launch their main attack in the southern sector as Blücher's army advanced on Leipzig from the northwest. A small operation would be conducted against the west side of Leipzig by an Allied corps of 19,000 men.[30]

Bernadotte planned to concentrate his army northwest of Leipzig at Landsberg on 16 October. Due to his phlegmatic habits, which included sleeping until noon, his staff did not issue orders until 11:00 A.M. on the sixteenth.[31] As a result the concentration did not occur until that evening.[32] Despite Bernadotte's delay, the Silesian and Bohemian Armies attacked Leipzig on the sixteenth. Heavy combat ensued along the northern, western, and southern sectors of the front, with the struggles centering around Möckern, Lindenau, and Wachau. Blücher's unexpected arrival and the confusion that it caused robbed Napoleon of the forces he planned to use to destroy Schwarzenberg. Had the 30,000 men left in Dresden been present, Napoleon could have crushed Schwarzenberg. By the end of the fighting on the sixteenth, Schwarzenberg's offensive in the Wachau area had been repulsed, and Napoleon had reestablished his line. French troops successfully defended Lindenau in the western sector but lost at Möckern, where Yorck's First Corps fought a savage battle. French losses for the sixteenth neared 25,000, while the Allies lost 30,000: an ominous ratio since Napoleon's reinforcements would only increase the Grande Armée to 200,000 men and 900 guns, while the Allies would reach 300,000 men and 1,500 guns with the arrival of the North German and Polish Armies.[33]

After the fighting ended on 16 October Napoleon considered a retreat to the Rhine. Although he issued preliminary orders for Bertrand to secure the bridge over the Saale, the emperor should have done more. Rather than throw additional bridges over the Elster and the Pleisse Rivers, he opted for a retreat over a single bridge through the west side of the city. Further discouraging news made a retreat inevitable. A force of 30,000 Bavarians under Gen. Karl Philipp von Wrede, posted on the Inn River, had made common cause with the Austrians and was preparing to march against Napoleon's lines of communication with France. A shortage of ammunition also became a factor; dwindling reserves would not support another day of intense fighting. After weighing these considerations, Napoleon still decided to postpone the retreat until the eighteenth in the hopes that the Allies might blunder. He also attempted to divide the Allies by offering an armistice to his father-in-law, Emperor Francis. His peace initiative not only failed but served to strengthen Allied resolve by convincing Napoleon's foes that he was spent. The heavy fighting of the day—particularly the events at Möckern—should have convinced him to retreat, but, as F. L. Petre notes, "the Emperor Napoleon was now, to a great extent, the master of General Bonaparte, and the Emperor could not bear to yield what practically meant his dominion in Germany, though the General saw that to do this was the only hope."[34]

Throughout the sixteenth Bülow had to listen to the sound of Yorck's guns at Möckern without being able to assist his countrymen. In the southern sector Kleist's Second Corps also fought. As his corps stood idle while the other Prussian corps commanders led theirs to battle, Bülow vainly attempted to convince Bernadotte to support Blücher's left flank. Where Bülow failed, a word from the representative of the British purse achieved some success; Bernadotte ordered the Russian cavalry to Möckern. Unfortunately for Yorck's corps, the Russians arrived after the battle had already ended.[35] Although Yorck's men secured the field, they lost 7,969 men out of 21,779. The French reportedly lost 9,000 men and 40 guns. Bernadotte could easily have supported the combat at Möckern. With his mere appearance on the right flank and rear of the enemy, he could have forced a decision and avoided the loss of several thousand Prussians. Bülow would not forget the shame he felt while his men stood and listened to the combat at Möckern.[36]

On the evening of 16 October Bernadotte issued his dispositions for the following day. Incredibly, the Army of North Germany would remain at Landsberg rather than advance on Leipzig.[37] This drew harsh criticism from his corps commanders. At midnight a second, more comprehensive order that would bring the army into the action circulated from the crown prince's headquarters. Upon receiving it all corps commanders were supposed to place their troops under arms. At daybreak the Russians, Prussians, and Swedes advanced toward Leipzig.[38] During the march Bülow advanced from Landsberg to Klein Podelwitz, while the Russians and Swedes took positions at Radefeld and Breitenfeld.[39]

Minimal fighting occurred on the seventeenth as both sides rested to renew the struggle on the following day. Taking advantage of the lull, the Silesian Army moved northwest of Leipzig to a position between the Elster and Parthe Rivers. Blücher believed that Bennigsen's Army of Poland would be able to cover his left wing. This, however, proved impossible since Bennigsen had advanced west and then veered southwest toward Schwarzenberg, exposing Blücher's left wing and creating a considerable gap in the Allied line. Blücher once again turned to Bernadotte and suggested that the Army of North Germany close the gap by taking a position at Taucha. Bernadotte agreed on the condition that Blücher reinforce him with one corps.[40] An exasperated Blücher complied, and the Russian corps of Gen. Andrault Langeron joined the Army of North Germany on the following day. Satisfied, Bernadotte proceeded to the Parthe River. He planned to cross the river and march on Leipzig from the northeast on the eighteenth. Simultaneously, Bennigsen's Army of Poland advanced from the east, while Schwarzenberg's Bohemian Army moved on the French positions south-southeast of Leipzig.

By the morning of 18 October 295,000 Allied soldiers, supported by 1,466 cannon, prepared to assault Leipzig. The Allies planned to launch six massive attacks along the entire front. Napoleon stood in the middle with 160,000 men. Early on the eighteenth he contracted his southern front by a few miles in preparation for the retreat. The French position catered solely to the defensive and allowed Napoleon to bolster weak spots quickly. The Allies facilitated the French defensive by attacking concentrically along the entire front rather than concentrating their superior combat power on one point.

In the northeastern sector the Army of North Germany for the last time faced its old adversary: Marshal Ney. His troops consisted of three corps, including Reynier's Seventh, Arrighi's cavalry, and Dombrowski's Poles. Several bends in the swampy Parthe offered Ney an excellent defense line. Its numerous bridges had been destroyed, and skirmishers supported by light artillery lined the houses and gardens. Ney held the Parthe with Reynier's 12,000 men, who arrived from Torgau just in time for the battle. With Reynier's main body posted at Paunsdorf on the Leipzig-Wurzen highway, French positions in this sector extended to Taucha.

On the eighteenth Bernadotte's army had to cross the Parthe and fill the gap between Blücher and Bennigsen. He ordered Bülow to move across the Parthe at Taucha and then send detachments eastward to Wurzen to open communications with Bennigsen's army. Wintzingerode would follow Bülow and dispatch cavalry eastward to Eilenburg and Wurzen in order to shield the left wing of the army. Langeron had to cross the Parthe below Taucha and maintain contact with Wintzingerode's right. Protected on both sides by the Russians, the Swedes would cross between Langeron and Wintzingerode.[41] Bernadotte refused to accelerate his march. "Provided the French are beaten," he supposedly sneered, "it is of no difference to me whether I or my army take part, and of the two, I had much rather we did not."[42] F. L. Petre notes that "for days past he had been hanging back; even on the 18th he might easily have been up three or four hours before he was. Then there would have been an overwhelming force against Napoleon's left on the Parthe. Even when he did arrive, Bernadotte acted very feebly. His Swedes did practically nothing."[43]

Bülow at last received the orders he had so anxiously awaited on the sixteenth. On the morning of the eighteenth he finally led his corps to battle. Two months and one day had passed since his corps had occupied the Nuthe-Notte line in anticipation of a French offensive against Berlin. Now his men had helped carry the war to Napoleon himself. The victor of Dennewitz reached Taucha around 2:00 P.M., but determined Saxon resistance repulsed his attacks—crossing the Parthe proved no easy task. Bülow brought up several batteries and the British rocket brigade to blast the Saxons from the village. Continuous bombardment brought no success. While his artillery shelled Taucha, Bülow's scouts searched for a river crossing. Reports soon arrived of a stone bridge north of Taucha. Although partially destroyed, it appeared strong enough to support the passage of artillery. Light artillery and Cossacks crossed and eventually opened fire on the Saxons. With enemy artillery in their rear and Cossacks closing on their line of retreat, the Saxons yielded the village. Although they regrouped and turned on the

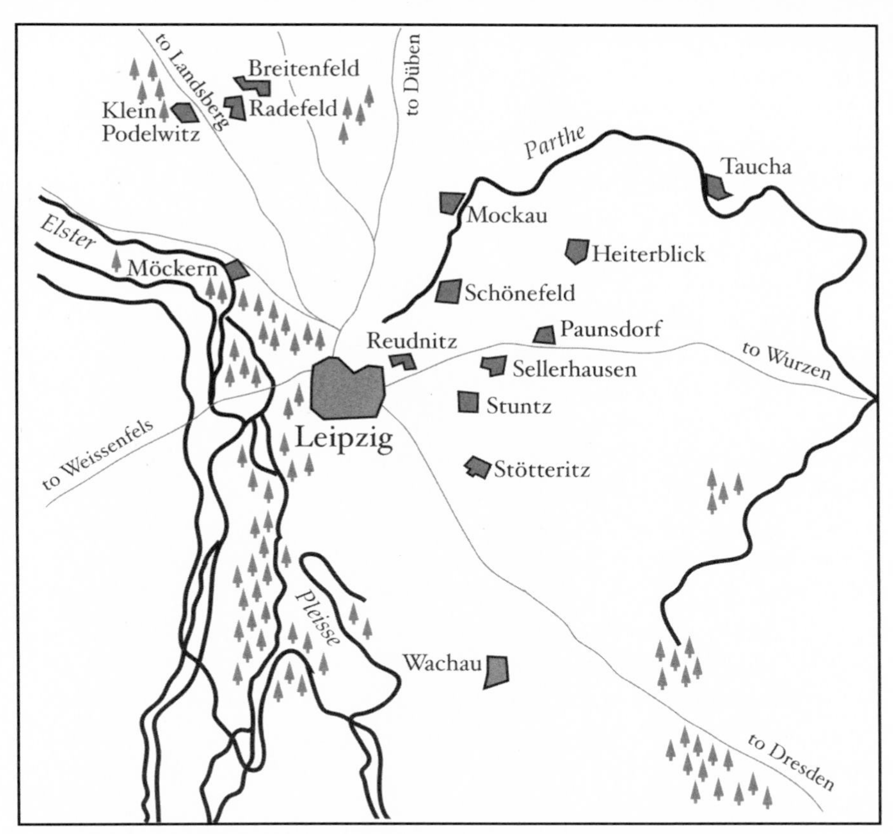

Leipzig and the Surrounding Area

pursuing Prussians, the rocket fire induced them to withdraw to Sellerhausen. Bülow's battalions moved through the village but found the roads clogged with overturned wagons. He sent a few squadrons east to establish communications with Bennigsen's right wing as the infantry slowly marched through Taucha en route to their next objective: Paunsdorf.

While Bülow's men contested Reynier's Saxons at Taucha, the Russians and Swedes crossed the Partha north of Taucha at 4:00 P.M. Convinced that Wintzingerode and Stedingk were within supporting distance, Bülow advanced along the main highway that ran from Torgau to Leipzig. He reorganized his brigades between Taucha and a hill chain west of the village. Hessen-Homburg formed the left, Borstell the middle, and Krafft the right. Oppen's cavalry proceeded along open terrain on the left wing. Although the hills concealed Bülow's approach and shielded his men from Ney's artillery, the Prussians could not see the French and Saxon batteries that awaited them at Paunsdorf. An overzealous Bülow, confident that resistance would again crumble, ordered Hessen-Homburg to advance before the other two brigades had come in line. As soon as Hessen-Homburg's battalions climbed the hilltops, Ney's artillery forced the Prussians to scramble for cover.

Luckily for Bülow, Langeron's Russian corps had crossed the Parthe at Mockau and advanced toward Schönefeld northwest of Paunsdorf. This new threat compromised Paunsdorf and forced Reynier to yield the village. He withdrew to a strong position between the villages of Sellerhausen and Stuntz, with his left still extended to the Parthe and his right at Stötteritz, where the French reserve stood. Ney then ordered Durutte's division to retake Paunsdorf. By this time Hessen-Homburg's first wave had already resumed its march. French and Prussian infantry collided in the village. Russian cavalry from Blücher's army appeared on Durutte's left flank, which prompted him to retreat toward Sellerhausen. Hessen-Homburg's lead battalion of the Fourth Reserve Regiment pursued the remains of Durutte's division to Sellerhausen, where French artillery prompted it to retreat.

At this point in the battle, units from Bennigsen's Army of Poland appeared in the sector. South of Paunsdorf the Austrian general Ferdinand von Bubna led the vanguard of Bennigsen's army to link with Bülow's left. Napoleon observed these developments and attempted to split the two Allied armies through a counterattack. French cavalry opened a gap between the Army of Poland and the Army of North Germany as Napoleon himself directed superior firepower at Hessen-Homburg's overextended and isolated brigade. After numerous casualties, the Prussians withdrew to Heiterblick on the Leipzig-Torgau highway, halfway between Taucha and Paunsdorf. A few anxious moments passed until it became clear that the French would not press the attack. This allowed Hessen-Homburg's brigade to reform, while Krafft and Borstell finally caught up to the action. Now that the Prussians had fought for nearly five hours, Bernadotte's Swedes and Russians entered the battle line.

Bülow counterattacked from Heiterblick with all three brigades and drove the French from Paunsdorf. On the hills adjacent to the village Swedish and Russian batteries unlimbered next to Bülow's artillery. Shells rained down on the French and their allies as they receded before the Prussian infantry. Ney's men regrouped between Stuntz and Sellerhausen. It appeared that Ney might salvage his sector when a fresh crisis shook the French line around 4:30 P.M.: Reynier's corps suffered the defection of 4,000 Saxons and a twelve-pounder battery. Finally fulfilling Ney's prophecy, the disaffected Saxons simply marched to the Allied side to await the outcome of the struggle. Ney filled the gap in his line and actually managed to organize another counterattack around 6:00 P.M. As his men doggedly advanced, the British rocket battery launched its missiles at close range and routed the French column. Boyen compared the effects of the rockets on the column to "disturbing an ant heap with a stick." He recalled that on the following day, when the Prussians "marched over the area upon which the French column had advanced, I was convinced of the significant effect of the rockets. Not only did a considerable number of dead lie there, but many of them had unusual burns on their faces and clothing; one could easily see why the enemy's composure had broken."[44]

Later in the evening, just before sunset, Bülow received orders to attack Stuntz and Sellerhausen. A full-scale bombardment by all of the army's artillery softened the French position prior to his advance. Although Bülow's line regiments had shouldered the bulk of the fighting throughout the day, the Landwehr of the Third Corps received the honor of leading the assault. Five militia battalions moved against Sellerhausen as two others attacked the burning remains of Stuntz. Unknown to the Allies, the French only held Sellerhausen and Stuntz as outposts. Smoke from the burning villages had concealed the French retreat to the eastern outskirts of Leipzig. Nevertheless, the Prussian Landwehr encountered spirited resistance from the rearguard in Sellerhausen and Stuntz. The French withdrew after a sharp skirmish, and the Prussians occupied both villages just as darkness blanketed the field.[45]

Once again Bülow's corps had shouldered the brunt of the fighting for the Army of North Germany. That night Bülow established his quarters in what remained of a schoolmaster's house in Paunsdorf. The only inhabitable room contained a long wooden bench that ran along the walls, one large table, and a very old piano. Later in the evening several members of Bülow's staff, as well as some of Bernadotte's, filled the room. Adlercreutz sat across from Bülow, who beat his fists on the table and appeared irate. The Prussian-born chief of staff received the unpleasant task of delivering Bernadotte's order for Bülow to dispatch a brigade to Eilenburg to attack an approaching enemy force. Earlier in the day Bülow had received information about this column and had sent two squadrons to the area. His scouts reported that they had found a Bavarian division that posed no threat. Bülow protested that with Thümen's brigade at Wittenberg his corps would be rendered useless by the loss of another brigade. He refused to weaken his corps further, especially since the battle had not been decided. When Adlercreutz relayed the message, the crown prince dropped the issue but would not let Bülow's defiance go unpunished.

Estimates vary for losses on both sides on 18 October. The Allies probably lost another 20,000 men, while the French sustained approximately 10,000 killed and wounded. Napoleon realized that he could no longer hold Leipzig and ordered the retreat to begin on the nineteenth. His dwindling ammunition reserves and the overall weight of Allied numerical superiority decided the issue. Late on the eighteenth the baggage and part of the reserve cavalry departed over the Lindenau causeway and crossed the Elster River on their way to the Rhine. At 2:00 A.M. on the nineteenth the reserve artillery followed by the Imperial Guard, Fourth Cavalry Corps, Tenth Corps, Second Corps, and Second Cavalry Corps began the retreat. A rearguard of 30,000 troops remained behind to hold Leipzig until the rest of the army had escaped. The French lines thinned before sunrise, but the departing troops left numerous campfires to deceive the Allies. Napoleon dispatched orders for the garrisons of Torgau and Wittenberg to capitulate as long as the men were granted free exit. The garrison at Dresden had to escape if it could. To the west Bertrand had already reached the Saale with orders to construct additional bridges. The emperor also dictated orders to summon the French National Guard to defend the country. Napoleon himself eventually made his way out of Leipzig around 11:00 A.M. on the nineteenth.[46] Germany was lost.

As the sky began to gray on the morning of 19 October, the Allies prepared to storm Leipzig. Schwarzenberg's unimaginative orders called for the four Allied armies to advance concentrically on Leipzig from the north, east, southeast, and south. Although the remaining French defenders had withdrawn to Leipzig's suburbs, the Allies did nothing to stop the Grande Armée's westward retreat to the Rhine. Instead Schwarzenberg remained fixated on capturing Leipzig rather than annihilating the enemy army.[47]

At 8:00 A.M. Bülow's corps began its advance against Ney's rearguard. Once again, as at Groß Beeren and Dennewitz, Bernadotte interfered and inexplicably ordered Krafft's brigade to join the Swedes as the rearguard—punishment for Bülow's defiance the previous evening. Stripped of a third of his infantry, Bülow had no other choice but to lead his Third and Fifth Brigades through Sellerhausen. Hessen-Homburg again formed the vanguard. Ney's men confronted the Prussians at Reudnitz. Disregarding the heavy artillery and small-arms fire, the Prussians penetrated the village and expelled the French, who fell back to the gardens and houses of the suburbs. As he rode through Reudnitz, Bülow observed for the first time the enemy troops entrenched behind Leipzig's defenses. On both sides of the highway lay hundreds of overturned wagons. It appeared that the enemy had no intention of surrendering. Estimates claim that the 30,000 defenders held a perimeter of 6,500 yards, or 4 men per yard.[48]

At 10:00 A.M. Bülow reached the eastern suburbs, but a ceasefire ordered by the tsar now circulated to the various armies. Alexander succumbed to the pleas of the king of Saxony to spare Leipzig—a delaying tactic masterminded by Napoleon. Bülow took advantage of the thirty-minute lull and rode to Bennigsen's headquarters to coordinate a joint assault. During his absence the battle resumed after the negotiations ended in failure. At this time Bernadotte reached the front, found Hessen-Homburg's brigade at the head of the Third Corps, and ordered an attack on the suburbs northeast of Leipzig. Unsupported, the Third Brigade marched into a meatgrinder. In a matter of minutes Hessen-Homburg lost 1,000 men, and the prince himself was wounded. French marksmen occupied the upper floors of the houses on both sides of the narrow street over which the Third Brigade advanced. Under this excellent cover, they cut down Hessen-Homburg's exposed men. Two of Bennigsen's heavy batteries came up to support but could provide little help since the Prussians and French were locked in hand-to-hand combat.

Bülow had observed Hessen-Homburg's advance from a distance. Furious over the ill-conceived attack, he returned to his position and ordered Borstell to advance. Borstell's artillery blasted the overturned wagons to open a path for the infantry. Meanwhile vicious street fighting continued. Hessen-Homburg's lead battalion of East Prussian Landwehr fought its way down a side street and was cut off; only half of its 400 men escaped. On the Prussian right, however, Borstell's attack steadily progressed and threatened the French line of retreat to Leipzig. His advance relieved the pressure on Hessen-Homburg and forced

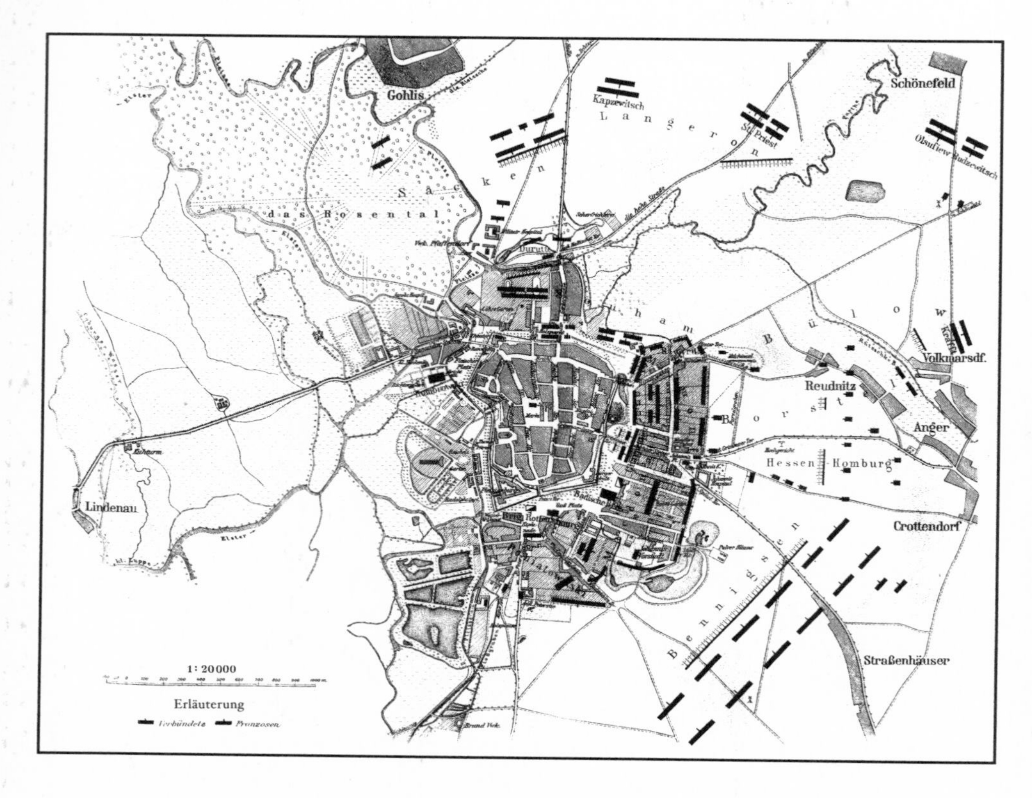

The Battle of Leipzig, 19 October 1813. From Friederich, *Die Befreiungskriege*, vol. 2.

the French to withdraw. Hessen-Homburg's Landwehr pursued and reached the Grimma Gate, the entrance to the eastern sector of Leipzig.

By 11:30 A.M. the French had been driven from the suburbs and into the inner city on all fronts. At the Grimma Gate, where the fighting has been described as "more desperate than anywhere," the Prussians confronted not only French soldiers but also Rheinbund troops that were still loyal to Napoleon.[49] Driven against the gate by Bülow's troops, the retreating French found it shut and held by their own German allies. They purportedly had instructions to allow no one to pass and thus refused to open the gate. The Prussians showed no mercy and massacred the French before the gate finally gave way. The lucky ones managed to scramble in before the Badeners again closed and barricaded the gate to prevent the Prussians from entering. Under canister and musket fire, Prussian skirmishers reached the wall of the barricaded Grimma Gate. From loopholes Hessian defenders fired volleys at point-blank range. The Prussians used the same loopholes to stab the Hessian marksmen with their bayonets and smash extended musket barrels. Hessen-Homburg's men reached the gate, but the Hessians repulsed their efforts to storm the barricades. At the gate house the Landwehr men breached the wall after pounding it with the butts of their muskets. The framework collapsed, and a few brave men passed through the breach to open the gate. Around 12:30 three battalions rushed in and forced the Hessians to surrender. The French soldiers who had not escaped quietly yielded to their fate. Borstell's brigade took many prisoners, including Reynier.[50] The rest of Bülow's corps pushed westward just as Blücher's men entered the city from the north. Dombrowski found his Poles trapped between Blücher and Bülow in the northwest corner of the city, where "the slaughter was so awful that in places the Pleisse River was choked by a gruesome dam of dead men and horses, across which their comrades found a means of escape to the gardens beyond, only to be surrounded there and forced to surrender."[51] The battle thus ended for Bülow, whose corps lost 78 officers and 2,186 men, mainly from Hessen-Homburg's brigade.

Meanwhile French resistance collapsed in all sectors of the city. Just before 1:00 P.M. a tremendous explosion rocked Leipzig and shattered the hopes of escape for the remaining defenders. Napoleon had ordered the bridge over the Elster mined and destroyed once the last French units had cleared the city. In a fit of confusion the unfortunate corporal who had been left behind to execute the orders became alarmed by the approach of some Russian skirmishers and lit the fuse. Soldiers, horses, and wagons lined the bridge when it blew. Once the charges detonated, "the air was filled with flying fragments of the bridge, with broken parts of wagons, and with the limbs of horses and men, which descended in a ghastly shower on the whole neighborhood."[52] Thousands of French soldiers found themselves stranded in Leipzig. Some tried to swim to safety and drowned in the process. Shortly afterward the tsar and king of Prussia entered Leipzig through the Grimma Gate. Soon the various army and corps commanders met the Allied sovereigns in Leipzig's marketplace. The battle had ended, and staggering losses characterized the four-day struggle. The Allies lost an estimated

54,000 men: the Russians suffered the highest casualty rate at 22,605 men, followed by 16,033 Prussians, and 14,958 Austrians; the Swedes sustained 178 casualties. Napoleon lost approximately 73,000 men, including 30,000 prisoners and 5,000 German deserters, as well as 325 guns and 40,000 muskets. Of the marshals, Prince Josef Anton Poniatowski drowned in the Elster just twelve hours after receiving his baton on the battlefield, while Ney, Macdonald, and Marmont were wounded. The Allies also captured thirty-six French generals.[53]

Like the Russian Campaign one year earlier, Napoleon's "Second Saxon Campaign" ended in failure; Germany was lost for good. Following Leipzig, the remnants of the Grande Armée of 1813 retreated to the Rhine River to defend France's natural frontiers as Napoleon's empire crumbled. Aside from a few isolated French garrisons, Berlin was safe. The liberation of Germany, which started on the fields of Groß Beeren, quickly accelerated after Leipzig as Napoleon's satellites withdrew from the Rheinbund one by one. According to David Chandler, the victory at Leipzig opened the door for Prussia to reemerge as a leading power in Germany and prepared the way for the birth of modern Europe.[54]

The war, however, did not end with Napoleon's defeat at Leipzig. Another bloody campaign would ensue before the French emperor finally abdicated on 6 April 1814. As for the Army of North Germany, Bülow's subordination to Bernadotte came to an end shortly after Leipzig. In November Bülow led his corps westward to liberate Holland and Belgium from French control. In early March 1814 he moved south, invaded northern France, and joined Blücher's army. Officially attached to the Silesian Army, he commanded Blücher's center during the Allied victory at the battle of Laon on 9 March 1814. Following this action, the old antagonisms resurfaced between the Prussian generals and threatened to split the army. But with Napoleon still in the field the Prussians cooperated long enough to reach the gates of Paris at last by 31 March.

As for Bernadotte, after the battle of Leipzig he proceeded northward, purportedly to finish the war in North Germany and to recover Hanover for the British; his real goal was to force the Danes to cede Norway. With 60,000 men he marched to take his long-awaited prize. On 14 January the prostrate Danes ceded Norway to Sweden in the Treaty of Kiel. Although Stockholm believed the war to be over for Sweden, Bernadotte turned south again. "Above all," as historian Alan

Palmer notes, "his greatest personal ambition remained unfulfilled, for the Prince-Royal of Sweden was still Jean-Baptiste Bernadotte, from Henry IV's Pau. With questionable sincerity the Tsar continued to tempt him, as in those desperate days at Abo: 'Soon France will have to settle her destiny,' wrote Alexander. 'You will be the mediator between her and Europe—and who knows where some happy star may lead you?'"[55]

Conclusion

The Armistice of Pläswitz provides a natural dividing line to evaluate Napoleon's strategy in 1813. In the operations prior to the armistice, Napoleon only partially resisted the "master plan's" strategy of maneuver and emphasis on a coup de théâtre. Initially he adhered to the one principle that had brought him so much success in the past: the annihilation of the main enemy army. After the Prussians and Russians solidified their alliance and formulated their own strategy, Napoleon turned his attention to destroying their combined army. Yet, unable to disregard his "master plan," he divided his forces for operations against Berlin on two occasions.

Ambitious indeed, the coup de théâtre had several shortcomings. The plan could only work by diverting French forces to North Germany and away from the main Allied army in Saxony. The initial operation against Berlin in mid-May failed when Ney turned his whole army south to join the battle at Bautzen. Not only did this postpone the operation against a weakly defended Berlin, but Ney's confusion cost Napoleon the manpower of his Second Corps—25,000 men—which could not reach Bautzen in time.[1] Consequently, this failure marks the first blunder that can be attributed to Napoleon's preoccupation with Berlin and the coup de théâtre. The operation not only failed to achieve its objective but prevented Napoleon from concentrating all of his available forces at Bautzen.

Oudinot's experience in June provided a lesson that Napoleon also failed to recognize. Unlike the impressive force of 84,000 men that Ney had assembled a few weeks earlier at Torgau, Oudinot had less than 20,000 men when he embarked on his mission against Bülow's corps. Napoleon believed that Oudinot had sufficient force to drive the Prussians across the Oder and take their capital.[2] Since Bülow's men actually outnumbered Oudinot's, his only chance for success would have been to isolate and destroy the Allied columns once they began to concentrate. With only a slim chance to concentrate superior combat power, how did Napoleon expect his marshal to succeed? The answer is that the emperor grossly underestimated the combat effectiveness and overall worth of the Prussian troops that guarded Berlin. Bülow defeated Oudinot in a hard-fought contest at Luckau. Although Napoleon acknowledged the improvement of the Prussian army since 1806, he refused to believe that it could match his troops in the field. This contempt plagued all of his calculations, much to the detriment of the subordinates who received independent commands.

Napoleon's correspondence and strategic planning in May and June do indeed place great emphasis on the capture of Berlin, which can be inferred as the preliminary step for the implementation of the master plan. Taking the Prussian capital may have been the initial phase of the larger operation, but circumstances prevented Napoleon from ever leading a campaign against Berlin himself. This meant that his battle-weary subordinates shouldered the responsibility of independent command. In May a confused Ney led his entire army to Bautzen. Napoleon had actually wanted Victor's 25,000 men to continue the operation against Berlin. Again, after the battle of Bautzen, the emperor ordered Oudinot to march *northwest* against Berlin with similar numbers, while Napoleon's army pursued the Allied army eastward. It remains doubtful that either Victor or Oudinot could have implemented the master plan with only 25,000 men, yet the emperor based his desire to take Berlin on the results he expected from a successful operation in North Germany. Without question, an aggressive move toward Berlin would test the strength of the Allied coalition as well as the resolve of the Prussians. Napoleon hoped that an operation against Berlin would induce the Prussians to bid farewell to their Russian benefactors and move with all possible speed to protect their capital. Had this been the case, the Sixth Coalition most likely would have dissolved. Russian sacrifices during their own war of liberation in 1812 had been immense, and their reaction to such a retrograde move by the Prussians might have been to withdraw from the war. Frederick William, however, avoided this pitfall. His reserved concern for Berlin and his aggressive attitude in the campaign could only have produced a positive impression on the one man who saw himself as the liberator of Europe, Tsar Alexander.

As for defenders, only a weak Allied corps guarded Berlin during most of April and May—a point that Napoleon should have considered in his assessment of that city's importance to the Allies. By mid-May Bülow's corps amounted to 16,000 men. Although the size of this corps doubled by June, it remains unlikely that it would have been able to stop a concerted French drive on Berlin.[3] The main Allied army's retreat eastward from Lützen isolated and exposed Bülow's corps. It is quite conceivable that Berlin would have fallen to a French offensive during the spring campaign. Unquestionably, its capture would have dealt a serious blow to Prussian morale. It is difficult to believe that the loss of the capital would have knocked the Prussians out of the coalition, however. For Frederick William, there would not and could not be another Tilsit. The loss of his capital would not have forced him to sue for peace. He had not done so in 1806. In January 1813 he fled to Silesia and prepared for war while the French still controlled Berlin. For the king of Prussia, the struggle in 1813 had to be a war to the death. The result either had to be the end of Napoleon's domination of Central Europe or the end of Hohenzollern Prussia.

After careful consideration, the idea that the fall of Berlin would have posed a serious obstacle to Prussian mobilization cannot be supported. Prussian mobilization, ordered on 12 January 1813 for the regular army, occurred as French units moved eastward through Brandenburg to meet the Russian advance. With Berlin completely under French control, the army concentrated mainly in Silesia. Provincial commanders in East Prussia, West Prussia, and Pomerania conducted their own mobilization as best they could, so that by 16 March 1813 Prussia fielded an army of 68,739 men. The armistice allowed the Prussians to double the size of their army by adding a militia consisting of 149 battalions and 113 squadrons, or 120,504 men.[4] Berlin's fall in May or early June undoubtedly would have hurt a portion of the militia's mobilization but would not have crippled the entire process. The decentralized mobilization of the Landwehr reduced Berlin's role, and the capital did not serve as the central hub of Prussian mobilization. In fact, when the armistice expired the entire Kurmark province, with Berlin at its center, produced only 20,560 Landwehr soldiers. Compared to the 50,000 provided by Silesia and the 42,000 raised in the provinces east of the Oder, the Kurmark's contribution—taking nothing away from the efforts of Bülow and Boyen—was not extraordinary.

Other exaggerated benefits of an operation in North Germany include the relief of veteran troops besieged in the garrisons on the Oder and the Vistula. This represents a misconception that Col. John Elting has termed pure myth. The majority of these garrison troops consisted not of the French veterans but of Polish, Lithuanian, Neapolitan, Spanish, Dutch, Italian, Croatian, Saxon, Bavarian, and other assorted German battalions. Elting has proven that generally weak "depot battalions of Polish or Lithuanian regiments, lines-of-communications detachments, and provisional units of stragglers and replacements" garrisoned the Oder and the Vistula fortresses. At Danzig the French garrison of 35,000 men consisted mostly of the "sick, wounded, or exhausted survivors of the great retreat out of Russia."[5] Hardly fit to serve as mobile field troops, these men probably performed a greater service by holding their respective posts, which in turn forced the Allies to allocate manpower to mask or besiege. Moreover, had Napoleon liberated the fortresses on the Oder and the Vistula, he still would have been obliged to provide garrisons.

If Napoleon's numerical superiority made the master plan feasible in May and early June, was it strategically sound? The answer must be no. Such a conclusion must not be based on the failures of Ney and Oudinot. Instead Napoleon's own principles of war dictate the answer. To achieve another victory on the scale of an Austerlitz, Jena, Friedland, or Wagram, Napoleon's objective had to be the main Allied army. He should have directed all strategic planning and offensive activity at the most effective and decisive means of attaining the objective. By defeating the armed might of his adversary, all secondary objectives such as Berlin would have been attained eventually.

Napoleon's overall mission in 1813 was to reassert French hegemony in Central Europe. The emperor had sufficient means to defeat the main enemy army decisively and thus destroy the Allied will to fight. Moreover, the coalition needed a victory. To attract allies, particularly Austria, and prove that the defeat at Lützen was not debilitating, the Russians and Prussians had to turn and fight, just as they did at Bautzen. By dividing his forces Napoleon denied himself the principle of mass. Had he retained Ney's army during the period between the battles of Lützen and Bautzen, he would have been able to concentrate superior combat power at the decisive place and time. In order to achieve conclusive results, Napoleon's strategy at all times should have been to concentrate superior combat power against his enemy's main army.

The emperor's plan for the fall campaign envisioned a defensive role for the army directly under his orders in Saxony. Meanwhile two other French armies would conduct offensive operations. Oudinot's Army of Berlin would advance against the Prussian capital and continue into North Germany, while Macdonald's Army of the Bober would march against the enemy forces in Silesia to shield Oudinot's right flank. Although Napoleon did not ascertain until very late that the main Allied army would operate from Bohemia, it remained clear that the enemy units assembled around Berlin did not constitute the main Allied host. Nevertheless, he allocated three infantry and one cavalry corps from his forces in Saxony to pursue the secondary objective of Berlin. Macdonald's army, which by 24 August also consisted of three infantry and one cavalry corps—approximately 100,000 men—extended eastward to hold Blücher's Army of Silesia. In a period of three days both French armies sustained defeats. Where Bülow merely checked Oudinot's advance at Groß Beeren, Blücher routed Macdonald's army at the Katzbach.

In these operations it is clear that Napoleon again allowed his strategy to be influenced by the results he expected from the master plan. Despite his calculations and personal feelings, a bold offensive against Berlin did not offer the same promise of easy success that it had in May or early June, when Bülow's small force guarded the Prussian capital. Numerical superiority no longer favored the French eagles, and the Allies no longer had to cover the vast area between Magdeburg and Crossen with 30,000 men. Instead the new Allied Army of North Germany—120,000 men—guarded Berlin. Such numbers now required a major French offensive and a decisive victory over the Army of North Germany in order for the master plan to achieve success. As for Berlin itself, the psychological effect of its fall indeed would have been worse in August or September than in May or June. By late August, however, Berlin was merely a geographic point. Possession of it would have afforded Napoleon no real political advantage unless he abandoned Saxony and established a new base in North Germany. As for the mobilization of the Prussian Landwehr and the regular army, Berlin no longer served the purpose of either. In fact, the Prussian capital did not even serve as a major supply depot; instead the fortress at Kolberg housed the arms, ammunition, and supplies that flowed in from Britain by way of the Royal Navy.

Careful scrutiny of Napoleon's strategy reveals that the battles of Groß Beeren and the Katzbach would have never taken place had the emperor forced himself to adhere to his own principle of mass and to concentrate on the annihilation of the main Allied army, which, by 16 August, he knew to be the enemy army in Bohemia.[6] The defeat of Oudinot and Macdonald is certainly not enough to condemn the emperor's strategy. Napoleon's inability to relinquish the offensive, however, combined with his desire to initiate the master plan with a bold stroke against Berlin, caused both defeats. Napoleon ordered Macdonald first to push back Blücher and then to maintain a defensive posture to protect Oudinot's flank. Thus as his first objective Macdonald had to pressure Blücher. Since the two armies had equal strength, Macdonald would have been hard-pressed to concentrate superior combat power at the critical place and time to attain decisive results. Regarding Macdonald's defensive role, Napoleon could have made better use of economy of force. Macdonald's extended army should have been pulled back to a more central location, such as the Spree River, and reduced in size, so that the emperor could have concentrated more combat power against the Army of Bohemia during the battle of Dresden. Although the aggressive Blücher did press the offensive once he realized that Napoleon had returned to Dresden, a commander more capable than Macdonald, even with a smaller force, could have held the Silesian Army long enough for the emperor to return after dealing with Schwarzenberg. Murat later performed this role in October, when he slowed Schwarzenberg's advance to a crawl; the Bohemian Army took two and one-half weeks to cover seventy miles.

To secure Oudinot's right flank, Napoleon could neither reduce the size of the Army of the Bober nor pull it back to the Spree. Oudinot also had difficulty concentrating superior combat power to defeat the Army of North Germany decisively. As with Macdonald's army, Napoleon would have been better served by implementing the principle of economy of force with the Army of Berlin. Despite any advantages that a successful operation in North Germany might have offered, it still remained a secondary theater. A decisive French victory over the main Allied army remained the best and proven means of unraveling the enemy coalition. Thus the Army of Berlin should not have existed.

Oudinot should have commanded two corps at the most to hold the crossings over the Elbe between Rosslau and Torgau. The rest of the forces that Napoleon allocated to the Army of Berlin would have better served the emperor had they remained with the Grande Armée. Consequently, in the case of both Macdonald and Oudinot, Napoleon should have redefined their objectives and allocated minimum essential combat power for their secondary efforts.

Although Napoleon inflicted over 35,000 casualties on Schwarzenberg's Army of Bohemia during the battle of Dresden, a decisive victory eluded him. Had a few additional French corps been at hand (the manpower spared by reducing the Army of Berlin and the Army of the Bober) the main Allied army might have been crushed. Regardless of "what if" scenarios, with the victory over Schwarzenberg the emperor believed that he had reached a point where he could personally implement his master plan. He planned to lead 30,000 men from Dresden to unite with the Army of Berlin and resume the operation against Berlin. Napoleon favored this as his next step rather than an operation against Prague.[7] After weighing the pros and cons of both operations, he found that the Berlin project offered a greater chance of success as well as additional benefits. Thus he decided to implement the master plan rather than oversee the pursuit of the badly mauled main Allied army, destruction of which might have brought Austria to terms. As it was, Macdonald's fiasco prevented Napoleon from marching against Berlin in early September.

From the start of the fall campaign, a defensive-oriented strategy would have afforded the emperor the best chance for success. Napoleon himself endorsed a defensive in a letter to his marshals on 12 August. "It seems to me," he noted, "that to bring about a decisive and brilliant result, the best way is to keep in close formation and allow the enemy to approach."[8] Five days later Napoleon again commented that "no one can turn an army of 400,000, planted on a system of fortresses, on a river like the Elbe, and able to deploy at will by Dresden, Torgau, Wittenberg, and Magdeburg."[9] Yet, try as he might, Napoleon could not convince himself to adopt a purely passive defensive. Hence the emperor could not refrain from adding offensive elements to his strategy, mainly an advance against Berlin. Consequently, the question once again reverts back to Napoleon's preoccupation with Berlin, North Germany, and the presumed results of the master plan. Contempt for the Army of North Germany may have made the revival of the master plan so appealing. Despite the admirable performance of the Prussian troops at the battles of Luckau and Groß Beeren, Napoleon's unwarranted disdain for them and their allies persisted, as is evident in his 2 September reference to the Army of North Germany as a "cloud of Cossacks and pack of bad Landwehr."[10] Ultimately the attempt to implement the master plan, with the conquest of Berlin as its centerpiece, was simply a mistake in August and September. Instead of committing combat forces to a secondary objective, Napoleon desperately needed to adhere to the one principle that had brought him so much success in the past: the concentration of superior combat power for the annihilation of the main enemy army.[11]

By far Napoleon's most feasible strategy in the Fall Campaign of 1813 would have been to concentrate his forces and exploit Allied mistakes. Connelly believes that with this strategy the emperor "could have preserved the strength of his men and waited for the enemy to make mistakes before striking, thus carrying another of his usual battlefield tactics to the strategic level."[12] Had he kept the Grande Armée massed, maintained a defensive posture, and utilized economy of force with Oudinot and Macdonald, he could have exploited a few key characteristics that had governed all of the coalitions arrayed against him in previous wars. First and foremost, the Allies needed a decisive victory. Eventually they would have to face Napoleon if they truly desired to liberate Central Europe. The Allies themselves could not afford a prolonged war of attrition and maneuver. Such a war would have deflated popular enthusiasm and might have subordinated military goals to political interests. In this epic struggle the collective fate of Central Europe and the great powers hung in the balance. During their councils of war in July the Russians and Prussians did not forget that nothing less than an unprecedented, massive undertaking would liberate Central Europe from French domination. Although the Austrians insisted on modifications that introduced more caution in the hopes of avoiding another catastrophe, prudence and calculated aggression characterized the actual execution of the Trachenberg Plan.[13] Finally, the British paymaster had to be considered. Certainly London would not have subsidized a prolonged war of attrition while the Duke of Wellington pressed the French in Iberia.

Whether Napoleon's personal supervision of the master plan in August or September would have been successful will never be known, but speculation may offer some insight. In reality the total success of the strategy outlined in the master plan required Napoleon strictly to adhere to its premises as established in early March. This would have required him completely to shift his base of operations to North Germany, to abandon Dresden, and to reconfigure his lines of communication. In his "Note" of 30 August 1813, however, the emperor speaks of maintaining his position in Saxony with the strong camp and vital supplies of Dresden at his disposal. When considering Allied strategy and the principles of the Trachenberg Plan, some obvious conclusions can be drawn. Once the Allies confirmed that Napoleon personally commanded the approaching French army, Bernadotte would have ordered a general retreat. The Russians, who placed no great value on Berlin, would have obeyed without question. Although Bülow and Tauentzien would have objected, they too would have followed. Just as with Blücher's Silesian Army, a demoralized Army of North Germany would have withdrawn before Napoleon's onslaught. The emperor would not have had the luxury of pursuing the fleeing Bernadotte before the other two Allied armies converged on their respective French holding forces. Napoleon then would have been forced to break off the pursuit of Bernadotte and race south to secure his lieutenants. This development, once known in Bernadotte's camp, would have caused the Prussians to drag the Army of North Germany forward to liberate their capital.

Throughout 1813 Napoleon's principal objective in North Germany was not the destruction of an enemy army, which represents a striking deviation from the emperor's principles of war.[14] Whether the goal was Berlin, Stettin, or Danzig, Napoleon's operations in North Germany consistently reverted to a strategy of maneuver rather than of annihilation. Had he effected this coup de théâtre and gained the Vistula, he still had to confront the enemy armies. In the fall campaign the emperor vigorously pressed the campaign north of the Elbe when the numerical advantage favored his adversaries. Not only was he outnumbered, but he desperately needed another Austerlitz. Such a victory had to be over the main Allied army in the hope that one of the belligerents would drop out of the war. Ultimately the operations against Berlin and the ensuing battles that resulted from Napoleon's almost obsessive wish to implement his master plan should not be judged by the losses incurred by the French armies involved, but rather by the way in which they limited the emperor's own ability to achieve decisive victory. Napoleon suffered defeat in 1813 "because he acted as if he possessed unlimited power," and the resources he expended on the campaigns for Berlin provide solid proof of his error in judgment.[15]

Failure in North Germany has been attributed to the marshals who led the operations. Both Ney and Napoleon deserve a fair share of blame for the miscarriage during the Bautzen operation. An insufficiently informed Ney misunderstood his role throughout the entire affair, and Napoleon's ambiguous directives did not provide the guidance needed by his impulsive marshal. Unfortunately for Napoleon, this early lesson went unheeded. Oudinot's subsequent failure to dislodge Bülow and secure the Prussian capital on the eve of the armistice also failed to make an impression on the emperor. Ney and Oudinot—men who at best had the talent to command a division—were indeed dubious choices when Marshal Davout, perhaps the greatest of Napoleon's marshals, languished in Hamburg.[16] Even more surprisingly, Napoleon selected the same men to command the Berlin operations in the fall campaign as he did in the spring campaign. Napoleon's failure to appoint adequate commanders after successive failures proved Ney and Oudinot incompetent remains symbolic of the errors in judgment that plagued the emperor's last campaigns.[17] His strategy and correspondence with his subordinates also reflect a tendency to view things as he wished, to underestimate the numbers of his adversaries and overestimate his own. Finally, Napoleon's less than clear instructions and the inability of his subordinates to coordinate large operations reveal the emperor's failure to grasp the importance of creating an adequate General Staff system.[18]

When examining the role of the Prussian army in 1813, it is important to note that the forces the Prussians unleashed on Napoleon were the fruits of their own labors. In 1806 Prussia lay prostrate at Napoleon's feet, similar to Austria in 1805 and 1809. Despite his overwhelming victories, Napoleon made no attempts to remove the monarchs of either Prussia or Austria, although the threat remained ever-present. The nineteenth-century French apologist Arthur Lévy believed that had the emperor taken this drastic step he would have put an end to the Allied coalitions.[19] Historian Pieter Geyl calls this conception of international politics "childish."[20] Although Geyl's assessment may be correct, Napoleon did fail to extend the reforms of the French Revolution—Liberty, Equality, and Fraternity—to the conquered areas of Central and Eastern Europe, especially Prussia. Unlike the Belgians, Dutch, Italians, Swiss, and Rhineland Germans, the Prussians were not granted the benefits of the Revolution by the emperor. He left the king of Prussia free to cope with the challenges posed by the French Revolution. Thus any reforms the king of Prussia did sponsor came as a response to French subjugation, the yoke of oppression, and newborn nationalism.[21] Moreover, any changes that could be interpreted as positive earned the monarch the gratitude of his people. In 1813 this fact became more apparent and more detrimental to French control in Prussia than in any other state.

The immediate effects of the Prussian reform movement of 1807–12 proved successful. Although smaller and unable to play an independent military role, the Prussian army of 1813 was superior to that of 1806.[22] Due to general social and military reforms, the soldier was elevated to a position of respect and looked upon as the savior of a "Fatherland." Within the army enlightened attitudes stressing civic responsibility replaced harsh discipline. Strict submission to lawful authority rather than feudal terror became the basis of obedience. By law the officer corps was opened to men of education and merit; a General Staff provided unity of command and direction.[23] The campaigns of 1813 provide adequate testimony to the army's improved technical efficiency.

Although tactical and organizational improvements enhanced the army's performance in 1813, evasion or outright abolition was the ultimate fate of several of Scharnhorst's key reforms. The principles that opened the officer corps to all classes suffered from conservative limitations and did not survive. Evidence also suggests that corporal punishment continued to be used by officers in 1813. Gneisenau, who had personally championed the abolition of flogging, was himself guilty. During the fall campaign the Silesian Landwehr of Yorck's corps particularly concerned him. He personally ordered the enforcement of strict discipline. A contemporary noted that after the battle on the Katzbach "the commanding officers of the battalions were punished with stern warnings, several officers were arrested, the majority of the Landwehr demoted to second class . . . punished with hunger and beatings; the only thing left to do was have them shot."[24] Moreover, the emasculation of the Landsturm in July—a time when a French invasion of the Kurmark to capture the national capital was imminent—provided an ominous sign of the king's reactionary conservatism, which would ultimately crush the reform movement in 1819.[25]

The Prussian reformers had labored to surpass the revolutionary theory of the French army. As early as 1807 the reformers wanted the entire male population, without exemption, to undergo military training.[26] Ultimately a small standing army with an immense reserve of trained men would be produced. The Krumper reserve system became the embodiment of this ideal. Time and resources, however, prevented the system from achieving the desired results.[27] With only 40,000 reservists in January 1813, the Prussian monarchy had to embrace universal conscription in order to field a sufficient army. By enacting the Landwehr decree, Prussia utilized the concept of levée en masse. Exemptions were limited and penalties made it clear that all except priests, teachers, and some civil servants had to serve. In their quest to create a national army of citizen-soldiers the reformers overestimated the strength of Prussian patriotism. Consequently, both the call for volunteers and the Landwehr decree sparked little enthusiasm.[28] Despite patriotic feelings, many subjects still feared and resisted military service. Widespread popular hostility to the French did not lead to mass volunteering.[29] As Bülow discovered in the Kurmark—the very heart of Prussia—it became crucial for the army to enforce the conscription edicts.

Although the Landwehr units that served in the Army of North Germany fought with distinction in several battles, the militia as an institution has been criticized for being a poor imitation of a standing army rather than something new and unique.[30] Regional loyalties bound them, but the concept of a Fatherland that had to be defended, liberated, and unified played less of a role.[31] The Landwehr, although created for the middle class and landed peasants, has been described as consisting of "the poor and dispossessed," who required substantial time to be properly organized, trained, and armed.[32] The expense of equipment often fell on the men or their district. A vast majority of the Landwehr received uniforms made of wretched cloth that shrank in the first rainstorm. Several militia units in Blücher's Silesian Army spent the majority of 1813 without shoes. After the battle on the Katzbach most of the men in Yorck's Landwehr units lacked shoes, trousers, and coats.[33] The next morning one battalion had only 202 of 510 men fit for action. In another the ratio was 271 out of 577.[34] After eighteen days of campaigning from 14 August to 1 September, Yorck's corps dwindled from 37,700 to 25,300 men. The Silesian Landwehr battalions suffered a much higher rate of loss than the line regiments. Another of the militia's problems was the use of inadequate and obsolete weapons.[35] Junior officers often lacked experience. As a result the overall military effectiveness of the Landwehr remained mixed. Some regiments, such as those that served in the Army of North Germany, proved just as effective as the line, while others, particularly in the Silesian Army, collapsed at the first exchange of fire. Regional loyalties and patriotic enthusiasm often did not overcome the Landwehr's insufficient training and lack of experience. Although the Landwehr had been a vital part of the reform program, its establishment reflected the demands of war rather than the triumph of enlightenment.[36]

For the Prussians, their war of liberation began at Tauroggen, which crowned three years of tense relations between the king and his army. In 1809 Frederick William had embittered the patriotic war hawks by refusing to assist the Austrians in the War of the Fifth Coalition. Three years later, when the king capitulated to Napoleon's pressure and placed Prussian troops at his disposal, "this feeling turned to a suppressed fury."[37] Retaliation took the form of Yorck's convention, which the king always resented. Nevertheless, Frederick William allowed himself to embrace the nationalistic fervor that it aroused and summon his people to arms.[38] Thomas Nipperdey describes the convention as "an amazing development . . . here was a general serving the militaristic state of Prussia (motto: obedience) . . . who took it upon himself to act independently, indeed claimed the right to disobey. He was putting patriotic and nationalist legitimacy higher than dynastic and military authority."[39] Yorck's act, notes Henry Kissinger, "became a symbol of national independence and freedom from foreign bondage."[40] Thus from the beginning the resurrected Prussian military establishment took the patriotic war movement out of the king's hands and determined that it would be more than a war of liberation—it would be a war of revenge.

When Frederick William fled to Breslau in January 1813, two-thirds of the Prussian army already operated independently of his command.[41] The four months between December 1812 and March 1813 provide little evidence of a change in the perplexing foreign policy that Frederick William had pursued prior to war in 1806. In the wake of Napoleon's destruction in Russia, neither the Russians nor the French could trust the Prussians, although both needed them desperately. As in 1805, the Prussians in December 1812 hoped to benefit from mediating between France and its enemies. Tauroggen, however, limited Frederick William's options.[42] During the first three months of 1813 the king was besieged by hopes and fears as he struggled to gain an advantageous diplomatic settlement with either France or Russia. Negotiating for Prussia's return to great power status proved erroneous, and very early it became clear that Berlin would have to fight for it—but on whose side? Napoleon helped answer the question by failing to offer the Prussians an attractive package that might make Berlin his main partner in German affairs. More importantly, the pressure exerted on the Prussian executive by the officer corps represents a thread of continuity that influenced Prussian policy in 1805–6 and again in 1813. After Napoleon crushed the Prussian army in 1806 and French troops began a humiliating six-year occupation of Prussia, the leaders of the Prussian military establishment labored to restore both national and international honor to their profession, their army, and, most of all, their state. Prussian generals took the initiative to precipitate a rupture with France, and personal feelings translated into political action.

In early 1813 Bülow and Yorck found themselves pulled in various directions. Although French misconceptions of the actual situation in Prussia aided the Prussian generals, both officers had to evade French and Russian demands for cooperative action. Their successful circumvention of both foreign armies came with very little direction from their king.[43] Bülow and Yorck had to decide their own courses of action by presuming what was best for the state, even if it did not coincide with their monarch's wishes. Only the careful judgment of Bülow and Yorck, the two officers most responsible for Prussia's drift toward war and the two commanders who kept the French and Russians guessing if Prussia was a friend or foe, prevented the state from becoming embroiled in a struggle with France before Frederick William concluded a Russian alliance.

To the Prussians, the war against Napoleon was not a political struggle. Instead it was an ideological "fight against evil, a struggle against the anti-Christ and his minions."[44] Unlike the Russians and Austrians, the Prussians turned their war against Napoleon into a holy crusade, a total war between two peoples—a Franco-Prussian war. Prussia's uprising produced a noteworthy spirit of sacrifice that enabled the government to collect 6.5 million thalers in the "gold for iron" fundraising campaign.[45] Enthusiasm and popular support did vary greatly, yet Prussian-German patriotism permeated the public mind.[46] The Prussians embraced the new patriotism "not for reform, constitutional liberty, and Prussian and/or German unity, but out of hatred of the foreign invader and a religiously based traditional loyalty to god, king, and country," which made the Prussian movement akin to those in Calabria, Spain, the Tyrol, and Russia.[47] Prussia's popular revolt—which the conservative Frederick William never wanted to approach the levels attained by the Spanish, Calabrian, or Tyrolean guerrillas—helped convince the king to renounce his alliance with Napoleon, perhaps out of fear that his own people might overthrow him. Yorck's convention initiated a period when the army appeared to pursue its own agenda, which also influenced Frederick William. Both the army's rebellion against royal prerogative and the popular rising steadily moved the cautious king to war. Credit must be given to Hardenberg for riding the storm long enough to secure favorable alliance terms from Russia. The ultimate result of the Prussian "rising" was for the Prussian people to perceive the struggle as their war.[48] The people not only convinced but in the case of East Prussia forced the king to allow the army to fight for Prussia's liberation.[49] They then supported the army in the field; and if enthusiasm waned, traditional Prussia militarism enabled the army to continue its "total" war.[50]

Craig notes that Prussian complaints over Allied war planning "were not really about strategy" but were "about something much more fundamental, about faith, about religion." Bülow, as a corps commander, and Blücher, as an army commander, both made critical decisions regardless of their superiors. Complaints, objections, and demands as well as "constantly reiterated opposition to any form of restraint" blended with Bülow's violent criticism of Bernadotte's strategy and Blücher's contempt for the machinations of Grand Allied Headquarters, which grew during 1813 and carried over into 1814. The Prussians pursued a different kind of war—a war guided by "mystical nationalism." At times this contradicted the designs of the Allied sovereigns and ministers, who strove to maintain the common interests of the alliance.[51] Schwarzenberg did not transmit orders to the North German or Silesian Armies. Instead the monarchs themselves, or their representatives on Schwarzenberg's staff, issued instructions to Blücher and Bernadotte, who sometimes loosely interpreted their meaning.[52] Bernadotte in particular "was suspicious of all orders emanating from the supreme command lest they overtax his resources and make it impossible for him to attain his real objective in the war, which was the acquisition of Norway for Sweden."[53]

Powerful personalities clashed and anarchy reigned at times in the high command of the Silesian Army, similar to the chaotic conditions at Grand Allied Headquarters. Thus in both auxiliary armies Schwarzenberg's orders were sometimes superseded by personal ambition and rivalry. Such tenuous central control actually benefited the Prussians by enabling them to ignore, modify, or emphasize directives from Grand Allied Headquarters in order to wage an almost fanatical national war against the French. Craig attributes Allied success in 1813 to Schwarzenberg's "patience and forbearance" as well as to "the general fear of Napoleon and the common awareness that he was still far from being beaten."[54] Time and again, however, Prussian impetuosity carried the war to the French and made the Trachenberg Plan a success. While Metternich, Schwarzenberg, Bernadotte, and at times even Alexander wanted to fight a "limited" war to attain "specific, minimal goals" (for which war was to be waged to a predesignated point and then stopped), the Prussian army waged an unlimited war and was allowed to do so by Napoleon's intransigence.[55]

The Prussian contribution in 1813 remains unparalleled. Financially devastated and an unwilling member of the Napoleonic system in 1812, the Prussians waged a total war against France in 1813. To challenge the French, a resurrected and reformed military establishment dragged its king forward—or completely disregarded him at times. The Prussians were directly responsible for many of the most decisive events in the Fall Campaign of 1813. Bülow defied Bernadotte on several occasions, which saved Berlin and altered the course of the war. Blücher's crushing victory on the Katzbach wrecked not only a French army but also Napoleon's plans to march on Berlin. Success on the Katzbach ultimately led to Ney's destruction at Dennewitz. Blücher's refusal to march to Bohemia in September and his subsequent march down the Elbe enabled the Allies to concentrate all of their combat power against a weakened Napoleon. Prussian triumphs at Groß Beeren, on the banks of the Katzbach, and at Hagelberg, Kulm, and Dennewitz countered Napoleon's victory at Dresden, reduced Prussia's dependence on Russia, and strengthened Prussia's claim to parity with Austria in Germany. "Those same unruly generals," asserts historian Enno Kraehe, ". . . were giving an account of themselves which filled everyone with pride. . . . Europe began to hear the names of Bülow and Kleist and Blücher."[56] The victory at Dennewitz provided a crucial turning point in the War of the Sixth Coalition and induced both sides to change strategy in its aftermath. Blücher brought both his Army of Silesia and the Army of North Germany over the Elbe; his decisions in early October and the efficient work of the Prussian General Staff throughout the campaign made Leipzig possible. Gneisenau and Blücher would see to it that the Prussians continued to wage their Franco-Prussian war of annihilation by pursuing Napoleon to the very gates of Paris in 1814.

The fanatical zeal with which Prussia's commanders pressed the war did not always correspond with Allied war aims, yet Allied diplomacy in part deserves some of the blame. The introduction of Bernadotte and Metternich not only changed the nature of the war but significantly influenced the type of war the Prussians wished to wage. Bernadotte's unrestrained personal considerations, dynastic concerns, and political machinations strangled and almost suffocated the Prussian war effort, while Metternich completely exchanged the patriotic and nationalist elements of a war that demanded total victory for clearly limited goals that favored restoration, legitimacy, and stability. With great mastery he succeeded in channeling Russia's "moralistic fervor" and Prussia's "national impetuosity" into a "concert of precise measures which imperceptibly transformed the moral basis of their efforts."[57] Frederick William accepted this arrangement because in the end he too was a conservative reactionary.[58] After the armistice the Prussian generals found themselves in a coalition whose goal was not ultimate military victory but peace with Napoleonic France through negotiation rather than military force. The very conditions that their monarch accepted as terms for peace fell far short of total victory and would have left Napoleon on his throne with France still the strongest power on the Continent.[59] Metternich may have succeeded in changing perceptions of peace and victory in the minds of Alexander and Frederick William, but Prussian commanders still measured victory the same way as Napoleon did: peace would be based on military success only.

At Grand Allied Headquarters the Allies settled into a policy of attaining peace without achieving total military victory, but constant dissension and confusion over strategic objectives proved divisive.[60] Although the Allies differed sharply over terms, Paul Schroeder notes that they "always sought a negotiated peace in one form or another and agreed that the war should be ended as soon as the right terms were attained."[61] Metternich faced two alternatives in 1813: a war of peoples or a war of states.[62] The treaties signed at Teplitz on 9 September settled the issue by making Austria the lead power in the coalition. Metternich, now the coalition's "quasi-prime minister," turned the peoples' war for liberation, independence, and national unity into a war of states for the restoration of the balance of power.[63] Moreover, Metternich led Austria into the war to end French hegemony, not as a crusade against Napoleon. For Austria's statesman, Napoleon's defeat was not as important as the creation of a coalition based on the principles of conservatism and stability.[64] The Prussian army, however, still preferred to fulfill a national desire for vengeance rather than comply with the international requisites for a durable peace.[65] Throughout the war in Germany the Austrians dominated the politics of the coalition and the Prussians represented the spirit of the coalition, while the Russians lacked the ability to do either.[66] "It was Prussian statesmen and Prussian generals," notes Showalter, "who stressed the importance of keeping the alliance intact by fighting the French wherever and whenever possible, leaving the aftermath of victory to take care of itself."[67]

The Prussian military establishment, committed to destroying the French Empire to satisfy its lust for revenge, simply could not adjust to Metternich's revolutionary change in strategy and war aims. In early 1813 Napoleon was not alone in his fear that rebels controlled the Prussian army. The Austrians in particular noted the manner in which the events between December and March allowed the military to push Prussia into a war with France.[68] During the first half of 1813 Metternich questioned whether the Prussian government could control its army. The fury with which the Prussians descended upon France in 1814 and their conduct that year as well as in 1815 earned nothing but suspicion, loathing, and contempt rather than gratitude from Prussia's allies. Tsar Alexander once informed his generals that in the future they might have to save the king of Prussia from his own army![69] Blücher's blind hatred of Napoleon, coupled with Gneisenau's desire to "answer the visits of the French to our cities by visiting them in theirs," meant that thousands of Prussian and Russian troops lost their lives in 1814, *after* Germany had been liberated.[70]

Whereas the tsar of Russia had the resources to replenish his losses, the king of Prussia did not. Just as Austria's combat power had given Schwarzenberg supreme command, so too did combat power directly determine a state's leverage at the peace table in the wake of Napoleon's abdication. There Prussia paid for the rash and bloody campaign of 1814 rather than reaping the rewards for its victories in 1813. Although Prussia received material compensation in the Rhineland as well as a generous chunk of Saxony, Metternich steered the Congress of Vienna to settle the much larger German Question in favor of Austria. Prussia had planned to annex all of North Germany, but Metternich realized that in the future Prussia could engineer German unification. He frustrated Prussian expansionist aims by proposing that the thirty-seven German states plus the ethnic German regions of Austria and Prussia be united in a confederation. Instead of facilitating German unity, Metternich sought to deny Germany's "immense wealth to a single great power by dissipating Germany's human and material resources among thirty-five princely states and four free cities."[71] As early as March 1813 Metternich had formulated Austria's objectives. Unfortunately for the Prussians, he "defined the object of the struggle as a war for an equilibrium, for a society of states and not of nations, for a Germany of many sovereignties, and for a conservative Europe."[72] Castlereagh supported Metternich's proposal and proved decisive in making the Austrian emperor the hereditary president of the German Confederation. The tsar's endorsement of Metternich's arrangement as a means to prevent future French encroachments in Germany dispelled any Prussian thoughts of challenging the Austrians and British. With an army that had been almost bled to death in the relentless pursuit of Napoleon, the Prussians did receive the material restoration of the state's strength but could do nothing to exploit the fervent nationalism that swept Germany in the wake of the Befreiungskriege. Metternich prevented the unification of Germany by either force of arms or national self-determination.[73]

In 1813 the Prussians created a citizens' army commanded by a professionalized officer corps and led by a highly efficient General Staff. Not only did the Prussians save their capital and change the course of the war, but the war effort represented the transition from the king's army to a national army and, to an extent, a people's army. When popular enthusiasm faltered, however, Prussian militarism took over to ensure the state's continued application of force. In this way the Prussian military establishment—separate from the king—waged an almost fanatical holy war against the French. Prussian victories in the Befreiungskriege laid the foundations that made future Prussian and German armies the envy of the world, yet they failed to transform the Prussian army permanently into a people's army. Moreover, Prussian victories not only liberated the state from Napoleon's yoke but freed the king from having to make liberal concessions to the middle and lower classes. No revolution against either absolute government or noble privilege occurred; conservatism triumphed, and the success of the army increased and extended the militaristic nature of Prussian culture. By the end of the struggle with Napoleon the military bureaucracy had freed itself from the personal interference of the monarch, and the army had become more of an active political force than ever before.[74] Despite the national awakening that gripped Prussia during the struggle against France, the citizens' army reverted back to a professional army, so that Prussia was again an army with a state. German unification through the "blood and iron" of the Prussian military establishment came fifty years later. The great omen for subsequent world history was that Prussia's uprising and victory in the Wars of Liberation failed to make the army more national and popular. Instead Prussia became more militaristic—a trend that continued in 1866, 1870, and 1914.[75]

Notes

PREFACE

1. I use the phrase "North Germany" to differentiate the Berlin campaigns from Napoleon's operations in Saxony. The events farther north, in Mecklenburg and around Hamburg, which are worthy of their own study, are mentioned only as they related to the Berlin campaigns.

2. In *The Politics of the Prussian Army*, 61–62, Gordon Craig notes that "much has been written about the popular enthusiasm of 1813 and doubtless much of it is exaggerated; but that there was a sharp contrast with the mood of 1806 there can be no doubt. The king himself was clearly surprised by the response to his message and by the floods of volunteers who applied at recruiting stations. Hatred of France was doubtless a primary motive in this upsurge of patriotism."

3. Nipperdey, *Germany from Napoleon to Bismarck*, 68.

4. Schroeder, *Transformation of European Politics*, 450.

5. The French levée en masse came in the form of Lazare Carnot's law of 23 August 1793 that conscripted unmarried men between the ages of eighteen and twenty-five with no exemptions or replacements. According to Paddy Griffith, the law stated "that all young men would go off to fight; the married men would do transport or munitions work; the women would make tents or uniforms and would serve in the hospitals; the children would comb lint; and the old men would stagger around the public squares raising the morale of the warriors." Griffith, *The Art of War*, 80–83.

6. Nipperdey, *Germany from Napoleon to Bismarck*, 69.

7. Ibid.

8. Schroeder, *Transformation of European Politics*, 473.

CHAPTER 1. FRANCE AND PRUSSIA

1. Blanning, *Origins of the French Revolutionary Wars*, 69.
2. See Hagen, "Partitions of Poland."
3. See Dwyer, "Politics of Prussian Neutrality," for a superb analysis of Prussia's neutrality between 1795 and 1806.
4. In *The Impact of Napoleon*, Simms provides an authoritative and well-researched study of Prussian high politics and foreign policy between the years 1797 and 1806.
5. See Dwyer, "Prussia and the Armed Neutrality."
6. Atkinson, *History of Germany*, 455–66.
7. For an interesting comparison of Frederick William III and Frederick II, see Arnheim, "Zur Charakteristik Friedrichs des Großen und seines Großneffen."
8. Oncken, *Österreich und Preußen*, 2:6 (quotation); Kissinger, *A World Restored*, 14.
9. Bailleu, *Preußen und Frankreich*, 2:354; Seeley, *Life and Times of Stein*, 11:235.
10. See Bitterauf, "Studien zur preußischen Politik."
11. Prussian troops had occupied Hanover in October 1805 in retaliation for Bernadotte's violation of Ansbach.
12. See Bailleu, "Die politische Haltung Friedrich Wilhelms III"; Griewank, "Hardenberg und die preußische Politik"; Simms, "The Road to Jena."
13. Atkinson, *History of Germany*, 497–98.
14. Showalter, "Hubertusberg to Auerstädt," 331.
15. Ritter, *Frederick the Great*, 131.
16. Chandler, *Atlas of Military Strategy*, 95.
17. Marshall-Cornwall, *Napoleon as Military Commander*, 25.
18. Chandler, *Atlas of Military Strategy*, 95.
19. Chandler, *Dictionary of the Napoleonic Wars*, 105–6.
20. Ritter, *Frederick the Great*, 132.
21. Petre, *Napoleon's Last Campaign*, 17. Count Philippe-Paul de Ségur noted that Napoleon could not be replaced "either because his subordinates' pride forbids them to obey another, or because . . . he had formed only able lieutenants, but no leaders." Ségur, *Napoleon's Russian Campaign*, 265.
22. See Eidahl, "Oudinot and Saint-Cyr in 1812," for the French problems with independent command in Russia; and Schneid, "Dynamics of Defeat," 8–15, for the collapse of the French high command after Napoleon left his army in Russia in early December.
23. Showalter offers an "alternative perspective on the evolution of the Prussian army" between the end of the Seven Years' War in 1763 and Prussia's debacle in 1806. According to his analysis, "the military logic of the Age of Reason combined with common sense evaluation of Prussia's strategic and economic positions to suggest that the state's optimal force structure should be front-loaded: geared for maximum immediate efficiency to produce maximum immediate results." Showalter, "Hubertusberg to Auerstädt," 308–33.

24. Chandler, *Campaigns of Napoleon*, 454.

25. Showalter describes the oblique order of battle as "the use of tactical and operational methods to solve strategic and grand-strategic problems." Showalter, *Wars of Frederick the Great*, 108–9.

26. Demeter, *German Officer-Corps*, 8.

27. Showalter, "Hubertusberg to Auerstädt," 308.

28. Ibid., 309.

29. Ibid.

30. Paret, *Yorck*, 19. "The approach march," notes Paret, "became a vital and complicated part of the battle—the most difficult part of the art of war it was often called, at least by staff officers."

31. Ibid., 15.

32. Palmer, "Frederick the Great," 57.

33. Paret, *Yorck*, 15–16.

34. Showalter, "Hubertusberg to Auerstädt," 310.

35. Ibid.

36. Paret, *Yorck*, 14–15.

37. Showalter claims that "Prussia's gun designers and practical soldiers alike favored ease of usage and enhanced rates of fire over ballistic qualities." "Hubertusberg to Auerstädt," 311.

38. Paret, *Yorck*, 15.

39. Kitchen, *Military History of Germany*, 21; Palmer, "Frederick the Great," 50; Duffy, *Army of Frederick the Great*, 54–68. Walter Simon adds that the army of 1806 still consisted of "ignorant peasants and mercenaries officered by petty noblemen whose arrogance all too often expressed itself in brutality." *Failure of the Prussian Reform Movement*, 146–47.

40. Showalter, "Hubertusberg to Auerstädt," 311.

41. Cited in Palmer, "Frederick the Great," 50, 55.

42. Paret, *Yorck*, 16–17.

43. Palmer, "Frederick the Great," 56.

44. Ibid., 55.

45. Jany, *Geschichte der königlichen preußischen Armee*, 3:50. In 1740 the Prussian army contained 26,000 foreigners out of 76,000 men; in 1752 the number of foreign born troops reached fifty percent. By 1763, however, the army consisted of only 37,000 foreigners and 103,000 natives. This number again rose to fifty percent in the 1780s before dropping to an estimated thirty-five percent by 1800. See also Ritter, *Frederick the Great*, 134–35.

46. Frederick also advised against camping near forests and suggested that the men be led to bathe by an officer. Palmer, "Frederick the Great," 55.

47. Ibid., 51; Paret, *Yorck*, 19.

48. Palmer, "Frederick the Great," 50.

49. Ibid., 51.

50. Kitchen, *Military History of Germany*, 22–34.

51. Simon, *Failure of the Prussian Reform Movement*, 147.

52. Paret, *Yorck*, 19.

53. Ibid. See also White, *Enlightened Soldier*, 1–56; Palmer, "Frederick the Great," 62–74.

54. Palmer, "Frederick the Great," 56.

55. Showalter, "Hubertusberg to Auerstädt," 330. Showalter suggests that the Prussian army "had adapted too well to what a later generation would call mid-intensity war and counterinsurgency operations, in the process taking for granted the continued ability to win a Leuthen or a Rossbach."

56. Ibid., 313. "Far from being the debacle or the farce often presented in narrowly focused military histories," notes Showalter, "the conflict provided the kind of diplomatic/political triumph Frederick had always hoped for from the army he had spent his life building."

57. Ibid., 319. The Prussians took huge chunks of Polish territory and renamed the provinces New East Prussia and South Prussia.

58. Ibid., 323.

59. Frederick William III has been criticized for not declaring war on France in 1805; it has been argued that the acquisition of Hanover hardly justified his vacillation, when participation in the War of the Third Coalition could have tipped the scales against France. Neither his state nor his army, however, was designed for the protracted struggles that accompanied the Wars of the First and Second Coalitions.

60. Showalter, in "Hubertusberg to Auerstädt," 331, adds that "this was not an optimal strategic situation, but neither was it generally perceived as being outside the capacities of Prussia's military establishment. The war hawks of 1806 included many of the officers most active in the military reform movement."

61. See the definition of limited war in Palmer, "Frederick the Great," 49–52; and the definition of total war in Ritter, *Frederick the Great*, 131. See also Connelly, "Napoleon and Frederick the Great," for an interesting comparison of their art of war.

62. Petre, *Napoleon's Conquest of Prussia*, 68–69.

63. Gen. Ernst Friedrich von Rüchel positioned his Prussian corps of 20,000 men between Gotha and Erfurt to support Brunswick.

64. Purportedly, the French took 7,262 medals and coins; 538 gems; 183 bronzes; 116 paintings; 96 busts and statues; and the Quadriga statue from atop the Brandenburg Gate. Bassewitz, *Die Kurmark-Brandenburg*, 1:154–56.

65. Shanahan, *Prussian Military Reforms*, 98.

66. The Prussians lost the provinces of New East Prussia and South Prussia to the Grand Duchy of Warsaw but kept West Prussia and East Prussia. Most of Prussia's western possessions, which included the Universities of Duisberg, Erlangen, and Halle, went to Jérôme Bonaparte's new Kingdom of Westphalia or to the Grand Duchy of Berg.

67. In the 12 July 1807 Convention of Königsberg, which was signed by the French marshal Louis-Alexandre Berthier and the Prussian field-marshal Friedrich Adolph von Kalkreuth, the French agreed to withdraw their forces from Prussia after the Prussians paid the indemnity. Napoleon did not set the specific amount of 140 million francs until August 1808; the Prussians paid it in full by 5 November 1808. *Recueil des traités de la France*, 2:272–73; *Sammlung von 1806 bis zum 27 Oktober 1810*, 136–38; *Napoleon's Conduct towards Prussia*, 9–10; Weinzierl, "Marshal Victor as Governor of Berlin," 216. In

Faust's Metropolis, 92, Richie provides some interesting details regarding the French occupation, but the information on this period of Berlin's history does suffer from inaccuracies.

68. The Prussians could no longer export grain, wood, and wool to Great Britain, while Silesian linen could no longer be exported to Italy and Spain. Along with the linen industry, the silk industry was virtually destroyed, and both fell by fifty percent. Grain prices fell by seventy percent, and the price of imports such as cotton, sugar, tobacco, and coffee rose sharply. Kitchen, *Military History of Germany*, 38.

69. For a description of the French occupation, see Granier, *Berichte aus der Berliner Franzosenzeit*, 89–90, 246–51, 278.

70. Paret, *Clausewitz*, 137–38.

71. Rosenberg, *Bureaucracy, Aristocracy, and Autocracy*, 203. His critical assessment of the 1807–12 Prussian Reform Era continues: "A streamlined system of political absolutism; a modified pattern of aristocratic privilege and social inequality; a redistribution of oligarchical authority among the revitalized segments of the traditional master class; a promotion of personal liberty and freedom of occupation and economic enterprise—these were the principal results of the bureaucratic saviors of Prussia." Craig, in *Politics of the Prussian Army*, 62, states that "it is reasonable to conclude that the reforms which had been primarily designed to appease the *bourgeoisie* and to reconcile it to the army had achieved their purpose."

72. Simon, *Failure of the Prussian Reform Movement*, 147.

73. Boyen, *Beiträge zur Kenntnis des Generals von Scharnhorst*, 25–100; Simon, *Failure of the Prussian Reform Movement*, 147–48; Shanahan, *Prussian Military Reforms*, 127–79; Scherbening and Willisen, eds., *Die Reorganisation der Preußischen Armee*, 1:24–52; White, *The Enlightened Soldier*, 56–121.

74. Nipperdey, *Germany from Napoleon to Bismarck*, 21–22.

75. See E. M. Arndt, "Zwei Worte über die Entstehung und Bestimmung der deutschen Legion," in Eckert, *Von Valmy bis Leipzig*, 215–22.

76. Feuchtwanger, *Prussia*, 113.

77. Paret, *Clausewitz*, 138–40.

78. Kitchen, *Military History of Germany*, 44.

79. The Edict of 9 October 1807 abolished serfdom and replaced a society based on estates with one divided into economic classes. The middle class and peasants received the right to purchase property from nobles, and nobles could engage in bourgeois occupations. See Demeter, *German Officer-Corps*, 13; Feuchtwanger, *Prussia*, 115.

80. Grunwald, *Life of Baron Stein*, 114.

81. Palmer, "Frederick the Great," 49.

82. See Hermann, "Friedrich Wilhelm III."

83. Craig provides a concise survey of Prussian military reforms in *Politics of the Prussian Army*, 37–60. See also Lehmann, "Zur Geschichte der preußischen Heeresreform von 1808"; Blanning, "Death and Transfiguration of Prussia." For Frederick William's role in the reform of the army, see Hermann, "Friedrich Wilhelm III."

84. Seeley, *Life and Times of Stein*, 2:480.

85. Feuchtwanger, *Prussia*, 126.

86. Out of the 8,000 officers that served in the Jena campaign, only 695 were non-noble. On 6 August 1808 the king decreed that "service cannot be monopolized by birth, for if birth is given too many rights then many undeveloped and unused strengths will slumber on the lap of the nation and the soaring wings of genius will be crippled . . . [this] new age needs more than old titles and parchments; it needs fresh deeds and strength." Kitchen, *Military History of Germany*, 42 (quotation); Palmer, "Frederick the Great," 54.

87. For the best treatment of the army's reform of the light infantry and adoption of open-order tactics, see Paret, *Yorck*, 154–90.

88. Vaupel, *Das Preußische Heer*, 361; *Sammlung von 1806 bis zum 27 Oktober 1810*, 253–64; Kitchen, *Military History of Germany*, 44.

89. Boyen, *Erinnerungen*, ed. Nippold, 1: 295; Vaupel, *Das Preußische Heer*, 817–22; Lehmann, *Scharnhorst*, 2:98–202, 289–96, 330–42; Meinecke, *Age of German Liberation*, 69–101; Simon, *Failure of the Prussian Reform Movement*, 160–61. Frederick William refused to enact a universal conscription decree between 1808 and 1812 not only because of his distrust of the lower classes and preoccupation with the pomp of a professional army, but also due to his fear of Napoleon's reaction.

90. Vaupel, *Das Preußische Heer*, 332 (quotation); Lehmann, *Scharnhorst*, 2:98–99; Shanahan, *Prussian Military Reforms*, 137.

91. According to Simon, the Prussian army of 1806 was "based on a semi-feudal social structure" adapted to the needs of eighteenth-century national warfare. Simon, *Failure of the Prussian Reform Movement*, 146. At the heart of the Prussian army was the canton system, which meant exemption from military service for all classes except the peasants. Lehmann, *Scharnhorst*, 2:60–83.

92. The system was used between the years 1809 and 1812. Jany, *Geschichte der königlichen preußischen Armee*, 3:464–66, and 4:13–68; Shanahan, *Prussian Military Reforms*, 159–178, 228–29.

93. See Weinzierl, "Marshal Victor as Governor of Berlin," for a balanced discussion of the first year of the French occupation of Prussia.

94. The Prussians bore the cost of the occupation. French troops were widely cantoned throughout Prussia to ease the problems of supply. Difficulties arose due to Prussia's poor resources. According to historian C. B. A. Behrens, of the 5,846 children born in Berlin between 1806 and 1808, 4,300 died in infancy. Thousands of peasant holdings and thousands of businesses were ruined by French requisitions. Behrens, *Society, Government, and the Enlightenment*, 191; Kitchen, *Military History of Germany*, 38. For French documents pertaining to the problems of the occupation of Prussia, see Granier, *Berichte aus der Berliner Franzosenzeit*, 84–85, 97, 113–15, 124–26, 131–33, 138, 142–43, 152–53.

95. *Recueil des traités de la France*, 2:272–73. In June 1808, prior to the ratification of the Treaty of Paris, the Prussian army numbered 50,047 officers and men, 23,683 of whom were regulars on leave. Shanahan, *Prussian Military Reforms*, 175.

96. See Garland, "L'amitié d'un grand homme."

97. Schill was killed at Stralsund on 31 May; his head was sent to Holland in a cask of wine. For the details of Schill's "ride," see Gill, *With Eagles to Glory*, 428–34.

98. Gneisenau continued to serve the Crown as a diplomatic agent, while Grolman eventually made his way to Spain, where he fought with distinction against the French between 1810 and 1812. Lehmann, *Scharnhorst*, 2:268–70. See Craig, *Politics of the Prussian Army*, 53–55. For an account of the problems between Borstell and Scharnhorst, see Stadelmann, "Das Duel."

99. Schroeder, *Transformation of European Politics*, 451. On 19 July 1810 Frederick William suffered the premature death of his wife. Queen Luise, purportedly referred to as the "only real man in Prussia," was mourned by the nation. See Bigelow, *History of the German Struggle for Liberty*, 1:38, for the unflattering French portrayal of the Prussian Queen as an Amazon and an Armida—the classic heroine who seduced several young men.

100. Seeley, *Life and Times of Stein*, 2:442.

101. Craig, *Politics of the Prussian Army*, 58–59.

102. Scharnhorst remained in Silesia as a royal advisor and joined a gloomy Blücher in Breslau.

103. Gneisenau quoted in Craig, "Problems of Coalition Warfare," 41.

104. Muir, *Britain and the Defeat of Napoleon*, 243.

105. The destruction had been most complete in the part of the Grande Armée that had retreated from Moscow. Davout's corps was reduced from 66,345 officers and men in June 1812 to a total of 2,281 by 13 January 1813. Of the 50,000-strong Imperial Guard, only 500 remained fit for service by 21 December. The combined strength of the First, Second, Third, and Fourth Corps had been over 125,000 men in June 1812; by February their musters reported a total of 6,400 effectives. Petre, *Napoleon's Last Campaign*, 9.

106. Bülow was to be relieved by Yorck as governor as soon as the latter returned from Russia.

107. Holleben, *Vorgeschichte und Geschichte des Feldzuges*, 41.

108. Auerswald to Hardenberg, 24 November 1812, and Schön to Hardenberg, 25 December 1812, in Schoenaich, ed., *Zur Vorgeschichte der Befreiungskriege*, 62–64.

109. Craig, *Politics of the Prussian Army*, 58–59.

CHAPTER 2. THE SIXTH COALITION

1. Napoleon to Maret, 23 September 1812, *Correspondance*, No. 19218, 24:226–27.

2. Napoleon to Frederick William, 14 December 1812, Germany, Geheimes Staatsarchiv Preußischer Kulturbesitz zu Berlin (hereafter cited as GStA), Rep. 92 Nachlaß Albrecht, Nr. 27; D'Ussel, *Études sur l'année 1813*, 146.

3. Schroeder, *Transformation of European Politics*, 456.

4. "March" units were replacements in march to the front that were combined in ad hoc formations for their journey from the homeland to their

regiments; these were known as "march battalions" or "march squadrons" and frequently were engaged in combat. See the glossary in Gill, *With Eagles to Glory*, 496.

5. Bülow's orders and correspondence with Thümen, Maj. Wilhelm Johann von Krauseneck, who commanded the garrison at Graudenz, and the West Prussian provincial government can be found in GStA, Rep. 15 A Nrs. 147, 154, and 341.

6. Reboul, *Campagne de 1813*, 1:163.

7. Seydlitz, *Tagebuch*, 2:278.

8. Frederick William to Bülow, 20 December 1813, GStA, Rep. 15 A, Nr. 334; Boyen, *Erinnerungen*, ed. Schmidt, 2:330; D'Ussel, *Études sur l'année 1813*, 146.

9. Bülow to Berthier, 25 December 1813, in Reboul, *Campagne de 1813*, 1:461–62.

10. Varnhagen von Ense, Bülow, 115–16; Reboul, *Campagne de 1813*, 1:160–66.

11. Schroeder, *Transformation of European Politics*, 448.

12. In the appendices of *Campagne de 1813*, Commandant Reboul of the historical section of the French General Staff provides complete copies of several of these letters.

13. Kissinger, *A World Restored*, 48–49.

14. After Prussia declared war on France in March 1813, Petre contends: "As for Prussia, a defeat such as Napoleon hoped to inflict on her and the Russians, must inevitably mean the end of her independent existence, at least during Napoleon's life-time, and the dethronement of Frederick William" (*Napoleon's Last Campaign*, 8).

15. Frederick William to Hardenberg, 25 December 1812, GStA, Rep. 92, Nachlaß Albrecht, Nr. 33.

16. Schroeder, *Transformation of European Politics*, 452–53.

17. Dunker, "Preußen während der französischen Okkupation," 157.

18. Schroeder, *Transformation of European Politics*, 453.

19. Quoted in Sweet, *Wilhelm von Humboldt*, 2:120.

20. Schroeder, *Transformation of European Politics*, 452.

21. Ibid., 463.

22. Nicolson, *Congress of Vienna*, 42–43.

23. Muir, *Britain and the Defeat of Napoleon*, 247.

24. Kraehe, *Metternich's German Policy*, 1:155. According to Kraehe, Knesebeck sought Austria's approval of a Russo-Prussian alliance because to the Prussians "Austria's approval would mean her assumption of responsibility if Prussia signed such a pact; Austria would be obligated not only to not strike at Prussia herself, but to come to her rescue if Russia failed to do so."

25. Schroeder, *Transformation of European Politics*, 463.

26. Oncken, *Österreich und Preußen*, 1:54; Kissinger, *A World Restored*, 49, 52.

27. Kraehe, *Metternich's German Policy*, 1:155–56.

28. Schroeder, *Transformation of European Politics*, 463.

29. Clausewitz, *The Campaign of 1812 in Russia*, 221.

30. Ross, *European Diplomatic History*, 326. According to Nipperdey, the convention "subsequently acquired a mythical significance in both liberal and conservative nationalist tradition before 1933, and indeed until the early days of the GDR. It became a symbol of Prussian (German)–Russian unity, as well as the symbol of the right of dissent." Nipperdey, *Germany from Napoleon to Bismarck*, 67.

31. Schroeder, *Transformation of European Politics*, 466.

32. Figures are cited in D'Ussel, *Études sur l'année 1813*, 153.

33. These were the men of the Eleventh Corps who garrisoned Stettin, Magdeburg, Spandau, Küstrin, and Glogau.

34. Napoleon's Austrian and Polish contingents—43,000 men and 127 guns—lingered close to Prussia's southeastern border. The Austrian auxiliary corps under Gen. Karl zu Schwarzenberg then withdrew through south-central Poland under strict orders from Emperor Francis not to sacrifice the troops in an engagement with the Russians. This allowed the Russians to occupy Warsaw and south Poland with little resistance. Schneid, "Dynamics of Defeat," 24–25; Cook, "Prince Schwarzenberg's Crises in 1812."

35. Kraehe, *Metternich's German Policy*, 1:154.

36. Donnersmarck, *Erinnerungen aus meinem Leben*, 155; Seydlitz, *Tagebuch*, 2:277.

37. Yorck's role at Tauroggen and the question of royal authority have been debated extensively. Although some claim that Yorck had authority, others maintain that his actions were totally independent. The king's renunciation of Yorck's actions was politically expedient and may not have reflected the monarch's true sentiments. Yorck did retain command of his corps throughout 1813 and 1814, but the king mistrusted him and harbored a grudge toward him throughout the war. For a discussion of Tauroggen, see Thimme, "König Friedrich Wilhelm III"; and the note in Craig, *Politics of the Prussian Army*, 59.

38. Varnhagen von Ense, *Bülow*. Napoleon revealed the military repercussions of Yorck's defection: "The immediate consequences of this act of treachery are that the King of Naples will have to withdraw behind the Vistula and that my losses will be increased by all of the sick left in the hospitals of old Prussia." Napoleon to Jérôme, 19 January 1813, *Correspondance*, No. 19462, 24:406.

39. Droysen, *Yorck*, 2:29; Reboul, *Campagne de 1813*, 1:307.

40. D'Ussel, *Études sur l'année 1813*, 123; Reboul, *Campagne de 1813*, 1:308; Seydlitz, *Tagebuch*, 2:279; Treuenfeld, *1813*, 229.

41. Seydlitz, *Tagebuch*, 2:280.

42. Murat especially desired that Bülow place the Prussian light cavalry at his disposal. Murat to Berthier, 8 January 1813; Berthier to Bülow, 9 January 1813 in Reboul, *Campagne de 1813*, 1:300.

43. Hake to Bülow, 6 January 1813, Friedrich Wilhelm Graf Bülow von Dennewitz: Dokumentation in Briefen-Befehlen-Berichten: Ehemals Mitteilungen aus dem Gräflichen Bülow Familien\-Archiv zu Grünhoff (hereafter cited as BFA) Nr. 123.

44. Bülow to Berthier, 10 January 1813, Archives Nationales (hereafter cited as AN), AF IV, Carton 1652.

45. For Borstell's activities, see Lehmann, "General Borstell."

46. Seydlitz, *Tagebuch*, 2:281.

47. For documents pertaining to Thümen's activities, see GStA, Rep. 15 A Nr. 341.

48. GStA, Rep. 15 A Nr. 147 contains Bülow's march route from East Prussia to Pomerania.

49. Seydlitz, *Tagebuch*, 2:281.

50. Varnhagen von Ense, *Bülow*, 123.

51. According to D'Ussel and Seydlitz, the Russians attempted to impose a convention on Bülow similar to that signed by Yorck. Reboul and Varnhagen von Ense do not mention any attempts to negotiate with Bülow. See ibid.; D'Ussel, *Études sur l'année 1813*, 147; Reboul, *Campagne de 1813*, 1:310; Seydlitz, *Tagebuch*, 2:281.

52. Reboul, *Campagne de 1813*, 1:310; Seydlitz, *Tagebuch*, 2:282.

53. Both the German and French accounts agree that Bülow's threat to employ force secured the release of his cavalry. See D'Ussel, *Études sur l'année 1813*, 147; Varnhagen von Ense, *Bülow*, 123; Reboul, *Campagne de 1813*, 1:310; Seydlitz, *Tagebuch*, 2:281.

54. Bülow's troops frequently crossed paths with French columns, and each time difficulties arose. D'Ussel, *Études sur l'année 1813*, 147.

55. GStA, Rep. 15 A Nr. 147.

56. Droysen, *Yorck*, 2:34; D'Ussel, *Études sur l'année 1813*, 227. Droysen relied on the unpublished *Tagebuch* of the president of the East Prussian government, Hans Jacob von Auerswald. According to Auerswald, "The mail from Berlin arrived—Yorck's convention was repudiated." Droysen, *Yorck*, 2:33–34, 39; D'Ussel, *Études sur l'année 1813*, 227.

57. Nipperdey, *Germany from Napoleon to Bismarck*, 67.

58. Yorck to Bülow, 13 January 1813, BFA, Nr. 24.

59. Droysen, *Yorck*, 1:235, and Varnhagen von Ense, *Bülow*, 47. Neither historian provides reasons for this abhorrence; Droysen claims that the problems started when the two officers commanded fusilier battalions in East Prussia. Varnhagen von Ense merely notes that "the dislike was caused by many factors."

60. Yorck to Scharnhorst, 22 August 1811, in Droysen, *Yorck*, 1:288–89.

61. Scharnhorst to Yorck, 29 August 1811, in Karl Linnebach, ed., *Scharnhorsts Briefe*, 1:418–21.

62. Bülow to Frederick William, 18 January 1813, BFA, Nr. 26.

63. Pertz, *Stein*, 267–97.

64. Parameters for service in the Landsturm were not established. Service in the Landwehr was made obligatory for all men between the ages eighteen and forty-five; substitutes could be purchased. See Shanahan, *Prussian Military Reforms*, 190–96, for a thorough discussion of the events in East Prussia.

65. Ross, *European Diplomatic History*, 327.

66. Although this was the first armed force in Prussia to call upon all citizens for service, the East Prussian model permitted the conscripted to purchase substitutes and thus ran counter to the reformers' belief that national defense was the obligation of every subject. Scharnhorst disagreed but reluc-

tantly allowed the substitutions to continue in East Prussia after he established the national Landwehr on 17 March 1813. Bezzenberger, *Urkunden des Provinzial-Archivs in Königsberg,* 15–19; Boyen, *Erinnerungen,* ed. Nippold 2:332–33; Lehmann, *Scharnhorst,* 2:538; Simon, *Failure of the Prussian Reform Movement,* 163–64.

67. Schroeder, *Transformation of European Politics,* 452.

68. Kissinger, *A World Restored,* 49.

69. Schroeder, *Transformation of European Politics,* 453.

70. This was not the course that some Russian officers wanted to take. Satiated by thoughts of the acquisition of East Prussia and the Grand Duchy of Warsaw, many Russian officers felt the war was over. Kraehe, *Metternich's German Policy,* 1:154.

71. Ibid.

72. Petre, *Napoleon's Last Campaign,* 7.

73. Schroeder, *Transformation of European Politics,* 449.

74. Hatzfeld to Hardenberg, 29 January 1813, in Oncken, *Österreich und Preußen,* 1:94.

75. Hardenberg's reply was contained in two notes to Antonio Maria Saint-Marsan, the French ambassador to Prussia, dated 13 and 15 February, in D'Ussel, *Études sur l'année 1813,* 262.

76. Napoleon to Maret, 10 February 1813, *Correspondance,* No. 19565, XXIV, 510; Napoleon to Eugène, 10 February 1813, ibid., No. 19567, 510.

77. Eugène to Napoleon, 28 January 1813, AN, AF IV, Carton 1651.

78. Augereau to Berthier and to Eugène, 11 February 1813, in Reboul, *Campagne de 1813,* 2:364.

79. Schroeder, *Transformation of European Politics,* 453.

80. Napoleon to Eugène, 8 February 1813, *Correspondance,* No. 19558, XXIV, 502. On 10 February Napoleon forbade further Prussian conscription.

81. Holleben, *Vorgeschichte und Geschichte des Feldzuges,* 126. A letter from Frederick William—one of the few Bülow received at this time—authorized him to disregard orders from French authorities and remain neutral. Frederick William to Bülow, 15 February 1813, GStA, Rep. 15 A Nr. 334.

82. Archives de l'Armée de Terre: Service historique de l'armée, Château de Vincennes, Paris (hereafter cited as AAT) MF 19 Dossier Marshal Victor, Victor to Clark, 3 March 1813; Reboul, *Campagne de 1813,* 2:426.

83. Eugène to Napoleon, 15 February 1813, in Beauharnais, *Mémoires,* 8:358.

84. In "The Dynamics of Defeat," 25–26, Schneid argues that the Prussians sought to reduce Eugène's ability to defend the Oder and that Bülow's neutrality "made the French position in Prussia less tenable."

85. D'Ussel, *Études sur l'année 1813,* 329. Occupying Brandenburg were 1,600 men of Gen. Joseph Lagrange's division. An additional 1,700 men were at Potsdam. The 14,000 men of Grenier's division and the rest of Lagrange's division, placed under the command of St. Cyr, were situated in Berlin. More than 15,000 men occupied the suburbs southeast of the capital at Fürstenwalde and Müllrose. The 3,100 men of Gen. Maurice Étienne Gérard's division served as rear-guard at Frankfurt-am-Oder.

86. Oncken, *Österreich und Preußen*, 1:130–31.
87. D'Ussel, *Études sur l'année 1813*, 311, 312.
88. Nipperdey, *Germany from Napoleon to Bismarck*, 70.
89. Schroeder, *Transformation of European Politics*, 454.
90. Quoted in D'Ussel, *Études sur l'année 1813*, 313–15.
91. Kutuzov to Wittgenstein, 17 February 1813, in Michaïlofsky-Danilefsky, *Kriege von 1813*, 21.
92. Knesebeck to Bülow, 17 February 1813, BFA, Nr. 29. Kutuzov to Wittgenstein, 17 February 1813, in Michaïlofsky-Danilefsky, *Kriege von 1813*; Knesebeck to Hardenberg, 17 February 1813, in D'Ussel, *Études sur l'année 1813*, 313–15; Reboul, *Campagne de 1813*, 2:411.
93. Droysen, *Yorck*, 2:136–37; Holleben, *Vorgeschichte und Geschichte des Feldzuges*, 131.
94. The next day Yorck wrote to Stein: "I still await precise instructions from the king; up until now I have acted according to my own views. At Breslau they seem to have forgotten me." Yorck to Stein, 23 February 1813, in Droysen, *Yorck*, 2:123.
95. The Prussian generals agreed to move their forces to the Oder by 8 March. Yorck to Bülow, 26 February 1813, GStA, Berlin, Rep. 15 A Nr. 248; Holleben, *Vorgeschichte und Geschichte des Feldzuges*, 131–32; Reboul, *Campagne de 1813*, 2:410–12.
96. Reboul, *Campagne de 1813*, 2:411; D'Ussel, *Études sur l'année 1813*, 308, 315.
97. Schroeder, *Transformation of European Politics*, 453, 454. According to Schroeder, Knesebeck "was concerned with Prussia's great-power status and realized that by controlling most of Poland, Russia would threaten Prussia strategically, make it [Prussia] dependent on Russia for its compensations in Germany, and push Prussia westward as a Russian buffer state."
98. Muir, *Britain and the Defeat of Napoleon*, 248.
99. Ibid., 247–48.
100. Kraehe, *Metternich's German Policy*, 1:157.
101. Ibid., 156–57.
102. Kissinger, *A World Restored*, 24, 48–49.
103. Ross, *European Diplomatic History*, 328–29.
104. Kissinger, *A World Restored*, 50–51, 158–60.
105. Nipperdey, *Germany from Napoleon to Bismarck*, 68.
106. Kraehe, *Metternich's German Policy*, 1:156–60; Schroeder, *Transformation of European Politics*, 453–56. As for the other states of Central Europe, the preamble of the Treaty of Kalisch promised independence to those that wanted "to free themselves from the French yoke." Russo-Prussian plans for the liberation and reconstruction of Germany centered on Stein's blueprints for a great popular uprising against Napoleon. Stein made several appeals to the German people to rise against the French. Not only did his machinations fail, but Napoleon exploited the scheme in his propaganda. On 25 March Kutuzov also issued a proclamation that described the Rheinbund as an "insidious fetter." It called on the princes and peoples of Germany to accept the tsar's protection and lead in creating a new Germany. He promised the destruction

of Napoleon's German allies should they refuse. Rather than sparking mass defections from the Napoleonic system, Stein's appeals and Kutuzov's declaration only served to terrify the Rheinbund princes and undermine Alexander's image. Metternich, who opposed nationalistic upheavals, benefited the most from the tsar's blunders.

107. Muir, *Britain and the Defeat of Napoleon*, 248.

108. Ibid., 244–45.

109. The siege corps of Stettin, Küstrin, and Glogau totaled 2,280 men, 1,570 Cossacks, and 16 guns. The siege corps of Danzig and Thorn numbered 21,289 men, 3,687 Cossacks, and 155 guns. A third group remained in the Grand Duchy of Warsaw and included the siege corps of Modlin, Zamosc, and the Warsaw garrison for a total of 27,115 men, 4,25 Cossacks, and 148 guns.

110. Ottomar Osten-Sacken und von Rhein, *Vom Niemen bis zur Elbe*, 1:448; D'Ussel, *Études sur l'année 1813*, 360.

111. "Situation," 13 March 1813, AN, AF IV, Carton 1651. This figure includes the Eleventh Corps, with 25,128 men and 46 guns. The Imperial Guard with 4,227 men and 9 guns as well as contingents of Poles, Saxons, and Bavarians provided an additional 14,755 men and 26 guns.

112. "Situation," 13 March 1813, AN, AF IV, Carton 1651. Stettin had 7,715 men and 148 guns; Küstrin, 3,372 men; Spandau, 2,926 men; Glogau, 4,501 men; Thorn, 3,908 men; Danzig, 27,328 men; Modlin, 4,300 men; Zamosc, 4,000 men; Czenstochau, 1,200 men; Magdeburg, 5,000 men; Wittenberg, 3,000 men; and Torgau, 2,000 Saxons.

113. "Situation," 13 March 1813, AN, AF IV, Carton 1651. Eugène expected to be reinforced by Gen. Jacques Lauriston's corps of 22,900 men and 34 guns. Serviceable divisions from the First and Second Corps yielded another 17,033 men and 24 guns. Gen. Marie-Charles de la Tour-Maubourg's First Cavalry Corps consisted of 1,481 men, while Gen. Horace Sebastiani's Second Cavalry Corps totaled 1,892.

114. "Situation," 13 March 1813, AN, AF IV, Carton 1651. Holding the lower Elbe, the troops of Gen. Charles Morand and Gen. Claude Carra Saint-Cyr totaled 6,000 men and 14 guns. Gen. Dominique Vandamme commanded an additional 20,000 men and 32 guns.

115. "Situation," 13 March 1813, AN, AF IV, Carton 1651.

116. Großer Generalstab, *Das Preußische Heer 1813*, 162–63, 421–57, 548–51.

117. Napoleon to Eugène, 9 and 15 March 1813, *Correspondance*, Nos. 19688 and 19721, 25:46–51, 88–93.

118. Petre, *Napoleon's Last Campaign*, 44–45.

119. Frederick William to Bülow, 24 and 26 March 1813, GStA, Rep. 15 A Nr. 248.

120. Bülow decided that his trusted subordinate Thümen would command the siege of Spandau. Thümen's troops consisted of three battalions, three Jäger companies, a six-pounder battery, a detachment of Russian cavalry, a light Russian battery, and three heavy Russian howitzers. From Graudenz arrived one twelve-pounder battery and half of a ten-pounder howitzer battery. This left Bülow with five battalions, eight squadrons, and one horse and two

foot batteries. Holleben, *Vorgeschichte und Geschichte des Feldzuges*, 279–80; Varnhagen von Ense, *Bülow*, 139.

121. Paret, *Yorck*, 195. The aged but inveterate Blücher had left retirement to take command of the First or Silesian Corps, which consisted of brigades from Brandenburg and Upper and Lower Silesia.

122. For documents pertaining to the formation of Bülow's, Yorck's, and Blücher's corps, see GStA, Rep. 15 A Nrs. 147, 148, 149, 150, 160, and 319.

123. Charras, *Histoire de la Guerre de 1813*, 468; Beauharnais, *Mémoires*, 188; Holleben, *Vorgeschichte und Geschichte des Feldzuges*, 443.

124. The Allies lost 28 officers and 953 men, while the French lost 21 officers, 738 men, 100 prisoners, and 1 gun. Holleben, *Vorgeschichte und Geschichte des Feldzuges*, 449; Vaudoncourt, *Histoire politique et militaire*, 2:167.

125. Bülow to Pauline, 6 April 1813, BFA, Nr. 35.

126. Wittgenstein to Yorck, 26 April 1813, GStA, Rep. 15 A Nr. 248.

127. Wittgenstein to Bülow, 20, 23, 24, 25, and 26 April 1813, and d'Auvray to Bülow, 27, 28, and 29 April 1813, GStA, Rep. 15 A Nr. 248.

128. "Notes pour le Vice-roi D'Italie," 11 March 1813, *Correspondance*, No. 19697, 25:61–62.

129. Napoleon to Bertrand, 12 April 1813, ibid., No. 19852, 25:189–90.

130. Wittgenstein to Bülow, 1 May 1813, and Yorck to Bülow, 1 May 1813, GStA, Rep. 15 A Nr. 248.

131. Caemmerer, *Die Ereignisse von Ende April bis zum Waffenstillstand*, 89. This force consisted of four and three-quarter battalions, nine squadrons, and three batteries.

132. Ibid., 89–92; Bülow to L'Estocq, 3 May 1813, GStA, Rep. 91 A Nr. 150; Clément, *Campagne de 1813*, 38–40; Petre, *Napoleon's Last Campaign*, 91.

133. Bülow to L'Estoq, 3 May 1813, GStA, Rep. 91 A Nr. 150; Caemmerer, *Die Ereignisse von Ende April bis zum Waffenstillstand*, 130.

134. Oppen to Bülow, 5 May 1813, GStA, Rep. 15 A Nr. 188; Bülow to L'Estoq, 5 May 1813, GStA, Rep. 91 A Nr. 150.

135. Caemmerer, *Die Ereignisse von Ende April bis zum Waffenstillstand*, 130; Varnhagen von Ense, *Bülow*, 157.

136. Frederick William to Bülow, 3 May 1813, GStA, Rep. 15 A Nr. 334; Caemmerer, *Die Ereignisse von Ende April bis zum Waffenstillstand*, 130.

137. Napoleon to Ney, 4 May 1813, *Correspondance*, 25:264–65; Napoleon to Ney, 13 May 1813, ibid., No. 20006, 25:292–93.

138. See Young, "Ney: The Bravest of the Brave," 358–81.

139. Chandler, *Dictionary of the Napoleonic Wars*, 312–15.

140. Petre, *Napoleon's Last Campaign*, 96.

141. Napoleon to Ney, 6 May 1813, *Correspondance*, No. 19972, 25:273–74.

142. According to Petre, "when one looks to the way in which he [Napoleon] cherished the hope of this division of the enemy's forces, one cannot help suspecting that the wish was the father of the thought. Moreover, Berlin was after all only a geographical point." Petre, *Napoleon's Last Campaign*, 94–95.

143. This coup de théâtre was by far the main characteristic of the "master plan of 1813."

CHAPTER 3. THE DEFENSE OF BERLIN

1. Due to his reputation as an educated man, Bülow became a mentor of princes. He started with Prince Louis Ferdinand von Hohenzollern in 1793. In 1813 Prince Wilhelm von Radziwill was assigned to his staff; the crown prince of Holland joined in the following year. Prince Wilhelm of Prussia, the future German emperor, commanded Bülow's cavalry in 1815. Lastly, Crown Prince Frederick William of Prussia, the future Frederick William IV, was assigned to Bülow's corps after the battle of Waterloo. BFA.

2. On 21 November 1808 Bülow had been promoted to Generalmajor; on 14 March 1813 he received his promotion to Generalleutnant. Bülow's service data can be found in GStA, VI, HA, Rep. 92 Nachlaß Friedrich Wilhelm Freiherr von Bülow, Graf von Dennewitz 1755–1816.

3. According to the Landwehr decrees of 17 March, the Military Governments oversaw the work of committees that were formed in each district to direct the mobilization of the militia (Prussian provinces were subdivided into districts, similar to counties). Caemmerer, *Die Ereignisse von Ende April bis zum Waffenstillstand*, 131.

4. For English accounts of the formation of the Prussian Landwehr, see Shanahan, *Prussian Military Reforms*, 201–30; Showalter, "The Prussian Landwehr"; and Simon, *Failure of the Prussian Reform Movement*, 168–97. For the conscription decrees for the army and Landwehr, see *Gesetz-Sammlung 1813*, 13–14, 36–37, 109–12.

5. Nipperdey, *Germany from Napoleon to Bismarck*, 41.

6. Shanahan, *Prussian Military Reforms*, 197.

7. See the discussion on the Landsturm in Simon, *Failure of the Prussian Reform Movement*, 168–80.

8. "Verordnung über den Landsturm," *Gesetz-Sammlung 1813*, 79–89; Eckert, *Von Valmy bis Leipzig*, 249–60.

9. Hardenberg sponsored the modifications, entitled "Verordnung vom 17ten Julius 1813: Betreff der Modifikationen des Landsturmedikts vom 21sten April," *Gesetz-Sammlung 1813*, 89–92; Eckert, *Von Valmy bis Leipzig*, 260–63.

10. Bezzenberger, *Urkunden des Provinzial-Archivs in Königsberg*, 21–28; Shanahan, *Prussian Military Reforms*, 208–9.

11. The four Military Governments were headquartered in Königsberg, Stargard, Berlin, and Breslau, corresponding to their respective territories: the regions between the Niemen and the Vistula, between the Vistula and the Oder, between the Oder and the Elbe, and Upper and Lower Silesia. The documents of the Military Government in Berlin can be found in GStA, Rep. 91 A Militärische Behörden: Der Militärgouvernement für das Land zwischen der Elbe und der Oder. For its general formation, see Rep. 91 A Nrs. 1, 3, 39.

12. Bülow to L'Estoq, 13 April 1813, GStA, Rep. 91 A Nr. 150. According to the Landsturm decree, army and corps commanders, as well as the military governors, could mobilize the Landsturm in local or provincial units. On the local level the country was divided into Landsturm districts and subdistricts analogous to the *Kreis* or district administrative unit. Local commanders were

appointed by the respective Military Governments. Towns with populations in excess of 2,000 appointed defense committees headed by the mayor. In rural areas all landowners of a district elected district defense committees composed of one deputy for each subdistrict. "These committees (*Schutzdeputationen*) in both town and country were to plan and execute local defense measures in consultation with the district commanders and with the military," notes Simon in *Failure of the Prussian Reform Movement*, 169–70.

13. L'Estoq and Sack to Bülow, 6, 13, and 20 April 1813, and L'Estoq to Bülow, 18 and 19 April 1813, GStA, Rep. 15 A Nr. 164; L'Estoq to Bülow, 24 April 1813, and Bülow to L'Estoq, 27 April 1813, GStA, Rep. 91 A Nr. 150.

14. The defense plans that were discussed in April and early May between Bülow and the Military Government in Berlin can be found in GStA, Rep. 91 A Nr. 150. After the news of the Allied defeat at Lützen, the Military Government in Berlin ordered Oberbaudirektor (chief building inspector) Johann Albert Eytelwein to draft a plan of defense for the Kurmark using the Landsturm. On 8 May he submitted a comprehensive report entitled "Ideas on the Defense of the Mittelmark with the Help of the Landsturm." Although Boyen soon modified the plan, its essential ideas remained, prompting the historical section of the Prussian General Staff to write in 1857 that Eytelwein's plan "formed the most direct official starting point for the development of the defense of the Mark." The plan is reproduced in its entirety in "Der Kriegsschauplatz der Nord-Armee," 32–35.

15. Frederick William to Bülow, 3 May 1813, GStA, Rep. 15 A Nr. 334; Frederick William to the Military Government in Berlin, 3 May 1813, in "Der Kriegsschauplatz der Nord-Armee," 31.

16. Boyen, *Erinnerungen*, ed. Schmidt, 2:576.

17. Both the Nuthe and the Notte, at the most 8–10 meters in width, flowed through swamp and marshland. Steep banks surrounded by boggy ground limited the crossing of horses and wagons to the few existing dams. Caemmerer, *Die Ereignisse von Ende April bis zum Waffenstillstand*, 137.

18. Boyen chaired the 9 May meeting and assumed direction of the defense plans. On 13 May he submitted his own defense plan entitled "Ideas on the Defense of the Kurmark." More extensive than Eytelwein's "Ideas," Boyen's scheme concentrated more on fortifications than on regular and irregular forces for the defense of the province. This plan can be found in the Prussian General Staff's "Der Kriegsschauplatz der Nord-Armee," 242–49. A copy of this plan can also be found in L'Estoq to Bülow, 13 May 1813, GStA, Rep 91 A Nr. 150. A redoubt is a "small detached work without bastions placed at some distance from a fortification to guard a vital position or obstruct the progress of an enemy in a given direction. Redoubts generally had ditches, parapets, some means of providing flanking fire, and a shelter for the garrison." Horward, *Napoleon and Iberia*, 403.

19. L'Estoq to Bülow, 12 May 1813, GStA, Rep 91 A Nr. 150; Markhoff to Bülow, 10 May 1813, in "Der Kriegsschauplatz der Nord-Armee," 36; Sack to Gunther, 10 May 1813, and Sack to Cochius, 10 May 1813, in ibid., 37–39. Pioneers are "soldiers employed to work with various tools or instruments such as picks, shovels, hatches, saws, etc. They were assigned work on the roads,

repairing fortifications and field works, clearing forests, and general construction work." Horward, *Napoleon and Iberia*, 402.

20. Oppen to Bülow, 7 and 9 May 1813, and Thümen to Bülow, 7 and 9 May 1813, GStA, Rep. 15 A Nr. 188; Sydow to Bülow, 9 May 1813, GStA, Rep 91 A. Nr. 150.

21. Wittgenstein to Bülow, 7 May 1813, in "Geschichte der Organisation der Landwehr," 83.

22. Frederick William to Bülow, 8 May 1813, GStA, Rep. 15 A Nr. 298; see also "Geschichte der Organisation der Landwehr," 83.

23. Prittwitz, *Beiträge*, 2:435. Bülow's Prussian contingent included thirteen battalions, two Jäger companies, four volunteer detachments, thirteen squadrons, and six batteries. Russian units amounted to five battalions, four squadrons, three and one-half Cossack regiments, and two batteries.

24. Marwitz to Bülow, 11 May 1813, in "Geschichte der Organisation der Landwehr," 73.

25. Marwitz to Bülow, 7 May 1813, in ibid., 73.

26. Bülow to L'Estoq, 5 and 6 May 1813, GStA, Rep. 91 A Nr. 150.

27. Friederich, *Die Befreiungskriege*, 1:253–55.

28. Napoleon to Ney, 6 and 13 May 1813, *Correspondance*, Nos. 19972 and 20006, 25:273–74, 292–93.

29. Caemmerer, *Die Ereignisse von Ende April bis zum Waffenstillstand*, 140–41. Here Generalleutnant von Caemmerer of the historical section of the Prussian General Staff cites Bülow's *Tagebuch*, which was formerly contained in the Kriegs-Archiv (I. E. 72). Although the staff of Berlin's Geheime Staatsarchiv recovered several Repositoria of this vital archive in 1995 and has since recategorized the documents, Bülow's *Tagebuch* remains lost.

30. Bülow to L'Estoq, 11 May 1813, GStA, Rep. 91 A Nr. 150. By mid-May the garrisons around the capital included a motley collection of units. Berlin had one reserve battalion from the Pomeranian Infantry Regiment, one convalescent battalion from Yorck's corps, two depot squadrons, and twelve guns. The Third Battalion of the Second East Prussian Infantry Regiment arrived on 18 May, while four East Prussian and Lithuanian reserve battalions were scheduled to arrive between 21 and 23 May. Ten other militia battalions were assembling north of the capital at Oranienburg. Potsdam had two Landwehr battalions, one Guard-Invalid battalion, two Guard depot-squadrons, and two cuirassier regiments; Saarmund: one Landwehr battalion and four guns; Trebbin: two Landwehr battalions, one Silesian march battalion, and one march squadron—both originally intended to replenish Yorck's corps; Zossen: one convalescent battalion assigned to Yorck's corps; Mittenwalde: three Landwehr companies, four guns, and another march squadron designated for Yorck's corps; Königs-Wusterhausen: one reserve battalion from the Leib Infantry Regiment and one Jäger detachment from Cottbus; Groß Machnow: one Silesian march battalion and the Ausländer Battalion. One squadron, posted in Trebbin, patrolled the defense line. Caemmerer, *Die Ereignisse von Ende April bis zum Waffenstillstand*, 139–40.

31. Hirschfeld to Bülow, 12 May 1813, GStA, Rep. 15 A Nr. 164.

32. Bülow to L'Estoq, 12 May 1813, GStA, Rep. 91 A. Nr. 150; Caemmerer, *Die Ereignisse von Ende April bis zum Waffenstillstand*, 140.
33. Bülow to Frederick William, 12 May 1813, BFA, Nr. 46.
34. Bülow to Carl John, 12 May 1813, GStA, Rep. 15 A Nr. 248; Caemmerer, *Die Ereignisse von Ende April bis zum Waffenstillstand*, 142.
35. Bülow to Frederick William, 12 May 1813, BFA, Nr. 46.
36. Caemmerer, *Die Ereignisse von Ende April bis zum Waffenstillstand*, 141.
37. Bülow to Wittgenstein, 14 May 1813, GStA, Rep. 15 A Nr. 248; Bülow to Frederick William, 14 May 1813, in Caemmerer, *Die Ereignisse von Ende April bis zum Waffenstillstand*, 142–43.
38. L'Estoq to Bülow, 13 May 1813; GStA, Rep. 91 A N5. 150.
39. Caemmerer, *Die Ereignisse von Ende April bis zum Waffenstillstand*, 138.
40. Bülow to Frederick William, 15 May 1813, in Caemmerer, *Die Ereignisse von Ende April bis zum Waffenstillstand*, 143.
41. According to the emperor's orders, Ney's own Third Corps was to reach Luckau with the advance guard in Lübben, the Fifth Corps in Dobrilugk, the Seventh Corps in Dahme, and the Second Corps and Second Cavalry Corps in Schönwald. Napoleon to Ney, 13 May 1813, *Correspondance*, No. 20006, 25:292–93.
42. Bülow to L'Estoq, 16 May 1813, GStA, Rep. 91 A Nr. 654.
43. "Der Kriegsschauplatz der Nord-Armee," 46.
44. Markhoff to Bülow, 16 May 1813, in ibid., 46–48.
45. Bülow to Frederick William, 15 May 1813, in Caemmerer, *Die Ereignisse von Ende April bis zum Waffenstillstand*, 143.
46. Borstell to Bülow, 17 May 1813, GStA, Rep. 15 A Nr. 164.
47. Bülow to L'Estoq, 18 May 1813, GStA, Rep. 91 A Nr. 150.
48. Ibid.
49. L'Estoq to Bülow, 18 May 1813, GStA, Rep. 91 A Nr. 150.
50. Bülow to Boyen, 20 May 1813, in Boyen, *Erinnerungen*, ed. Nippold, 3:384–85; Meinecke, *Boyen*, 1:279–80; Boyen, *Erinnerungen*, ed. Schmidt, 2:584.
51. Günther to Bassewitz, 17 May 1813, in "Der Kriegsschauplatz der Nord-Armee," 57–58.
52. Günther to Sack, 14 May 1813, GStA, Rep. 91 A Nr. 153.
53. Cochius to Sack, 23 May 1813, GStA, Rep. 91 A Nr. 153.
54. Cochius to Sack, 16 May 1813, GStA, Rep. 91 A Nr. 153.
55. Foucart, *Bautzen*, 1:217–18; Petre, *Napoleon's Last Campaign*, 107–8.
56. Caemmerer praises Bülow's assessment of the need to pursue and attack Ney's withdrawing army, but is very critical of Bülow's decision to grant his corps a day of rest due to supply problems. The Prussian General Staff historian notes that "we can only judge such concerns in the supposition that Napoleon would have rejected them. In 1812 innumerable thousands had starved under him and in 1813 large numbers deserted because of hunger." Caemmerer, *Die Ereignisse von Ende April bis zum Waffenstillstand*, 144, 145.

CHAPTER 4. LUCKAU

1. Plotho, *Der Krieg,* 1:217. In a letter of 17 May Wittgenstein authorizes Bülow to proceed according to his own judgment but makes no mention of an advance by Bülow on Napoleon's flank and rear. Wittgenstein to Bülow, 17 May 1813, GStA, Rep. 15 A. Nr. 248; Caemmerer, *Die Ereignisse von Ende April bis zum Waffenstillstand,* 295–6.

2. Boyen, *Erinnerungen,* ed. Schmidt, 2:584.

3. The discerning Caemmerer does point to Wittgenstein's letter of 17 May as well as Bülow's responsibility for defending Berlin as possible explanations for his lethargy. "It is thus humanly conceivable," maintains Caemmerer, "that Bülow did not undertake the difficult task of launching an offensive on Napoleon's flank and rear because he was not expected to. If high command only required him to execute a defensive, then he had other reasons besides the supply problems to refrain from a far-reaching attack. Since Bülow's main task was the defense of the Mark, his corps, the only regular unit among very questionable forces, was of great importance. Without his corps the Landwehr and Landsturm were incapable of serious resistance, and the Swedes certainly would not cooperate unless [Prussian] line troops were available in some strength. Thus, the idea of conserving his troops for future, larger tasks . . . was obviously at work." Caemmerer, *Die Ereignisse von Ende April bis zum Waffenstillstand,* 296–97.

4. Borstell to Bülow, 20 May 1813, GStA, Rep. 15 A. Nr. 164. Caemmerer agrees with Borstell and argues that the appearance of Borstell's brigade near Görlitz on 23 May "would unquestionably have provoked great uneasiness in the enemy's headquarters." Caemmerer, *Die Ereignisse von Ende April bis zum Waffenstillstand,* 297.

5. Caemmerer states that Bülow's march to Baruth on 19 May "completed the first step for an operation on the flank and rear of Napoleon. Then, however, it degenerated into quite regrettable inactivity, which could no longer be justified by concerns over supply." Caemmerer does claim that although Bülow's complaints to the Kurmark commissariat were justified, the lack of supplies was no reason to halt operations. Echoing Scharnhorst's assessment of Bülow, Caemmerer notes that "from his remarks, Bülow gives the impression that to him the rigid magazine system of the eighteenth century was still the real rule from which he would deviate only under particularly favorable circumstances. Had Bülow divided his corps into two columns of 8,000 to 10,000 men each, avoided the enemy's main areas of operation, and had the troops been given some flour, rice, oat rations, and a meat reserve, then an advance in the rear of the enemy would have been quite possible." Caemmerer, *Die Ereignisse von Ende April bis zum Waffenstillstand,* 295.

6. Bülow also mentions his responsibility of maintaining communications with the other Allied commanders in North Germany, mainly Gen. Ludwig Georg Count von Wallmoden and Vorontsov. The journeyman Wallmoden, now in Russian service, commanded a motley corps of 11,600 Russian, Prussian, Hanoverian, Mecklenburger, Dessauer, and Hanseatic soldiers, whose responsibility was to observe the lower Elbe and the French forces

in Hamburg. Vorontsov's small Russian brigade was positioned on the middle Elbe to mask Magdeburg. For Wallmoden's operations, see Pierer, *Der Feldzug*; Bülow to Wittgenstein, 20 May 1813, in Caemmerer, *Die Ereignisse von Ende April bis zum Waffenstillstand*, 297–98.

7. Bülow to Boyen, 22 May 1813, in Boyen, *Erinnerungen*, ed. Nippold, 3:388–89.

8. Caemmerer, *Die Ereignisse von Ende April bis zum Waffenstillstand*, 299.

9. Bülow to Thümen, 24 May 1813, GStA, Rep. 15 A Nr. 342; Plotho, *Der Krieg*, 1:217.

10. Bülow to Boyen, 24 May 1813, in Boyen, *Erinnerungen*, ed. Nippold, 3:390–91.

11. Although Caemmerer makes no mention of these orders, Varnhagen von Ense, in *Bülow*, 171, claims that the instructions reached Bülow on the night of 25 May. The historian also notes that the king's emphasis on defending Berlin and Potsdam justified Bülow's opposition to Borstell's request to march to Bautzen. In his letter to Boyen, Bülow claims that he has just met with Captain von Blankenburg, who delivered the report from Gen. Friedrich Heinrich von Kleist that 60,000 Austrians were poised to cross the Saxon frontier near Pirna. Bülow to Boyen, 26 May 1813, in Boyen, *Erinnerungen*, ed. Nippold, 3:393.

12. Bülow to L'Estoq, 25 May 1813, GStA, Rep. 91 A Nr. 153.

13. Marwitz to Bülow, 11 May 1813, GStA, Rep. 15 A Nr. 164.

14. Hirschfeld to Bülow, 12 May 1813, GStA, Rep. 15 A Nr. 164.

15. Hirschfeld to the Military Government in Berlin, 18 May 1813, in "Geschichte der Organisation der Landwehr," 90–91. See also Boyen, *Erinnerungen*, ed. Schmidt, 2:578–80.

16. "Geschichte der Organisation der Landwehr," 136.

17. Bassewitz to the Military Government, 20 May 1813, in ibid., 77.

18. Borstell to L'Estoq, 27 May 1813, GStA, Rep. 91 A Nr. 150; Caemmerer, *Die Ereignisse von Ende April bis zum Waffenstillstand*, 300.

19. Reports on the Neumark Landwehr from the authorities in Stargard, mainly military governor general Bogislaw Friedrich Count von Tauentzien and civil governor Karl Friedrich von Beyme, reached Bülow on 22, 23, and 27 May. GStA, Rep. 15 A Nr. 164.

20. "Der Kriegsschauplatz der Nord-Armee," 95.

21. Frederick William to Bülow, 23 May 1813, GStA, Rep. 15 A Nr. 164; "Der Kriegsschauplatz der Nord-Armee," 97–98.

22. Dobschütz to Bülow, 27 and 28 May 1813, GStA, Rep 15 A Nr. 164.

23. "Geschichte der Organisation der Landwehr," 106–7.

24. Napoleon to Berthier, 24 May 1813, *Correspondance*, No. 20037, 25:312–13.

25. Austin, "Oudinot: The Father of the Grenadiers," 384–402 (quotation on 384).

26. In *Beiträge*, 2:202, Prittwitz, who served on Bülow's staff, claims that Bülow decided to march northeast to reach Müllrose by 30 May.

27. Plotho, *Der Krieg*, 1:218.

28. Bülow to Boyen, 27 May 1813, in Boyen, *Erinnerungen*, ed. Nippold, 3:394–95.

29. Plotho, *Der Krieg*, 1:218; Caemmerer, *Die Ereignisse von Ende April bis zum Waffenstillstand*, 301, 302, 305. Caemmerer correctly calls Bülow's decision to attack with only half of his available strength an "outright mistake." "He should have calculated," notes Caemmerer, "that more enemy troops would be following, and if 8,000 of his own men appeared sufficient to meet the enemy, the 16,000 could probably achieve great success." Moreover, if Bülow had in fact decided to march east, "it would have been imprudent to divide his forces and march in opposite directions." Ultimately, the Prussian historian asserts that "the combat at Hoyerswerda exposes in an exceedingly clear way Bülow's faulty strategy." Despite Caemmerer's keen knowledge of military matters, he undermines his case against Bülow by claiming that a decisive defeat over Oudinot at Hoyerswerda would have "facilitated the first operative steps" in an Austrian declaration of war on France.

30. Lejeune, *Memoirs*, 2:275.

31. Battle accounts are found in ibid.; GStA, Rep. 15 A Nr. 342 Disposition zum Angriff auf Hoyerswerda; Oudinot to Berthier, 28 May 1813, AAT, C^2 146; Caemmerer, *Die Ereignisse von Ende April bis zum Waffenstillstand*, 304–5.

32. Bülow to Boyen, 28 May 1813, in Boyen, *Erinnerungen*, ed. Nippold, 3:395–97.

33. Boyen, *Erinnerungen*, ed. Schmidt, 2:586–87.

34. Bassewitz to Boyen, 27 May 1813, in "Geschichte der Organisation der Landwehr," 97–98.

35. Caemmerer, *Die Ereignisse von Ende April bis zum Waffenstillstand*, 306.

36. Bülow's main body advanced to Cottbus on the Spree; Borstell moved to Forst on the Neisse; and Oppen to Drebkau. Bülow's *Tagesbefehl* for 30 May 1813, signed 29 May 1813, GStA, Rep. 15 A Nr. 342.

37. Cossacks raided Senftenberg on the Black Elster, Spremberg on the Spree, Naumburg on the Queiss, and Sagan on the Bober.

38. Caemmerer, *Die Ereignisse von Ende April bis zum Waffenstillstand*, 307.

39. Wittgenstein to Bülow, 25 May 1813, GStA, Rep. 15 A Nr. 248.

40. Muir, *Britain and the Defeat of Napoleon*, 245.

41. Schroeder, *Transformation of European Politics*, 430.

42. Kalkreuth to Frederick William, 31 May 1813, BFA, Nr. 50.

43. A copy of Bülow's orders can be found in Bülow to Thümen, 31 May 1813, GStA, Rep. 15 A Nr. 342. Caemmerer, *Die Ereignisse von Ende April bis zum Waffenstillstand*, 307.

44. Bülow to Boyen, 31 May 1813, in Boyen, Erinnerungen, ed. Nippold, 3:397–99.

45. GStA, Rep. 15 A Nr. 396 Marwitz Tagebuch; Boyen, *Erinnerungen*, ed. Schmidt, 2:587.

46. Hinrichs to Bülow, 1 and 2 June 1813, GStA, Rep. 15 A Nr. 164.

47. Bülow to L'Estoq and Sack, 25 May 1813; L'Estoq and Sack to Putlitz, 27 May 1813; L'Estoq and Sack to Hirschfeld, 27 May 1813, GStA, Rep.

91 A Nr. 153; Putlitz to Bülow, 3 June 1813, GStA, Rep. 15 A. Nr. 164. See also the May and June reports to the Military Government in Berlin in GStA, Rep 91 A Nr. 226 Dislokation von Truppenabteilungen.

48. Caemmerer, *Die Ereignisse von Ende April bis zum Waffenstillstand*, 307.

49. Bülow's operations in May sparked historiographic debate. In Stralsund the crown prince of Sweden often discussed Bülow's movements, purportedly exclaiming: "Ah, these are the operations of an experienced captain." Despite this dubious endorsement, writers such as Caemmerer and Meinecke criticize Bülow for clinging to obsolete eighteenth-century tactics. Contemporaries like Boyen also rebuke him for remaining north of the Elbe. These assessments fail to take into consideration the restraints placed on Bülow as well as the orders he received from the king of Prussia to defend the capital with all means. As Caemmerer concedes, Bülow proved during the Fall Campaign of 1813 that he could adhere to the principles of modern warfare. See Boyen, *Erinnerungen*, ed. Schmidt, 2:585–88; Varnhagen von Ense, *Bülow*, 168–69; Caemmerer, *Die Ereignisse von Ende April bis zum Waffenstillstand*, 300–306.

50. Barclay de Tolly to Bülow, 30 May 1813, GStA, Rep. 15 A Nr. 248.

51. Bülow's main body would march from Cottbus to Kalau, Oppen's brigade to Groß Räschen, and Borstell's to Forst.

52. Varnhagen von Ense, *Bülow*, 168–69.

53. Caemmerer, *Die Ereignisse von Ende April bis zum Waffenstillstand*, 308.

54. Lejeune, *Memoirs*, 2:277.

55. Caemmerer, *Die Ereignisse von Ende April bis zum Waffenstillstand*, 308–10.

56. Boyen, *Erinnerungen*, ed. Nippold, 3:401–2.

57. Lejeune, *Memoirs*, 2:277.

58. Battle accounts are found in Bülow to L'Estoq, 6 June 1813, GStA, Rep. 91 A Nr. 154; Oudinot to Berthier, 7 June 1813, AAT, C^2 147; Boyen, *Erinnerungen*, ed. Schmidt, 2:588; Burstini, *Darstellung des Treffens bei Luckau*, 10–20; Lejeune, *Memoirs*, 2:276–77; Caemmerer, *Die Ereignisse von Ende April bis zum Waffenstillstand*, 310–13; Plotho, *Der Krieg*, 1:221–24.

59. Varnhagen von Ense, *Bülow*, 184.

60. Boyen, *Erinnerungen*, ed. Schmidt, 2:588.

61. Frederick William to Bülow, 4 June 1813, GStA, Rep. 15 A Nr. 334.

62. Ross, *European Diplomatic History*, 331.

63. A copy of the provisions of the armistice can be found in GStA, Rep. 91 A Nr. 656.

64. Bassewitz to Boyen, 27 May 1813, in "Geschichte der Organisation der Landwehr," 97–98.

CHAPTER 5. MUSKETS, SADDLES, AND SHOES

1. Frederick William to Bülow, 8 June 1813, BFA, Nr. 69. Gneisenau and Gen. Friedrich Wilhelm von Zastrow assumed responsibility for finishing

the mobilization of the Silesian Landwehr. Gneisenau's 3 and 9 July reports on his progress are reproduced in Eckert, *Von Valmy bis Leipzig*, 243–44. See also "Organisation der Landwehr," 407–10.

2. Frederick William to Bülow, 8 June 1813, BFA, Nr. 69; Boyen, *Erinnerungen*, ed. Nippold, 3:419–20; "Geschichte der Organisation der Landwehr," 110.

3. Boyen, *Erinnerungen*, ed. Nippold, 2:332–33; see the discussion in Jany, *Geschichte der königlichen preußischen Armee*, 4:83; Shanahan, *Prussian Military Reforms*, 202–4, 211–12.

4. See the discussion in Showalter, "The Prussian Landwehr," 13.

5. Simon, *Failure of the Prussian Reform Movement*, 162; Shanahan, *Prussian Military Reforms*, 209–10; 219–20.

6. "Geschichte der Organisation der Landwehr," 63.

7. Showalter, "The Prussian Landwehr," 10.

8. According to the Landwehr decrees of 17 March, manpower would be levied according to the density of the population of a given locality and assembled locally and provincially in squads, companies, and battalions; four companies would form a battalion of 800 men. Like the regular army, the militia had to swear an oath and was subject to martial law. Pay was suspended indefinitely; compensation was not to be sought during the early stages of the war. The king appointed the battalion, brigade, and division commanders; the district commissions selected the junior officers from the entire population without consideration of age, yet all selections had to be confirmed by the king. Each recruit was expected to uniform and equip himself; if he was unable, the district would supply his gear. The state would provide weapons and ammunition. For the time being the first line would be armed with pikes. Caemmerer, *Die Ereignisse von Ende April bis zum Waffenstillstand*, 131.

9. Shanahan, *Prussian Military Reforms*, 205.

10. Showalter, "The Prussian Landwehr," 12; see Boyen, *Erinnerungen*, ed. Nippold, 3:430–33.

11. "Geschichte der Organisation der Landwehr," 134–35.

12. For example, by the end of May the cavalry squadron furnished by the Second Jerichow District had earned sharp criticism for equipment shortages. Blame fell on the district mayor, von Katte, who claimed that due to the lack of funds the district commission could not afford the necessary equipment. Katte was reported to the king and removed from office. Bassewitz to Katte, 29 June 1813, in ibid., 136–37.

13. Boyen, *Erinnerungen*, ed. Schmidt, 2: 578–80.

14. Letters to Bassewitz from the District Commissions of Anclam and Demmin, 11 June 1813, in "Geschichte der Organisation der Landwehr," 131–32.

15. L'Estoq to Bassewitz, 12 June 1813, in ibid., 137.

16. GStA, Rep 91 A Nr. 14 Sammlung der Edikte und Verordnungen.

17. The Neumark's population was 258,784 in 1813.

18. Hinrichs to Bülow, 1 June 1813, GStA, Rep. 15 A Nr. 164.

19. Bülow to Tauentzien, 17 and 18 June, GStA, Rep. 15 A Nr. 250; Bülow to Frederick William, 18 June 1813, in "Geschichte der Organisation der Landwehr," 114–15.

20. Krafft to Bülow, 26 June 1813, GStA, Rep. 15 A Nr. 164.

21. Krafft to Bülow, 22 June 1813, GStA, Rep. 15 A Nr. 164.

22. Eisenhardt to Bülow, 1 July 1813, GStA, Rep. 15 A Nr. 164; Tauentzien to Frederick William, 1 July 1813, in "Geschichte der Organisation der Landwehr," 147–48.

23. Krafft to Bülow, 22 June 1813, GStA, Rep. 15 A Nr. 164.

24. Frederick William to Bülow, 8 June 1813, BFA, Nr. 69; Boyen, *Erinnerungen*, ed. Nippold, 3:419–20; "Geschichte der Organisation der Landwehr," 13.

25. Krafft to Bülow, 22 June 1813, GStA, Rep. 15 A Nr. 164; "Geschichte der Organisation der Landwehr," 141. Due to the local nature of the recruiting, which enabled conscripts to serve with friends and relatives, many commanders disregarded the king's suggestion out of fear that separating the men would lower morale. See Showalter, "The Prussian Landwehr," 10.

26. Wißmann to Frederick William, 4 July 1813, in "Geschichte der Organisation der Landwehr," 148–50.

27. For a detailed discussion of the early development of the Kurmark Landwehr, see "Geschichte der Organisation der Landwehr," 1–75; Shanahan, *Prussian Military Reforms*, 209–10, provides a concise discussion of the philosophical and ideological issues that surfaced during the mobilization of the Landwehr.

28. Shanahan, *Prussian Military Reforms*, 204–7.

29. L'Estoq and Sack to Bülow, 11 June 1813, GStA, Rep. 15 A Nr. 164; Bülow to L'Estoq, 11 June 1813, GStA, Rep. 91 A Nr. 236.

30. GStA, Rep. 91 A Nr. 236 Dislokation von Truppen infolge des Waffenstillstandes; Boyen, *Erinnerungen*, ed. Nippold, 3:413. The brigades of Bülow's corps also needed quarters and thus compounded the problems for the Military Government. Reports over the dislocation of Bülow's brigades can be found in GStA, Rep. 91 A Nr. 233.

31. L'Estoq and Sack to Bülow, 11 June 1813, GStA, Rep. 91 A Nr. 236; L'Estoq and Sack to Putlitz, 11 June 1813, GStA, Rep. 15 A Nr. 164.

32. "Dislocation of the Seven Kurmark Landwehr Brigades" and "Cantonments for Kurmark Landwehr Brigades I–IV," in Putlitz to Bülow, 16 June 1813, GStA, Rep. 15 A Nr. 164; Bülow to Frederick William, 18 June 1813, in "Geschichte der Organisation der Landwehr," 114–16.

33. L'Estoq to Bülow, 16 June 1813, GStA, Rep. 91 A Nr. 236 (italics mine).

34. Bülow to L'Estoq, 20 June 1813, GStA, Rep. 91 A Nr. 236.

35. Bülow to Frederick William, 18 June 1813, in "Geschichte der Organisation der Landwehr," 114–16. The king assured Bülow that he was not surprised by the discrepancies in the development of the Kurmark brigades. Frederick William promised that the supplies in Kolberg would be distributed to meet the Landwehr's needs. Frederick William to Bülow, 25 June 1813, GStA, Rep. 15 A Nr. 334.

36. Cavaignac, *La formation de la Prusse*, 2:458; Showalter, "The Prussian Landwehr," 9. In *Preußen*, 421, 447, Ibbeken claims that the Prussian army between 1813 and 1815 numbered 279,000 men, of which 27,763 were volun-

teers, or ten percent of the total strength of the army. He includes the Jäger in his total of volunteers, which accounts for the discrepancy in the number of volunteers.

37. Showalter, "The Prussian Landwehr," 9.

38. Letter from the Berlin Commission to the Military Government, 6 June 1813, in "Geschichte der Organisation der Landwehr," 135.

39. "Geschichte der Organisation der Landwehr," 139.

40. Between June and September 1813 the Prussians received 113,000 muskets complete with powder and flints, while the Russians received 100,000 muskets, 116 cannon, and 1,200 tons of ammunition. Muir claims that in 1813 the British sent more than £1 million worth of military stores to the Baltic. See Muir, *Britain and the Defeat of Napoleon*, 292.

41. The British agreed to provide an annual subsidy of £666,666 if the Prussians maintained an army of 80,000 men. On 24 June six British ships arrived in Kolberg, four carrying arms for the Russians and two for the Prussians. They delivered 15,000 muskets with 3,000,000 cartridges; 2,000 sabers; 1,045 ninety-pound casks of powder; 2,183 ammunition pouches; 2,375 bayonets; 2,368 bandoliers; 1,473 musket slings; 3,000 frock coats; 2,500 vests; 2,000 greatcoats; 4,000 shakos; 1,500 pairs of shoes; and 3,000 woolen blankets. On 20 July a British transport docked in Stralsund and delivered 12,000 muskets for Prussian use. Three more transports arrived in Kolberg on 7 August carrying 7,000 muskets with bayonets and accessories; 700 cavalry sabers; 700,000 musket cartridges; 70,000 flints; 400 vests; 6,200 pairs of black boots; 1,900 greatcoats; and 1,660 rucksacks. On 14 August three British ships delivered 4,000 muskets; 400 sabers; 400,000 musket cartridges; and 30,000 flints. In Stralsund 30,000 muskets and 2,000 ninety-pound casks of gunpowder arrived on 22 August. Kolberg received another cargo of 2,000 ninety-pound casks of gunpowder on 3 September. Finally, 10,000 muskets arrived in Kolberg on 22 September. Großer Generalstab, *Das Preußische Heer 1813*, 179–81, 417–18.

42. Bülow to Tauentzien, 29 and 30 June 1813, and 4, 6, 9, 10, 24, and 30 July 1813, GStA, Rep. 15 A Nr. 250.

43. Boyen to Bülow, 1, 2, and 3 July 1813, GStA, Rep. 15 A Nr. 164; "Geschichte der Organisation der Landwehr," 114–135.

44. Boyen to Bülow, 1 July 1813, GStA, Rep. 15 A Nr. 164; Boyen, *Erinnerungen*, ed. Nippold, 3:430–33.

45. Showalter, "The Prussian Landwehr," 9–10.

46. "Geschichte der Organisation der Landwehr," 142–43.

47. Boyen to Bülow, 1 July 1813, GStA, Rep. 15 A Nr. 164.

48. Boyen added that "if his progress continues, he will make an excellent staff officer." Grolman's brother, Karl, served on Blücher's staff.

49. Boyen to Bülow, 1 and 3 July 1813, GStA, Rep. 15 A Nr. 164.

50. "Geschichte der Organisation der Landwehr," 140.

51. Shanahan, *Prussian Military Reforms*, 208. This held true in every Prussian province.

52. Frederick William to Bülow, 7 May 1813, GStA, Rep. 15 A Nr. 298.

53. Bülow, Parolbefehl of 5 July, "Angelegenheiten der Landwehr und Landsturm, 1813–1815," GStA, Rep. 89 Nr. 32318; "Geschichte der Organisation der

Landwehr," 140–42; *Gesetz-Sammlung 1813*, 13–14; Großer Generalstab, *Das Preußische Heer 1813*, 395; Shanahan, *Prussian Military Reforms*, 201–2.

54. See the discussion in Showalter, "The Prussian Landwehr," 10–12, on the reluctance of line and Jäger personnel to transfer to the Landwehr.

55. Vaupel, *Das Preußische Heer*, 187–91, 533–36; law of 6 August 1808 as listed in *Sammlung von 1806 bis zum 1810*, 275–77; Höhn, *Revolution-Heer-Kriegsbild*, 92–93, 435–36.

56. Demeter, *The German Officer-Corps*, 12–14.

57. Bülow to Frederick William, 16 July 1813, GStA, Rep. 15 A Nr. 238.

58. Hirschfeld to Bülow, 15 July 1813, GStA, Rep. 15 A Nr. 164.

59. Bülow to Frederick William, 15 July 1813, in "Geschichte des Organisation der Landwehr," 157; and Bülow to Frederick William, 16 July 1813, GStA, Rep. 15 A Nr. 238.

60. Frederick William to Bülow, 22 July 1813, GStA, Rep. 15 A Nr. 334.

61. Frederick William to Bülow, 21 July 1813, GStA, Rep. 15 A Nr. 334.

62. See "Die Formation der freiwilligen Jäger-Detachments."

63. Großer Generalstab, *Das Preußische Heer 1813*, 143; Showalter, "The Prussian Landwehr," 11–12.

64. East Prussia contributed twenty battalions and sixteen squadrons; West Prussia: eleven battalions and nine squadrons; Pomerania: twelve battalions and twelve squadrons. See Jany, *Geschichte der königlichen preußischen Armee*, 4:90.

65. "Geschichte der Organisation der Landwehr," 159.

66. Boyen, *Erinnerungen*, ed. Nippold, 3:479; Frederick William to Putlitz, 15 July 1813, in "Geschichte der Organisation der Landwehr," 161.

67. Frederick William to Bülow, 15 July 1813, in Boyen, *Erinnerungen*, ed. Nippold, 3:479; Frederick William to Hirschfeld, 15 July 1813, in "Geschichte der Organisation der Landwehr," 162.

68. Shanahan, *Prussian Military Reforms*, 225–30.

69. *Gesetz-Sammlung 1813*, 13–14.

70. Shanahan, *Prussian Military Reforms*, 229.

71. Scharnhorst authored the decrees, entitled "Verordnung über die Organisation der Landwehr," which are reproduced in Eckert, *Von Valmy bis Leipzig*, 238–41. See also *Gesetz-Sammlung 1813*, 36–37, 109–19; Bezzenberger, *Urkunden des Provinzial-Archivs in Königsberg*, 15–19; Boyen, *Erinnerungen*, ed. Nippold, 2:332–33; Lehmann, *Scharnhorst*, 2:538; Simon, *Failure of the Prussian Reform Movement*, 163–64.

72. Shanahan, *Prussian Military Reforms*, 202–3. There is much debate over the role of a militia in Prussia's mobilization plans. Boyen, Jany, and Shanahan all claim that the establishment of the East Prussian and national Landwehr "upset" the original rearmament plans that featured the creation of a small professional army. The Kalisch Treaty required Prussia to field a militia, but as late as 21 February mobilization plans concentrated on arming the regular army. Armament shortages and the king's aversion to a levée certainly support Shanahan's argument that the East Prussian Landwehr was "decisive" for the creation of the national Landwehr. See Boyen, *Erinnerungen*, ed. Schmidt, 2:332–33; Jany, *Geschichte der königlichen preußischen Armee*, 4:83.

73. Jany, *Geschichte der königlichen preußischen Armee*, 4:93–94. According to Generalmajor Jany, Prussia's population numbered 4,600,000. Of the 120,504 Landwehr soldiers, 20,560 came from the Kurmark; 7,941 from the Neumark; 15,409 from Pomerania; 49,974 from Silesia; East and West Prussia and Lithuania fielded 26,620. Shanahan, *Prussian Military Reforms*, 219.

CHAPTER 6. AXES, SPADES, AND WATER

1. Rhaden to L'Estoq, 28 May 1813, GStA, Rep. 91 A Nr. 153.
2. Cochius to Sack, 2 June 1813, GStA, Rep. 91 A Nr. 153.
3. L'Estoq to Bülow, 8 June 1813, GStA, Rep. 91 A Nr. 153.
4. "Der Kriegsschauplatz der Nord-Armee," 157.
5. L'Estoq to Bülow, 12 July 1813, GStA, Rep. 91 A Nr. 154.
6. Meyer to Bülow, 19 July 1813, GStA, Rep. 91 A Nr. 155.
7. Borstell to Bülow, 8 August 1813, GStA, Rep. 91 A Nr. 155. In this letter Borstell recommended that four battalions, eight squadrons, and one horse battery be posted in the Beeskow-Storkow District. On 12 August Borstell's chief-of-staff, Rüchel-Kleist, completed an inspection of the Spree defense line. His report to Borstell contained similar suggestions for defending the Beeskow-Storkow District, namely to augment the local Landsturm with "three or four battalions of light infantry and Jäger, four or five squadrons of cavalry, and some horse artillery." The only defense measure taken in this region was the fortification of Köpenick, which was completed on 16 August after numerous delays caused by the shortage of workers. Borstell to Bülow, 8 August 1813, GStA, Rep. 15 A Nr. 298; Rüchel-Kleist to Borstell, 12 August 1813, in "Der Kriegsschauplatz der Nord-Armee," 161.
8. Bülow to Borstell, 10 August 1813, in "Der Kriegsschauplatz der Nord-Armee," 160.
9. "Der Kriegsschauplatz der Nord-Armee," 150.
10. Eytelwein to Sack, 23 June 1813, GStA, Rep. 91 A Nr. 154.
11. L'Estoq to Bülow, 27 June 1813, GStA, Rep. 91 A Nr. 154.
12. Markhoff to Bülow, 10 August 1813, in "Der Kriegsschauplatz der Nord-Armee," 155.
13. Bülow to Meyer, 10 August 1813, in ibid., 156.
14. Günther to Sack, 11 June 1813, GStA, Rep 91 A Nr. 154.
15. Bülow to L'Estoq, 13 June 1813, GStA, Rep. 91 A Nr. 154. Cochius received this task and opened the dams along the Nuthe on 20 June. "Der Kriegsschauplatz der Nord-Armee," 122.
16. Rüchel-Kleist to Borstell, 25 July 1813, GStA, Rep. 91 A Nr. 155.
17. Cochius to Sack, 30 June 1813, GStA, Rep. 91 A Nr. 154.
18. Rhaden to L'Estoq, 24 June 1813, GStA, Rep. 91 A Nr. 154.
19. Bülow to L'Estoq, 8 July 1813, GStA, Rep. 91 A Nr. 154.
20. "Der Kriegsschauplatz der Nord-Armee," 128.
21. Ibid., 134.
22. L'Estoq to Bülow, 15, 17, and 23 July 1813; Bülow to L'Estoq, 16, 22, and 28 July 1813, GStA, Rep 91 A Nr. 155.

23. L'Estoq and Sack to Frederick William, 12 June 1813, in "Der Kriegsschauplatz," 134–36.

24. Reiche's *Memoiren*, 1:289–92, outlines the efforts at Spandau and contains letters from the king to Blücher and the Military Government in Berlin on 7 June 1813 that describe the royal prerogative for rebuilding the fortress's defenses.

25. L'Estoq to Bülow, 15 June 1813, GStA, Rep. 91 A. Nr. 154.

26. "Der Kriegsschauplatz der Nord-Armee," 193, 194.

27. Heune to Bülow, 19 June 1813, GStA, Rep. 91 A Nr. 154.

28. Bülow to L'Estoq, 21 June 1813, GStA, Rep. 91 A Nr. 154.

29. L'Estoq and Sack to Bülow, 23 June 1813, GStA, Rep. 91 A Nr. 154.

30. "Der Kriegsschauplatz der Nord-Armee," 165.

31. Ibid., 169.

32. Bülow to L'Estoq, 30 June 1813, GStA, Rep. 91 A Nr. 154.

33. L'Estoq and Sack to Bülow, 1 July 1813, GStA, Rep. 91 A Nr. 154.

34. L'Estoq and Sack to the Berlin Committee for Landwehr and Landsturm, 1 July 1813, GStA, Rep. 91 A Nr. 154.

35. Loos to L'Estoq, 4 July 1813, GStA, Rep. 91 A Nr. 154.

36. L'Estoq to Loos, 5 July 1813, GStA, Rep. 91 A Nr. 154.

37. L'Estoq and Sack to the Berlin Committee for Landwehr and Landsturm, 5 July 1813, GStA, Rep. 91 A Nr. 154. The Military Government wrote: "The Civic Guard will no longer receive preferential treatment; rather it now has reason to complain of discrimination."

38. Chief of Police Lecocq, a reactionary who also served as the chairman of the Berlin Committee for Landwehr and Landsturm, had earlier complained to the Military Government that the use of the Landsturm for guard duty was not only unconstitutional but interfered with the operation of municipal government and threatened the tranquility and security of the city. More to the point was his comment that service in the Landsturm gave certain segments of the urban population, especially craftsmen and those who worked with their hands, ludicrous ideas of equality. This was making it increasingly difficult for the authorities to enforce the necessary obedience and respect. Simon, in *Failure of the Prussian Reform Movement*, 173, notes that Lecocq's real complaint was that commoners were tempted to commit excesses under the cover of patriotism. Although Sack supported the Landsturm, Lecocq's protests eventually reached sources much closer to the king.

39. L'Estoq and Sack to the Berlin Committee for Landwehr and Landsturm, 5 July 1813, GStA, Rep. 91 A Nr. 154.

40. Sack to Büsching, 10 July 1813, in "Der Kriegsschauplatz der Nord-Armee," 173.

41. Bülow to L'Estoq, 13 July 1813; and L'Estoq to Bülow, 14 July 1813, GStA, Rep. 91 A Nr. 155; L'Estoq to Büsching, 14 July 1813, in "Der Kriegsschauplatz der Nord-Armee," 174–75 (quotation).

42. Loos to L'Estoq, 16 July 1813, GStA, Rep. 91 A Nr. 155.

43. "Der Kriegsschauplatz der Nord-Armee," 175.

44. Loos to L'Estoq, 16 July 1813, GStA, Rep. 91 A Nr. 155.

45. According to Simon, "vocal and effective resistance to the Landsturm was centered in Berlin," where there was "the largest concentration of wealth and hence the greatest fear of its destruction" through either the scorched-earth policy or the Landsturm itself. Simon, *Failure of the Prussian Reform Movement*, 172–73.

46. The decree, which dissolved the defense committees and fatally restricted the universal obligation to serve in the Landsturm, was a step to appease conservatives and soothe the king, who, in the midst of a life or death struggle with the French Empire, was becoming increasingly reactionary. "Verordnung vom 17ten Julius 1813: Betreff der Modifikationen des Landsturmedikts vom 21sten April," in *Gesetz-Sammlung 1813*, 89–92; Eckert, *Von Valmy bis Leipzig*, 260–63.

47. "Der Kriegsschauplatz der Nord-Armee," 176. Elsewhere the authority to mobilize the Landsturm was placed solely in the hands of the Military Governments, who could only act on the orders of the king. See Simon, *Failure of the Prussian Reform Movement*, 172–81.

48. Loos to L'Estoq, 22 July 1813, GStA, Rep. 91 A Nr. 155.

49. L'Estoq to Bülow, 23 July 1813, GStA, Rep. 91 A Nr. 155.

50. Bülow to L'Estoq, 28 July 1813, GStA, Rep. 91 A Nr. 155. "Concerning the remark stated in the letter regarding His Royal Majesty the king," noted Bülow, "this matter is completely unknown to me. The king had expressed his displeasure over the entrenchments along the Schaf-Graben, and felt that they had such a weak profile that they could be destroyed by a 3-pounder." Donnersmarck later recalled that "on 14 July, the king and I drove around Berlin to Charlottenburg, where at the *Chausseehause* a small *flèche* had been raised which the king labeled as 'child's play' and he sought to set things right." "Der Kriegsschauplatz der Nord-Armee," 177.

51. The Military Government of Berlin to Büsching, 30 July 1813, in "Der Kriegsschauplatz der Nord-Armee," 182.

52. The Military Government of Berlin to Frederick William, 4 August 1813, in ibid., 179. This report claimed that Bernadotte "was generally very content with everything" regarding the military preparations.

53. Bülow to L'Estoq, 31 July 1813, GStA, Rep. 91 A Nr. 155.

54. "Der Kriegsschauplatz der Nord-Armee," 179.

55. L'Estoq to Büsching, 3 August 1813, in ibid., 180.

56. Bülow to L'Estoq, 4 August 1813, GStA, Rep. 91 A Nr. 155.

57. The Military Government to Büsching, 4 August 1813, in "Der Kriegsschauplatz der Nord-Armee," 181.

58. The Military Government to Büsching, 7 August 1813, in ibid.

59. Bülow to L'Estoq, 7 August 1813, GStA, Rep. 91 A Nr. 155.

60. The Military Government to Büsching, 7 August 1813, in "Der Kriegsschauplatz der Nord-Armee," 182.

61. The Military Government to Büsching, 11 August 1813, in ibid.

62. Kolberg mediated at the request of the Military Government.

63. Bülow to L'Estoq, 15 August 1813, GStA, Rep. 91 A Nr. 155.

64. The Military Government to Büsching, 16 August 1813, in "Der Kriegsschauplatz der Nord-Armee," 182.

65. Büsching to the Military Government, 16 August 1813, GStA, Rep. 91 A Nr. 156.

CHAPTER 7. PLANS AND PREPARATIONS

1. Schroeder, *Transformation of European Politics*, 458–59.
2. Nicolson, *Congress of Vienna*, 55–56.
3. Kissinger, *A World Restored*, 38–39.
4. Muir, *Britain and the Defeat of Napoleon*, 257. The British representative in Prussian Headquarters, Charles Stewart, advanced the Prussians £100,000 to cover immediate needs, but further payments were suspended for the duration of the armistice.
5. Schroeder, *Transformation of European Politics*, 457.
6. Kraehe, *Metternich's German Policy*, 1:178. The return of Hanover to Great Britain was not an insignificant point considering that Prussia's expansionist goals prior to 1806 had centered on the North German electorate.
7. Muir, *Britain and the Defeat of Napoleon*, 246–47.
8. Schroeder, *Transformation of European Politics*, 459.
9. Ross, *European Diplomatic History*, 329.
10. Oncken, *Österreich und Preußen*, 1:416.
11. Schroeder, *Transformation of European Politics*, 460–61.
12. Nicolson, *Congress of Vienna*, 52.
13. Kraehe, Metternich's German Policy, 1:167, 169.
14. Oncken, *Österreich und Preußen*, 2:318.
15. Ross, *European Diplomatic History*, 332; Kissinger, *A World Restored*, 73.
16. Kraehe, *Metternich's German Policy*, 1:174.
17. Nicolson, *Congress of Vienna*, 53.
18. Not only did Napoleon end Habsburg familial control or influence over much of northern Italy between 1797 and 1801, but he also stripped Austria of the Illyrian provinces between 1805 and 1809. Thus the Austrians sought to regain the preponderance of power they once held among the German and Italian states. This meant limiting both Prussia's influence in South and Central Germany and Russia's presence west of Poland.
19. Schroeder, *Transformation of European Politics*, 460–61.
20. Ibid.
21. Nicolson, *Congress of Vienna*, 39.
22. Schroeder and Kissinger disagree over the nature of Metternich's peace plan. See Schroeder, *Transformation of European Politics*, 461, 462 (quotation); and Kissinger, *A World Restored*, 73.
23. Metternich, *Mémoires*, 1:124.
24. Schroeder, *Transformation of European Politics*, 463.
25. Ibid., 465.
26. Ross, *European Diplomatic History*, 341–42.
27. Schroeder, *Transformation of European Politics*, 464.
28. Nipperdey, *Germany from Napoleon to Bismarck*, 70.
29. Muir, *Britain and the Defeat of Napoleon*, 281.

30. Nicolson, *Congress of Vienna*, 42–43.
31. Kissinger, *A World Restored*, 30.
32. Nicholson, *Congress of Vienna*, 42, 60.
33. Ibid., 40.
34. Schroeder, *Transformation of European Politics*, 467–68.
35. Napoleon quoted in Nicolson, *Congress of Vienna*, 43.
36. Schroeder, *Transformation of European Politics*, 467–70.
37. Kissinger, *A World Restored*, 74.
38. Kraehe, *Metternich's German Policy*, 1:177. Metternich worded the language regarding Prussia's expansion in Poland to undermine the Kalisch pact.
39. Kissinger, *A World Restored*, 76.
40. Muir, *Britain and the Defeat of Napoleon*, 248.
41. Metternich, *Mémoires*, 2:187–89. In his pro-British interpretation of the diplomacy that took place during the armistice, Riley claims that when Napoleon received the news of the Duke of Wellington's victory over the French at Vitoria on 21 June 1813 he realized that it would strengthen Allied resolve to fight and so agreed to the extension of the armistice. Riley goes on to argue the debatable points that Vitoria limited Metternich's plan for dealing with the British and that "the victory at Vitoria, stiffening the resolve of the Allies [at Pläswitz], pointed the way to Leipzig." Riley, *Napoleon and the World War*, 113–14, 366.
42. The Austrian High Command informed Metternich that if he could provide them with four more weeks of peace they could field an additional 75,000 men. Nicolson, *Congress of Vienna*, 45.
43. Kraehe, *Metternich's German Policy*, 1:180–81; Nicolson, *Congress of Vienna*, 41.
44. Chandler, *Campaigns of Napoleon*, 898–99.
45. Muir, *Britain and the Defeat of Napoleon*, 284.
46. Ross, *European Diplomatic History*, 333.
47. Kissinger, *A World Restored*, 82.
48. Nicolson, *Congress of Vienna*, 56.
49. Nipperdey, *Germany from Napoleon to Bismarck*, 70.
50. Kissinger, *A World Restored*, 82.
51. Ibid., 49.
52. Ibid., 11.
53. Muir, *Britain and the Defeat of Napoleon*, 285–86.
54. See White, "Defeating Napoleon."
55. Metternich quoted in Craig, "Problems of Coalition Warfare," 26.
56. Craig, "Problems of Coalition Warfare," 24.
57. Ibid., 27.
58. Ibid., 28–29.
59. Boyen, *Erinnerungen*, ed. Schmidt, 2:611.
60. This included the four battalions of the Second Kurmark Landwehr Regiment, the four battalions of the First Neumark Landwehr Regiment, and the Second and Fourth Kurmark Landwehr Cavalry Regiments. The remaining Landwehr regiments came from East Prussia and Pomerania.

61. Goerlitz, *History of the German General Staff*, 19 (quotation); Dupuy, *Genius for War*, 17–36.

62. Goerlitz, *History of the German General Staff*, 18. Yorck opposed Scharnhorst's plans to open the officer corps to commoners and mocked the notion that "a hidden talent can be found under every peasant's jacket." He added that just because Pope Sixtus V had been a swineherd in his youth, it would be ludicrous "to consider all such possible candidates, lest some divine swineherd perish unnoticed." Yorck cited in Droysen, *Yorck*, 1:130. Dupuy notes that although Yorck and Scharnhorst "were poles apart in social and political outlook, Scharnhorst had so respected Yorck's military competence that in 1809 he had appointed Yorck Inspector of Infantry." Dupuy, *Genius for War*, 32.

63. Demeter cites two key points from the memoirs of the Brandenburg Junker Friedrich August von der Marwitz. First, the main defect of the Prussian army of 1806 "was at the top." Second, "the commanders who from 1813 onwards won glory for the name of Prussia, inflicting such defeats upon the enemy that they entered his capital twice as conquerors, had all been officers in the Prussian Army in the year 1806 and were in most cases already serving as its commanders." Marwitz concluded that among the officers who served in 1813 were sixty commanders of corps, divisions, and brigades and more than a hundred regimental commanders, all of whom had served in 1806. Marwitz also found that all but 10 of 300 battalion commanders and 100 of 2,000 company and squadron commanders who commanded in 1813 were veterans of the 1806–7 campaigns. He declared that "if the same men could produce one result in 1806 and the opposite in 1813, the cause must be sought not in the officers themselves, but in the decisions taken higher up—in the regulations, the equipment and the circumstances: but first and foremost in the grace of God." Demeter, *The German Officer-Corps*, 9–10. See also Demeter's chart on p. 8, which lists the age groups of the Prussian officer corps from generals to captains in 1806.

64. Boyen, *Erinnerungen*, ed. Schmidt, 2:614.

65. For a thorough review of Dietrich's ideas, see Palmer, "Frederick the Great," 69–74. For the troubled relationship of the two Bülow brothers, see Bülow, *Aus Dietrich Bülows Leben*, 7–21.

66. Varnhagen von Ense, *Bülow*, 54.

67. Meinecke, *Boyen*, 1:306.

68. For an account of the Superior Investigating Commission, see Kitchen, *Military History of Germany*, 40–42. A cabinet order of 4 June 1808 established a committee to draft new army training regulations. Paret provides a description of the committee's work in *Yorck*, 140–45.

69. Varnhagen von Ense, *Bülow*, 69. To Bülow and others such as Marwitz, Borstell, and for a time Yorck, none of whom were opposed to military reform, Scharnhorst represented a "new and alien force operating within their special preserve, the army." Simon, in *Failure of the Prussian Reform Movement*, 153, notes that Scharnhorst's "disrespect for traditions which he himself had not enjoyed infuriated them." In *Boyen*, 1:171, Meinecke claims that they saw in Scharnhorst's emphasis on education and on opening the officer

corps to commoners a "sinister plot to cause the internal disintegration of the army."

70. Scharnhorst to Yorck, 29 August 1811, in Droysen, *Yorck*, 1:289–90.

71. See the discussion on "dual command" in Goerlitz, *History of the German General Staff*, 41; White, *The Enlightened Soldier*, 165.

72. Yorck's First Corps was assigned to Blücher; Kleist's Second Corps to Schwarzenberg; Bülow and Tauentzien to Bernadotte.

73. Boyen, *Erinnerungen*, ed. Schmidt, 2:613.

74. Meinecke, *Boyen*, 1:306.

75. Boyen, *Erinnerungen*, ed. Schmidt, 2:614. "We separated from each other on friendly terms at the end of the war," recalled Boyen, who had no reason to write favorably of Bülow in his memoirs. Many of Boyen's closest associates, including Scharnhorst, Gneisenau, Grolman, and Müffling, were Bülow's enemies.

76. Petre, *Napoleon's Last Campaign*, 170. Allied reserves and besieging forces numbered an additional 143,000 men, while Napoleon had 77,000 men garrisoned in fortresses on the Elbe, Oder, and Vistula.

77. Marmont, *Mémoires*, 5:139.

78. Napoleon to Ney and Marmont, 12 August 1813, *Correspondance*, No. 20360, 26:34–36; Napoleon to Oudinot, 12 August 1813, ibid., No. 20365, 26:37–38.

79. Berthier to Sébastiani, Mortier, Victor, Latour-Maubourg, and Poniatowski, 12 August 1813, AAT, C^{17} 179; Napoleon to Berthier, 11 August 1813, *Correspondance*, No. 20348, 26:24–25.

80. Berthier to Girard, 12 August 1813, and Berthier to Lemarois, 13 August 1813, AAT, C^{17} 179; Napoleon to Davout, 12 August 1813, *Correspondance*, No. 20353, 26:28.

81. Berthier to Davout, 13 August 1813, AAT, C^{17} 179; Napoleon to Davout, 13 August 1813, *Correspondance*, No. 20374, 26:47–48.

82. Napoleon to Berthier, 11 August 1813, *Correspondance*, No. 20348, 26:24; Napoleon to Oudinot, 12 August 1813, ibid., No. 20365, 26:37–38; Napoleon to Davout, 12 August 1813, ibid., No. 20357, 26:32–33.

83. Napoleon to Berthier, 11 August 1813, ibid., No. 20348, 26:24; Napoleon to Oudinot, 12 August 1813, ibid., No. 20365, 26:37–38. Gen. Henri Bertrand commanded the 21,173 infantry, 672 cavalry, and 72 guns of the Fourth Corps. Gen. Jean-Louis-Ebénézer Reynier's Seventh Corps numbered 17,200 infantry, 1,200 cavalry, and 68 guns. Oudinot's own Twelfth Corps totaled 15,818 infantry, 1,529 cavalry, and 58 guns. Gen. Jean-Toussaint Arrighi de Casanova commanded the Third Cavalry Corps, consisting of 5,607 men and 18 guns. Quistorp, *Geschichte der Nord-Armee*, 3:63–71.

84. Berthier to Oudinot, 13 August 1813, AAT, C^{17} 179; Napoleon to Oudinot, 12 August 1813, *Correspondance*, No. 20365, 26:39.

85. Oudinot to Berthier, 14 August 1813, AAT, C^{2} 153.

86. Chandler maintains that Davout was the ablest of Napoleon's twenty-six marshals "but paradoxically never enjoyed his master's unquestioning trust." Moreover, Chandler notes that after Davout's great victory over the Prussians at Auerstädt, Napoleon harbored a "tincture of envy and suspicion" despite the

marshal's "unquestioning loyalty." Philipp Coates-Wright claims that St.-Cyr had never been one of Napoleon's favorites and had not received his appointment to the marshalate until 1812, apparently as punishment for failing to sign the proclamation congratulating Napoleon on the declaration of the empire in March 1804. As for Marshal Marmont, his appointment to the marshalate in 1809 came on the strength of his personal friendship with Napoleon rather than his proven skills. After his debacle at Salamanca on 22 July 1812, Napoleon could simply not afford to give his friend another chance at independent command. David G. Chandler, "Davout: The Iron Marshal," 94, 110; Coates-Wright, "Gouvion St.-Cyr: The Owl"; Pimlott, "Marmont: Friendship's Choice."

87. Oudinot's Twelfth Corps contained one Bavarian and two French divisions; Reynier's Seventh Corps had one French and two Saxon divisions; Bertrand's Fourth Corps contained one division each of French, Italian, and Württemberger troops. "Situation of the 4th Corps," 16 August 1813, AAT, C^2 539; "Situation of the 12th Corps," 1 July 1813, and "Situation of the 7th Corps," 1 August 1813, AAT, C^2 541; "Situation of the 3rd Cavalry Corps," 1 August 1813, AAT, C^2 544.

88. Berthier to Poniatowski, 13 August 1813, AAT, C^{17} 179; Napoleon to Berthier, 23 August 1813, *Correspondance*, No. 20442, 26:414–15; Petre, *Napoleon's Last Campaign*, 172. These units included the Third, Fifth, Sixth, and Eleventh Corps and Second Cavalry Corps.

89. Napoleon to Berthier, 13 August 1813, *Correspondance*, No. 20371, 26:42–44; Napoleon to Ney, Saint-Cyr, Macdonald, and Marmont, ibid., No. 29373, 26:45–47; Petre, *Napoleon's Last Campaign*, 172.

90. Marmont, *Mémoires*, 5:140.

91. Cited in Petre, *Napoleon's Last Campaign*, 185.

92. Napoleon to Macdonald, 16 August 1813, *Correspondance*, Nos. 20390 and 20391, 26:69–70.

93. Napoleon to Berthier, 23 August 1813, ibid., Nos. 20441, 20442, and 20443, 26:414–18.

94. Wintzingerode's Russian corps contained 13,622 infantry, 14,096 cavalry, and 1,639 gunners with 92 pieces; Stedingk's Swedes numbered 19,047 infantry, 2,755 cavalry, and 1,647 gunners with 54 cannon. Tauentzien's Fourth Corps was subdivided into a corps for field operations and two siege brigades. His field corps consisted of 30,169 infantry, 2,789 cavalry, and 675 gunners with 42 guns. The two siege brigades consisted of Hinrichs's 6,630 infantry, 492 cavalry, and 8 guns; and Plötz's 10,015 infantry, 533 cavalry, and 8 guns. Quistorp, *Geschichte der Nord-Armee*, 3:2–20.

95. Boyen, *Erinnerungen*, ed. Schmidt, 2:625.

96. Charles John to Tauentzien, 13 August 1813, in Quistorp, *Geschichte der Nord-Armee*, 1:139.

97. Charles John to Wintzingerode, 13 August 1813, *Recueil*, 79–80.

98. Bülow to Frederick William, 15 August 1813, GStA, Rep. 15 A Nr. 238.

99. Boyen, *Erinnerungen*, ed. Schmidt, 2:619–20.

100. Kalckreuth to Köckritz, 28 June 1813, in Meinecke, "Zur Beurteilung Bernadottes im Herbstfeldzuge 1813," 7:164–65.

CHAPTER 8. OPENING MOVES

1. *Recueil*, 83–85.

2. Borstell to Bülow, 14 August 1813, in Quistorp, *Geschichte der Nord-Armee*, 1:193. For this phase of the campaign, the Geheime Staatsarchiv has been able to relocate only the Repositorium containing the August correspondence between Thümen and Bülow, Thümen and the other Third Corps brigade commanders, and Thümen and his forward posts (GStA, Rep. 15 A Nr. 344). We can only hope that more of these precious documents are rediscovered as the Germans conclude the long process of reunifying their archival system.

3. Bülow to Charles John, 14 August 1813, in ibid.; Swederus, *Schwedens Politik und Kriege*, 1:26–28.

4. Boyen, *Erinnerungen*, ed. Schmidt, 2:619.

5. Fabry, *Étude sur les opérations dur maréchal Oudinot*, 43–44; Quistorp, *Geschichte der Nord-Armee*, 1:198–200.

6. Although hostilities were not scheduled to resume until 12:00 A.M. on 17 August, Blücher had led the entire Silesian Army into the twenty-mile-wide neutral zone that separated the contending forces in Silesia on 13 August. He justified his actions by citing the need to be in contact with the enemy to have ample warning of their movements.

7. "Order of the Day," 15 August 1813, *Recueil*, 81.

8. Charles John to Blücher, 19 August 1813, ibid., 102–3.

9. Fabry, *Étude sur les opérations du maréchal Oudinot*, 61.

10. A copy of Bülow's Tagesbefehl for the movements on 17 May can be found in GStA, Rep. 15 A Nr. 344. Charles John to Bülow and Tauentzien, 16 August 1813, *Recueil*, 88–89.

11. Charles John to Wintzingerode, Hirschfeld, and Stedingk, 16 August 1813, ibid., 91–92.

12. Bülow to Friedrich Wilhelm, 18 August 1813, GStA, Rep. 19 A Nr. 238.

13. Hirschfeld to Tauentzien, 15 August 1813, ibid., 113. Tauentzien had forwarded this report to Bernadotte's headquarters.

14. Charles John to Blücher, 16 August 1813, *Recueil*, 93. Bernadotte also informed Hirschfeld that "Napoleon has marched from Luckau to Baruth in the direction of Berlin." Charles John to Hirschfeld, 16 August 1813, *Recueil*, 93.

15. Boyen, *Erinnerungen*, ed. Schmidt, 2:620–21.

16. Boyen described Bülow's second plan as "the best." Boyen, *Erinnerungen*, ed. Schmidt, 2:620.

17. Ibid., 622; Meinecke, *Boyen*, 1:314.

18. Meinecke, *Boyen*, 1:309. "Bülow," notes Meinecke, "who could now and then depart from his old methodical manner of warfare, now showed in his military plans something related to Gneisenau's strategy."

19. Charles John to Bülow, 17 August 1813, *Recueil*, 94.

20. Charles John to Wintzingerode, 17 August 1813, ibid., 95–96.

21. "Der Kriegsschauplatz der Nord-Armee im Jahre 1813," 186.

22. Bülow to L'Estoq, 17 August 1813, GStA, Rep. 91 A Nr. 156; L'Estoq and Sack to Bülow, 18 August 1813, GStA, Rep. 15 A Nr. 298.

23. Loos to the Military Government in Berlin, 22 August 1813, GStA, Rep. 91 A, Nr. 156.

24. Bülow to Thümen and Thümen's reports to Bülow, 18 August 1813, GStA Rep. 15 A Nr. 344; Charles John to Wintzingerode, 17 May 1813, *Recueil*, 95–96; Quistorp, *Geschichte der Nord-Armee*, 1:212–13.

25. Charles John to Bülow, 18 August 1813, *Recueil*, 97; Charles John to Tauentzien, 18 August 1813, ibid., 98.

26. "Historique des opérations des 4, 7 et 12 corps, et du 3 corps de cavalerie, depuis la rupture de l'armistice le 17 August jusqu'au 4 septembre, par le général de brigade du génie Blein." AAT, MR 688; Reynier to Berthier, 19 August 1813; Oudinot to Berthier, 26 August 1813; "Report of the 7th Corps," 26 August 1813; "Report of the 4th Corps," 27 August 1813, AAT, C^2 154.

27. Thümen to Bülow, 19 August 1813, GStA Rep. 15 A Nr. 344; Quistorp, *Geschichte der Nord-Armee*, 1:215–16.

28. Reynier to Berthier, 20 August 1813, AAT, C^2 154.

29. Borstell to Bülow, 19 August 1813, in Quistorp, *Geschichte der Nord-Armee*, 1:215.

30. Tauentzien's "corps" only consisted of Dobschütz's brigade and the reserve artillery and cavalry. The other three brigades were operating on the army's flanks.

31. A copy of Bülow's Tagesbefehl for the movements on 20 May can be found in GStA, Rep. 15 A Nr. 344. Charles John to Bülow, 19 August 1813, *Recueil*, 101; Charles John to Tauentzien, 19 August 1813, ibid., 102; Charles John to Wintzingerode, 19 August 1813, ibid., 98–99. Wintzingerode's 3,000 Cossacks continued to observe the Elbe from Zerbst to Jessen.

32. Bülow to Friedrich Wilhelm, 19 August 1813, BFA, Nr. 63.

33. Fabry, *Étude sur les opérations du maréchal Oudinot*, 69–70.

34. "Historique des opérations," AAT, MR 688; Reynier to Berthier, 20 August 1813; Oudinot to Berthier, 26 August 1813; "Report of the 7th Corps," 26 August 1813; "Report of the 4th Corps," 27 August 1813, AAT, C^2 154; Fabry, *Étude sur les opérations du maréchal Oudinot*, 75–76.

35. Fabry, *Étude sur les opérations du maréchal Oudinot*, 75; Boyen, *Erinnerungen*, ed. Schmidt, 2:623.

36. "Order of the Day," 20 August 1813, *Recueil*, 104–6. Some of Tauentzien's Landwehr battalions occupied the entrenchments on the Tempelhof hill chain.

37. Wiehr, *Napoleon und Bernadotte*, 126.

38. For general accounts of the combats on 21 August, see "Historique des opérations," AAT, MR 688; Oudinot to Berthier, 26 August 1813; "Report of the 7th Corps," 26 August 1813; "Report of the 4th Corps," 27 August 1813, AAT, C^2 154; Fabry, *Étude sur les opérations du maréchal Oudinot*, 77–79; Quistorp, *Geschichte der Nord-Armee*, 1:229–235.

39. Bülow to Thümen, 21 May 1813, Boyen to Thümen, 21 May 1813, and a copy of Bülow's Tagesbefehl for the movements on 22 May can be found in GStA, Rep. 15 A Nr. 344. "Order of the Day," 21 August 1813, *Recueil*, 110–12. Even at this late hour Bernadotte still feared for his left. Tauentzien was to direct Wobeser to Lieberose to "ascertain the movements and forces of

the enemy between Luckau and Baruth." See Charles John to Tauentzien, 21 August 1813, ibid., 109–10.

40. Quistorp, *Geschichte der Nord-Armee*, 1:239–40.

41. Fabry, *Étude sur les opérations du maréchal Oudinot*, 65.

42. Although some historians, including the German authority on the Army of North Germany Generalleutnant Barthold von Quistorp, have claimed that Bülow uttered these words during this meeting, Joachim-Albrecht Count Bülow von Dennewitz insists that Bülow actually said this phrase to his brother-in-law, Ludwig von Auer, after a 13 August council of war in Oranienburg. Unlike those of his wife Friederike, Auer's unpublished memoirs were lost in the family estate at Grünhoff when the Red Army invaded East Prussia in 1945.

43. Quistorp, *Geschichte der Nord-Armee*, 1:242–43.

44. "Order of the Day," 22 August 1813, *Recueil*, 113–15.

45. On 19 August Bernadotte informed Blücher that the Army of North Germany "has been without subsistence for two days; this misfortune has delayed my dispositions." On the twenty-first he wrote that "the unexpected difficulties of supply have increased due to the army's concentration in the vicinity of this city." See Charles John to Blücher, 19 August 1813, *Recueil*, 103; "4th Bulletin of the Army of North Germany," 21 August 1813, ibid., 107.

46. "Historique des opérations," AAT, MR 688; Oudinot to Berthier, 26 August 1813; "Report of the 7th Corps," 26 August 1813; "Report of the 4th Corps," 27 August 1813, AAT, C^2 154.

47. Thümen to Bülow, 21 August 1813, GStA, Rep. 15 A Nr. 298. This Repositorium, which contains a portion of Bülow's correspondance with his brigadiers, is part of the rediscovered Repositoria of the Kriegs-Archiv of the Großer Generalstab now housed in the Geheime Staatsarchiv.

48. Thümen to Bülow, 22 August 1813, GStA, Rep. 15 A Nr. 298.

49. Boyen to Rottenburg, 21 August 1813, in Quistorp, *Geschichte der Nord-Armee*, 246.

50. For general accounts of the combats on the twenty-second, see "Historique des opérations," AAT, MR 688; Oudinot to Berthier, 26 August 1813; "Report of the 7th Corps," 26 August 1813; "Report of the 4th Corps," 26 August 1813, AAT C^2 154; Boyen, *Erinnerungen*, ed. Schmidt, 2:624–27; Varnhagen von Ense, *Bülow*, 200–202; Fabry, *Étude sur les opérations du maréchal Oudinot*, 90–100; Quistorp, *Geschichte der Nord-Armee*, 1:244–61; Wagner, *Pläne der Schlachten und Treffen*, 2:39–43.

51. Order of the Day, 22 August 1813, *Recueil*, 113–14. On 23 August (*Recueil*, 115) Bernadotte issued further instructions for Bülow to order Borstell to withdraw to Heinersdorf and Groß Beeren in order to support Tauentzien. Had Borstell executed this order, he would not have been in position to make his flank attack on Reynier on the twenty-third. Quistorp, *Geschichte der Nord-Armee*, 1:261–63.

52. Boyen to Rottenburg, 22 August 1813, in Quistorp, *Geschichte der Nord-Armee*, 1:263.

53. Bülow to Thümen, 22 August 1813, GStA, Rep. 15 A Nr. 343.

54. "Report of the 5th Brigade," 31 August 1813, in Boyen, *Erinnerungen*, ed. Nippold, 3:125, 564. Bülow initially ordered Borstell to Groß Ziethen and later redirected him to Birkholz.

55. Charles John to Bülow, 23 August 1813, BFA, Nr. 65.

CHAPTER 9. GROß BEEREN

1. Wagner, *Pläne der Schlachten und Treffen*, 2:41.
2. Förster, *Geschichte der Befreiungskriege*, 1:765, 772.
3. In the position around Ruhlsdorf, the Sputendorf forest faced the right wing of the Allied army; the narrow Ruhlsdorf gorge hindered movement by the center; a marsh before the front and flank of the left wing limited mobility in that sector. Boyen, *Erinnerungen*, ed. Schmidt, 2:627.
4. Auer, "Erinnerungen aus der Jugendzeit für meine Kinder," BFA, Nr. 67.
5. Boyen, *Erinnerungen*, ed. Schmidt, 2:628.
6. Ibid., 628–29.
7. "Report of the 3rd Brigade," 28 August 1813, in Boyen, *Erinnerungen*, ed. Nippold, 3:559. At Heinersdorf the Third Brigade took a position on the right wing, beside it the Sixth, and then the Fourth. The reserve cavalry camped north of the village, with the reserve artillery beside it to the right, and behind the Third Brigade. One fusilier battalion occupied Klein Beeren. For troop dispositions, see Wagner, *Pläne der Schlachten und Treffen*, 2:45.
8. For accounts of the combat at Blankenfelde, see "Report of the 4th Corps," 27 August 1813, AAT, C[2] 154; "Historique des opérations," AAT, MR 688; Fabry, *Étude sur les opérations du maréchal Oudinot*, 108–10; Quistorp, *Geschichte der Nord-Armee*, 1:272–76; Wagner, *Pläne der Schlachten und Treffen*, 2:43–45.
9. Wagner, *Pläne der Schlachten und Treffen*, 2:46.
10. "Report of the 6th Brigade," 1 September 1813, in Boyen, *Erinnerungen*, ed. Nippold, 3:561.
11. Bülow to Frederick William, 24 August 1813, in Quistorp, *Geschichte der Nord-Armee*, 1:306–7.
12. Wagner, *Pläne der Schlachten und Treffen*, 2:44.
13. Oudinot to Berthier, 26 August 1813, AAT, C[2] 154. Odeleben, *Napoleons Feldzug im Sachsen*, 153; Fabry, *Étude sur les opérations du maréchal Oudinot*, 114.
14. Bülow to Frederick William, 24 August 1813, GStA, Rep. 15 A Nr. 238.
15. Bernadotte quoted in Reiche, *Memoiren*, 1:300.
16. Finley, *The Most Monstrous of Wars*, 17–18.
17. Boyen, *Erinnerungen*, ed. Schmidt, 2:630.
18. Bülow's reserve artillery contained the Prussian twelve-pounder batteries Nos. 4 and 5, consisting of eight guns each, and the Russian heavy batteries Nos. 7 and 21, consisting of ten and twelve guns each respectively. Altogether Bülow's reserve artillery consisted of fifty-four pieces, thirty-eight of which were twelve-pounders. The remaining sixteen guns were the eight six-pounders of battery No. 19 and the eight guns of the horse battery No. 11.

19. Boyen, *Erinnerungen*, ed. Schmidt, 2:631. According to Boyen, this "proved that in the present employment of artillery and by the utilization of any terrain, an advance in combat with long, thin lines is impossible and should thus be stricken from the regulations." For a discussion on the Prussian army's use of lines and columns, see Paret, *Yorck*, 183–84.

20. Boyen, *Erinnerungen*, ed. Schmidt, 630.

21. Förster, *Geschichte der Befreiungskriege*, 1:772.

22. Oudinot to Berthier, 25 August 1813, AN, AF IV, Carton 1660.

23. Battle accounts can be found in Oudinot to Berthier, 26 August 1813, and "Report of the 7th Corps," 26 August 1813, AAT, C^2 154; Bülow to Frederick William, 24 August 1813 in Quistorp, *Geschichte der Nord-Armee*, 1:306–7; "Report of the 4th Brigade," 28 August 1813; "Report of the 3rd Brigade," 28 August 1813; "Report of the 5th Brigade," 31 August 1813; "Report of the 6th Brigade," 1 September 1813, in Boyen, *Erinnerungen*, 3: ed. Nippold, 559–67; Boyen, *Erinnerungen*, ed. Schmidt, 2:628–32; Odeleben, *Napoleons Feldzug in Sachsen*, 155–57; Fabry, *Étude des opérations du maréchal Oudinot*, 117–25; Eidahl, "Napoleon's Faulty Strategy."

24. Varnhagen von Ense, *Bülow*, 213.

25. Wagner, *Pläne der Schlachten und Treffen*, 2:54.

26. Boyen, *Erinnerungen*, ed. Schmidt, 2:631.

27. GStA, Rep. 91 A Nr. 97.

28. "Beiträge zur militärischen Geschichte Sachsens," 230.

29. Rehtwisch, *Aus dem Tagebuch eines Freiwilligen*, 75–76.

30. Oudinot to Berthier, 26 August 1813, AAT, C^2 154.

31. Oudinot to Berthier, 26 August 1813, and "Report of the 7th Corps," 26 August 1813, AAT, C^2 154.

32. Oudinot had not maintained communication with Davout, who "had very little information of the enemy's strength or position." Davout did not begin his retreat until 2 September. Gallaher, *The Iron Marshal*, 281–82.

33. Petre, *Napoleon's Last Campaign*, 263.

34. White claims that "more than likely it was Boyen's resolution that had saved the day." According to Boyen himself, "Bülow had certainly undertaken the battle upon his own initiative. He could unpretentiously say that he had prevented the Army of North Germany from a retrograde movement and thus had saved Berlin. If Bülow would have been defeated . . . Berlin would probably have been relinquished." Boyen, *Erinnerungen*, 2:633; White, *The Enlightened Soldier*, 167.

35. GStA, Rep. 15 A Nr. 238.

36. Bülow to Pauline, 25 August 1813, BFA, Nr. 69.

37. "Tagesbefehl," 24 August 1813, in Varnhagen von Ense, *Bülow*, 216.

38. "Report of the 3rd Brigade," 28 August 1813, in Boyen, *Erinnerungen*, ed. Nippold, 3:561.

39. Swederus, in *Schwedens Politik und Kriege*, 30–75, uses documents from the Swedish archives to refute the Prussian General Staff's interpretation of the battle and to argue that Bülow and the Prussians greatly undermined Bernadotte's strategy. Hans Delbrück, in *Weltgeschichte*, 4:468, 479, limits Bülow's credit and terms Bernadotte's strategy before Groß Beeren flawless.

He notes that "the opportunity for a decisive victory (at Groß Beeren) was lost by Bülow's unauthorized action." Konrad Lehmann's exhaustive study, *Die Rettung Berlins im Jahre 1813*, 253, also ultimately praises Bernadotte's conduct. Meinecke, in *Boyen*, 1:310, 316, 329, describes Bernadotte's strategic plan before Groß Beeren as "expedient and clever" but regrets that its author lacked "the determined offensive spirit" for its execution. Friederich, in *Der Befreiungskriege*, 2:144, claims that Bernadotte lacked energy in his operations: "So we see in the crown prince in the year 1813 a remarkable mixture of ingenuity and inability, of courage and timidity bordering on the absurd, of determination and indecision—all in all a psychological riddle, which up until now none could satisfactorily solve." Heinrich Ulmann, in *Geschichte der Befreiungskriege*, 2:85, labels Bülow "the hero of Groß Beeren" and says that irresolution marred Bernadotte's leadership.

CHAPTER 10. THE POLITICS OF DISSENSION

1. Auer, "Erinnerungen aus der Jugendzeit für meine Kinder," BFA, Nr. 67.
2. Ibid.; Boyen, *Erinnerungen*, ed. Schmidt, 2:632; Reiche, *Memoiren*, 1:303–4.
3. Boyen, *Erinnerungen*, ed. Schmidt, 2:636; Reiche, *Memoiren*, 1:304.
4. Auer, "Erinnerungen aus der Jugendzeit für meine Kinder," BFA, Nr. 53.
5. Boyen, *Erinnerungen*, ed. Schmidt, 2:632, 635.
6. Charles John to Bülow, Tauentzien, and Wintzingerode, 24 August 1813, *Recueil*, 118–19.
7. Bertrand's Fourth Corps withdrew to Saalow; Reynier's Seventh Corps to Gottow; and Oudinot's Twelfth Corps and the Third Cavalry Corps to Baruth. Charles Jean to Bülow, 24 August 1813, *Recueil*, 124.
8. Charles John to Tauentzien, 25 August 1813, ibid., 128.
9. *Fifth Bulletin*, 24 August 1813; *Recueil*, 120–22; Philippart, *Memoirs and Campaigns of Charles John*, 216; Pflugk-Harttung, "Bülows Bericht," 172.
10. Bülow to Pauline, 27 August 1813, BFA, Nr. 70.
11. Gill, "Bernadotte and the Saxon Army at Wagram." See also commentary by Donald D. Horward, ibid., 284–87.
12. Boyen noted that Bülow "liked glory, but placed little value on decorations. He was unselfish and respected people." Boyen, *Erinnerungen*, ed. Schmidt, 2:636.
13. Pflugk-Harttung, "Bülows Bericht," 172.
14. Sack to Boyen, 27 August 1813, in Boyen, *Erinnerungen*, ed. Nippold, 3:567–68.
15. Pflugk-Harttung, "Bülows Bericht," 172.
16. Other recipients included Blücher, Kleist, Yorck, Tauentzien, and the Russian A. I. Osterman-Tolstoy. Bülow won his in September 1813.
17. Auer, "Erinnerungen aus der Jugendzeit für meine Kinder," BFA, Nr. 67.

18. "Order of the Day," 25 August 1813, *Recueil*, 129–30.

19. GStA, Rep. 15 A Nr. 396 Marwitz Tagebuch.

20. Girard's French troops consisted of six line battalions, two light battalions, and five squadrons. In addition to these units, he commanded one Westphalian, one Croatian, and two Saxon battalions.

21. Putlitz to Gneisenau, 24 and 27 August 1813, GStA, Nachlaß Gneisenau, Packet Nr. 18; GStA, Rep. 15 A Nr. 396 Marwitz Tagebuch. Sources for the encounter at Hagelberg include Friederich, *Die Befreiungskriege*, 2:167–71; Plotho, *Der Krieg*, 2:151–55; Quistorp, *Geschichte der Nord-Armee*, 1:407–22; Wagner, *Pläne der Schlachten und Treffen*, 2:93–108.

22. Bülow to Pauline, 27 August 1813, BFA, Nr. 70.

23. Bülow to Pauline, 28 August 1813, BFA, Nr. 71.

24. Charles John to Wintzingerode, Tauentzien, and Bülow, 28 August 1813, *Recueil*, 145–46; Bülow to Pauline, 29 August 1813, BFA, Nr. 72.

25. Boyen, *Erinnerungen*, ed. Schmidt, 2:638.

26. Lejeune, *Memoirs*, 2:284–85.

27. Bülow to Pauline, 29 August 1813, BFA, Nr. 72.

28. Bülow to L'Estoq, 29 August 1813, GStA, Rep. 91 A Nr. 156.

29. Boyen, *Erinnerungen*, ed. Schmidt, 2:636, 639.

30. Bülow's Tagesbfehl for 30 August 1813, GStA, Rep. 15 A Nr. 343; Charles John to Bülow, 30 August 1813, *Recueil*, 159.

31. Bülow's Tagesbefehl for 31 August 1813, GStA, Rep. 15 A Nr. 343; Charles John to Bülow, 31 August 1813, ibid., 163.

32. Boyen, *Erinnerungen*, ed. Schmidt, 2:639; Varnhagen von Ense, *Bülow*, 222.

33. The Allied ring slowly closed around Oudinot. Bülow marched to Schwabeck and moved his advance guard to Marzahna. Dobschütz moved to Kurzlipsdorf, the Russian cavalry to Lobbese and Niemegk, and Hirschfeld to Görzke, while the Swedes remained at Treuenbrietzen and Wintzingerode by Pflügkuff. Tauentzien's main body remained at Luckau.

34. Bülow had gained extensive knowledge of the terrain around Wittenberg during the spring campaign. In a letter to Adlercreutz he explained that from west to east on the right bank of the Elbe the suburbs of Apollensdorf, Kropstädt, and Gallin formed an arc around Wittenberg. The terrain in the middle and eastern regions offered Oudinot many advantages, including entrenchments. The sector's right or eastern flank was covered by a brook flowing from Zahna to the Elbe. An attack from Kropstädt in the center was complicated by thick woodlands that extended to Thießen. Boyen, *Erinnerungen*, ed. Nippold, 3:136–37, 568–70.

35. Boyen, *Erinnerungen*, ed. Schmidt, 2:641.

36. Wagner, *Pläne der Schlachten und Treffen*, 2:61.

37. Charles John to Dobschütz, 2 September 1813, *Recueil*, 173. Bülow's corps increased to 37,800 men.

38. Charles John to Tauentzien, 3 September 1813, ibid., 174–75.

39. Wagner, *Pläne der Schlachten und Treffen*, 2:62.

40. Bülow to Charles John, 4 September 1813, BFA, Nr. 73.

41. Ibid.

42. Bernadotte's apologists claimed that his strategy following Groß Beeren adhered strictly to the Trachenberg Plan; see Scott, *Bernadotte*, 94.

CHAPTER 11. DENNEWITZ

1. Napoleon to Berthier, 23 August 1813, *Correspondance*, No. 20442, 26:115–16.
2. See Cook, "Schwarzenberg at Dresden," 645–49.
3. For Napoleon's strategic considerations regarding projects against either Berlin or Prague, see "Note sur la situation général de mes affaires," 30 August 1813, *Correspondance*, No. 20492, 26:153–57.
4. Ibid.; Quistorp, *Geschichte der Nord-Armee*, 1:442.
5. Napoleon to Berthier, 2 September 1813, *Correspondance*, No. 20502, 26:162–63.
6. Ibid.; Berthier to Oudinot, 2 September 1813, AAT, C^{17} 180.
7. Berthier to Ney, 2 September 1813, AAT, C^{17} 180.
8. Ibid.
9. Berthier to Ney, 3 September 1813, AAT, C^{17} 180. According to Berthier, Napoleon would reach Macdonald's army at Bautzen on the fourth and then attack Blücher. "After the battle, His Majesty will march in great haste on Berlin."
10. "Ordre de mouvement pour 5 septembre 1813," 4 September 1813, AAT, C^{2} 155; Oudinot to Berthier, 7 September 1813, AAT, C^{2} 155; "Report of the 7th Corps," 9 September 1813, and "Report of 4th Corps," 9 September 1813, AAT, C^{2} 155.
11. Oudinot to Berthier, 7 September 1813, AAT, C^{2} 155; Wagner, *Pläne der Schlachten und Treffen*, 2:64–67.
12. Boyen, *Erinnerungen*, ed. Schmidt, 2:642–43.
13. Bülow to Adlercreutz, 5 September 1813, in Quistorp, *Geschichte der Nord-Armee*, 1:469.
14. Bülow to Charles John, 5 September 1813, in ibid., 468–69.
15. Charles John to Bülow and Wintzingerode, 5 September 1813, *Recueil*, 186.
16. Boyen, *Erinnerungen*, ed. Schmidt, 2:643. Boyen and his excellent staff work deserve the credit for correctly orienting Bülow. According to Bülow's report to the crown prince at 1:30 p.m., he had planned to withdraw northwest toward Bernadotte and away from Tauentzien and Ney.
17. Reiche, *Memoiren*, 1:307.
18. Boyen, *Erinnerungen*, ed. Schmidt, 2:643.
19. German archival material for this phase of the campaign unfortunately is very limited. The two Repositoria that contain Bülow's military correspondance, Rep. 15 A. Nrs. 250 and 298, have few documents pertaining to the first two weeks of September. "Geschichte der Nord-Armee im Jahre 1813, Drittes Heft," 26; Quistorp, *Geschichte der Nord-Armee*, 1:470.
20. Charles John to Bülow, 5 September 1813, Recueil, 187–88.
21. "Order of the Day," 5 September 1813, ibid., 189–90.
22. Bülow to Tauentzien, 5 September 1813, in Quistorp, *Geschichte der Nord-Armee*, 1:471.

23. The theory that Ney was leading his army eastward in an attempt to outflank and destroy Blücher's Army of Silesia does not enjoy the support of the archival and published registers of the French army. See Berthier to Ney, 3 September 1813, AAT, C[17] 180.

24. "Orders," 5 September 1813; Oudinot to Berthier, 7 September 1813; Reynier to Berthier, 7 September 1813; "Report of the 4th Corps," 9 September 1813; Bertrand to Ney, 10 September 1813; "Report of the 7th Corps," 9 September 1813, AAT, C[2] 155; Petre, *Napoleon's Last Campaign*, 272–75. There are several discrepancies in the after-action reports filed by the French commanders regarding Ney's orders for the morning of the sixth. Confusion and poor maps played a role, while the "blame-game" accounts for the attempts of each corps commander to clear his name.

25. Boyen, *Erinnerungen*, ed. Schmidt, 2:645.

26. Bülow to Charles John, 6 September 1813, in Quistorp, *Geschichte der Nord-Armee*, 1:473.

27. Wagner, *Pläne der Schlachten und Treffen*, 2:67.

28. Boyen, *Erinnerungen*, ed. Schmidt, 2:645.

29. "Geschichte der Nord-Armee, Drittes Heft," 32–33; Wagner, *Pläne der Schlachten und Treffen*, 2:70.

30. "Report of 4th Corps," 9 September 1813; Bertrand to Ney, 10 September 1813; "Report of the 15th Division of the 4th Corps," 9 September 1813, AAT, C[2] 155.

31. Reiche, *Memoiren*, 1:311.

32. The battlefield at Dennewitz is well preserved and looks much as it did in 1813. With the exception of Niedergörsdorf, which has expanded somewhat, the other three villages have experienced little growth. The district government in Jüterbog is working to preserve the battlefield as a historic park. Numerous monuments, a battlefield walking tour, and a museum in Dennewitz dedicated to the battle make a trip to the battlefield worthwhile. By train the trip from Berlin takes almost two hours, and visitors can stay at the Wirtshaus zum Grafen Bülow, a cozy inn with comfortable beds, modern bathrooms, and an interesting menu that features such dishes as "General Bülow's Siegesschmaus" (victory feast) and "Napoleon's Henkersmahlzeit" (last meal before execution).

33. The Nuthe was later extended south to Dennewitz, so that modern maps no longer use the name Ahebach.

34. "Geschichte der Nord-Armee, Drittes Heft," 39–40; "Report of the 4th Corps," 9 September 1813, and "Report of the 7th Corps," 9 September 1813, AAT, C[2] 155; Meinecke, *Boyen*, 1:325–26; Wagner, *Pläne der Schlachten und Treffen*, 2:69.

35. "Order of the Day," 6 September 1813, *Recueil*, 193–94.

36. Bernadotte quoted in Schinkel, *Minnen ur Sveriges nyare historia*, 7:242. Bülow's actions sparked a historiographic debate. He has been accused of ruining Bernadotte's plans to concentrate the entire army at Lobbese to destroy Ney. Had it not been for the Prussians, however, Ney's army would have cleared Jüterbog and reached Dahme before the slow-moving Army of North Germany would have been able to react. Ernst Wiehr, in *Napoleon und Bernadotte*, 251, supports Bernadotte's conduct, particularly in the days prior

to Dennewitz. As with Groß Beeren, Swederus, in *Schwedens Politik und Kriege*, 137–219, devotes three chapters in his engaging attempt to refute Prusso-German interpretations of Bernadotte's lethargy before and during the battle of Dennewitz. The Swedish historian blames inaccurate reports from the Prussians for Bernadotte's conduct at Dennewitz. Moreover, he vehemently denies that the crown prince ordered Borstell to Eckmannsdorf. Richard Haedecke's 1915 psychological critique of Bernadotte's action before Dennewitz favors him rather than Bülow in "Bernadotte und die Schlacht bei Dennewitz," 46. Concerning Dennewitz, Delbrück, in *Weltgeschichte*, 4:479, states that "Bülow has the claim to fame as a heroic soldier, but no more." Meinecke, in *Boyen*, 1:329, claims that Bernadotte could have arrived earlier and more decisively at Dennewitz if he had been more animated. Ulmann, in *Geschichte der Befreiungskriege*, 2:85, exclusively credits the Prussians with the victory at Dennewitz. In *Napoleon's Last Campaign*, 277–78, Petre, who follows Friederich's *Die Befreiungskriege*, 2:190–92, claims that Bernadotte cannot be blamed for delay or inactivity since Ney's objective was not clear and the Swedes and Russians marched fifteen miles in six and one-half hours.

37. Tauentzien's Landwehr included two regiments from the Kurmark, one from the Neumark, and one from Silesia. His cavalry consisted of Landwehr regiments from Neumark, East Prussia, Pomerania, and Berlin.

38. Ney to Napoleon, 7 September 1813, AN, AF IV, Carton 1662^{B}, plaquette 3.

39. Boyen, *Erinnerungen*, ed. Schmidt, 2:649.

40. Quistorp, *Geschichte der Nord-Armee*, 1:476.

41. Reiche, *Memoiren*, 1:313; Schinkel, *Minnen ur Sveriges nyare historia*, 7:243.

42. Oudinot to Berthier, 7 September 1813, AAT, C^2 155.

43. Friedrich was the brother of Carl von Clausewitz.

44. "Geschichte der Nord-Armee, Drittes Heft," 101. The First Battalion of the Fourth Reserve Regiment lost 7 officers and 318 men in the battle.

45. Boyen, *Erinnerungen*, ed. Schmidt, 2:651.

46. The battle account has been drawn from "Report of the 7th Corps," 9 September 1813; "Report of the 4th Corps," 9 September 1813; and Bertrand to Ney, 10 September 1813; Reynier to Berthier, 7 September 1813; and "Report of the 15th Division of the 4th Corps," 9 September 1813, AAT, C^2 155; Boyen, *Erinnerungen*, ed. Schmidt, 2:649–51; Friccius, *Geschichte des Krieges*, 1:343, 349; "Geschichte der Nord-Armee, Drittes Heft," 29–80; Petre, *Napoleon's Last Campaign*, 272–78; Quistorp, *Geschichte der Nord-Armee*, 1:488–531.

47. Quistorp, *Geschichte der Nord-Armee*, 1:524–31.

48. GStA Rep. 91 A Nrs. 97 and 100.

49. Quistorp, *Geschichte der Nord-Armee*, 1:542.

50. Charles John to Bülow, 7 September 1813, BFA, Nr. 80a.</>

CHAPTER 12. AT THE RUBICON

1. Reynier to Berthier, 7 September 1813; "Report of the 7th Corps," 9 September 1813; "Report of the 12th Corps," 7 September 1813; "Report of

the Chief of Staff of the Saxon Army von Holtzendorff," 8 September 1813, AAT, C2 155; Ney to Napoleon, 7 September 1813, AN, AF IV, Carton 1662B, plaquette 3; Lebrun to Napoleon, 7 September 1813, Fabry, *Étude sur les opérations de l'empereur*, 21–22.

2. Reynier to Berthier, 7 September 1813, and "Report of the 7th Corps," 9 September 1813, AAT, C2 155; Holtzendorff, *Geschichte der Königlich Sächsischen Leichten Infanterie*, 140–41.

3. "Geschichte der Nord-Armee, Drittes Heft," 84–85.

4. Ney to Napoleon, 7 September 1813, AN, AF IV, Carton 1662B, plaquette 3; Lebrun to Napoleon, 7 September 1813, in Fabry, *Étude sur les opérations de l'empereur*, 21–22.

5. Wobeser's infantry consisted of six West Prussian Landwehr battalions, one East Prussian Landwehr battalion, and one Neumark Landwehr battalion.

6. "Geschichte der Nord-Armee, Drittes Heft," 90–97; Petre, *Napoleon's Last Campaign*, 275–76.

7. Quistorp, *Geschichte der Nord-Armee*, 1:538–41.

8. "Geschichte der Nord-Armee, Drittes Heft," 92–93.

9. Bülow to Pauline, 7 September 1813, BFA, Nr. 79.

10. Bülow to Pauline, 19 September 1813, BFA, Nr. 90. Bülow wrote that the Grand Cross of the Swedish Order of the Sword "does not matter much to me."

11. Ney to Berthier, 8 and 10 September 1813, AAT, C2 155.

12. Ney to Napoleon, 7 September 1813, AN, AF IV, Carton 1662B, plaquette 3.

13. Ney to Napoleon, 7 September 1813, AN, AF IV, Carton 1662B, plaquette 3; Ney to Berthier, 8 and 10 September 1813, AAT, C2 155; Lebrun to Napoleon, 7 September 1813, in Fabry, *Étude sur les opérations de l'empereur*, 21–22; "Geschichte der Nord-Armee, Drittes Heft," 94–95.

14. Franquemont cited in Fabry, *Étude sur les opérations de l'empereur*, 52–54.

15. Ney to Berthier, 8 and 10 September 1813, AAT, C2 155.

16. Fabry, *Étude sur les opérations de l'empereur*, 52–54.

17. La Poype to Berthier, 9 September 1813, AAT, C2 155.

18. Berthier to Ney, 9 September 1813, AAT, C17 180.

19. Berthier to Ney, 10 September 1813, AAT, C17 180; Napoleon to Berthier, 10 September 1813, *Correspondance*, No. 20537, 26:184–85.

20. Berthier to Ney, 10 September 1813, AAT, C17 180.

21. Fabry, *Étude sur les opérations de l'empereur*, 104.

22. Ney to Berthier, 13 September 1813, AAT, C2 155; Fabry, *Étude sur les opérations de l'empereur*, 143–44.

23. Reynier to Berthier, 7 September 1813, AAT, C2 155.

24. "Situation de la 7e corps," 14 September 1813, AAT, C2 541; "Beiträge zur militärischen Geschichte Sachsens," 231. The Saxons claimed to have lost 28 officers and 3,313 men between 30 August and 7 September, of which 16 officers and 1,082 men were killed and wounded. Material losses amounted to 312 horses, 7 six-pound guns, 2 twelve-pound guns, 3 eight-pound howitzers, and 40 wagons.

25. "Situation de la 4^{e} corps," 14 September 1813, AAT, C^{2} 539.

26. "Situation de la 12^{e} corps," 14 September 1813, AAT, C^{2} 539.

27. "Geschichte der Nord-Armee, Drittes Heft," 98.

28. Oudinot to Berthier, 8 September 1813, AAT, C^{2} 155; Ney to Berthier, 12 September 1813, AAT, C^{2} 155; Ney to Berthier, 13 September 1813, AAT, C^{2} 155; Bertrand to Berthier, 13 September 1813, AAT, C^{2} 155.

29. Ney to Berthier, 10 September 1813, AAT, C^{2} 155.

30. Fabry, *Étude sur les opérations de l'empereur*, 93.

31. Ney to Berthier, 10 September 1813, AAT, C^{2} 155.

32. Oudinot to Berthier, 8 September 1813, AAT, C^{2} 155.

33. Bertrand to Berthier, 13 September 1813, AAT, C^{2} 155.

34. Raglowich to Maximilian, 9 September 1813, in Fabry, *Étude sur les opérations de l'empereur*, 34.

35. Franquemont to Friedrich, 10 September 1813, in ibid., 43–44.

36. Schroeder, *Transformation of European Politics*, 478–79.

37 Kraehe, *Metternich's German Policy*, 1:197–98.

38. Schroeder, *Transformation of European Politics*, 478; Nipperdey, *Germany from Napoleon to Bismarck*, 71.

39. Kraehe, *Metternich's German Policy*, 1:203.

40. Kissinger, *A World Restored*, 97–98.

41. Kraehe, *Metternich's German Policy*, 1:205, 207.

42. "It has commonly been held," maintains Kraehe, "that Metternich scored a smashing victory over the gullible Prussians, persuading them that the phrase meant merely immediate liberation from Napoleon and not, as he really intended, lasting independence from a future central authority. This charge is not entirely unfounded, but it arises from a distorted conception of the situation. In arguing against a German-union clause at this point Metternich probably did call it inopportune rather than intrinsically wrong, and maintained that the wording finally adopted simply kept the issue open. But this was his honest opinion." Ibid., 205–6.

43. Ross, *European Diplomatic History*, 342. "How can one achieve unity," asked the Hanoverian minister, Count Ernst von Münster, "when one begins by guaranteeing the absolute independence of the states of Germany?" Quoted in Kraehe, *Metternich's German Policy*, 1:217.

44. Schroeder, *Transformation of European Politics*, 478–82. Schroeder argues that Russia maintained its leadership of the coalition, while the older works of Kissinger, *A World Restored*, 82, and Kraehe, *Metternich's German Policy*, 1:206–7, although they differ in their interpretations of Metternich's motives, claim that leadership of the alliance securely belonged to Austria.

45. Ney to Berthier, 9 September 1813, and Ney to Berthier, 10 September 1813, AAT, C^{2} 155.

46. Ney to Napoleon, 7 September 1813, AN, AF IV, Carton 1662^{B}, plaquette 3.

47. Ney to Berthier, 8 September 1813, AAT, C^{2} 155.

48. Ney to Reynier, 8 September 1813, AN, AF IV, Carton 1662^{B}, plaquette 3.

49. Fabry, *Étude sur les opérations de l'empereur*, 52–54.

50. Reynier to Ney, 10 September 1813, AN, AF IV, Carton 1662[B], plaquette 3.

51. Reynier to Berthier, 10 September 1813, AAT, C^2 155.

52. Raglowich to Maximilian, 9 September 1813, in Fabry, *Étude sur les opérations de l'empereur*, 34.

53. Ney to Berthier, 12 September 1813, AAT, C^2 155.

54. Boyen, *Erinnerungen*, ed. Nippold, 3:571–72.

55. Tenth Bulletin, "Battle of Dennewitz," 8 September 1813, in *Recueil*, 201–8; Philippart, *Memoirs and Campaigns of Charles John*, 231–38.

56. Scott, *Bernadotte and the Fall of Napoleon*, 101.

57. Varnhagen von Ense, *Bülow*, 252–53.

58. Bülow to Pauline, 19 September 1813, BFA, Nr. 90.

59. Bülow to Pauline, 29 September 1813, BFA, Nr. 101.

60. According to Scott, after Dennewitz a biased Pozzo's "suspicions of Bernadotte were as strong as his hatred of Napoleon." Scott speculated that perhaps Pozzo felt slighted since two commoners had been elevated to thrones, while "the genius of Pozzo di Borgo" had been overlooked. Nesselrode to Pozzo, 12 August 1813, in Scott, *Bernadotte and the Fall of Napoleon*, 98.

61. Pozzo di Borgo to Nesselrode, 7 September 1813, and Vincent to Metternich, 7 September 1813, in Scott, *Bernadotte and the Fall of Napoleon*, 96.

62. Thornton to Castlereagh, 8 September 1813, in Castlereagh, *Correspondence, Despatches and Other Papers*, 9:49.

63. Skjölderbrand, *Excellensen Grefve A. F. Skjölderbrands Memoarer*, 5:51; Scott, *Bernadotte and the Fall of Napoleon*, 96.

64. Thornton to Castlereagh, 8 September 1813, Castlereagh, *Correspondence, Despatches and Other Papers*, 9:49.

65. Pozzo di Borgo to Nesselrode, 7 September 1813, in Pflugk-Harttung, *Illustrierte Geschichte der Befreiungskriege*, 2:234–35.

66. Scott, *Bernadotte and the Fall of Napoleon*, 97.

67. Alexander to Charles John, 7 September 1813, in Scott, *Bernadotte and the Fall of Napoleon*, 104.

68. Castlereagh to Thornton, 24 September 1813, Castlereagh, *Correspondence, Despatches and Other Papers*, 9:51.

69. Apologists claim that Schwarzenberg's inactivity prevented Bernadotte from crossing the Elbe. See Scott, *Bernadotte and the Fall of Napoleon*, 102; Swederus, *Schwedens Politik und Kriege*, 2:249–77.

70. Charles John to Wallmoden, 8 September 1813, *Recueil*, 213–15.

71. Boyen, *Erinnerungen*, ed. Schmidt, 2:657.

72. Charles John to Bülow, 8 September 1813, *Recueil*, 211–12; Charles John to Tauentzien, 8 September 1813, ibid., 208.

73. Charles John to Wintzingerode, 8 September 1813, ibid., 209–11.

74. "Order of the Day," 9 September 1813, ibid., 215–16.

75. "Order of the Day," 10 September 1813, ibid., 222–23.

76. Bülow to Pauline, 9 September 1813, BFA, Nr. 85.

77. Krusemarck to Bülow, 12 September 1813, GStA, Rep. 92, Nachlaß Albrecht, Nr. 43.

78. Charles John to Tauentzien, 11 September 1813, *Recueil*, 228–29.

79. "Order of the Day," 11 September 1813, ibid., 229–32; Charles John to Bülow, 12 September 1813, ibid., 233; "Order of the Day," 13 September 1813, ibid., 238–42.

80. Bülow to Adlercreutz, 14 September 1813, in Boyen, *Erinnerungen*, ed. Nippold, 3:162–63, 578–81.

CHAPTER 13. CROSSING THE RUBICON

1. Chandler, *Campaigns of Napoleon*, 916.
2. Napoleon to Daru, 23 September 1813, *Correspondance*, No. 20619, 26:236–38.
3. Petre, *Napoleon's Last Campaign*, 279.
4. Marmont quoted in ibid., 281.
5. Berthier to Ney, 10 September 1813, AAT, C^{17} 180; Napoleon to Berthier, 10 September 1813, *Correspondance*, No. 20537, 26:184–85.
6. Petre, *Napoleon's Last Campaign*, 292.
7. Gneisenau quoted in Friederich, *Die Befreiungskriege*, 2:214.
8. Ibid.
9. Blücher quoted in ibid., 2:215.
10. Ibid.
11. Charles John to Tauentzien, 15 September 1813, *Recueil*, 248–49.
12. "Order of the Day," 15 September 1813, ibid., 254–55.
13. Charles John to Blücher, 15 September 1813, ibid., 250–52. Bernadotte obviously exaggerated the importance of Berlin.
14. Ibid.
15. Bülow to Adlercreutz, 14 September 1813, in Boyen, *Erinnerungen*, ed. Nippold, 3:162–63, 578–81. Since the Prussians would remain on the right bank of the Elbe, Wittenberg could maintain communications with Ney's army on the left bank. Bülow argued that military history provided several examples of the consequences of failing to encircle a fortress totally: either the besieging force suffered considerable losses or the operation had to be aborted.
16. Charles John to Bülow, 15 September 1813, *Recueil*, 253–54.
17. Barton, *Bernadotte: Prince and King*, 92–95; Scott, *Bernadotte and the Fall of Napoleon*, 104; Londonderry, *Narrative of the War in Germany and France*, 120 (quotation).
18. Boyen, *Erinnerungen*, ed. Schmidt, 2:660.
19. "Order of the Day," 15 September 1813, *Recueil*, 254–56.
20. Boyen, *Erinnerungen*, ed. Schmidt, 2:661–62.
21. As for the charge of insubordination, apologists have attempted to vindicate Bernadotte's operations in 1813. They follow the crown prince's example and accuse Bülow of insubordination and interfering with Bernadotte's strategic plans. The Swedish historian Swederus, in *Schwedens Politik und Kriege*, 1:249–55, claims that Bernadotte's army was too small to carry the war across the Elbe and that due to Schwarzenberg's inactivity following the defeat at Dresden on 27 August Bernadotte did not cross the Elbe. Scott, in *Bernadotte and the Fall of Napoleon*, 97–98, claims that after Dennewitz the campaign settled into a war of attrition and that Bernadotte "dared not advance

with his Swedes" but that the "hot-headed Prussians and the military-political agents urged Bernadotte to press boldly forward." Scott maintains that Bernadotte would not move forward until Schwarzenberg began offensive operations and that the crown prince "insisted on possessing the French posts before he advanced." As for Wittenberg, Scott notes that disputes began when the crown prince ordered Bülow, "who itched for action, to take the important fortification of Wittenberg." Scott concedes that the task was "beyond Bülow's means and filled to overflowing his cup of resentment; he remonstrated in offensive terms." A contemporary of the period, Robert Wilson, in *General Wilson's Journal*, ed. Anthony Brett-James, 124–25, remarks that the sacrifice of Bernadotte's communications by crossing the Elbe "was too much to require of him." Barton equates Bernadotte's crossing of the Elbe with the Rubicon, since he would be "face to face with Napoleon, with the Elbe between him and Sweden, and a network of fortresses threatening his rear and flanks." Barton, *Bernadotte: Prince and King*, 95.

22. Boyen, *Erinnerungen*, ed. Schmidt, 2:661–62. Boyen recalled that "ironically, if it was a crime to be a member of the Tugenbund, this crime I had committed, but not Bülow, who was never a member of this society."

23. Ibid.

24. Charles John to Tauentzien, 15 September 1813 and 16 September 1813, *Recueil*, 249, 260; "Order of the Day," 15 September 1813, ibid., 257. As for the rest of the Fourth Corps, Dobschütz remained with Tauentzien, but the crown prince had transferred Hirschfeld's brigade to Bülow to conduct the siege of Wittenberg, and Putlitz occupied the right bank of the Elbe between Magdeburg and Havelberg.

25. Tauentzien quoted in Fabry, *Étude sur les opérations de l'empereur*, 191.

26. Charles John to Tauentzien, 16 September 1813, *Recueil*, 260–61.

27. Fabry, *Étude sur les opérations de l'empereur*, 211.

28. Bülow to Charles John, 17 September 1813, in ibid., 223. Fabry is very critical of Bülow's suggestion to retreat to Dahme. He notes that "Bülow's proposal proves that he could easily allow himself to be influenced . . . the movement that he proposed would have certainly had a deplorable effect on morale and would have allowed the Emperor to obtain the result that he sought: to relieve Leipzig." Fabry is likewise critical of the accounts furnished by Quistorp and Boyen. The French historian accuses his German counterparts of intentionally ignoring Bülow's suggestion and unfairly condemning the prince-royal for refusing to consider offensive operations.

29. Charles John to Bülow, 17 September, *Recueil*, 263.

30. Charles John to Tauentzien, 17 September 1813, ibid., 262–63.

31. Quistorp, *Geschichte der Nord-Armee*, 2:29.

32. Tauentzien to Blücher, 18 September 1813, in Fabry, *Étude sur les opérations de L'empereur*, 241.

33. Charles John to Tauentzien, 19 September 1813, *Recueil*, 265–66.

34. Bülow to Adlercreutz, 18 September 1813, in Boyen, *Erinnerungen*, ed. Nippold, 3:595–97.

35. Berthier to Ney, 19 September 1813, AAT, C^{17} 180.

36. Adlercreutz to Bülow, 22 September 1813, BFA, Nr. 92a.

37. Adlercreutz to Bülow, 20 September 1813, BFA, Nr. 90a.

38. Varnhagen von Ense, *Bülow*, 258.

39. Charles John to Bülow, 23 September 1813, *Recueil*, 279–81.

40. Märtens to Knesebeck, 6 October 1813, in Quistorp, *Geschichte der Nord-Armee*, 2:20–21.

41. Vincent to Metternich, 24 September 1813, and Pozzo to Nesselrode, 25 September 1813, in Scott, *Bernadotte and the Fall of Napoleon*, 103; Barton, *Bernadotte: Prince and King*, 96; Pingaud, *Bernadotte, Napoléon et les Bourbons*, 226.

42. Krusemarck to Knesebeck, 27 September 1813, in Quistorp, *Geschichte der Nord-Armee*, 2:87.

43. Vincent to Metternich, 24 September 1813, in Scott, *Bernadotte and the Fall of Napoleon*, 105.

44. Petre, *Napoleon's Last Campaign*, 295.

45. Horward, "Napoleon and the Transformation of War," 84.

46. Chandler, *Campaigns of Napoleon*, 916.

47. Napoleon to Murat, 23 September 1813, *Correspondance*, No. 20618, 26:235–36.

48. Maude, *Leipzig Campaign*, 237.

49. Napoleon to Macdonald, 4 October 1813, *Correspondance*, No. 20693, 26:290.

50. Bülow to Adlercreutz, 23 September 1813, BFA, Nr. 91b.

51. Bülow to Charles John, 24 September 1813, BFA, Nr. 93; Charles John to Bülow, 24 September 1813, *Recueil*, 283.

52. "Order of the Day," 24 September 1813, BFA, Brief Nr. 94.

53. Boyen, *Erinnerungen*, ed. Schmidt, 2:666.

54. Bülow to Thornton, Vincent, Pozzo, and Krusemarck, 25 September 1813, BFA, Nr. 96. Bülow outlined two projects, which he insisted "could change the course of the war at this very moment." His first plan called for a simultaneous crossing of the Elbe at Rosslau and Elster to envelop Ney's army near Kemberg. After such a devastating victory, he predicted the Saxons would defect. Bülow believed the final destruction of the Army of Berlin would force Napoleon to detach a new force to hold the Army of North Germany. This further attrition of French forces would facilitate Blücher's advance to the Elbe and Schwarzenberg's march from Bohemia to Saxony. Bülow's second plan called for the Army of North Germany to leave one corps to mask Wittenberg, while the remainder marched southeast along the right bank of the Elbe to locate and destroy French forces between Torgau and Grossenhain. The Army of North Germany would operate in the rear and the flank of the French army facing Blücher so that he could reach the Elbe unhindered. All three Allied armies would then unite in a joint operation. To justify this operation Bülow used Bernadotte's own concern for Berlin and North Germany. If Napoleon defeated Blücher, the Army of Silesia would be forced to retreat to Silesia. In this case Bülow believed that Napoleon would reinforce Ney, who would cross the Elbe at Torgau and continue his operation against Berlin and North Germany. In defense of Prussia as well as Bernadotte's line of retreat through North Ger-

many to Sweden, Bülow explained that the theater of war had to be transferred once and for all to Saxony.

55. Adlercreutz to Bülow, 24 September 1813, *Recueil*, 281; Charles John to Hirschfeld, ibid., 283.

56. Boyen, *Erinnerungen*, ed. Schmidt, 667; Tauentzien quoted in Quistorp, *Geschichte der Nord-Armee*, 2:86.

57. Bülow to Pauline, 25 September 1813, BFA, Nr. 97.

58. Charles John to Bülow, 27–28 September 1813, *Recueil*, 295–96.

59. The Swedes lost a little over 600 men during the fighting on 28 and 29 September. Quistorp, *Geschichte der Nord-Armee*, 2:90–97.

60. Bülow to Pauline, 29 September 1813, BFA, Nr. 100.

61. Donald D. Horward to the author, "Notes at Wittenberg, 15 August 1978," n.d.

62. Boyen, *Erinnerungen*, ed. Schmidt, 2:668.

63. Quistorp, *Geschichte der Nord-Armee*, 2:56–57.

64. Varnhagen von Ense, *Bülow*, 266.

65. Bülow to Blücher, 1 October 1813, BFA, Nr. 102a.

66. Bülow to Pauline, 2 and 3 October 1813, BFA, Nr. 105.

67. Gneisenau to Boyen, 23 September 1813, GStA, Rep. 92 Nachlaß Gneisenau Packet Nr. 53a.

68. Gneisenau to Clausewitz, 26 September 1813, GStA, Rep. 92, Nachlaß Gneisenau Packet Nr. 53a. Clausewitz, who served as a Russian lieutenant-colonel, was chief of staff of Wallmoden's corps on the lower Elbe.

69. Boyen, *Erinnerungen*, ed. Schmidt, 1:362–63.

70. Varnhagen von Ense, *Bülow*, 90–91.

71. Krusemarck to Frederick William, 2 October 1813, GStA, Rep. 92, Nachlaß Albrecht, Nr. 43.

72. Frederick William to Bülow, 3 October 1813, GStA, Rep. 15 A Nr. 334.

73. Petre, *Napoleon's Last Campaign*, 357.

74. See Scott, *Bernadotte and the Fall of Napoleon*, 99.

75. Petre, *Napoleon's Last Campaign*, 295.

76. Nicolson, in *Congress of Vienna*, 51, adequately summarizes the spirit of coalition warfare that Bernadotte at times blatantly disregarded: "The basis of any alliance, or coalition, is an agreement between two or more sovereign states to subordinate their interests to a single purpose."

77. Rochechouart, *Souvenirs sur la révolution, l'empire, et la restauration*, 245–57 (quotation on 253). For a thorough discussion of Bernadotte's aims, see Pingaud, *Bernadotte, Napoléon et les Bourbons*, 213–313.

CHAPTER 14. LEIPZIG

1. Napoleon to Clark, 27 September 1813, *Correspondance*, No. 20646, 26:256–57.

2. Various accounts stated Yorck's losses at around 1,600, while Bertrand lost 2,000 and 11 guns. See Friederich, *Die Befreiungskriege*, 2:229–34; Petre, *Napoleon's Last Campaign*, 297–99.

3. Charles John to Vorontsov, 3 October 1813, *Recueil,* 322.

4. Charles John to Bülow, 3 October 1813, *Recueil,* 320; Charles John to Hirschfeld, 3 October 1813, ibid., 321; Charles John to Stedingk, 3 October 1813, ibid.; Charles John to Tauentzien, 3 October 1813, ibid., 323; Charles John to Wintzingerode, 3 October 1813, ibid.

5. Charles John to Bülow, 3 October 1813, ibid., 320.

6. Charles John to Wintzingerode, 3 October 1813, ibid.; Charles John to Tauentzien, 3 October 1813, ibid.; Adlercreutz to Boyd, 3 October 1813, ibid., 323–24.

7. Adlercreutz to Bülow, 4 October 1813, ibid., 329.

8. Boyen, *Erinnerungen,* ed. Schmidt, 2:674.

9. Adlercreutz to Bülow, 5 October 1813, *Recueil,* 334.

10. Adlercreutz to Wintzingerode, 5 October 1813, ibid., 332–33.

11. Petre, *Napoleon's Last Campaign,* 307.

12. "Order of the Day," 6 October 1813, *Recueil,* 338–40.

13. Petre, *Napoleon's Last Campaign,* 306.

14. Gneisenau to Boyen, 7 and 8 October 1813, GStA, Rep. 92, Nachlaß Gneisenau Packet Nr. 53a; "Order of the Day," 8 October 1813, *Recueil,* 347.

15. Napoleon to Murat, 5 October 1813, *Correspondance,* No. 20698, 26:292–93.

16. Napoleon to Marmont, 6 October 1813, ibid., No. 20705, 26:296.

17. Napoleon to Berthier, 9 October 1813, ibid., No. 20731, 26:311–12; Napoleon to Murat, 9 October 1813, ibid., No. 20735, 26:313–14.

18. Wartenburg, *Napoleon as a General,* 2:338.

19. Chandler, *Campaigns of Napoleon,* 917.

20. The account of this meeting can be found in Maude, *Leipzig Campaign,* 243.

21. On the eleventh Bülow and Wintzingerode crossed the Saale at Wettin, while the Swedes crossed at Alsleben. Thümen remained at Wittenberg, and Wobeser reached Torgau. "Order of the Day," 10 and 11 October 1813, in Boyen, *Erinnerungen,* ed. Nippold, 3:185, 657–58. Charles John to Bülow, 8 October 1813, *Recueil,* 345–46; "Order of the Day," 10 October 1813, ibid., 354–55.

22. Adlercreutz to Bülow, 10 October 1813, *Recueil,* 355.

23. Boyen, *Erinnerungen,* ed. Schmidt, 2:676.

24. Ibid.

25. Napoleon to Ney, 12 October 1813, *Correspondance,* No. 20765, 26:332.

26. Bernadotte quoted in Boyen, *Erinnerungen,* ed. Schmidt, 2:678.

27. Gneisenau to Boyen, 13 October 1813, GStA, Rep. 92, Nachlaß Gneisenau Packet Nr. 53a.

28. "Order of the Day," 14 October 1813, *Recueil,* 366.

29. "Order of the Day," 15 October 1813, ibid., 369–71.

30. Chandler, *Campaigns of Napoleon,* 924.

31. "Order of the Day," 16 October 1813, *Recueil,* 372.

32. Boyen, *Erinnerungen,* ed. Schmidt, 2:679.

33. Chandler, *Campaigns of Napoleon,* 932.

34. Petre, *Napoleon's Last Campaign,* 353.

35. Varnhagen von Ense, *Bülow*, 273.

36. Boyen, *Erinnerungen*, ed. Schmidt, 2:679; Petre, *Napoleon's Last Campaign*, 341–47.

37. "Order of the Day," 16 October 1813, *Recueil*, 374.

38. "Order of the Day," 17 October 1813, ibid., 375.

39. "Korpsbericht über die Schlacht bei Leipzig," in Boyen, *Erinnerungen*, ed. Nippold, 3:663.

40. Charles John to Blücher, 17 October 1813, GStA, Rep. 92 Nachlaß Gneisenau Packet Nr. 18.

41. "Order of the Day," 18 October 1813, *Recueil*, 378–79.

42. Scott, *Bernadotte and the Fall of Napoleon*, 114.

43. Petre, *Napoleon's Last Campaign*, 370.

44. Boyen, *Erinnerungen*, ed. Schmidt, 2:684.

45. Accounts of Bülow's operations on the eighteenth have been drawn from "Korpsbericht über die Schlacht bei Leipzig," in Boyen, *Erinnerungen*, ed. Nippold, 3:192–93, 663–64; Friederich, *Die Befreiungskriege*, 2:330–49; Varnhagen von Ense, *Bülow*, 275–82.

46. Chandler, *Campaigns of Napoleon*, 935; Petre, *Napoleon's Last Campaign*, 368, 373–75, 378.

47. Petre, *Napoleon's Last Campaign*, 373.

48. Ibid., 377.

49. Ibid., 379.

50. Boyen, *Erinnerungen*, ed. Schmidt, 2:687.

51. For accounts of Bülow's operations on the nineteenth, see "Korpsbericht über die Schlacht bei Leipzig," in Boyen, *Erinnerungen*, ed. Nippold, 3:193–95, 664–65; Friccius, *Geschichte des Krieges*, 1:507–45; Petre, *Napoleon's Last Campaign*, 381 (quotation); Varnhagen von Ense, *Bülow*, 282–89; Friederich, *Die Befreiungskriege*, 2:349–60.

52. Petre, *Napoleon's Last Campaign*, 380.

53. Friederich, *Die Befreiungskriege*, 2:349–60.

54. Chandler, *Campaigns of Napoleon*, 936.

55. Palmer, *Bernadotte*, 207–9.

CONCLUSION

1. According to Petre, these forces "would probably have made all the difference at the battle." Petre, *Napoleon's Last Campaign*, 108.

2. Napoleon to Berthier, 24 May 1813, *Correspondance*, No. 20037, 25:312–13.

3. Such a French operation would have to consist of a significant number of troops.

4. Jany, *Geschichte der königlichen preußischen Armee*, 4:90.

5. Elting, "Myths of the Napoleonic Period," 503.

6. Napoleon to Macdonald, 16 August 1813, *Correspondance*, No. 20390, 26:69–70.

7. According to Napoleon's "Note sur la situation général de mes affaires," 30 August 1813, *Correspondance*, No. 20492, 26:153–57, with his reinforcements

the Army of Berlin would exceed 80,000 men. Davout's force at Hamburg would have provided an additional 25,000. Even so, Bernadotte's army still would have maintained a numerical superiority. Napoleon's presence on the field would have been more than enough compensation, however, had the Army of North Germany accepted battle, which would not have been the case. In accordance with the Trachenberg Plan, Bernadotte would have had full justification to order a general retreat before Napoleon's onslaught, just as Blücher had in August.

8. Napoleon to Ney, 12 August 1813, *Correspondance*, No. 20360, 26:34–36.

9. Napoleon to St.-Cyr, 17 August 1813, ibid., No. 20398, 26:77–78.

10. Napoleon to Berthier, 2 September 1813, *Correspondance*, No. 20502, 26:162–63.

11. Wartenburg, *Napoleon as a General*, 2:280.

12. Connelly, *Blundering to Glory*, 190.

13. Although the Trachenberg Plan was rooted in the eighteenth-century concepts of maneuvering against an enemy's communications and avoiding a confrontation with Napoleon, the battles at Groß Beeren, the Katzbach, Hagelberg, Dresden, Dennewitz, and Leipzig suggest that the Allies were well aware of the need to engage and destroy the enemy army. Prudence should not be confused with ignorance. See the discussion in Gallaher, "Strategic Success and Failure in 1813: A Commentary."

14. Petre, *Napoleon's Last Campaign*, 48.

15. Kissinger, *A World Restored*, 65.

16. For a discussion on the importance of Hamburg, see Muir, *Britain and the Defeat of Napoleon*, 252.

17. Napoleon was well aware of the shortcomings of his chief lieutenants. On 22 August he wrote that in his current situation his greatest obstacle was the lack of confidence his generals had in themselves; "wherever I am not personally present, the enemy's forces appear considerable to them." Napoleon to Maret, 22 August 1813, *Correspondance*, No. 20437, 26:112–13.

18. Yorck von Wartenburg alleges that as early as 26 January 1813 Napoleon's orders no longer "showed the clearness of judgement with which he formerly estimated facts." Instead Yorck finds evidence "of that falsifying and self-deceiving process which had taken such fast hold on his mind." Wartenburg, *Napoleon as a General*, 2:237.

19. Lévy, *Napoléon intime*, 161.

20. Geyl, *Napoleon: For and Against*, 253.

21. Rosenberg contends that after 1807 French occupation troops diverted the discontent of Prussia's lower classes and "had a profound effect upon the alignment of social forces." Rosenberg, *Bureaucracy, Aristocracy, and Autocracy*, 204.

22. Showalter explains that "operationally the Prussian army of the Wars of Liberation was much more the force of a *Kleinstaat* than its Frederician predecessor had ever been. Not intended to strike decisive, independent blows, it was governed by tactical doctrines stressing the use of combination punches to develop and discover weak spots, followed by breakthroughs. . . .

It would be another half-century before Prussia sought to play an independent military role." Showalter, "Hubertusberg to Auerstädt," 333.

23. Kitchen, *Military History of Germany*, 57.

24. Ibid., 55.

25. The Prussian official Theodor von Schön lamented that the enthusiasm for king and country that the Landsturm had inspired was viewed as Jacobinism and sansculottism. Meinecke, *Boyen*, 1:299.

26. Grunwald, *Life of Baron Stein*, 126. In France, according to the Law of 19 Fructidor An VI (September 1798), "the defense of his country" was "the duty of every citizen," but only "when the country was declared in danger." Apart from this emergency, the French army was recruited by voluntary enlistment and by conscription, under which a conscript of means could find a substitute.

27. Kitchen, *Military History of Germany*, 48. Nationalist historians created the legend that the Krumper system enabled the Prussians to train a reserve army of 150,000. This legend was so widely believed throughout Europe that provisions against the recreation of such a system were incorporated into the 1919 Treaty of Versailles.

28. Nipperdey, *Germany from Napoleon to Bismarck*, 68. Nipperdey maintains that "it was the educated youth who answered the call for volunteers, and the *Freikorps* (10% of the armed forces at the outset and over 12.5%, or 20,000, at the end) were what gave this war its special character."

29. Muir, *Britain and the Defeat of Napoleon*, 289.

30. Kitchen, *Military History of Germany*, 55.

31. Muir, *Britain and the Defeat of Napoleon*, 289. Muir makes an interesting argument that "the greatest importance of the Wars of Liberation in the creation of modern nationalism was in providing material for patriotic legends and the sense of a shared national past which developed during the nineteenth-century."

32. Kitchen, *Military History of Germany*, 55.

33. Brett-James, *Europe against Napoleon*, 44.

34. Petre, *Napoleon's Last Campaign*, 256.

35. Brett-James, *Europe against Napoleon*, 43, 44. The Silesian Landwehr experienced the most problems during the mobilization. The men were armed with 20,000 Austrian muskets in which the makers had failed to bore any touch holes.

36. Simon, *Failure of the Prussian Reform Movement*, 167.

37. Craig, "Problems of Coalition Warfare," 41.

38. Ibid., 42.

39. Nipperdey, *Germany from Napoleon to Bismarck*, 67.

40. Kissinger, *A World Restored*, 47.

41. Schroeder, *Transformation of European Politics*, 453.

42. See the debate over Yorck's insubordination in Craig, *Politics of the Prussian Army*, 59.

43. The French experienced a similar situation in December 1812, when an entire month passed before French commanders in Prussia and Poland received any correspondance from Napoleon. Schneid notes that "never in the

life of the Empire had such a period gone by where Napoleon's lieutenants were without instructions from their master. Despite the hardship and lack of clear direction, the marshals and generals did their best to carry on." Schneid, "Dynamics of Defeat," 16.

44. Craig, "Problems of Coalition Warfare," 43.

45. Nipperdey, *Germany from Napoleon to Bismarck*, 68.

46. Ibid., 68–69. In the book *Leyer und Schwert*, Theodore Körner, a Saxon who served in a Prussian volunteer unit (the Lützow Freikorps), reflected the mood of the educated and the young when he wrote: "It is not a war of the kind the kings know about, 'tis a crusade, 'tis a holy war."

47. Schroeder, *Transformation of European Politics*, 451–52.

48. Nipperdey, *Germany from Napoleon to Bismarck*, 68.

49. Schroeder, *Transformation of European Politics*, 452.

50. The fact that the Prussian armies of 1813, 1814, and 1815 did not disintegrate after devastating defeats, especially those suffered by Blücher in 1814 and 1815, also provides proof that the reformers had achieved the basic goal of creating a Prussian national consciousness.

51. Craig, "Problems of Coalition Warfare," 42, 43.

52. This situation was intolerable for Schwarzenberg. "It is really inhuman what I tolerate and bear; I am surrounded by fools of all kinds . . . gossips, and critics. Vermin in countless multitudes gnaw at me and torment me to the marrow of my bones. More than once I have felt in danger of being overwhelmed." Schwarzenberg to his wife, 5 September 1813, in Cook, "Schwarzenberg at Dresden," 642.

53. Craig, "Problems of Coalition Warfare," 31.

54. Ibid.

55. Schroeder, *Transformation of European Politics*, 472–73.

56. Kraehe, *Metternich's German Policy*, 1:201.

57. Kissinger, *A World Restored*, 51.

58. Nipperdey, *Germany from Napoleon to Bismarck*, 70–71.

59. Schroeder, *Transformation of European Politics*, 472–73, 477.

60. Nicolson, *Congress of Vienna*, 48.

61. Schroeder, *Transformation of European Politics*, 477.

62. Kissinger, *A World Restored*, 47.

63. Nipperdey, *Germany from Napoleon to Bismarck*, 71.

64. Kissinger, *A World Restored*, 25, 51.

65. Nicolson, *Congress of Vienna*, 51.

66. Frederick Schneid to the author, "Notes on Austria's Strategy in 1813," 24 October 2000.

67. Showalter, "Hubertusberg to Auerstädt," 332–33.

68. Lehmann, *Scharnhorst*, 2:514.

69. Gneisenau quoted in Meinecke, *Boyen*, 2:73.

70. In *Transformation of European Politics*, 451, Schroeder describes the nationalism that beset the Prussian army during the War of Liberation as "harmful and counterproductive."

71. Wawro, *Austro-Prussian War*, 36.

72. Kissinger, *A World Restored*, 56.

73. Ibid., 51.

74. Rosenberg, *Bureaucracy, Aristocracy, and Autocracy,* 203, 216. "The legal removal of special noble privilege in the military service," notes Rosenberg, "led, eventually, to the qualified sharing of professional status prerogatives by a rising number of non-nobles. But more important than the broadening of the social base of personnel recruitment was the strengthening of the officer corps as a self-governing bureaucratic corporation perpetuating itself through the method of cooptation. The Military Service state profited greatly from reform. For the establishment of bureaucratic absolutism buttressed its position as a highly favored professional status group and privileged social elite."

75. Schroeder, *Transformation of European Politics*, 452.

Bibliography

ABBREVIATIONS

AAT	Archiv de l'Armée de Terre, Paris.
AN	Archives Nationales, Paris.
BFA	Bülow Familienarchiv.
CEH	*Central European History.*
CRE	*Consortium on Revolutionary Europe, 1750–1850: Selected Papers.*
FBPG	*Forschungen zur brandenburgischen-preußischen Geschichte.*
GH	*German History.*
GStA	Geheimes Staatsarchiv Preußischer Kulturbesitz, Berlin.
HZ	*Historische Zeitschrift.*
IHR	*International History Review.*
MR	Mémoires-Reconnaissances (AAT), Paris.
MW	*Militär-Wochenblatt. Redigirt von der historischen Abteilung des Generalstabes.*
PStA	*Publikationen aus den Preußischen Staatsarchiven.*
ZKWK	*Zeitschrift für Kunst, Wissenschaft und Geschichte des Krieges.*

I. ARCHIVAL SOURCES

Germany

Ehemals Mitteilungen aus dem Gräflichen Bülow Familien-Archiv zu Grünhoff (BFA), Baden-Baden. Friedrich Wilhelm Graf Bülow von Dennewitz. Dokumentation in Briefen-Befehlen-Berichten. Gesammelt, Übertragen und mit Anmerkungen Versehen von Joachim-Albrecht Graf Bülow von Dennewitz.

Geheimes Staatsarchiv Preußischer Kulturbesitz zu Berlin (GStA). Consulted: Rep. 89 Zivilkabinet Befehle Nrs. 32314, 32302 Bd. 2, 32303 Bd. 3, 32318; Rep. 91 A Militärische Behörden, Der Militärgouvernement für das Land zwischen der Elbe und Oder: Nrs. 1, 2, 3, 4, 14, 15, 48, 96, 97, 100, 123, 150, 153, 154, 155, 156, 189, 226, 236, 237, 654, 669, 684, 782, 887, 1050; Rep. 92 Nachlaß Albrecht: Nrs. 17, 18,19, 20, 22, 27, 33, 41, 42, 43, 44, 54, 55; Rep. 92 Nachlaß Bülow von Dennewitz; Rep. 92 Nachlaß Gneisenau Packet Nrs. 20b, 21, 22, 23, 24; Rep. 92 Nachlaß Hardenberg L 33–38; Rep. 92 Nachlaß Scharnhorst: Nrs. 217/30, 217/88, 217/92, 217/93, 217/96, 217/97, 217/100, 217/100–105; IV. Hauptabteilungen Preußischer Heeresarchiv und Heeresgeschichtliche Sammlung: Rep. 15 A Nrs. 19, 22, 147, 148, 149, 150, 154, 160, 164, 175, 188, 238, 243, 248, 250, 261, 298, 319, 334, 341, 342, 343, 344, 359, 395, 396; Rep. B Nrs. 188, 275, 698; BPH, Rep. 192 Wittgenstein V, 5.1.

France

Archives de l'Armée de Terre (AAT): Service historique de l'armée, Château de Vincennes, Paris. Consulted: Correspondance et Registres, Cartons: C2 141, C2 142, C2 153, C2 155, C2 168, C2 316, C2 320, C2 322, C2 539, C2 541, C2 544, C17 178, C17 180; Mémoires-Reconnaissances (MR) 688, 696, 698, 699, 898.

Archives Nationales (AN) Paris. Consulted: AF IV 1651[A], AF IV 1651[B], AF IV 1652, AF IV 1659[B], AF IV 1660[A], AF IV 1660[B], AF IV 1661[B], AF IV 1662[A], AF IV 1662[B].

II. PRIMARY WORKS

Bailleu, Paul, ed. *Briefwechsel König Friedrich Wilhelms III und der Königin Luise mit Kaiser Alexander I nebst ergänzenden fürstlichen Korrespondenzen. PStA*, vol. 75. Leipzig, 1900.

———. *Preußen und Frankreich von 1795 bis 1807: Diplomatische Correspondenzen. PStA*, vol. 8. 2 vols. Leipzig, 1881–87.

Bassewitz, Magnus Friedrich von. *Die Kurmark-Brandenburg im Zusammenhang mit den Schicksalen des Gesamtstaats Preußen während der Zeit vom 22 Oktober 1806 bis zum Ende des Jahres 1808*. 2 vols. Leipzig, 1851–52.

Beauharnais, Eugène de. *Mémoires et correspondance politique et militaire du prince Eugène*. Ed. and annotated by Baron Albert Du Casse. 10 vols. Paris, 1858–60.

"Beiträge zur militärischen Geschichte Sachsens, oder Blätter aus dem Tagebuch eines königlich Sächsischen Offiziers, der den Feldzügen von 1812 und 1813 im 7. Korps der französischen Armee beiwohnte." *ZKWK* 40 (1837): 220–47.

Berthier, Louis Alexandre. *Registre d'ordres du maréchal Berthier pendant la campagne de 1813*. 2 vols. Paris, 1909.

Bezzenberger. A., ed. *Urkunden des Provinzial-Archivs in Königsberg und des gräflich Dohnaschen Majorats-Archivs in Schlobitten betreffend die Erhebung Ostpreußens im Jahre 1813 und die Errichtung der Landwehr*. Königsberg, 1894.

Blücher, Gebhard Leberecht von. *Ausgewählte Briefe des Feldmarschalls Leberecht von Blücher*. Leipzig, n.d.

———. *Blüchers Briefe*. Ed. Wolfgang von Unger. Stuttgart, 1912.

Boyen, Hermann von. *Beiträge zur Kenntnis des Generals von Scharnhorst und seiner amtlichen Thätigkeit in den Jahren 1808–1813*. Berlin, 1833.

———. *Denkwürdigkeiten und Erinnerungen, 1771–1813*. 2 vols. Stuttgart, 1899.

———. *Erinnerungen aus dem Leben des General-Feldmarshalls Hermann von Boyen*. Ed. Friedrich Nippold. 3 vols. Leipzig, 1889–90.

———. *Erinnerungen aus dem Leben des General-Feldmarshalls Hermann von Boyen*. Ed. Dorothea Schmidt. 2 vols. Berlin, 1990.

Brett-James, Antony. *Europe against Napoleon: The Leipzig Campaign, 1813, from Eyewitness Accounts*. London, 1970.

Burstini, Baron von. *Darstellung des Treffens bei Luckau den 4 Juni 1813*. Berlin, 1813.

Castlereagh, Robert Stewart. *The Correspondence, Despatches and Other Papers of Viscount Castlereagh*. Ed. Charles Vane. 12 vols. London, 1848–53.

Cathcart, George. *Commentaries on the War in Russia and Germany in 1812 and 1813*. London, 1850.

Clausewitz, Carl von. *The Campaign of 1812 in Russia*. Berlin, 1843; reprint ed., London, 1992.

———. *Der Feldzug 1812 in Rußland und die Befreiungskriege von 1812–15*. Berlin, 1906.

———. *Nachrichten über Preußen in seiner großen Katastrophe*. Kriegs-geschichtliche Einzelschriften, Vol. 10. Berlin, 1888.

Davout, Louis-Nicholas. *Correspondance du maréchal Davout, prince d'Eckmühl, ses commandements, son ministère, 1801–1815*. Ed. Charles de Mazade. 4 vols. Paris, 1885.

Donnersmarck, Wilhelm Ludwig Victor, Graf Henckel von. *Erinnerungen aus meinem Leben*. Zerbst, 1846.

Fezansac, Raymond. *Souvenirs militaires de 1804 à 1814*. Paris, 1870.

Förster, Friedrich. *Geschichte der Befreiungskriege 1813, 1814, 1815*. 3 vols. Berlin, 1857–58.

Frederick II, King of Prussia. *Die Werke Friedrichs der Großen*. 10 vols. Berlin, 1912–14.

Friccius, Carl. *Geschichte des Krieges in den Jahren 1813 und 1814 mit besonderer Rücksicht auf Ostpreußen und das Königsbergische Landwehrbataillon*. 2 vols. Berlin, 1848.

Gesetz-Sammlung für die Königlichen Preußischen Staaten 1813. Berlin, n.d.

Gneisenau, August von. *The Life and Campaigns of Field-Marshal Prince Blücher*. London, 1815.

Granier, Hermann, ed. *Berichte aus der Berliner Franzosenzeit, 1807–1809*. *PStA*, vol. 88. Leipzig, 1913.

Griewank, Karl, ed. *Gneisenau: Ein Leben in Briefen*. Leipzig, 1939.

Hassel, Paul, ed. *Geschichte der preußischen Politik: 1807–1808*. *PStA*, vol. 6. Leipzig, 1881.

Hassenkamp, Heinrich von. *General Graf Bülow von Dennewitz in den Feldzügen von 1814 und 1815*. Leipzig, 1843.

Hellinghaus, Otto, ed. *Denkwürdigkeiten aus der Freiheitskriege 1813–1815*. Freiburg, 1913.

Hofmann, Georg von. *Zur Geschichte des Feldzuges von 1813*. Berlin, 1843.

Holtzendorff, Albrecht von. *Geschichte der Königlich Sächsischen Leichten Infanterie von Ihrer Errichtung bis zum 1 Oktober 1859*. Leipzig, 1860.

Karl XIV, King of Sweden. *Recueil des ordres de mouvement, proclamations et bulletins de S.A.R. le prince royal de Suède, commandant en chef l'armée combinée du nord de l'Allemagne en 1813 et 1814*. Stockholm, 1838.

Körner, Theodore. *Leyer und Schwert*. Berlin, 1814.

Lejeune, Louis-François. *Memoirs of Baron Lejeune, Aide-de-Camp to Marshals Berthier, Davout and Oudinot*. Trans. and ed. Mrs. Arthur Bell. 2 vols. London, 1897.

Linnebach, Karl, ed. *Scharnhorsts Briefe*. Vol. 1 in *Privatbriefe*. Leipzig, 1914; reprint ed., with commentary by Heinz Stübig. Munich, 1980.

Londonderry, Lieut.-Gen. Charles William Vane, Marquess [Sir Charles Stewart]. *Narrative of the War in Germany and France in 1813 and 1814*. London, 1830.

Luvaas, Jay, ed. and trans. *Frederick the Great on the Art of War*. New York, 1966.

Marmont, A. de. *Mémoires du Duc de Raguse*. 9 vols. Paris, 1857.

Marwitz, Friedrich von. d. *Aus dem Nachlaß Friedrich August Ludwig von der Marwitz*. 2 vols. Berlin, 1852.

———. *Friedrich August von der Marwitz: Ein märkischer Edelmann im Zeitalter der Befreiungskriege*. Ed. Friedrich Meusel. 3 vols. Berlin, 1908–13.

Meltzer, Carl. *Geschichtliche Darstellung meist unbekannter Kriegs-Scenen oder Feldzüge der Sachsen deren Kantonnements sowie Lützows Jagd und des zweiten franz. Ausländer Regiment in den Jahren 1811 bis 1819*. 2 vols. Dresden, 1845.

Metternich-Winneburg, Clemens Lothar Wenzel. *Mémoires, documents et écrits divers laissés par le prince de Metternich, chancelier de cour et d'état*. Ed. Alfons von Klinkowström. 8 vols. Paris, 1880–86.

Müffling, Friedrich Karl von. *Aus meinem Leben*. Berlin, 1851.

———. *Passages from My Life: Together with Memoirs of the Campaign of 1813 and 1814*. Trans. and ed. Philip Yorke, London, 1853.

Napoléon I, Emperor of the French. *La correspondance de Napoléon Ier, publiée par ordre de l'empereur Napoléon III*. 32 vols. Paris, 1858–69.

Napoleon's Conduct towards Prussia since the Peace of Tilsit: From the Original Documents Published under the Authority of the Prussian Government. London, 1814.

Odeleben, E. O. von. *Napoleons Feldzug im Sachsen im Jahre 1813*. Dresden, 1816.

Philippart, John. *Memoirs and Campaigns of Charles John, Prince Royal of Sweden*. Baltimore, 1815.

Pierer, H. A. *Der Feldzug des Corps des Generals Grafen Ludwig von Wallmoden-Gimborn an der Nieder-Elbe und in Belgien in den Jahren 1813 und 1814*. Altenburg, 1848.

Plotho, Carl von. *Der Krieg in Deutschland und Frankreich in den Jahren 1813 und 1814*. 3 vols. Berlin, 1817.

Prittwitz, Karl Heinrich. *Beiträge zur Geschichte des Jahres 1813: Von einem höheren Offizier der Preußischen Armee*. 2 vols. Potsdam, 1843.

Quistorp, Barthold von. *Geschichte der Nord-Armee im Jahre 1813*. 3 vols. Berlin, 1894.

Ranke, Leopold von. *Denkwürdigkeiten des Staatskanzlers Fürsten von Hardenberg*. 5 vols. Leipzig, 1877.

Rau, Karl Ferdinand von. *Der Krieg der Verbundeten gegen Frankreich in den Jahren 1813, 1814 und 1815*. Berlin, 1833.

Recueil des traités de la France, publié sous les auspices du ministère des affaires étrangères. 23 vols. Paris, 1864–1907.

Rehtwisch, Theodor, *Groß Beeren, 23 August 1813; Hagelberg, 27 August 1813; Theodor*

Körners Tod, 26 August 1813. Vol. 3 of *Schlachtenbilder der Befreiungskrieg*. Leipzig, 1912.

———, ed. *Aus dem Tagebuch eines Freiwilligen: Bilder aus den Jahren 1813 und 1814*. Leipzig, 1911.

Reiche, Ludwig von. *Memoiren des königlichen preußischen Generals der Infanterie Ludwig von Reiche*. Ed. Louis von Weltzien. 3 vols. Leipzig, 1857.

Rochechouart, Louis Victor Léon. *Souvenirs sur la révolution, l'empire et la restauration*. Paris, 1933.

Sammlung der für die Königlichen Preußischen Staaten erschienenen Gesetze und Verordnungen von 1806 bis zum 27 Oktober 1810. Berlin, 1822.

Scharnhorst, Gerhard von, ed. *Auszug aus den Verordnungen über die Verfassung der Königlichen Preußischen Armee, welche seit dem Tilsiter Frieden ergangen sind*. Berlin, 1810.

Scherbening, R. K. von, and K. W. Willisen, eds. *Die Reorganisation der Preußischen Armee nach dem Tilsiter Frieden*. 2 vols. Berlin, 1862–66.

Schinkel, Öfverste von. *Minnen ur Sveriges nyare historia*. 12 vols. Stockholm, 1855.

Schoenaich, Adolf, ed. *Zur Vorgeschichte der Befreiungskriege: Kriegsberichte von 1812*. Berlin, 1912.

Ségur, Philippe-Paul de. *Napoleon's Russian Campaign*. New York, 1976.

Seydlitz, August von. *Tagebuch des Königlich Preußischen Armee Korps unter Befehl des Generalleutnant von Yorck im Feldzuge von 1812*. 2 vols. Berlin, 1812.

Temperley, Harold, and Penson, Lilian. *Foundations of British Foreign Policy from Pitt to Salisbury on Documents, Old and New, Selected and Edited with Historical Introductions*. Cambridge, 1938.

Valentini, Georg von. *Der große Krieg*. 2 vols. Berlin, 1833.

———. *Lehre vom Kriege*. 2 vols. Berlin, 1835.

Varnhagen von Ense, Karl August. *Fürst Blücher von Wahlstadt*. Berlin, 1933.

———. *Das Leben der Generals Gräfen Bülow von Dennewitz*. Berlin, 1853.

Vaudoncourt, Guillaume. *Histoire de la guerre soutenue par les français en Allemagne en 1813*. Paris, 1819.

———. *Histoire politique et militaire du Prince Eugène Napoléon*. 2 vols. Paris, 1928.

Vaupel, Rudolf, ed. *Das Preußische Heer vom Tilsiter Frieden bis zur Befreiung: 1807–1814*. Part 2 of *Die Reorganisation des Preußischen Staates unter Stein und Hardenberg*. *PStA*, vol. 94. Leipzig, 1938.

Venturini, Carl. *Rußlands und Deutschlands Befreiungskriege von der Franzosen-Herrschaft unter Napoleon Buonaparte in den Jahren 1812–1815*. 4 vols. Altenburg, 1816–18.

Voss, Julius von. *Heinrich von Bülow*. Berlin, 1807.

Wagner, C. A. von. *Pläne der Schlachten und Treffen von der preußischen Armee in den Feldzügen der Jahre 1813, 1814 und 1815*. 4 vols. Berlin, 1821.

Wilson, Robert. *General Wilson's Journal, 1812–1814*. Ed. Antony Brett-James. London, 1964.

———. *Private Diary of Travels, Personal Services, and Public Events: During the Mission Employed with the European Armies in the Campaigns of 1812, 1813, 1814*. London, 1861.

Winter, Georg., ed. *Die Reorganisation des Preußischen Staates unter Stein und Hardenberg*. Part 1: *Allgemeine Verwaltungs- und Behördenreform*. *PStA*, vol. 93. Leipzig, 1931.

III. SECONDARY WORKS

Anderson, Eugene. *Nationalism and the Cultural Crises in Prussia, 1806–1815*. New York, 1976.

Arnheim, Fritz. "Zur Charakteristik Friedrichs des Großen und seines Großneffen, des nachmaligen Königs Friedrich Wilhelm III." *FBPG* 18 (1905): 229–36.

Atkinson, C. T. *A History of Germany, 1715–1815*. London, 1908.

Austin, Paul Britten. "Oudinot: The Father of the Grenadiers." In *Napoleon's Marshals*, ed. David G. Chandler. New York, 1987.

Bailleu, Paul. "Aus einem Stammbuch der Königin Luise." *FBPG* 8 (1895): 251–53.

———. "Haugwitz und Hardenberg." *Deutsche Rundschau* 20 (1879): 268–98.

———. "Die politische Haltung Friedrich Wilhelms III vor Ausbruch des Krieges von 1806." *FBPG* 12 (1889): 250.

Barton, D. Plunket. *Bernadotte: Prince and King, 1810–1844*. London, 1925.

Bauer, Frank. *Groß Beeren 1813: Die Verteidigung der preußischen Hauptstadt*. Potsdam, 1996.

Behrens, C. B. A. *Society, Government, and the Enlightenment: The Experiences of Eighteenth-Century France and Prussia*. London, 1985.

Bigelow, Poultney. *The History of the German Struggle for Liberty*. 2 vols. New York, 1896–1903.

Biro, Sydney. *The German Policy of Revolutionary France: A Study in French Diplomacy during the War of the First Coalition, 1792–1797*. 2 vols. Cambridge, 1957.

Bitterauf, Theodor. "Studien zur preußischen Politik im Jahre 1805." *FBPG* 27 (1914): 431–515.

Blanning, T. C. W. "The Death and Transfiguration of Prussia." *Historical Journal* 29, no. 2 (1986): 433–59.

———. *The French Revolution in Germany: Occupation and Resistance in the Rhineland, 1792–1802*. Oxford, 1983.

———. *The Origins of the French Revolutionary Wars*. London, 1986.

Bowden, Scott. *Napoleon's Grande Armée of 1813*. Chicago, 1990.

Bränner, R. *Geschichte der preußischen Landwehr: Historische Darstellung und Beleuchtung ihrer Vorgeschichte, Errichtung und späteren Organisation*. 2 vols. Berlin, 1863.

Brunschwig, Henri. *Enlightenment and Romanticism in Eighteenth-Century Prussia*. Trans. F. Jellinek. Chicago, 1974.

Bülow, Eduard von. *Aus Dietrich Bülows Leben*. Berlin, 1853.

Caemmerer, R. von. *Die Befreiungskriege, 1813–1815: Ein Strategischer Überblick*. Berlin, 1907.

———. *Die Ereignisse von Ende April bis zum Waffenstillstand*. Part 2 of *Geschichte des Frühjahrsfeldzuges 1813 und seine Vorgeschichte*. Berlin, 1909. Geschichte der Befreiungskriege. 9 vols. Berlin 1903–9.

Carsten, F. L. *From Scharnhorst to Schleicher: The Prussian Officer Corps in Politics, 1806–1933*. London, 1957.

Cavaignac, J. M. E. G. *La formation de la Prusse contemporaine*. 2 vols. Paris, 1897–98.

Chandler, David G. *Atlas of Military Strategy*. London, 1996.

———. *The Campaigns of Napoleon*. New York, 1966.

———. "Davout: The Iron Marshal." In *Napoleon's Marshals*, ed. David G. Chandler. New York, 1987.

———. *Dictionary of the Napoleonic Wars*. New York, 1979.

Charras, J. B. A. *Histoire de la Guerre de 1813 en Allemagne. Derniers jours de la retraite, insurrection de l'Allemagne, armements, diplomatie, entrée en campagne*. 2nd ed. Paris, 1870.

Clément, G. *Campagne de 1813*. Paris, 1904.

Coates-Wright, Philipp. "Gouvion St.-Cyr: The Owl." In *Napoleon's Marshals*, ed. David G. Chandler. New York, 1987.

Connelly, Owen. *Blundering to Glory: Napoleon's Military Campaigns*. Wilmington, 1987.

———. "Napoleon and Frederick the Great." *CRE* (1995): 507–11.

———. *Napoleon's Satellite Kingdoms: Managing Conquered Peoples*. Malabar, Fla., 1990.

Conrady, Emil von. *Leben und Wirken des Generals Carl von Grolman*. 3 vols. Berlin, 1933.

Cook, Llewellyn. "Prince Schwarzenberg's Crises in 1812: In the Service of Two Emperors." *CRE* (1995): 351–58.

———. "Schwarzenberg at Dresden: Leadership and Command." *CRE* (1994): 642–51.

Craig, Gordon A. *The Politics of the Prussian Army: 1640–1945*. Oxford, 1956.

———. "Problems of Coalition Warfare: The Military Alliance against Napoleon, 1813–14." In *War, Politics, and Diplomacy: Selected Essays by Gordon Craig*. London, 1966.

Delbrück, Hans. *Weltgeschichte*. 5 vols. Berlin, 1925–29.

Delbrück, Hans, and G. H. Pertz. *Das Leben des Feldmarschalls Grafen Neithardt von Gneisenau*. 5 vols. Berlin, 1864–80.

Demeter, Karl. *Das deutsche Heer und seine Offiziere*. Berlin, 1930.

———. *The German Officer-Corps in Society and State, 1650–1945*. Trans. Angus Malcolm. New York, 1965.

Droysen, Johann. *Das Leben des Feldmarshalls Grafen Yorck von Wartenburg*. 2 vols. Leipzig, 1851.

Du Casse, Albert. *Le général Arrighi de Casanova, duc de Padoue*. 2 vols. Paris, 1866.

Duffy, Christopher. *The Army of Frederick the Great*. New York, 1974.

———. *Frederick the Great: A Military Life*. London, 1985.

Dunker, Max. "Preußen während der französischen Okkupation." In *Aus der Zeit Friedrichs des Großen und Friedrich Wilhelms III: Abhandlungen zur preußischen Geschichte*. Leipzig, 1876.

Dupuy, Trevor. *A Genius for War: The German Army and General Staff, 1807–1945*. Englewood Cliffs, N.J., 1977.

D'Ussel, Jean. *Études sur l'année 1813: La défection de la Prusse, décembre 1812–mars 1813*. Paris, 1907.

Duval, J. C. X. A. *Napoleon, Bülow et Bernadotte, 1813*. Paris, 1906.

Dwyer, Philip. "The Politics of Prussian Neutrality, 1795–1806." *GH* 12 (1994): 351–74.

———. "Prussia and the Armed Neutrality: The Invasion of Hanover in 1801." *IHR* 15 (1993): 661–87.

Eckert, Georg. *Von Valmy bis Leipzig: Quellen und Dokumente zur Geschichte der preußischen Heeresreform*. Hanover, 1955.

Eidahl, Kyle. "The Military Career of Nicolas Charles Oudinot, 1767–1847." Ph.D. diss.,

Florida State University, 1990.
———. "Napoleon's Faulty Strategy: Oudinot's Operations against Berlin, 1813." *CRE* (1995): 395–403.
———. "Oudinot and Saint-Cyr in 1812: The Problems of Independent Command." *CRE* (1993): 65–71.
Elting, John. "Myths of the Napoleonic Period." *CRE* (1995): 502–6.
———. *Swords around a Throne: Napoleon's Grande Armée*. New York, 1988.
Elting, John, and Vincent Esposito. *A Military History and Atlas of the Napoleonic Wars*. New York, 1964.
"Die Erhaltung von Crossen im Jahre 1813: Aus dem hinterlassenen Tagebuche des Generals von Dobschütz." *ZKWK* 39 (1837): 257–69.
"Errichtung der Landwehr und des Landsturms in Ostpreußen, Westpreußen, am rechten Weichselufer und Litthauen im Jahre 1813." *MW* (1846): 1–146.
Fabry, Gabriel Joseph. *Étude sur les opérations de l'empereur, 5 septembre au 21 septembre 1813*. Paris, 1910.
———. *Étude sur les opérations du maréchal Oudinot du 15 août au 4 septembre: Groß Beeren*. Paris, 1910.
Feuchtwanger, E. J. *Prussia: Myth and Reality*. New York, 1973.
Finley, Milton. "The Career of Count Jean Reynier, 1792–1814." Ph.D. diss., Florida State University, 1972.
———. *The Most Monstrous of Wars: The Napoleonic Guerrilla War in Southern Italy, 1806–1811*. Columbia, S.C., 1994.
Fisher, H. A. L. *Napoleonic Statesmanship in Germany*. Oxford, 1903.
Ford, G. S. *Hanover and Prussia: A Study in Neutrality, 1795–1803*. New York, 1903.
———. *Stein and the Era of Reform in Prussia, 1807–1815*. Princeton, 1922; reprint ed., Glouchester, 1965.
"Die Formation der freiwilligen Jäger-Detachments bei der preußischen Armee im Jahre 1813." *MW* (1845): 449–515.
Fortescue, J. W. *British Statesmen of the Great War, 1793–1814*. Oxford, 1911.
Foucart, P. J. *Bautzen: 20–21 mai 1813*. 2 vols. Paris, 1897.
Friederich, Rudolf von. "Die Auffassung der strategischen Lage seitens der Verbündeten am Schlusse des Waffenstillstandes von Poischwitz 1813." *MW* (1902): 1–36.
———. *Die Befreiungskriege, 1813–1815*. 4 vols. Berlin, 1911–13.
———. *Geschichte des Herbstfeldzuges 1813*. 3 vols. Berlin, 1903–6. Geschichte der Befreiungskriege 1813–1815. 9 vols. Berlin, 1903–9.
———. "Die strategische Lage Napoleons am Schlusse des Waffenstillstandes von Poischwitz." *MW* (1901): 1–36.
Gallaher, John. *The Iron Marshal: A Biography of Louis N. Davout*. Carbondale, Ill., 1976.
———. "Strategic Success and Failure in 1813: A Commentary." *CRE* (1995): 411–13.
Garland, Phil. "L'amitié d'un grand homme: Napoleon and Alexander at Erfurt, 1808." *CRE* (1995): 334–42.
"Geschichte der Nord-Armee im Jahre 1813, Zweites Heft: Rückzug der französischen Armee nach der Schlacht bei Groß Beeren bis Wittenberg und das Treffen bei Hagelberg." *MW* (1863): 1–120.
"Geschichte der Nord-Armee im Jahre 1813, Drittes Heft: Zweite französische Offensive gegen die Mark und die Schlacht bei Dennewitz." *MW* (1865): 1–132.

"Geschichte der Organisation der Landwehr in der Kurmark nebst den drei Vorpommerschen Kreisen in der Neumark im Jahre 1813." *MW* (1857): 1–166.

Geyl, Pieter. *Napoleon: For and Against*. New Haven, 1949.

Gill, John H. "Bernadotte and the Saxon Army at Wagram." *CRE* (1994): 266–75.

———. *With Eagles to Glory: Napoleon and His German Allies in the 1809 Campaign*. London, 1992.

Goerlitz, Walter. *History of the German General Staff, 1657–1945*. Trans. Brian Battershaw. New York, 1954.

Goltz, Colmar von der. *Von Rossbach bis Jena und Auerstädt*. Berlin, 1906.

Gooch, George P. *Germany and the French Revolution*. London, 1920.

Griewank, Karl. "Hardenberg und die preußische Politik, 1804 bis 1806." *FBPG* 47 (1935): 227–308.

Griffith, Paddy. *The Art of War of Revolutionary France, 1789–1802*. London, 1998.

Großer Generalstab, Kriegsgeschichtliche Abteilung. *1806: Das preußische Offizierkorps und die Untersuchung der Kriegsereignisse*. Berlin, 1906.

———. *Das Preußische Heer der Befreiungskriege*. Part 1. *Urkündliche Beiträge und Forschungen zur Geschichte des Preußischen Heeres*. Berlin, 1912.

———. *Das Preußische Heer der Befreiungskriege*. Part 2: *Das Preußische Heer im Jahre 1813*. Berlin, 1914.

Grunwald, Constantin de. *The Life of Baron Stein: Napoleon's Nemesis*. Trans. C. F. Atkinson. New York, 1936.

Haedecke, Richard. "Bernadotte und die Schlacht bei Dennewitz." Ph.D. diss., Großherzoglich Hessischen Ludwigs-Universität, 1915.

Hagen, William. "The Partitions of Poland and the Crises of the Old Regime in Prussia." *CEH* 9 (1976): 115–28.

Hausherr, Hans. "Hardenberg und der Friede von Basel." *HZ* 184 (1957): 292–335.

———. "Stein und Hardenberg." *HZ* 190 (1960): 267–89.

Heidrich, Kurt. *Preußen im Kampfe gegen die französische Revolution bis zur zweiten Teilung Polens*. Berlin, 1908.

Henderson, Ernest F. *Blücher and the Uprising of Prussia against Napoleon, 1806–1815*. London, 1911.

Hermann, Alfred. "Friedrich Wilhelm III und sein Anteil an der Heeresreform bis 1813." *Historische Viertelsjahresschrift* 11 (1908): 484–516.

Höhn, Reinhard. *Revolution-Heer-Kriegsbild*. Darmstadt, 1944.

Holleben, A. von. *Vorgeschichte und Geschichte des Feldzuges bis zum 26 April 1813*. Part 1 of *Geschichte des Frühjahrsfeldzuges 1813 und seine Vorgeschichte*. Berlin, 1904. Geschichte der Befreiungskriege. 9 vols. Berlin 1903–9.

Horward, Donald D. *The French Revolution and Napoleon Collection at Florida State University: A Bibliographical Guide*. Tallahassee, 1973.

———. *Napoleon and Iberia: The Twin Sieges of Ciudad Rodrigo and Almeida, 1810*. Tallahassee, 1980.

———. "Napoleon and the Transformation of War." In *Napoleon and America*, ed. Robert B. Holtman. Pensacola, Fla., 1988.

Ibbeken, Rudolf. *Preußen, 1807–1813: Staat und Volk als Idee und in Wirklichkeit*. Cologne and Berlin, 1970.

Jany, Curt. *Geschichte der königlichen preußischen Armee*. 4 vols. Berlin, 1929.

Kissinger, Henry. *A World Restored: Metternich, Castlereagh and the Problems of Peace,*

1812–22. Boston, 1957.
Kitchen, Martin. *A Military History of Germany*. London, 1954.
Koch, H. W. *A History of Prussia*. New York, 1987.
Kraehe, Enno. *Metternich's German Policy*. 2 vols. Princeton, 1963.
"Der Kriegsschauplatz der Nord-Armee im Jahre 1813." *MW* (1858): 1–249.
Lehmann, Konrad. *Die Rettung Berlins im Jahre 1813*. Berlin, 1934.
Lehmann, Max. "Boyens Denkwürdigkeiten." *HZ* 67 (1891): 40–54.
———. *Freiherr vom Stein*. 3 vols. Leipzig, 1902–5.
———. "General Borstell und der Ausbruch des Krieges von 1813." *HZ* 37 (1877): 55–76.
———. "Ein Regierungsprogramm Friedrich Wilhelms III." *HZ* 61 (1889): 441–60.
———. *Scharnhorst*. 2 vols. Leipzig, 1886–87.
———. "Zur Geschichte der preußischen Heeresreform von 1808." *HZ* 126 (1922): 436–57.
Lévy, Arthur. *Napoléon et la paix*. Paris, n.d.
———. *Napoléon intime*. Paris, 1933.
Luvaas, Jay. *Frederick the Great on the Art of War*. New York, 1966.
Lynn, John. *The Bayonets of the Republic: Motivation and Tactics in the Army of Revolutionary France, 1791–1794*. Champaign, Ill., 1984.
Marriott, J. A. R., and C. G. Roberston. *The Evolution of Prussia: The Making of an Empire*. Oxford, 1915.
Marshall-Cornwall, *Napoleon as Military Commander*. London, 1967; reprint ed., New York, 1998.
Maude, F. N. *1806: The Jena Campaign*. New York, 1909.
———. *The Leipzig Campaign, 1813*. London, 1908.
McKay, Derek, and H. M. Scott. *The Rise of the Great Powers, 1648–1815*. London, 1983.
Meinecke, Friedrich. *The Age of German Liberation, 1795–1815*. Trans. and ed. Peter Paret. Berkeley, 1977.
———. *Das Leben des Generalfeldmarschalls Hermann von Boyen*. 2 vols. Stuttgart, 1896–99.
———. "Zur Beurteilung Bernadottes im Herbstfeldzuge 1813." *FBPG* 7 (1894): 161–78.
Meusel, Friedrich. "Die Besoldung der Armee im alten Preußen und ihre Reform 1808." *FBPG* 21 (1908): 243–49.
Muir, Rory. *Britain and the Defeat of Napoleon, 1807–1815*. London, 1996.
Munchow-Pohl, Bernd von. *Zwischen Reform und Krieg: Untersuchungen zur Bewußtseinlage in Preußen 1809–1812*. Göttingen, 1987.
Nafziger, George. *Napoleon at Dresden: The Battles of August 1813*. Chicago, 1994.
Nicolson, Harold. *The Congress of Vienna: A Study in Allied Unity*. New York, 1946.
Nipperdey, Thomas. *Germany from Napoleon to Bismarck, 1799–1866*. Trans. Daniel Nolan. Princeton, 1996.
Nord, Reinhold. *Die Deutsche Heeresverfassung nach dem Gewaltfrieden von Tilsit und Versailles*. Berlin, 1936.
Oncken, Wilhelm. *Österreich und Preußen im Befreiungskrieg*. 2 vols. Berlin, 1876–79.
"Die Operationspläne Napoleons von der Schlacht bei Groß Beeren bis zur Schlacht bei Dennewitz." *MW* (1863): 1–40.
"Organisation der Landwehr, Landwehr-Reserven und des Landsturms der Provinz Schlesien im Jahre 1813." *MW* (1845): 307–420.
Osten-Sacken und Rhein, Ottomar von. *Vom Niemen bis zur Elbe*. Vol. 1 of *Militärisch-*

politische Geschichte des Befreiungskrieges im Jahre 1813. 2 vols. Berlin, 1813.

Pallmann, Reinhold. *Die Schlacht bei Groß Beeren und General von Bülow*. Berlin, 1872.

Palmer, Alan. *Bernadotte: Napoleon's Marshal, Sweden's King*. London, 1990.

Palmer, Robert R. "Frederick the Great, Guibert, Bülow: From Dynastic to National War." In *Makers of Modern Strategy: Military Thought from Machiavelli to Hitler*, ed. E. M. Earle. Princeton, 1971.

Paret, Peter. "Clausewitz and the Nineteenth Century." In *The Theory and Practice of War*, ed. Michael Howard. New York, 1966.

———. *Clausewitz and the State*. Oxford, 1976.

———. *Yorck and the Era of Prussian Reform, 1807–1815*. Princeton, 1966.

Parkinson, Roger. *Clausewitz: A Biography*. New York, 1971.

Pertz, G. H. *Das Leben des Ministers Freiherrn vom Stein*. 6 vols. Berlin, 1849–55.

Petre, F. L. *Napoleon's Conquest of Prussia, 1806*. London, 1907; reprint ed., London, 1993.

———. *Napoleon's Last Campaign in Germany, 1813*. London, 1912; reprint ed., London, 1992.

Pflugk-Harttung, Julius. "Bülows Bericht über die Schlacht bei Groß Beeren und die preußische Zensur." *FBPG* 23 (1910): 156–79.

———. *Illustrierte Geschichte der Brefreiungskriege 1813–1815*. Stuttgart, 1913.

Pierer, H. A. *Der Feldzug des Corps des Generals Grafen Ludwig Georg Thedel von Wallmoden-Gimborn an der Nieder-Elbe und in Belgien in den Jahren 1813 und 1814*. Altenburg, 1848.

Pimlott, John L. "Marmont: Friendship's Choice." In *Napoleon's Marshals*, ed. David G. Chandler. New York, 1987.

Pingaud, Léonce. *Bernadotte, Napoléon et les Bourbons, 1797–1844*. Paris, 1901.

Rachfahl, Felix. "Bernadotte und Bülow vor Wittenberg: Kritische Studien zur Schlacht von Dennewitz." Parts 1 und 2. *FBPG* 25 (1913): 159–225; 26 (1913): 87–147.

Reboul, Frédéric. *Campagne de 1813: Les préliminaires*. Publié sous la direction de la Section Historique de l'État-Major de l'Armée. 2 vols. Paris, 1910–12.

"Die Reorganisation der Preußischen Armee nach dem Tilsiter Frieden: Die Jahre 1809 bis 1812." *MW* (1866): 1–407.

Richie, Alexandra. *Faust's Metropolis: A History of Berlin*. New York, 1998.

Riley, John P. *Napoleon and the World War of 1813: Lessons in Coalition War Fighting*. London, 2000.

Ritter, Gerhard. *Frederick the Great*. Trans. Peter Paret. Berkeley, 1974.

———. *The Sword and the Scepter: The Problem of Militarism in Germany*. Trans. Heinz Norden. 4 vols. Coral Gables, Fla., 1969–73.

Rosenberg, Hans. *Bureaucracy, Aristocracy, and Autocracy: The Prussian Experience, 1660–1815*. 3rd ed. Cambridge, 1968.

Ross, Steven. *European Diplomatic History, 1789–1815: France against Europe*. New York, 1969.

Rothenberg, Gunther. *Napoleon's Great Adversary: The Archduke Charles and the Austrian Army, 1792–1814*. London, 1982; reprint ed., New York, 1995.

Schmeidler, Bernhard. "Bernadotte vor Groß Beeren." *FBPG* 29 (1916): 159–72.

Schmidt, Kunhardt von. "Statische Nachrichten über das Preußischen Offizierkorps von 1806 und seine Opfer für die Befreiung Deutschlands." *MW* (1901): 431–82.

Schneid, Frederick. "The Dynamics of Defeat: French Army Leadership, December 1812–March 1813." *Journal of Military History* 63, no. 1 (January 1999): 7–28.

Schroeder, Paul. *The Transformation of European Politics, 1763–1848*. Oxford, 1994.

Scott, Franklin D. *Bernadotte and the Fall of Napoleon*. Cambridge, 1934.

Scott, H. M. "Introduction: Prussia from Rossbach to Jena." *GH* 12 (1994): 279–85.

Seeley, J. R. *Life and Times of Stein or Germany and Prussia in the Napoleonic Age*. 3 vols. New York, 1969.

Shanahan, William. *Prussian Military Reforms, 1786–1813*. New York, 1945.

Sherwig, John. *Guineas and Gunpowder: British Foreign Aid in the Wars with France 1793–1815*. Cambridge, Mass., 1969.

Showalter, Dennis E. "Hubertusberg to Auerstädt: The Prussian Army in Decline?" *GH* 12 (1994): 308–33.

———. "The Prussian Landwehr and Its Critics, 1813–1819." *CEH* 4 (1971): 3–33.

———. *The Wars of Frederick the Great*. London, 1996.

Simms, Brendan. *The Impact of Napoleon: Prussian High Politics, Foreign Policy and the Crises of the Executive, 1797–1806*. Cambridge, 1997.

———. "The Road to Jena: Prussian High Politics, 1804–1806." *GH* 12 (1994): 374–94.

Simon, Walter. *The Failure of the Prussian Reform Movement, 1807–1819*. Ithaca, 1955.

Six, Georges. *Dictionnaire biographique des généraux et amiraux français de la révolution et de l'empire*. 2 vols. Paris, 1934.

Skjölderbrand, A. F. *Excellensen Grefve A. F. Skjölderbrands Memoarer*. Ed. Henrik Schück. 5 vols. Stockholm, 1904.

Stadelmann, Rudolf. "Das Duel zwischen Scharnhorst und Borstell im Dezember 1807." *HZ* 161 (1940): 263–76.

Stamm-Kuhlmann, Thomas. *König in Preußens großer Zeit: Friedrich Wilhelm III, der Melancholiker auf dem Thron*. Berlin, 1992.

Straube, Fritz. *Frühjahrsfeldzug 1813: Die Rolle der russischen Truppen bei der Befreiung Deutschlands vom Napoleonischen Joch*. Berlin, 1963.

———, ed. *Das Jahr 1813: Studien zur Geschichte und Wirkung der Befreiungskriege*. Berlin, 1963.

Stulz, Percy. *Fremdherrschaft und Befreiungskampf: Die preußische Kabinettspolitik und die Rolle der Volksmassen in den Jahren 1811 bis 1813*. Berlin, 1960.

Swederus, G. *Schwedens Politik und Kriege in den Jahren 1808 bis 1814 vorzüglich unter Leitung des Kronprinzen Carl Johan*. Trans. into German by C. F. Frisch. 2 vols. Leipzig, 1866.

Sweet, Paul. *Wilhelm von Humboldt: A Biography*. 2 vols. Columbus, 1980.

Thimme, Friedrich. "König Friedrich Wilhelm III, sein Anteil an den Konventionen von Tauroggen und an der Reform von 1807–1812." *FBPG* 18 (1905): 1–59.

Thiry, Jean. *Leipzig, 30 juin–7 novembre*. Paris, 1972.

Tingsten, Lars. *Huvuddragen av Sveriges Krig och Yttre Politik augusti 1813–januari 1814*. Stockholm, 1924.

Treuenfeld, Bruno von. *Das Jahre 1813: Bis zur Schlacht von Groß Görschen*. Leipzig, 1901.

Ulmann, Heinrich. *Geschichte der Befreiungskriege 1813 und 1814*. 2 vols. Munich, 1914–15.

Wartenburg, Yorck von. *Napoleon as a General*. 2 vols. Ed. Walter H. James. London, n.d.

Wawro, Geoffrey. *The Austro-Prussian War: Austria's War with Prussia and Italy in 1866*. Cambridge, 1996.

Webster, Charles K. *British Diplomacy, 1813–1815: Select Documents Dealing with the Reconstruction of Europe*. London, 1921.

———. *The Foreign Policy of Castlereagh, 1812–1815: Britain and the Reconstruction of Europe*. London, 1931.

Weinzierl, John. "Marshal Victor as Governor of Berlin." *CRE* (1996): 216–23.

White, Charles E. "Defeating Napoleon: The Trachenberg Concept of 1813." *CRE* (1997): 411–19.

———. *The Enlightened Soldier: Scharnhorst and the Militärische Gesellschaft in Berlin, 1801–1805*. Westport, Conn., 1989.

Wiehr, Ernst. *Napoleon und Bernadotte im Herbstfeldzuge 1813*. Berlin, 1893.

Williamson, Gordon. *The Iron Cross: A History, 1813–1957*. Denison, Tex., 1994.

Wittichen, Friedrich Carl. "Zur Geschichte der öffentlichen Meinung in Preußen vor 1806." *FBPG* 23 (1910): 35–70.

Young, Peter. "Ney: The Bravest of the Brave." In *Napoleon's Marshals*, ed. David G. Chandler. New York, 1987.